CITIBANK

Also Available:

WHISTLE BLOWING: *The Report on the Conference on Professional Responsibility,* edited by Ralph Nader, Peter Petkas, and Kate Blackwell

WHO RUNS CONGRESS? by Mark J. Green, James M. Fallows, and David R. Zwick

THE WORKERS: *Portraits of Nine American Jobholders,* by Kenneth Lasson

YOU AND YOUR PENSION: *Why You May Never Get a Penny/What You Can Do About It,* by Ralph Nader and Kate Blackwell

Ralph Nader's Study Group Report
on First National City Bank

CITIBANK

by David Leinsdorf & Donald Etra

Foreword by Ralph Nader

Grossman Publishers / New York / 1973

First National City Bank Task Force*

David Leinsdorf, Project Co-Director and Author
    B.A., Columbia College
    LL.B., Columbia University
    Trial Attorney, U.S. Department of Justice,
      Antitrust Division, 1967–70

Donald Etra, Project Co-Director and Author
    B.A., Yale University
    J.D., Columbia University
    M.B.A., Columbia University
    Member of the Bar, State of New York

Peter Thomas Bepler, II
    B.A., Fordham College
    M.A., University of Virginia
    First-year law student, New York University

Michael Berger
    B.S., Yale University
    Second-year law student, Columbia University

Peter Buchsbaum
    B.A., Cornell University
    Third-year law student, Harvard University

Matthew Daynard
    B.A., Ohio Wesleyan University
    Second-year law student, Columbia University

Mark W. Foster
    B.A., Yale University
    Second-year law student, Harvard University

Philip M. Gassel
    B.S., Northwestern University
    First-year law student, Columbia University

* Task force members are described as of the time they worked on the study.

Eric Peter Geller
    B.A., George Washington University
    First-year law student, Harvard University

Marjorie Golding
    Student, Vassar College

Hunter D. Hale
    B.A., Emory University
    First-year law student, Columbia University

Gregory Hiestand
    B.A., Columbia University
    Third-year law student, Columbia University

Richard Alan Janis
    First-year undergraduate, Northwestern University

Douglas Kass
    B.A., Alfred College
    M.B.A., University of Pennsylvania

William Klein
    First-year undergraduate, Cornell University

Barbara Kronman
    B.B.A., College of the City of New York

Sandra Kunsberg
    B.A., Brandeis University
    Second-year law student, Columbia University

Nancy Levine
    High-school senior, River Edge, N.J.

Steven Ney
    B.A., Columbia College
    First-year law student, Yale University

Stuart M. Nierenberg
    B.A., Princeton University
    First-year law student, Columbia University

Pierce Henry O'Donnell
  B.A., Georgetown University
  First-year law student, Georgetown Law Center

Steven Henry Rosen
  B.A., University of Maryland
  M.P.A., Syracuse University
  First-year law student, New York University

Michael Stolzar
  B.A., University of Rochester
  First-year law student, Columbia University

Astrida Woods
  Student, Barnard College

Editorial Assistance

Professor Fairfax Leary, Jr., University of Pennsylvania Law School
Karen W. Ferguson, Attorney, Public Interest Research Group
Professor John A. Spanogle, University of Maine Law School

Special Projects
Miriam Cutler
Robert Lighthizer

Production
Susan Fagin
Theo Page
Connie Jo Smith
Anne Ulinski

Foreword by Ralph Nader

The powers and doings of bankers have fostered much speculation throughout our history by those who considered themselves aggrieved or denied by their services and influence. Farmers, small merchants, inventors, homeowners, minority groups, and consumer loan recipients, among others, have been dealt with by banks in markedly one-sided contractual relationships. Because banks and their regulatory agencies treasure secrecy to an extreme, what goes on behind the marble pillars is, to the public, off limits.

Secrecy breeds ignorance, lack of interest, and despair on the part of those citizens who are affected adversely by irregular, discriminatory, or predatory banking behavior. Secrecy also denies citizens any right of access to information that could establish standards of evaluation for bank activity or passivity. Finally, secrecy permits and shields complicity between banks themselves, banks and politicians, banks and regulatory or other government agencies, and banks and their large corporate depositors.

Such information about banks that is publicly available—through regulatory bodies—involves largely aggregate data that banks want but cannot compile for themselves. On the other hand, the government rarely provides citizens with bank information which they need for intelligent consumer decisions and citizen action. This report dwells on how valuable such information would be and what kinds of information are not available. Clearly, there are the most compelling reasons for a thorough examination of the gross inadequacy of performance by government agencies in refusing to disclose data which they have in their possession and the refusal of banks to disclose selective and specific information to their shareholders and customers. Information is the currency both of democracy and a free marketplace of quality competition and consumer sovereignty. For a bank customer to obtain those facts that he needs to make intelligent decisions, the darkness must withdraw from the corridors of modern banking institutions.

It was the belief that the public's information about banks

should be greatly increased, particularly as banks prepared to spread out into other economic activities via their holding companies, that prompted this study. One bank—First National City Bank—was chosen as a case study of intrinsic importance, because of the institution's size, leadership, and comparative significance, to highlight the need to study banks from a consumer standpoint. To our knowledge, no analysis of a bank and its impact on its community, such as essayed here, has been done before. A consumer-citizen evaluation of a bank's activities also seemed novel to Walter Wriston and William Spencer, respectively chairman and president of Citibank, as the company is called, when we visited them to inform them of the project and ask their cooperation. Mr. Wriston was a bit taut and challenging about what we wished to discover; while Mr. Spencer used his more amiable disposition to suggest right off some reasons for the bank's information policy (discussed in the report). Customers' rights of privacy and competition were the two main reasons given but, as the summer unfolded, these were expanded far beyond their legitimate ambit. Banks such as Citibank know far more about one another voluntarily than they are willing to tell the public. Privacy for *individual* customers is extended to all aspects of *corporate* customers and other impersonal data categories relating, for example, to the distribution by geography and industry of deposits and loans.

Citibank made it apparent to the study team in the first few weeks that a very limited cooperation would be extended, notwithstanding the fact that some members of the team had shareholder and consumer relationships with the bank. These two types of contractual relationships did not deter bank officials from rejecting their company's slogan—"First National City hates to say no." Given the sprawling business involvement of the bank, this report does not pretend to treat all the bank's major activities. Its foreign banking affairs are not included, for example, nor are such areas as tax and loan accounts or property tax payments. The report's emphasis is on the community-consumer-employee-city-regulatory agency dimensions of Citibank's world and its relationship to some large corporate customers.

What banks do and do not do should be matters made interesting, understandable, pertinent, and engaging of people's efforts as citizens and consumers. Banking news should not be restricted to business pages and highly formalized reporting primarily for banking and commercial readers. Historically, banks have described themselves as performing a "public trust" and as "serving the community." It is time to examine the reality and implications of these pretensions. It is also time to assess the degree of their compliance with banking and other laws, and to call for broader representation of the community on banks' boards of directors and in the banks' managerial ranks through wiser employment and promotion policies. Urgently, the impact on competition and economic concentration that will assuredly result from the one-bank holding company movement requires an independent base for continual scrutiny that is not likely to come from the compliant Federal Reserve Board.

The growth of a phenomenon known as "refusal to deal" presages new regulatory policies to deal with such undeclared practices. Marking off whole urban sectors as tabu for bank loans can spark a series of similar "red-linings" by other businesses (such as insurance) and quickly propel the sector into rapid deterioration. Institutions that possess legal monopolies over demand deposits and receive a variety of direct and indirect governmental subsidies should observe open standards for doing business, which can be challenged by those who are aggrieved. Debt-to-income guidelines and credit granting criteria should be made available to the public by the issuing bank. New ideas—such as Citibank holding public hearings concerning bank forms it uses or is revising—should be explored. The legal responsibility of Citibank for the outrageous practice of "sewer service," discussed in subsequent pages, should be acted upon by law enforcement officials.

A substantial section of this report is devoted to Citibank's management of over $14 billion in trust funds—mostly employee benefit accounts (pension monies) and personal trust accounts. Chairman Wriston decreed that no bank employees were to discuss, or reply to any questions by the study group about, the bank's trust department and its handling of what Justice Louis Brandeis called "other people's money." But the important public issues surrounding the trust department's obscured operations were not so easily camouflaged.

As Donald Etra, who directed the trust study, describes, there is a tremendous concentration of control by a few banks over the more than $300 billion in bank trust departments nationally. The conflicts of interest between bank commercial and trust departments regularly favor the enrichment of the former. Trust beneficiaries and pension plan participants are deprived of the information and rights they may want to participate in the management and investment of their money. Trust and estate lawyers work closely with the bank to perpetuate this oligarchic condition. While surveying members of Citibank's outside directors and trust board members, Etra found a remarkable amount of ignorance and inattention, which attest to their function as protective window dressing for the all-dominant Citibank managers led by Wriston.

The recommendations for private pension plan and trust account reform in this book focus on the overriding question: How can such massive accumulations of people's money under highly centralized control be deconcentrated, subjected to fuller disclosure of operations and policy, and directed toward investments that serve the interests of the many instead of a few giant corporations?

It is clear that neither the Securities and Exchange Commission nor the bank-indentured state bank regulatory agencies will address themselves to this question. The contrived complexity and cultivated secrecy about banks are traditional shields. They keep ordinary people and bank consumers from finding out what is going on. In this way the public is prevented from correcting abuses and directing wealth toward capital-starved and innovative uses that could benefit those people whose money the banks are using.

The new "profit-center" banks are seriously disturbing many older or retired bank executives who see the trust function of banks being ramshackled by the supermoney and superconglomerate dealings of the new bank managers. Some of them have discussed these matters with the study group, but still more are needed to speak and act to further those ideals that they believe are being violated wholesale in the pell-mell rush for profits. The specific proposals for change submitted by David Leinsdorf and Donald Etra may stimulate more bankers to candor. Already, after hearing of this study, Mills B. Lane,

Jr., the Chairman of Citizens and Southern Bank of Georgia, the state's largest, ridiculed Citibank's excuses for secrecy. He exposed their rationale by disclosing to researchers far more information about his bank than Citibank said would permit accepted banking practices—and still protected the personal confidences of his customers. There is a need for a gathering of socially-minded bankers who do not approve of the current concentration trends in banking nor the increasing misdirection of banks away from their community and into the megacorporate world of fast money for ego-gratifying corporate mergers and powerplays.

I hope this report will stimulate response from within Citibank's ranks and the banking industry and its constituency, generally. For the consumer movement is on the threshold of interacting with this vast subeconomy. A two-way process of specific communication involving consumers with bank employees, executives, and regulatory officials will enhance the process of documenting the issues and advancing the cause of responsive and accountable banking.

Ralph Nader
February, 1973
Washington, D.C.

Preface

During the summer of 1970, we embarked on a study of First National City Bank, New York's largest bank. The task force conducted over 400 interviews of bankers, corporation officers, bank customers, government money managers, regulatory agency personnel, and congressional committee staff members. We sent questionnaires to individual and corporate bank customers, examined government files and congressional committee reports, researched published materials, and followed developments in the trade press, notably the excellent daily banking journal, the *American Banker*.

When we took stock of the material gathered at the end of that summer, we realized that much work remained to be done. Major areas of FNCB's activities, such as the trust and international departments, had scarcely been touched. Still, because it could take years to cover every significant area, we decided to put together a preliminary report focusing on the bank's commercial activities. This preliminary report was released in mimeograph form in June, 1971. First National City responded to that report and the task force answered FNCB's response. The response and answer are to be found in the Appendix. Most of the data collected for this study was assembled during the summer of 1970 and during 1971. Many of the conclusions and recommendations that we have made are, therefore, based on that data. However, wherever feasible, we have updated statistics in order to present as current as possible a picture of Citibank and the banking industry.

In October, 1971, we began a major study of FNCB's trust activities. Announcement of this study was greeted by a memo from Walter Wriston, Chairman of FNCB. Mr. Wriston's memo, sent to all 37,000 employees of the bank, ordered every employee to refrain from speaking with members of the task force. Undaunted, the task force continued its study of FNCB's trust activities. We contacted over 100 beneficiaries of personal trusts managed by the bank and close to 400 companies whose pension funds are managed by FNCB. We researched published material, scoured surrogate's court files and interviewed more than 50 trust and money management experts, some of whom were Citibankers.

Along with an updated version of our 1971 study of FNCB's commercial activities, we publish here for the first time the results of our trust study.

The task force thanks David Caplovitz, Professor at Columbia University's Bureau of Applied Social Research, for giving us access to the vast files of information gathered for his massive book, *Debtors in Default* (1970). The project directors are greatly indebted to Professor John A. Spanogle, of the University of Maine Law School, and Professor Fairfax Leary, Jr., of the Temple University School of Law, who patiently read and criticized draft after draft of this report.

David Leinsdorf
Donald Etra

Contents

Introduction

A commercial bank is a merchant of money. It accumulates money from people, corporations, and governments and lends it to people, corporations, and governments. The difference between the cost of attracting funds and the price charged for lending is the bank's profit. The key to the banks' profitability is growth. Although bank profit *margins* have declined dramatically in recent years, banks have expanded their operations fast enough to offset the lower rate of profit earned on each dollar of gross revenue. This growth has been achieved —even during the recession of 1970—for a variety of reasons.

One reason is the fact that banks have exclusive control over 75% of America's money supply. The principle economic function of commercial banks is to operate the nation's payments mechanism, i.e., to hold demand (checking) deposits and honor checks drawn against them. No other institutions have the right to receive such deposits which, in the United States, are the equivalent of currency and coin and constitute 75% of the nation's money supply. As the Federal Reserve Board increases the money supply to meet the needs of our ever-expanding economy, commercial banks are guaranteed a minimum rate of growth.

The power to make loans with these deposits gives banks another exceptional prerogative—the capacity to create money. An example will show how this process works.

Banks must set aside part of their deposits as legal reserves at the district Federal Reserve banks. Legal reserves are designed to ensure that banks have enough funds to honor checks presented for payment, and to provide the Federal Reserve Board with a means of regulating the amount of money that member banks can create. Presently, 17.5% of demand deposits must go into reserves.* For the sake of simplicity, however, the following description of how banks create money assumes a 20% demand deposit reserve requirement.

---

* The actual demand deposit reserve requirements are 17% on deposits under $5 million, and 17.5% on deposits over $5 million.

Suppose that someone deposits $1,000 in newly printed currency in a Citibank checking account. Given our hypothetical 20% reserve requirement, FNCB puts $200 of the $1,000 deposit into its reserve account at the Federal Reserve Bank of New York. Suppose that FNCB makes an $800 vacation loan with the balance, which the borrower uses to pay his travel agent. If the travel agent deposits the $800 in an account at Chase Manhattan Bank, the original $1,000 has expanded to $1,800 in demand deposits—the man who sold the bond has $1,000 at FNCB which he can withdraw at any time and the travel agent can do the same with his $800 at Chase.

Chase, too, will put 20% of the deposit, or $160, into its reserve account, but can lend out the remaining $640 to its customers. If Chase lends the $640 to a customer who pays the money to a used car dealer who has a Chemical Bank account, the bank deposits flowing from the original $1,000 now total $2,440—$1,000 at FNCB, $800 at Chase, and $640 at Chemical. As the process continues, the bank following Chemical will add four-fifths of $640 to the banking system's demand deposits and so on until finally, the original $1,000 deposited at FNCB will have expanded to $5,000 of demand deposits in the banking system.

Another factor behind the growth rate of the banking industry is the fact that banks have expanded into new fields of activity from which they have traditionally been excluded. With the Comptroller of the Currency leading the way with novel reinterpretations of long-standing laws and FNCB initiating a veritable stampede by banks to diversify through the creation of one-bank holding companies, banks have obtained new freedom to compete with nonbank corporations.

Another reason for the growth of banks—and this applies primarily to the largest banks—is the fact that the top priority of the billion-dollar banks is meeting the needs of the fastest growing companies in America's economy, the giant national and multinational corporations. As FNCB and the other money-market banks apply their best talent, the largest part of their funds, and their new technology to handling the global financial transactions of large corporations, they ensure that, as an increasing share of America's productive resources come under the control of fewer and fewer giant corporations, the large banks that serve those corporations will achieve similar growth for themselves. Consequently the concentration of America's productive resources is reflected in a corresponding concentration in the banking industry. Although there are more than 13,000 commercial banks in the United States, 100 banks hold half of all deposits and ten banks hold one-quarter. The three largest banks have 13% of all deposits and Citibank alone has 4%—$1 out of every $25.

The corporate merger boom has been another means of promoting FNCB's growth. Citibank has acted as a marriage broker by maintaining a list of acquisition-minded companies for its customers. It has waived covenants in bank loan agreements that would otherwise prohibit acquisitions and it has financed acquisitions by customers with a virtual rubber stamp. Citibank thus allies itself with many of the most aggressive conglomerate companies in the economy, and the bank and its corporate customers each nurture the growth of the other.

The merger movement has had important ramifications on competition in the banking industry and on local economic development. Small, local banks are precluded from competing for local deposits; when a national company buys a local business, the acquired company's bank deposits are typically transferred to the acquiring company's money-market banks. This removes funds from the local economy and fosters economic colonialism.

Although the central role of commercial banks in our economy imbues bank activities with the character of a "public trust," there have been virtually no attempts to study banks in terms of how they serve their individual, corporate, and government customers, what they do with their depositors' money, how they affect the communities in which they operate, how they deal with their employees, and how they affect economic priorities. This report is a first step toward developing the information needed to make an informed evaluation of how commercial banks affect people. We have concentrated on one bank in order to develop as much concrete, specific informa-

xxiv   INTRODUCTION

tion as possible on the framework within which priorities are formulated and far-reaching decisions are made and implemented.

FNCB was chosen as the subject of our study for a variety of reasons. It is the largest bank in New York City, which is the most important money market in the world. With 25% more branches than Chase Manhattan, the second largest bank in New York, it is the city's largest consumer bank, attracting more individual deposits and extending more consumer credit than any other New York City bank. Citibank is also very innovative in developing new deposit gathering and financing devices. It was the first New York City bank to lend money to consumers, the first to open overseas branches, the first to form a one-bank holding company, and the first to develop the important negotiable certificate of deposit, thus offering corporations, wealthy individuals, and other large investors with a short-term investment alternative to U.S. Treasury Bills. In all of these developments, other banks followed Citibank's lead. Thus, by studying FNCB, it is possible to better understand the direction in which the banking industry is moving.

Forbes magazine calls banking America's fastest growing industry and Citibank the fastest growing of the 20 largest banks. Citibank's growth has been staggering. Deposits have doubled in seven years, loans and assets in six years, profits in nine years, and employees in ten years. Although California's Bank of America is larger than Citibank, Bank of America has it easier because it can branch and gather up deposits all over one of America's largest, fastest growing states. Citibank's domestic operations, on the other hand, have been confined to New York City and two suburban counties. Consequently, Citibank has had to rely more on innovation and aggressiveness to offset the inherent comparative advantage that California's unrestricted branching laws give to Bank of America.*

Although Bank of America ($28 billion in assets) is somewhat larger than Citibank ($26 billion), Citibank is very large nonetheless. Only AT&T, Prudential Life, and Metropolitan

* The New York State legislature recently amended New York's branching laws to allow statewide branching, starting January 1, 1976. This will permit the large New York City banks to expand their share of the market further.

Life have more assets. In addition to the $26 billion of assets owned by FNCB, the bank's trust department manages another $14 billion in assets for pension funds, personal trusts, investment advisory accounts, and estates and has exclusive investment discretion over almost half of these assets.

As might be expected, the information gathered by the task force indicates that Citibank is a microcosm, albeit a large one, of the contradictions and distortions, the strengths and weaknesses found throughout the American business community. Citibank's hiring and promotion practices provide a good case in point. Until a few years ago, when the tight New York City labor market induced Citibank to reexamine its hiring policies, it adhered to needlessly high employment standards. Although most jobs at Citibank require few or easily taught skills, the bank required applicants to have a high-school diploma, thereby excluding thousands of people from jobs for which they were otherwise qualified. Blacks and other poorly educated minorities were especially likely to be excluded.

Although Citibank was forced to relax its hiring standards to replace the 5,000–6,000 employees who leave each year and to support the bank's high growth rate, the opportunities for blacks, women, Jews, and other groups to move into positions of responsibility are still very limited. This is largely because there are more promotable employees than responsible positions, giving Citibank the opportunity to pick and choose, and locking thousands of employees into dull jobs for which they are overqualified and underpaid. Consequently, employee alienation and turnover are extremely high, undermining management's capacity to retain control over its rapidly expanding activities.

Widespread employee dissatisfaction takes its toll on the bank's customers—especially the individual customers of the retail branch network. Service in Citibank's branches is inadequate. Customers have to wait even when the branch is not busy. Operating policies are implemented haphazardly, resulting in wide variations from branch to branch in the quality of customer service. Customers are confused about the operation and cost of services and branch officers fail, with distressing frequency, to enlighten customers and end the confusion. Lending criteria are frequently ignored, resulting in extensions of credit to tens of thousands of people who cannot afford to meet their monthly payments.

Despite Citibank's failure to service its present volume of retail business adequately, FNCB has had great success expanding the range of its services, the number of its branches, and its share of the market. Deceptive advertising, descriptive brochures that don't describe, and volume-oriented employee incentive programs are all used to maximize growth without regard to the human toll. And the human toll is substantial.

One result of Citibank's slovenly but ever-expanding operation is that the bank is New York City's number one plaintiff. In 1969, FNCB sued 10,000 people (increasing to 15,000 in 1970), more than five times as many lawsuits as any other bank. Adjusted for the volume of consumer credit outstanding, Citibank's rate of suit is more than double that of any other bank. Ninety-five per cent of the judgments are default judgments and impose an additional 25% in attorney fees, court costs, and interest charges on the average judgment debtor (70% of whom earn less than $6,000 a year). Furthermore, Citibank's practice of calling and threatening to call the debtor's employer exploits the fact that many employers illegally fire employees rather than deduct 10% of the judgment debtor's wages pursuant to a garnishment order. As a result, many debtors must refinance the debt by taking out a new loan in order to avoid being fired. Another component of FNCB's collection operation is widespread "sewer service," i.e., the practice by which process servers fail to serve the summons and complaint properly, preventing the defendant from finding out about the lawsuit against him and insuring a high default judgment rate.

In sharp contrast to its aggressive posture in the retail banking market, FNCB virtually ignores the credit-starved residential mortgage market, aggravating New York City's housing crisis. Though in 1970 FNCB held nearly $2 billion of peoples' savings deposits, the bank's residential mortgage loan portfolio was only one-fourth as large. Yet savings deposits are long-term, stable funds that are ideally suited to long-term residential mortgage lending. Citibank's refusal to provide the funds needed to preserve, rehabilitate, and construct housing underscores the bank's obliviousness to the needs of the community from which it draws its deposits. The branch network thus operates like a system of receptacles where people deposit their money to be siphoned off into the bank's "central pool" and made available to the giant corporations. Meanwhile, the people who provide the funds must suffer deteriorating housing conditions because FNCB and other banks have virtually unfettered discretion to lend the peoples' money where they want. Citibank's retail branch operation, therefore, is like a regressive tax, taking money from those who can least afford to lose it and giving it to those who need it the least.

Though Citibank gathers up billions of dollars from individuals and then ignores the critical shortage of long-term residential mortgage money, it is not so oblivious to corporate needs. With a board of directors composed almost exclusively of top executives from its large corporate customers, Citibank's sensitivity to corporate wants contrasts sharply with its contempt for human needs. In 1970, FNCB was interlocked with 40 of the 300 largest industrial corporations in the United States, including 7 of the top 10, plus 6 of the 15 largest life-insurance companies, 2 of the 4 largest retailers, and the 2 largest utilities.

But interlocking directorates constitute just one factor behind Citibank's obeisance to corporate wants. More important is the bank's fetish with preserving and strengthening in every possible manner the total account relationship between the bank and its corporate customers. Because corporations have numerous alternative sources of credit both within and without the banking system and because the deposit balances of individual corporations are so substantial, corporations have the leverage to obtain a vast array of services in exchange for their deposits, a volume of credit that far exceeds the amount of corporate deposits, and favorable credit terms.

As a result, financially hard-pressed corporations in America obtain huge amounts of credit at the "prime rate," the lowest corporate lending rate that is purportedly reserved for only the most creditworthy companies. Citibank is not the only bank to behave in this manner. Indeed, the typical loan to a giant corporation is made through a multibank lending syndicate in

which most or all of the large New York City banks participate, with interest rates fixed by agreement instead of competitive forces.

Citibank's aggressive development of its relationships with
national and multinational corporations contrasts sharply with
its niggardly involvement in fostering local economic development by minority business enterprises. Although the bank pays
lip service to the policy of promoting minority economic development, its small-business investment company avoids small
neighborhood businesses of the type that could significantly
increase grass-roots entrepreneurship, preferring to invest in
million-dollar enterprises that have high growth potential. Similarly, the bank has a passive approach to making economic
development loans in the ghettos of New York, waiting for
borrowers to seek out the bank instead of drumming up business. It has also failed to require its loan officers to apply
their expertise to counseling minority enterprises.

The financial crisis that plagues New York City has been
aggravated by FNCB and the other large banks. Preferential
bank income taxes cost New York City $10 million a year in
lost revenues. The fact that the banks have provided the city
with relatively few services in exchange for hundreds of millions of dollars of interest-free demand deposits has cost New
York City many millions of dollars in excess costs each year
($8 million in 1969 alone). And the banks' abandonment of
the municipal bond market, especially in times of tight money,
has weakened the market for municipal securities, adding millions of dollars a year to New York City's borrowing costs.

At the same time that FNCB has been receiving preferential
tax treatment, earning exorbitant profits on New York City's
accounts and adding to New York City's borrowing costs, Citibank has wielded considerable influence over public spending
decisions through its membership on public bodies and private
civic associations. FNCB was represented on a commission
appointed by Governor Rockefeller that recommended a $65
million giveaway to purchase the bankrupt Long Island Railroad from a major FNCB debtor. FNCB is a member of the
Downtown Lower Manhattan Association, the financial community's local planning board, that initiated the Port of New
York Authority's giant World Trade Center, the largest office

building in the world. As lead bank for the Port Authority, FNCB played a central role in the financial arrangements for the World Trade Center. Having participated in the creation of the World Trade Center, FNCB uses its membership on the Metropolitan Transit Authority to accelerate the construction, at taxpayers' expense, of new subway facilities to handle the World Trade Center's additional burden on New York's already crowded transit facilities.

Citibank also performs governmental functions for New York City, such as processing New York City's personal income-tax returns. Although the contract with the city prohibits the bank from using the information extracted from the income-tax returns for any private purpose, Citibank retains copies of the computer tapes and city officials admit that they have no way of ensuring that the bank does not utilize the information for its own credit files. At a time when massive, computerized data banks are proliferating, compiling secret dossiers on all citizens, this Citibank practice raises the possibility of further invasions of citizens' rights to privacy.

Citibank not only provides commercial services to individuals, corporations, and municipalities, it also provides trust services. Citibank manages $14 billion in its trust department, most of which is in personal estates and trusts, and corporate and municipal pension funds. While almost complete yet unwarranted secrecy surrounds the trust activities of banks, the public has been, of late, becoming increasingly aware of the conflicts that arise when a commercial bank also provides trust services. Some of the conflicts are blatant: a trust department can invest a pension fund in a company deeply indebted to the commercial side of the bank. Some of the conflicts are more subtle: a trust department can deliberately keep a portion of a trust fund uninvested and leave the uninvested cash in demand deposits with the commercial bank. The presence and potential for such conflicts demand that the public ask whether trust departments have any place as part of a commercial bank.

Because commercial banking is imbued with a "public trust," banking has always been a regulated industry. Permission to open a bank or new branches has always required government approval and a showing of community need.

Branching has been restricted, in part, to preserve local control over local funds and to ensure that citizens' deposits remain available for reinvestment in the local economy. The freedom of banks to engage in nonbanking activities has been circumscribed severely to prevent banks from using their access to interest-free demand deposits to gain unfair competitive advantage over nonbank competitors and to avoid conflicts of interest that could arise from bank diversification.

But the bank regulatory agencies have failed to monitor banks to ensure that community needs are met, and have steadily relaxed the traditional restrictions on bank expansion into new activities and territories. The Comptroller of the Currency, who is responsible for regulating national banks, has been particularly responsive to the banks' desire for greater freedom to expand. Branch applications are routinely approved despite findings by the Comptroller's own examiners that the community to be served already has enough banks. Contrary to the statutory requirement that the Comptroller observe state branching laws in acting on branch applications by national banks, the Comptroller has allowed national banks to open branches where state banks could not. Regulations and rulings were rewritten to permit banks to carry on some of their operations through subsidiaries and to allow banks to expand into travel agency services, including automobile rentals and trip insurance, warehousing, data processing, leasing of personal property, mutual funds, messenger services, and the selling of insurance. Bank mergers, too, were approved almost with a rubber stamp.

The Comptroller's *laissez-faire* approach to bank regulation affected the Federal Reserve Board, which regulates state-chartered banks that are members of the Federal Reserve System. As it became increasingly apparent that national banks were obtaining unique advantages despite the long-standing statutory policy of putting national and state banks on a competitively equal footing, Chase Manhattan Bank, the largest state bank in the country, and more than 160 other state banks converted to national charters during the 1960s. The Fed, as the Federal Reserve Board is called, under pressure from state member banks to restore competitive equality, followed the Comptroller's lead and permitted state banks to engage in many of the activities permitted by the Comptroller, leading one Fed member to characterize bank regulation as "competition in laxity."

This permissiveness also prevails in the examinations that the regulatory agencies are supposed to make of bank operations. This is especially true of the Comptroller's examination of the largest banks, which are examined less frequently than the law requires and with a disproportionately small amount of examination resources. Although Bank of America, Citibank, and Chase have one-fifth of all national bank assets, the Comptroller allocates a total of only 3% of his examination resources to them, because he has so much confidence in their solvency. The Comptroller gives little or no attention to many other important areas that bear on compliance with the law by the giant banks.

Citibank also has a high degree of autonomy from Fed monetary policy. In 1969 and early 1970, FNCB continued expanding its loan portfolio despite Fed monetary policy designed to slow down the economy and inflation by restricting bank credit growth. Citibank did this by borrowing billions of dollars in the unregulated international Eurodollar market and from its one-bank holding company which raised funds in the unregulated commercial paper market. As a result of these activities by FNCB and other large banks, it took longer than anticipated for the economy to respond to the Fed's credit restraint policies. Furthermore, the impact of credit restraint was distributed unevenly throughout the economy because the large banks, with vast overseas branch networks and holding companies, could continue to finance their customers' expansion plans while smaller banks were required to restrict their loans.

The latest, and potentially most far-reaching, development in the area of bank regulation has been the development of one-bank holding companies. In order to escape some of the restrictions on bank activities, FNCB created a corporation to own the bank. Because Citicorp, as the holding company is called, is not itself a bank—it just owns a bank—it can engage in many activities prohibited to banks. When Citicorp tried to take over a large insurance company, it became apparent that bank holding companies could change the entire structure of the American economy. After two years of legislative battling, Congress, at the end of 1970, passed legislation requiring bank holding companies to obtain approval from the Federal Reserve Board before acquiring or creating new subsidiaries. The statutory formula, however, gives the Fed a large amount of discretion to determine what activities are closely related to banking.

Though nominally independent, bank holding companies are, in fact, mere extensions of the banks they own. They share the same directors, managers, offices, technological resources, customers and, most important of all, they generate their funds by virtue of their affiliations with banks. Accordingly, bank holding companies have competitive advantages that independent, nonbank competitors cannot match, making it safe to predict that if the Fed allows substantial expansion into new fields, the long-range consequence will be to reduce the rapidly-diminishing diversity and countervailing economic powers in our economy.

The fundamental issue facing the American banking system is whether the people and government will reassert the concept that banking is a "public trust" to be operated as objectively, independently, and free from conflicts of interest as possible. If banks and their government regulators continue to make growth and profits a higher priority than ensuring an equitable distribution of financial resources across all sectors of the economy, then it is safe to predict that the distortions that pervade America's economy today—such as the dearth of money to finance the preservation, rehabilitation, and expansion of the nation's housing, the higher cost of borrowing by state and municipalities to construct needed public facilities, the increasing concentration of our economic resources, the inability of local communities to influence local economic decisions, and the powerlessness of millions of consumers to transcend the anonymity of an account number—will grow worse, not better, in the coming years.

The banks, dominating the financial lifeblood of the American economy and participating, actively or passively, in virtually every significant financial transaction, have a unique capacity to devise and implement solutions to many of America's most pressing economic problems. Because the banks, as the following chapters demonstrate, have little incentive to apply their financial, managerial, and technological resources to meet the unmet human needs, citizens and their government representatives must apply every means of pressure at their disposal to increase the banks' willingness to deal with problems that are presently ignored.

The first priority, however, must be to generate sufficient information about banks' activities so that informed responses to the unsolved problems may be devised, something that is extremely difficult to do when the bureaucrats—the bankers, the executives of the bank customers, and the officials of the bank regulatory agencies—have virtually exclusive access to the relevant data. This raises the fundamental question of what information banks should be required to disclose.

Gathering data for this report was like putting together a jigsaw puzzle without all the pieces. Although Citibank cooperated by making employees available for interviews, the number of interviews permitted—53, or fewer than five interviews for each task force member—provided a very limited sampling of the bank's 37,000 employees. Furthermore, the bank's extensive monitoring of the interviews provided a strong reminder for officers to be careful not to disclose unfavorable information about the bank:

1. A representative of Citibank's senior management—Vice Chairman J. Howard Laeri or Senior V.P. and Cashier Carl Desch—attended the interviews; and
2. Donald Colen, FNCB Vice President in charge of Public Relations, attended the interviews; and
3. An attorney from Citibank's law firm, Shearman and Sterling, attended the interviews; and
4. All interviews were tape-recorded (one copy of the tape was provided to the task force); and
5. Interviews took place in a conference room in the executive suite, not in the interviewee's office.

The bank also laid down stringent restrictions on what information it would disclose. It refused to disclose anything about any customer relationship, information deemed of competitive significance, or information deemed within the area of management concern and responsibility.[1]

When the bank wanted to withhold information that did not clearly fall within the prohibited categories, it trotted out new excuses. Thus, Citibank refused our request for a list of the corporate securities for which FNCB is trustee—information that is public but would require many weeks to compile from public sources—on the grounds that the bank would not act as our "file clerk." [2] Citibank could have compiled this data with relative ease. Similarly, the bank refused to provide a complete list of its lawyers on the grounds that such information was "out of bounds." [3]

Our effort to examine the stockholder list of First National City Corporation (FNCC) provides a good illustration of Citibank's grudging response to our requests for information. In early October, 1970, the project co-director (DL) called Carl Desch, FNCB's Senior Vice President and Cashier and said that, as a stockholder, he wanted to examine the holding company's stockholder list. An appointment was arranged and on October 13, DL went to the bank. Samuel Lord, Jr., a Vice President who works under Mr. Desch, ushered him into a conference room, where he sat down to examine five three-inch-thick volumes of computer printouts listing the names, addresses, and stockholdings of FNCC's 66,000 stockholders.

When DL started taking notes—his purpose was to identify the corporation's largest stockholders—Mr. Lord, who had stayed in the room, objected and said no notes could be taken. DL protested that stockholders have a legal right to inspect and copy the stockholder list and expressed surprise because Mr. Desch had not indicated that note taking would be prohibited. Mr. Lord, however, reaffirmed his instructions that notes could not be taken. When DL asked to see Mr. Desch, he was told Mr. Desch was out of the country. When he asked to speak to another member of senior management, Mr. Lord replied that the stockholders' list was within Mr. Desch's province.

Realizing the futility of further argument or of examining the list without taking notes, DL left and sent a registered letter to Mr. Desch, claiming that the refusal to allow copying subverted the stockholder's right to inspect the list. Later that month, J. Howard Laeri, FNCB Vice Chairman, called to say that there had been a "misunderstanding," and that the stockholders' list could be inspected and copied, which was later done.

Another example of difficulty in obtaining information involved our interview with William Spencer, FNCB's President, a friendly man who spoke more openly than anyone else interviewed at the bank. Early in the interview, we queried Mr. Spencer about the capacity of the management to keep track of what goes on in all of the bank's far-flung activities. When Spencer answered "You've probably seen our policy manual" which contains the "general policies how we aspire, as best we can identify, the way the bank is to be run . . . ," [4] Donald Colen, Vice President in charge of Public Relations, gesticulated from across the table to indicate that we could not have access to the policy manual. Readers who may be surprised that the public-relations vice president would tell the president what can and cannot be disclosed, should note this incident as evidence of how difficult it is for corporate employees—even the president—to depart from the "company line."

Citibank withheld a large amount of vital information. The bank offered various excuses for denying this information. The insubstantiality of these excuses is best illustrated by the fact that a major Georgia bank, Citizens and Southern National Bank, made much of this kind of information available to another group which was examining that bank. Following is a partial list of the data that FNCB refused to disclose; where C&S appears in parentheses it is to indicate that Citizens and Southern made comparable data available to the C&S study group.

Loans to companies that share directors with the bank and holding company [5]

Loans to directors (C&S) [6]

Loans to affiliates and subsidiaries (C&S) [7]

The names of companies whose loans had been written off as losses [8]

The size of its loans to such troubled borrowers as Lockheed and the Chrysler Corporation [9]

Total loan commitments (C&S) [10]

The size of its loans to aerospace companies,[11] airlines,[12] oil companies,[13] stock brokers,[14] banks and other financial institutions, or any industry breakdown of its loan portfolio [15]

The volume of Master Charge credit and other revolving credit plans (C&S) [16]

The geographic distribution of the mortgage portfolio and a breakdown by type of building (C&S) [17]

Deposits over and under $800 [18] (which is the dividing line between accounts which are free of monthly service charge [19])

A breakdown of checking or time deposits into those of individuals, corporations, and partnerships (C&S) [20]

A breakdown of checking or time deposits by size [21]

The attendance record of directors (C&S) [22]

Litigation filed against the bank of holding company (C&S) [23]

The names of companies whose pension funds it manages (C&S) [24]

The average salary paid to different categories of employees [25]

The profitability of the bank's major divisions (C&S) [26]

Reinvestment of foreign profits [27]

Municipal bond issues underwritten, bidding procedures, and investment criteria (C&S) [28]

Master Charge merchant discount schedule [29]

A comprehensive list of subsidiaries [30]

The percentage of checking and time deposits generated by each of FNCB's major divisions [31]

The tax effect of FNCB's leasing activities [32]

The volume of Eurodollar borrowings (C&S) [33]

Procedures for lending money to borrowers whose credits have been classified by the Comptroller of the Currency as doubtful, substandard, and loss [34]

The bank's role in financing mergers in the oil industry [35]

Reasons for giving investment advice on New York City pension funds without fee [36] and

Identities of insurance companies writing credit-line insurance for FNCB borrowers (C&S) [37]

Much of the information was refused, not because of the need to preserve confidential customer relationships or keep other banks from obtaining "competitive" information, but because Citibank feels that the data shed too much light on what the bank does with depositors' money. For example, at the 1971 Annual Meeting of Citicorp stockholders, Chairman Walter Wriston was asked to disclose the bank's outstanding loans and commitments to the troubled aerospace-airline industry. When Wriston refused on the grounds that it was "competitive market information," he was asked to divulge aerospace-airline "loans and commitments in which other banks participate . . . ," i.e., arrangements of which Citibank's competitors already have knowledge.[38] Again, he refused, this time on the grounds that "different banks are in different circumstances and it would be very difficult." [39] The fact is, the other banks already have the figures or can easily compile them. Large loans of the type made in the aerospace-airline industry typically involve multibank syndicates with a relatively stable cast of participants among the large banks. Thus, Citibank withheld the information, not for "competitive" reasons, but to deny the public information needed to help make an informed evaluation of the bank's lending policies.

Another illustration of how difficult it is to extract information from Citibank involves another exchange that occurred at the 1971 Annual Stockholders Meeting. When asked "Why are the bank's investments in state and municipal securities so low at this time? . . . ," Chairman Wriston responded, "Our states and municipals are basically unchanged from a year ago, if I am not mistaken." [40] Chairman Wriston failed to mention, however, that in the first quarter of 1971, which ended the day after the annual meeting, the bank had liquidated $272,255,000 or one-fourth of its state and municipal bond portfolio.[41]

Citibank also refused to provide the task force with material which, by law, the bank is required to furnish upon request to members of the public. During the course of the trust study, four separate requests were made, each at different branch locations of the bank, for copies of FNCB's common trust fund reports. These are reports of the performance and portfolio composition of the collective investment funds that FNCB manages for the personal trusts. By law,[42] such reports must be furnished to any member of the public who requests them. Each time, an officer at the branch would take down the name of the task force member requesting the report and would promise to send him the reports by mail. These promises were never kept. Finally, the task force co-director (DE), went to the main headquarters of FNCB, at 53rd Street and Park Avenue.

Wearing a three-piece suit and striped tie, DE walked into the building. He was stopped by a security guard and asked to sign his name and destination in the building, the trust department. He signed in and went to the personal trust floor. DE asked the secretary for FNCB's common trust fund reports from 1960 to the present date. The secretary started toward the storeroom closet until she was stopped by a Mr. Manning Voorhees. Mr. Voorhees ushered DE into his office and asked DE where he was from. When DE replied, "The Center for Study of Responsive Law," Mr. Voorhees called in a Mr. Raymond Dobosiewiscz, another man from the Personal Trust Division, who asked DE how he had gotten into the building.

"Through the front door," DE replied.

"Weren't you stopped?" Mr. Dobosiewiscz asked.

"No," DE stated, "I signed in that I was going to the trust department and that was that."

"Oh," Mr. Dobosiewiscz exclaimed. "We have elaborate security provisions, not only to prevent people like you from getting in, but to stop strangers as well."

Mr. Voorhees asked DE what his educational background was, and then responded, "Well, we're glad to see you've had training. We really resent Nader sending in people with just B.A.'s."

Voorhees then told DE that the bank would mail the common trust fund reports requested. Voorhees helped DE on with his coat and escorted him down the elevator and walked him through the lobby to the Park Avenue entrance to the bank. That week Mr. Voorhees mailed DE copies of the common trust fund reports for just the 1969–71 period. DE had requested all the reports from 1960. The purpose of the request was to help the study group analyze the performance of FNCB's trust department and to determine the extent to which the trust department invested in companies having other commercial dealings with the bank.

Since Mr. Voorhees did not mail all of the reports requested and since, legally, DE, as a member of the public, had a right to such reports, DE and another member of the task force, Michael Berger, returned to FNCB three weeks later. Upon reaching the personal trust floor, DE asked to see Mr. Voorhees. While DE and MB were waiting for Voorhees, Mr. Dobosiewiscz rushed out of his office. DE started to reintroduce himself to Mr. Dobosiewiscz, who cut him off with, "I know who you are."

Mr. Dobosiewiscz led them into his own office. DE explained that he had come for the earlier common trust fund reports which Mr. Voorhees had promised to send but which never were sent. Mr. Dobosiewiscz said, "All I can talk to you about is the weather." Finally, Mr. Voorhees came in, but instead of bringing the common trust fund reports he handed DE a general brochure describing FNCB's trust services.

Voorhees then said, "Well, I guess you got what you came for." DE explained that such was not the case, since what was wanted was FNCB's common trust fund reports.

Voorhees stated, "We do not plan to give them to you." DE asked why not.

Voorhees answered, "We have come to the point where I feel we should terminate the conversation." He continued, "I feel that I must tell you that we'd prefer if you did not come into the building again. If you do, we will be forced to take sterner measures."

The Comptroller of the Currency is in charge of enforcing the law which guarantees the public access to a national bank's common trust fund reports. The task force requested, in person and by registered mail, that the Comptroller order FNCB to make the common trust fund reports available. The task force never received any response to these requests. Incidentally the Comptroller's office is paid for not by the public treasury, but by the banks themselves.

Banks should be required to disclose much information that they presently withhold. The most important need is for data on the banks' performance of their basic intermediary function—i.e., where they get their money and what they do with it. Thus, banks should be required to disclose their deposits by geographic location of depositors. Furthermore, deposits should be broken down by type of depositor—individuals, corporations, and government units—and by size of account.

Banks should also be required to disclose more information about the application of these funds. Residential mortgage loans —broken down by geography and into single and multiple dwellings—should be disclosed so that an assessment of each bank's role in meeting community housing needs can be made. Commercial and industrial loans should be broken down by industry and geography. This would permit an analysis of the extent to which banks are siphoning off one community's financial resources to meet the credit needs of another and to determine which industries are obtaining funds at the expense of others. This is not to say that there should be a rigid formula requiring banks to direct their credit back to the sources from which they obtain their deposits, but only that the basic data needed for an informed assessment of commercial bank activities is not available in systematic, up-to-date, and comprehensive form.

It is also important to require banks to disclose information concerning their lending rates. At a minimum, banks should be required to further refine the geographic and industry breakdown of their loan portfolios to indicate, for example, what proportion of commercial and industrial loans in each territory and industry are at the prime rate, a quarter over prime, and so on. This would permit an analysis—thus far precluded by bank secrecy—of whether banks are granting credit in a nondiscriminatory manner and whether certain sectors of the economy are obtaining preferential terms.

Even more detailed disclosure should be required of credit granted to companies with which the banks are interlocked through shared directors. Although Citibank asserts that credit is granted to the companies with which it shares directors on the terms generally available to other customers, the bank refuses to divulge data to substantiate this claim. The fact that two financially troubled interlocked companies—Pan American World Airways and the Boeing Company—have obtained vast sums of prime rate credit provides some grounds for skepticism. Representative Wright Patman, Chairman of the House Banking and Currency Committee, has long tried to ascertain the names of prime rate borrowers, but banks, citing the sanctity of the bank-customer relationship, have refused Patman's requests.

This raises another problem that deserves some discussion —the fact that banks do not distinguish between individual, corporate, and government customers when it comes to disclosing information. There are strong policy reasons for distinguishing between individuals and corporations in requiring the disclosure of data pertaining to bank relations. The fact that banks perform a "public trust," the fact that they have a monopoly over demand deposits, gives the public the right to have specific, detailed information on how banks exercise their credit-granting, money-creating powers. The fact that corporations are chartered by the government and have pervasive influence over the economic, physical, and sociopolitical environment, gives the people the right to information that would illuminate the extent to which—and the terms on which—their money is being distributed among various competing sectors of the economy.

Although it might, at the present time, be impractical to require disclosure of credit agreements between banks and all corporate customers, we believe that syndicate credit agreements in which two or more banks lend money to the same corporation should be made public. Not only would this shed some light on the banks' allocation of America's financial resources to the largest corporations, it would tend to encourage greater price competition by providing credit applicants with a yardstick for negotiating credit terms. If corporations sought to avoid the disclosure requirements by making separate credit agreements with different banks, this too would encourage price competition. Independent negotiations would tend to undermine the price uniformity that obtains from the present practice of banks working out the credit terms in concert.

We believe that the major reason for Citibank's refusal to disclose any information about its customer relationships is to withhold the information necessary for an informed assessment of how bank activities affect people's lives. If banks are to preserve their virtually limitless autonomy to decide to whom, at what price, and on what terms they will extend credit, they cannot afford to have the public find out what is done with its money. For full and frank disclosure would inevitably lead to demands that banks respond to some considerations that transcend their own immediate profit and loss and improve their compliance with the spirit and the letter of the laws that govern our economic system. Accordingly, the process of devising feasible and equitable means of financing the credit-starved sectors of the economy must start by piercing the veil of secrecy that presently surrounds the activities of commercial banks. This report is a step in that direction.

I

Citibankers

I absolutely believe that the greatest single fundamental strength of this organization is the old bit about the V.P. title on every briefcase, that unless you can maintain— and it's becoming increasingly difficult to maintain with all the idiot jobs created by the computer—but unless you can maintain for every individual that comes into this bank an atmosphere in which they can grow, then you've lost.

> —Robert Feagles
> Senior Vice President (Personnel)
> First National City Bank

Tom Wilcox, who's running our urban and public affairs program and is Vice Chairman of the bank, came into the bank at age sixteen as a pageboy. We sent him to Princeton.

> —J. Howard Laeri
> Vice Chairman
> First National City Bank

Women are better bankers than men, according to a management consultant's study recently completed for Citibank. They are more polite and more efficient in their dealings with the customers of Citibank's retail branch network—the one part of Citibank's commercial banking operation in which women have been accorded the opportunity to advance into positions of responsibility. In light of their superior performance in serving Citibank's individual customers, it seems reasonable to assume that, given an equal opportunity to move into responsible positions in the corporate (wholesale) banking field, women would perform at least as well as, if not better than men. So far, however, women, like blacks, Jews, and other minority groups, have been virtually excluded from positions of responsibility in the Corporate Banking Group.

Although Citibank calls itself an open society, in which the

1

only determinant of an employee's "career path" is her *
ability and determination to work hard, the fact is that jobs
entailing high levels of responsibility, discretion, and compensation are closed to thousands of qualified Citibankers. Although more than half of Citibank's employees are women
and more than 35% are black, there is not one woman or
black vice president in the Corporate Banking Group, the department that handles most of the bank's money and deals
with America's giant national and multinational corporations.
To say that most promotions are based on ability does not
mean that most capable, deserving employees are promoted.
For Citibank, in common with other pyramidal bureaucracies,
has many more competent, promotable employees whose abilities are being underutilized than it has responsible, challenging
positions to offer them.

Lack of opportunity for promotion is only one of Citibank's
personnel problems. Another is low pay. Banks pay notoriously low wages to the thousands of assembly-line clerical
employees who process tons of checks, securities, and other
papers and Citibank is no exception. Although Citibank's officers are well paid—virtually all officers earn over $12,000
and FNCB Chairman, Walter Wriston, earns $250,000, un-
skilled, entry-level clerical employees start at $4,400 a year,
employees who can do some typing start at $4,700 and high-
school graduates with business training get $5,000.² Although
these employees can expect about $600 in wage increases dur-
ing the first year if they perform well, salary progression
slows down once the employee approaches the midpoint in
the salary range that FNCB assigns to a given function.³ A
detailed study of hiring practices at the large New York City
banks, conducted in 1970 by Professor R. David Corwin of
New York University, noted that in banks' mid-range salary
grades (6–9) "approximately 90% of the employees make
$6,500 or less." ⁴ In light of the fact that over 90% of
the new clerical workers start in grades 1–9,⁵ it seems reasonable to conclude that the vast majority of Citibank's clerical
workers earn less than $6,500. This income is well below
the $7,183 that the U.S. Department of Labor estimated was

*More than 50% of Citibank's employees are women.

necessary in early 1970 to sustain a low standard of living for a New York City family of four.[6] In sum, most of FNCB's clerical employees receive wages that are only marginally adequate to support a family in New York City.

A third major personnel problem is working conditions, especially in the back office. Like workers on industrial assembly lines, the 5,000 clerical workers in Citibank's Operating Group, perform dull, repetitive tasks under exacting production schedules in noisy, uncomfortable surroundings. (See the discussion of Operating Group working conditions, pp. 12–18.)

As a result of the limited promotion opportunities, low wages, and poor working conditions, Citibank's employees quit in droves. In 1969, more than one out of every three domestic employees—or 6,000 people—left the bank. In the recession year of 1970, when it was more difficult to go down the street and get another job, the rate of turnover dropped to 29%, but over 5,000 people still left Citibank. Surprisingly, employee dissatisfaction is highest among long-service employees.[8]

In recent years, as the manpower requirements at the large New York City banks escalated due to their growth and enormous turnover rates, the banks have begun hiring more minority employees. Personnel managers convinced the bank management that employment hiring standards had to be relaxed to fill their manpower needs. The high-school diploma requirement disappeared as banks focused increasingly on the prospective employee's performance capability instead of her credentials, as Professor Corwin notes:

> All the [large New York City banks] realized that the "standards" which seemed to be prerequisite for performing a task were not in fact necessary but rather had become barriers to employment for individuals perfectly capable of doing the work but unable to marshall the formal and informal credentials necessary to do the job.[9]

As the New York City labor market became tighter and tighter in the boom of the late 1960s, Congress created the JOBS (Job Opportunity in the Business Sector) program to encourage the training of "hard-core" unemployed. Although most New York City banks participate in the JOBS program run by the New York Chapter of the American Institute of Banking (AIB), FNCB, like Chase Manhattan Bank, chose to set up its own program. AIB and Chase began with an attempt to provide trainees with high-school equivalency training. FNCB however concentrated on job skills.*

FNCB's JOBS program has two tracks—a 16-week course for general clerks and machine operators and a 20-week course for typists. Virtually all of the trainees are black and Puerto Rican women. The program focuses on job-related skills and provides counseling and some remedial academic work. A key element is the early establishment of an employer-employee relationship by paying trainees. Although Department of Labor guidelines suggest that JOBS program trainees receive entry-level wages during the training period, FNCB pays only $70 a week—$15 below the $85 starting wage. Nonetheless, the trainees do get paid.[10] The Department of Labor pays for the entire program, except for those costs that the bank would ordinarily incur in training employees hired off the street. Citibank received $2,200,000 and laid out $300,000 of its own money to train about 1,000 graduates of the program.[11]

Forty per cent of the trainees drop out during the program. Robert Feagles, FNCB's Senior Vice President in charge of Personnel Administration, says that this compares favorably with the normal dropout rate. Of the 1,000 graduates, 500–600 were still at FNCB during the summer of 1970. According to Feagles, the first group of trainees performed so well that some supervisors specifically request JOBS-trained employees for their departments. Once they start work, the bank treats the trainees like other employees.

FNCB's JOBS program has been successful—up to a point. Although it has brought people with no job skills and nonexistent or spotty employment histories into the labor force, it has done little to deal with the most important bank personel problem—upgrading entry level employees. The JOBS program also provides businesses with federal money to upgrade disadvantaged employees, but thus far Citibank has not utilized this option. Feagles noted that there were 50% more minority supervisors than the year before, but when queried as to the number, he couldn't remember.[12]

---

*However, Citibank takes only people who can read at the sixth-grade level.

Despite the increased rate of hiring minority employees, "at the management levels," as Professor Corwin's study noted, "minorities are incidental to the world of banking." [13] Most of the blacks and other minority employees on Citibank's payroll are concentrated at the lower pay grades. Thus Citibank's back office paper processing factory is mostly staffed by black and Puerto Rican women. The night shift, in particular, is a ghetto—except for the supervisors. Branch platform personnel (i.e., the officers who sit at the desks on the main floors of the branches) are almost exclusively white, though a substantial proportion—roughly 30% according to a recent management consulting study—are women.[14] Tellers, clerks, and guards are a mixture of black and white men and women.[15] The corporate lending department, however, is overwhelmingly white and male.[16]

1. Corporate Bankers

Women, blacks, and other minority employees have been virtually excluded from the corporate lending area. Of the 288 officers in the Corporate Banking Group on July 1, 1969, there was one black and three women, all assistant cashiers in non-lending jobs.[17] A major reason for the absence of women and blacks in the corporate lending area is the fact that a large part of the job involves, as many bankers put it, "being a face man." Much bank-corporation business is transacted in informal and recreational settings, in which blacks, women, and other minorities just don't "fit."

The women who do get hired are assigned less responsible tasks and receive lower salaries than their male counterparts. One woman, with a graduate degree in business administration, received $8,000, compared to the $12,000 paid male trainees. She was assigned to an essentially public-relations-type job without lending authority. She was called upon to provide cooking and fashion services. Similarly, the only black officer in the Corporate Banking Group was in the Corporate Services Division and had no lending authority.[18]

Jews do not fare better. When asked why there were so few Jewish Vice Presidents at FNCB, one officer, who recently left after more than five years with the bank, replied:

I can't think of any. All organizations have an ethnic character
—law firms, investment banking houses, and banks. First National City Bank's character is WASP, that's all. Jews make it
if they can assimilate and fit in. An organization will bend to
make room for someone not their own kind if the guy is so extremely capable that they have to put up with him and if he'll
change halfway.

Chase Manhattan and Manufacturers Hanover are even more
anti-Semitic than Citibank, according to many bankers. "The
brightest MBA [Master of Business Administration]," noted
one bank personnel specialist, "will fail to get ahead at Chase
because he looks like he comes from the Garment District."

Citibank pays its officers well. The bank uses a "base plus
system with additives" for starting college graduates. A college
degree is worth $9,000 a year in base salary, plus another
$500–$700 for employees with relevant summer work experience, $500 for a record of academic excellence, $300 for
each year of military service as an enlisted man, and $500
for each year of military service as an officer. The average
college graduate entrant gets about $1,500–$1,700 in "additives," for a total starting salary of $10,500–$10,700.[19]

New employees with a two-year graduate degree, typically
an MBA, do better. Their base salary is $12,000. The same
additives apply for summer work experience, academic excel-
lence, and military service and the average MBA is paid
about $2,000 over the base, for a starting salary of $14,000
a year.[20]

As of July, 1969, assistant cashiers, the lowest ranking officers, were paid from $10,400 to $33,500. Assistant vice
presidents received from $17,000 to $38,000 and vice presidents earned from $18,750 to $67,000.[21] Although we were
unable to obtain specific figures on salaries paid to senior vice
presidents and executive vice presidents, we estimate that salaries for senior vice presidents start in the upper region of the
vice president salary range and go up to about $100,000. Execu-
tive vice presidents probably earn about $100,000.

FNCC's 1971 proxy material indicates that Vice Chairman
Thomas Wilcox receives $144,370. George C. Scott, the other
vice chairman, probably gets the same amount, as did his predecessor. Executive Committee Chairman Edward L. Palmer is

paid $160,840, and President William Spencer receives $189,840. Chairman Walter Wriston is paid $257,820.[22]

Despite the widespread belief that promoting blacks, women, and other discriminated-against groups to responsible positions is an act of corporate charity that conflicts with profit maximization, there is substantial reason to believe that just the opposite is true. In fact, Citibank's personnel and promotion policies have increased the turnover rate, decreased the quality of the service offered to FNCB's customers, and eliminated qualified blacks, women, and noncollege-trained employees from consideration for promotion.

In 1970, FNCB hired Cresap, McCormick & Paget, a New York management consulting firm, to do a shopping survey of a cross-section of Citibank branches in order to determine how FNCB could increase the quality of its customer service and its share of the retail banking market. The results of the study disprove some widely held misconceptions about personnel policies.

According to the Cresap study, FNCB's general requirement that platform officers be college educated may be too stringent:

—The level of education does appear to have some positive correlation with desire to serve, but these benefits are open to question when the relatively narrow difference between the performance of high-school and college graduates is considered in the light of the substantially higher salaries which employees with college degrees can command.
—The desire to serve ratings accorded platform personnel with college degrees was less than 1 per cent greater than those who only have some college education.
—The level of education attained also appears to have a positive correlation with the impact of the banker's personality traits, but these benefits should again be questioned in the light of incremental salary costs.

The Cresap study noted that probable causes of Citibank's personnel problems included:

—Job specifications which are too high in light of current conditions, because of the traditional concept of the banker's role.
—Assumption that a higher level of education will necessarily result in a corresponding improvement in performance on the platform.

The study concluded:

> —The company is not taking full advantage of a large supply of potential employees.
> —The payroll costs of supplying a given level of service to customers is higher than is necessary.
> —The company's hiring and promotional policies and practices relating to minority and lower income groups may be open to question.
> —Morale on the platform may be lower and turnover higher than they should be because some employees are over-qualified for the positions which they hold.[23]

The study also concluded that "it is more important that [the banker] develop a high degree of skill in interpersonal relations and communications than a high level of technical product knowledge." [24] Thus, long term-credit experience or training did not result in superior branch officer performance. On the contrary,

> *Long-term Service, Or A Specific Type of Functional Experience May Not Be Desirable Requirements for Advancement To The Platform* [emphasis in original]
> —Shoppers' rating of the banker's desire to serve, efficiency and politeness generally began to decline after 14 years of service, but the average length of service of the 131 bankers who were shopped and identified was 15.7 years.
> —The composite percentage of excellent and good ratings of the impact of bankers' personality traits actually decreased somewhat for bankers with more than nine years of service, and the efficiency of those people employed for more than 15 years was actually rated lower than those with less than five years of service.
> —Efficiency and politeness appears highest in those bankers under 30, while desire to serve was most apparent in the 30–39 age group. Nevertheless, the average age of the bankers who were shopped and identified was 42.2 years.
> — . . . it would [probably] be desirable to lower the overall average for both length of service and age of the platform staff by placing qualified candidates in platform positions as soon as their experience (of whatever type) allows, at a relatively younger age, if possible.[25]

Another finding of the survey was that women bankers perform better than their male counterparts:

> *The Proportion Of Females on the Platform May Not Be As Great As It Should Be.* [emphasis in original]

—Only one-third of the 131 platform bankers who were shopped and identified during the study were women.

—An analysis of the survey findings reveals the following about their performance:

*Females on the platform were accorded a higher proportion of excellent and good ratings on their desire to serve than men.

*Women were rated substantially better than men in the impact of their personality traits on customers for each of the five factors that were tested.

*Women were rated almost 11% better than men in politeness and efficiency, the two traits which customers considered to be the most important.[26]

Accordingly, Cresap recommended that *"Capable Women Should Be Assigned To Fill Openings On The Platform Staff Whenever Possible."* [27] There is, however, no indication that recognition of this superiority will lead to expanded promotion of women beyond the platform. On the contrary, Cresap takes it for granted that, unlike men, women platform officers will neither expect nor receive promotions into positions of greater responsibility because they "would be quite satisfied to assume platform responsibilities as a permanent assignment." [28] Thus, despite the evidence that "women can function at least as well (and possibly better) than men," [29] they are not accorded the opportunity to compete with men for the more important positions in the bank.

The fact that only one of Citibank's 300 vice presidents is a woman while more than half of its employees are female [30] indicates how limited the promotion opportunities for women are. Citibank didn't have one woman vice president until May, 1971, when it promoted a woman in the International Banking Group who had been a Citibanker for 28 years.[31]

The Cresap study demonstrates that it is in FNCB's interest to accelerate promotion for women, people with less education, employees in clerical and operating positions without specific credit training or experience, and young people. Women, blacks, and other minorities are heavily represented in these groups. Adoption of the recommendations, however, will not be easy. Though many current platform officers are performing below par, at least in part, according to the study, because their abilities are being underutilized, it would be inequitable to discharge them. The problem is not of their making, but rather stems from the fact that their training qualified them for jobs that entail discretion, initiative, and responsibility, while their jobs are largely clerical and administrative. Furthermore, FNCB cannot create openings on the platform for women, blacks, clerks, and less-educated operations personnel by promoting the present platform employees into jobs more suited for their training and talents because "the number of promotable candidates [on the platform] is greater than the number of opportunities which are available." [32] Change, therefore, will be slow.

In 1970, FNCB was challenged under New York State's Human Rights Law for discriminating against women.[33] Beverly Wadsworth, a *cum laude* graduate from Radcliffe College, sued FNCB alleging that during her employment at the bank she was the object of subtle and blatant discrimination. In hearings before the New York State Human Rights Division, Ms. Wadsworth explained that because she was a woman the bank thwarted her attempts to become a corporate lending officer and instead directed her to the personal banking group. Ms. Wadsworth explained that despite high ratings from other bank officers, her superiors treated her as a file clerk. Ms. Wadsworth introduced evidence during the hearings illustrating that she was assigned fewer accounts to manage than men at her level, and that she was paid less well than those men.

The Wadsworth hearings also portrayed some of Citibank's overall personnel practices. When the FNCB's personnel directory was introduced into evidence, the almost total lack of women officers became apparent. Even when a woman had an official title, she was listed in the directory at the end of the section, her title was omitted, and, unlike the men, her marital status was noted. The hearings also highlighted the fact that Citibank did no recruiting at any all-women colleges.

Ms. Wadsworth's testimony described the attitudes of other officers of the bank, such as Donald Evans, a vice president. According to Ms. Wadsworth, during a conversation on January 13, 1970, Evans told her that women were proven to be poor at getting new business; therefore Evans was unwilling to give Wadsworth new business names to go after. To which Wadsworth replied, "Why not—I would be glad to call on new business names." Ms. Wadsworth recounted the two reasons Evans gave her for the bank's increasing interest in promoting women: first, women are more adept at handling certain situations because bank customers are less likely to swear at women; and second, Citibank wants to promote women so as not to be accused of discriminating against them. Mr. Evans, in testifying about the January 13 conversation, noted, "In the course of the conversation I did indicate that I had observed that men are less likely to lose their tempers when complaining to a woman."

Ms. Wadsworth's was not the only challenge to Citibank's employment practices during the past year. During 1972 a group of women from the National Organization of Women (NOW) picketed FNCB's branch at the bank's corporate headquarters. The women demanded to see a woman officer, and, when the bank refused· to let the group meet with one, the women closed out their accounts with the bank. Quite possibly, the bank's lack of cooperation with the NOW group was based on inability to find a woman officer in their ranks for, of the 300 vice presidents in the Corporate Banking Group, not one is a woman.

In 1972 New York City Councilwoman Carol Greitzer tried to do a study of employment practices in New York banks. Her conclusion was that the largest banks discriminate against women by demoting and underpaying them and denying them educational opportunities necessary for advancement. Councilwoman Greitzer said that FNCB was "very uncooperative in making information available." [34]

One unequivocal way to evaluate Citibank's efforts in the area of minority employment would be to examine the bank's EEO–1 forms which contain complete data on employment of minority groups. Citibank refused the study group's request for these forms. In our opinion, FNCB's unwillingness to make public this data casts serious doubt on the honesty of its minority hiring and promotion efforts. It is very nice to hear William Spencer, FNCB President, tell others that "Corporations, whenever possible, should seek to employ and promote qualified women, blacks, and minority groups," [35] but these words ring hollow without evidence that such policies are the policies of Mr. Spencer's own corporation. It is well and good that FNCB subscribes to New York State's Division of Human

Rights program "to voluntarily increase the number of minority and female employees in bank middle management and professional executive positions," [36] but this, too, is hollow when the bank does not actually demonstrate that it is promoting qualified employees.

According to William H. Brown, Chairman of the Equal Employment Opportunity Commission (EEOC), "equal employment opportunity hasn't happened in the banking industry." There are a large percentage of women who are "invariably congregated in lower positions. If you have a large reservoir of women and have really given them the opportunity to rise, a significant portion should be in top management and this is not true in the banking industry." [37]

2. The Factory

Factory type operations . . . are the task performed largely and increasingly by minorities. In fact much of the Wall Street operations are in the process of becoming ghetto-ized.[38]

—*Professor R. David Corwin*

Speed and low cost are the major objectives of the Item Processing Division (IPD) of the Operating Group of FNCB, which processes millions of checks each day. Speed is important because the sooner the checks can be processed and collected, the sooner the funds are available for the bank to put into loans and investments. A reduction in this "float," the time between presentation and collection, makes Citibank more efficient and profitable.

Until a few years ago, FNCB's back office operation was dreadfully inefficient. The bank had projected that if existing trends continued, within five years it would have been impossible to make any money.[39] FNCB reacted by naming William Spencer, the top corporate loan officer (and now president), to the task of shaping up the Operating Group. Spencer and his 31-year-old successor, John Reed, an MIT-trained specialist in industrial management, undertook a detailed cost-analysis of the Operating Group in order to find out how they could reduce costs and float time. As John Reed noted:

> We found that there was no record of what resources were being consumed to produce what. The departments were organized in a helter-skelter manner. There were no clean flows of activity. . . .
>
> We have created the mechanism to inject productivity changes just like General Motors or Standard Oil, or anybody else, which will serve to absorb the very legitimate and necessary labor cost increases.
>
> We hired from a friendly auto manufacturer some people who know something about how to develop the types of managerial support systems you need to run a factory.[40]

Like many factories, FNCB's back office operates 24 hours a day in order to increase the use of the expensive computer facilities and to reduce the "float" time. Unlike many factories, however, Citibank's back office is manned by nominally white-collar, unorganized employees, receiving relatively low wages.

Despite the fact that FNCB's check processing operation is extensively automated, it is still a relatively labor-intensive operation. When checks are deposited in a Citibank account they are forwarded to the Item Processing Division located in a new building at 111 Wall Street in downtown Manhattan. The IPD counts the 2,000,000 checks that arrive each day by weighing them (300 checks per pound, or three tons a day).[41] The checks then go to the operators of 200 mica encoding machines, who print the dollar amount on each check in magnetic ink, which can be read by the computers. A proficient operator can handle 1,000 checks per hour, or better than 16 checks per minute. The account number is already printed on the check in magnetic ink. The checks are then fed into a computer, which transfers the information onto a transaction tape, and sorts the checks into two categories, those drawn on Citibank accounts (posted checks) and those which are drawn on accounts at other banks (cleared checks). The transaction tape, which contains a record of all transactions handled within the previous 24 hours, is run through another computer in order to transfer the information onto a history tape, containing a record of all transactions in each account since the last monthly statement.

Checks are sorted a second time—posted checks according to customer account, and cleared checks according to geographical location of the drawee bank. This is done by computerized sorting machines that can process 2,000 to 3,000 checks per minute. The posted checks go to the Services Operations Department where employees make sure that there are no stop orders before filing them into each customer's account along with cleared checks from other banks drawn on Citibank. The employees in this department also answer inquiries from depositors who have lost track of their balances. Every month, the checks are pulled from each account file and sent out with the monthly statement, which is printed out by computers.

Cleared checks are sent to the local clearinghouse, the Federal Reserve banks or to correspondent banks, which forward them to the banks on which they are drawn. Somewhere along the line, all the checks are photocopied by the bank.[42]

Another labor-intensive function that the Operating Group performs is processing corporate stock transfers. When a sale of corporate stock occurs, the stockbroker sends the securities to the bank that acts as the corporation's stock transfer agent. The bank cancels the old securities and issues new ones, and the name of the purchaser is printed on the securities. Although part of this operation has been automated at Citibank, it still requires a large amount of routinized clerical work.[43]

Citibank's paper processing factory, the Operating Group, has the highest turnover rate in the bank, and it's not difficult to understand the reason. A comprehensive attitude survey of the Operation Group's 5,602 workers, performed in 1970 by the Opinion Research Corporation, of Princeton, New Jersey, discloses profound employee dissatisfaction over promotion opportunities, working conditions, pay scales, fringe benefits, and employee-management relations.

Oppressive working conditions is a major grievance of Citibank's 4,937 Operating Group clerical employees, who constitute 88% of the Operating Group work force (200 officers and 465 supervisors account for 3.6% and 8.4%, respectively).[44] An extraordinary proportion of Operating Group clerical employees complain of inadequate space and equipment, too much noise, uncomfortable temperatures, too many rush jobs and insufficient staff to handle the work load, inadequate advance notice of overtime and changes affecting the job, too much duplication, and too much work piled on the good employees.

Thirty-seven per cent of all Operating Group clerical employees rated the space they had to work in as "poor" or "very poor." [45]

Thirty per cent of all Operating Group clerical employees commented unfavorably on the equipment and machines. In both areas, long-term employees had the highest proportion of negative responses. [46]

Noise was another source of complaints. Thirty-four per cent of all Operating Group clerical employees responded negatively when asked to rate "noise in your work area" with the highest proportion of "poor" and "very poor" ratings from Spanish Americans. [47]

Although the Operating Group is located in a three-year-old air-conditioned building, 39% rated temperature as "poor" or "very poor," with long-term employees the most dissatisfied. [48]

In addition to dissatisfaction with the physical environment in which they work, 32% of all Operating Group clerical workers said that there were not enough people to do the work, and 25% stated that Citibank was "poor" or "very poor" in avoiding duplication of work. [49] Moreover, more than 75% of the employees agreed that "People who do the best work often find more and more work piled on them."

Similarly, 46% of all Operating Group clerical employees agreed that "often the daily work must be put aside in order to do rush jobs that come in without much advance notice." [50]

In light of the high volume of work and the frequency with which rush jobs come in, it is not surprising that a significant minority of employees in different departments disagree with the statement that "[we] receive sufficient advance notice when we have to work overtime." Although only 31% of all Operating Group clerical employees disagreed, 47% of the night shift employees in the Input Section of the Item Processing Division agreed. [51]

Similarly, a high proportion of Operating Group clerical employees responded negatively when asked whether the bank informed them in advance of changes affecting their work. Overall, 34% rated FNCB as "poor" or "very poor" in this respect.

The clerical employees also expressed significant dissatisfaction with their wages and fringe benefits. Again, one-third rated their pay as "poor" or "very poor." Almost two-thirds felt that salary levels are lower at Citibank than in other large companies in New York City. Forty-one per cent disagreed with the statement that "pay raises in my area are given fairly." [52]

Notwithstanding Citibank's professed devotion to promoting employees into more responsible positions whenever possible, these workers do not believe that their chances of getting ahead are primarily dependent on performance. On the contrary, 55% of them agreed with the statement that employees are "[held] back from promotion because [the] boss feels that you are too valuable to lose." [53] In fact, 39% of all Operating Group clerical employees disagreed with the statement that "[at] Citibank, staff members who do the best work are promoted more rapidly and receive better raises than those whose work isn't very good." [54]

Thirty-five per cent of all Operating Group clerical workers rated Citibank as "poor" or "very poor" in "making it possible for you to transfer from one job to another." In the Input Section of the Item Processing Division, 46% of night shift employees gave negative ratings in this area.[55] And 40% of all Operating Group clericals rate as "poor" or "very poor" Citibank's provision for job training to help employees qualify for better jobs.[56]

The oppressiveness of the work cannot be overemphasized. Despite the mod-decorated interior and piped-in Muzak, Citibank's factory workers, like those interviewed for Professor Corwin's study, "referred to the tedium and boring character of the operations they performed, the heaviness of the work production quotas, the compulsory overtime rules, and the social remoteness of their supervisors." [57] "It's such a drag," said one woman who operated a mica encoding machine. "Imagine if you had to type numbers all your life. It's horrible. I hate it but I can't get transferred to another job. I'd like to quit but I can't seem to find another job. And I need the money."

Another echoed similar sentiments: "The pay's lousy. I earn ninety bucks a week and after the deductions, I still can't pay the rent," noted one clerk. "But the worst part is the boredom. I hardly do anything but count papers and carry them around. Man, there's no way out. Nobody gets promoted and if you quit, it's the same scene everywhere else." One bank conducted a study of the employees who quit and, not surprisingly, discovered that employees with higher employment test scores were quitting sooner than those with lower scores.[58]

The limited opportunities for advancement make it very difficult for blacks and other minorities, who are concentrated in low-level jobs, to move into more responsible positions. "Virtually all supervisory personnel," noted Corwin's study, "are hostile to accelerated promotion of minority persons." [59] The prevailing attitude is "It took me ten years and I don't care what your color is." But this attitude ignores the fact that the minority employees would be more evenly spread out in higher grades if the banks had not long maintained excessive barriers to hiring and promotion.

Employee dissatisfaction and alienation by oppressive working conditions is not, of course, peculiar to Citibank and the other large New York City banks. Unlike other industries, however, in which union power has enabled workers to obtain higher wages to compensate for the dreariness of the daily routine, virtually no efforts have been made to organize bank employees. The nature of the work performed by many bank employees, however, has a lot in common with traditional blue-collar work. Yet Citibank's back-office employees receive wages that are only marginally adequate to support a family in New York City. In a very real sense, therefore, the huge profits earned by Citibank in recent years are subsidized by its workers.

Unions should make a concerted effort to organize the 5,000 factory workers in Citibank's back office. Citibank is much more vulnerable to traditional union organization methods than many industries that have already been organized. Every department of the bank is highly dependent on the factory. The entire factory operation is located in one building. Shutting down the factory for even a few days, and perhaps even a walkout by a substantial number of key employees, would immobilize the entire bank. Most efforts to unionize banks, however, have focused on organizing at the branch level, where relatively better working conditions, higher salaries, and far-flung branch networks have made success more difficult. By concentrating on the factory, however, unions would find it relatively easy to organize the workers and compel management to pay wages that compensate for the dehumanizing toll of the factory's "idiot jobs."

II

Retail Banking for Individuals

First National City Bank is the largest retail bank in New York City. It has more branches, more individual checking deposits, more passbook savings deposits, more credit cardholders, and more credit customers than any other commercial bank in New York City.

Growth, however, not service, has been the hallmark of Citibank's retail operation. FNCB's striking expansion of retail banking services and volume has not been accompanied by a corresponding improvement in the quality of service offered to its individual customers. Consultant studies, commissioned by the bank in 1959, 1962, and 1970, show that Citibank's service was relatively good in 1959, improved measurably by 1962, but deteriorated sharply thereafter.

Because most people base their choice of bank on convenient location and because Citibank has 25% more branches than its nearest competitor, slovenly service costs Citibank very little. Accordingly, in terms of the "trade-off" between the cost of improving service and the business lost by not doing so, it may be more profitable for Citibank to continue growing in size and complexity without much attention to service.

The major burden of Citibank's poor service falls on the customer, not the bank; people waste their time, suffer confusion and frustration from their inability to understand the operation and cost of bank services, and incur needless service and finance charges. Particularly hard hit are low-income debtors, who frequently obtain credit they cannot repay because the bank fails to ensure that its minimum credit standards are applied by branch personnel. Consequently, Citibank is New York's largest plaintiff; within a two-year period Citibank filed over 25,000 lawsuits to recover money from debtors in default.[1]

Citibank is also contemptuous of its customers' legal rights:

it violates the "truth-in-lending" laws, the "due process" clause of the U.S. Constitution and the process-serving laws, and it exploits the illegal behavior of others by threatening to inform the debtor's employer of an impending garnishment. Although these practices are open and notorious, as we will see, the government agencies responsible for enforcing the laws have done virtually nothing to end them.

1. Expanding Everything But Service

In 1959, when Citibank had 85 domestic branches,[2] all located in New York City, it hired the management consulting firm of Cresap, McCormick and Paget to perform a shopping survey of its branches.* The bank wanted to find out how well its branch platform personnel (the officers at the desks, as opposed to the tellers) were performing their duties and to compare FNCB's service with that of other New York City banks. The survey discovered that FNCB had a "less than satisfactory competitive standing in the retail customer service offered by its platform personnel"; platform personnel "took comparatively little advantage of the opportunities for cross-selling" (i.e., pushing other services); shoppers reported "a widespread lack of interest in them as individual bank customers"; and "in particular, National City personnel appeared not to be making full use of their opportunities to present the Bank to the retail customer as one best qualified to serve him in all his banking needs." [3]

The "First Service Shopping Program," as the 1959 study was called, led to a new conference training program between branch personnel and top management of the bank. In 1962, when FNCB's branch network had 104 offices,[4] Cresap was hired to perform a "Second Service Shopping Program" to evaluate the effectiveness of the new training program. Cresap

---

* Incidentally, in December, 1970, FNCC purchased all the outstanding stock of Cresap. Then in June, 1972 the Fed ruled that management consulting does not qualify as an activity "closely related to banking." Thus it is not a permissible activity for a bank holding company. FNCC, however, has until 1980 to divest itself of Cresap.

discovered that Citibank's service had improved to the point where "on an over-all basis, National City now has the slight service advantage which its competition enjoyed in 1959."

The most striking aspect of the 1962 survey was that it revealed a high proportion of platform personnel able to explain clearly the operation and costs of at least some of the bank's services. More than 95% of Citibank's platform personnel clearly explained the differences between, and comparative costs of, special and regular checking accounts, up from 89% in 1959.[5] When shoppers inquired about opening a savings account, however, the performance of platform personnel fell down. Only 40% could describe the basic rules pertaining to savings accounts.[6]

The overall personal impact of FNCB's platform personnel in depositor shopping situations, according to the 1962 Cresap study, was very good: 95% acknowledged the shopper's presence promptly and courteously, 94% were alert and businesslike, 88% created a friendly feeling, and 87% gave a feeling of confidence in their ability.[7]

The performance of Citibank's platform personnel varied considerably when shoppers inquired about credit services. Eighty-four per cent of the bankers clearly explained the operation of auto loans and 77% of the officers explained the operation of home mortgage loans, but only 37% of the bankers clearly explained the operation of small business loans.[8]

Having concluded that in 1962 FNCB was doing comparatively well, Cresap made few recommendations. It suggested that Citibank: develop personnel standards for individuals who deal with retail customers; decentralize and improve its training programs; and consider assigning all retail business development to one person in each branch, supervised by one individual at headquarters.[9]

By the time Cresap performed the "Third Service Shopping Program" in 1970, when FNCB had expanded to 200 branches,[10] Citibank's overall retail service had deteriorated sharply.

Overall, Citibank's branch platform officers explained the services available only 61% of the time.[11] With few exceptions, the quality of service is below average for the most basic credit and deposit services. As Cresap noted:

Composite ratings of the banker's knowledgeability in two of
the most basic retail banking transactions (Opening A Checking
Account and Opening A Passbook Savings Account) were both
below the average of the thirteen roles in this group, while their
performance in the role of dealing with an automobile loan was
the second highest.[12]

When shoppers inquired about opening a special checking account, only 65% of the bankers could explain clearly how
the account worked, down from 89% in 1962. Only 47%
"scored composite affirmative ratings" on opening a checking
account.[13] Only 40% of the bankers could explain the comparative costs of different types of checking accounts, down
from 79% in 1962.[14] There was, however, some improvement in the ability of bankers to explain savings accounts,
from 63% to 66%.[15]

The overall performance in explaining credit services was
dismal. Only 35% of the platform personnel could explain the
essential requirements to qualify for "Ready-Credit," Citibank's
"instant loan," [16] whereby customers apply, in advance, for a
"line of credit." [17] "Product knowledge displayed in connection with another important service [Master Charge] was
also rated well below the average of the 13 roles in this group,
with a composite score of 49.6%." [18] When shoppers asked
about the computation of Master Charge credit card costs, only
46% of the bankers could spell out the costs.[19] "Checking
Plus," which allows a checking account depositor to write a
check for more money than he has in his account, was cor-
rectly explained 56% of the time.[20] By comparison, the best
performance by platform personnel—78%—occurred in the
relatively unimportant area of explaining Citibank's multitude
of personalized, mod-colored checks, which, by the way, are
available in "exclusive" Pucci-decorated checkbooks.[21]

Service at branches varies tremendously. Suburban and
smaller branches consistently received relatively high scores:

[There was a] . . . wide variation in the customer's ratings of
the bankers' desire to serve—from a high of 100.0% excellent
and good ratings at Rye, Bronxville, and Armonk [located in
suburban Westchester County] to a low of 57.1% at Eighty-
Sixth Street [and Broadway in Manhattan].
There was also a 42.9% spread in the rating of the quality of

service obtained at different branches, with Armonk and Castleton Corners [located in Staten Island] the highest (92.9%), and Broadway–56th Street the lowest (50.0%).[22]

Cresap concluded that the "probable causes" for the variations in the level of customer service were:

> A lack of clearly established customer service policies and standards which can be uniformly applied throughout the retail banking organization. A lack of uniform standards by which customer service performance can be measured and compared.[23]

In light of these findings, it is not surprising that when shoppers attempted to redeem a "Golden Growth Bond," a consumer time deposit that can be cashed only at three-month intervals,[24] they encountered different receptions from branch to branch:

> . . . shoppers at nine branches were successful in their request to redeem their Golden Growth Bonds, while the same request made by the same people was refused at 16 others . . .[25]

Not only do Citibank's customers receive poor service, they have to wait for it, as the Cresap study noted: "[More] than 18% of the customers at all branches had to wait more than 5 minutes for service—even though the bank was not at all busy.[26] This, the study concluded, was due to poor platform coverage:

> . . . the variations in the length of time which shoppers had to wait for service indicates there are some basic differences between platform coverage and customer demand.[27]

Like the quality of customer service, waiting time varied from branch to branch. It is interesting to note that Cresap found a "tendency . . . of the larger branches to give a lower quality of service."[28] Cresap concluded that this was due to:

> Lack of policies defining what a desirable and minimum level of platform coverage should be.
> Lack of policies defining what an adequate level of customer service actually is.
> Lack of standards to measure and compare the platform coverage and customer service rendered at different branches.[29]

One reason Citibank's service deteriorated so dramatically

is that between 1962 and 1970 the bank doubled the size of its domestic branch network, ignoring the administrative problems generated by such rapid expansion. The Comptroller of the Currency, the regulatory agency responsible for passing on branch applications, has approved the applications with a virtual rubber stamp, never questioning the ability of management to monitor service at the branch level. Time and again, the Comptroller approved the applications, despite opposition from other banks and despite findings by its own examiners that the area to be served by the new branches was already being served adequately.[30]

Another reason for the deterioration is that Citibank has focused its primary attention on expanding the number of services without ensuring that its branch personnel were adequately trained or equipped with explanatory materials to understand and communicate the operation and costs of the various services to bank customers.

Finally, as noted, the bank has had no economic inducement to improve the quality of service because most retail customers choose a bank for its convenient location and Citibank has 25% more branches than its nearest competitor, Chase Manhattan.

Cresap's recommendations best summarize the disorganized and haphazard nature of Citibank's customer service:

Policies
The Personal Banking Group should clarify its policies regarding promptness of service, platform coverage, customer service versus other duties and service standards generally.

Organization
The arrangements for providing continuing training to platform personnel in explaining and selling the Bank's services (products) should be improved.
The management organization in the larger branches should be strengthened.
The specifications for recruiting platform personnel should be refined.

Methods of Communication
Communications should be improved in at least three areas:
   —Regarding the importance of product knowledge
   —Regarding the inter-relationships among products and groups of products

—Regarding the need for flexibility in explaining products under various conditions.

The relative importance should be clarified of:
—The various types of transactions
—The various aspects of these transactions

Platform personnel should be taught:
—Efficiency
—Salesmanship
—How to view problems from the customers' viewpoint rather than from the bank's viewpoint.

Selling aids and how-to-sell instructions should be provided for platform personnel.

Greater knowledge of the specifications of the merchandise selected for promotion should be imparted.

The basic concepts of scheduling personnel to cover customer traffic should be developed and communicated to branch management.

The training efforts directed at former operations and personal credit bankers should be continued and intensified.

Methods of Motivation

Standards for measuring performance and incentives to encourage improved performance should be developed and installed.

Other techniques to inspire personnel to perform to potential should be devised and implemented.

The rating of selling results should be more precise and the rewarding of outstanding efforts should be speeded.

All of the possible methods should be used to convince platform personnel that the customer is king.

Methods of Control

Improved methods of controlling individual branch performance should be developed and installed.

Cross-selling and other basic objectives should be defined by branch size.

Better controls for the scheduling of platform personnel to serve customers should be established.

Facilities

Platform layouts should be revamped only where experience dictates.[31]

We now turn our attention to the area of consumer credit in order to evaluate the consequences of Citibank's poor level of retail customer service. This area illustrates how what economists call the "externalities" of poor or grasping bank sales practices take their human toll.

2. Consumer Credit

In dollar volume FNCB's retail credit operation is much larger than that of any other commercial bank in New York City. On December 31, 1969, FNCB's "Loans to individuals for household, family, and other consumer expenditures" (including credit card accounts) amounted to $1,059,079,000. This equals 4.3% of its total assets.[32] For comparison purposes, Chase Manhattan's volume was $572,773,000 (2.6% of assets);[33] Manufacturers Hanover's was $472,413,000 (3.9% of assets);[34] Chemical's was $478,624,000 (4.9% of assets),[35] and all commercial banks held $63,355,683,000, equal to 12% of their assets.[36]

Citibank is New York's leading retail bank because its passive approach to customer service, detailed in Cresap's 1970 survey, does not extend to marketing. Citibank is very aggressive when it comes to selling its "products," but it is much more concerned with market penetration through gimmicky advertising, cross-selling, promotional offerings, and volume-oriented employee incentive programs than with explaining the operation and cost of its rapidly proliferating services to its customers.

FNCB extends retail credit in many different forms. The largest category is personal loans[37] on the borrower's signature or with a co-maker jointly assuming liability in case the borrower defaults or on collateral. The average personal loan is for $1,450.[38] Automobile loans, i.e., direct loans to the purchaser secured by the automobile, represent the second largest category of retail credit. Citibank also makes indirect auto loans, buying retail installment sales contracts from dealers and finance companies.[39] The average auto loan is for $2,850.[40] Home improvement loans, secured by a mortgage interest in the residence on which the improvements are made, is the third largest category of consumer credit.[41] The average home improvement loan is for $3,100.[42]

Citibank also extends credit through various revolving credit plans. Checking Plus permits depositors to overdraw on their accounts, automatically converting the overdraft into a personal loan, and Ready Credit establishes a similar "line of credit" for nondepositors. Master Charge enables a cardholder to make purchases with a credit card and pay the bank at the end of the month or over a two-year period. FNCB also makes boat loans, government-guaranteed student loans, and loans under its own money-for-college program without a government guarantee.

FNCB's leading role in retail credit stems back to 1928, when it became the first large New York City commercial bank to enter the market, as noted by John Mosier, FNCB Assistant Vice President in charge of Branch Installment Loan Coordination and Training:

> The very first day that we opened, there were 3,000 people in a line that circled around Madison and 42nd Street, three times, and the police were there to keep the people in line . . . I believe our history is best explained in that we got there the "firstest with the mostest." And, hell, when the competition got into the act, we didn't sit on our hornshoes, no! [43]

Seven years passed before the other large banks followed suit. FNCB's jump on the competition helped the bank build up a large base of customers, many of whom return again and again when they need credit. Over 80% of FNCB's retail borrowers have had previous credit experience with the bank.[44]

Advertising is another important element in FNCB's retail operation. Most of FNCB's $8–$9 million advertising budget is directed to the retail market. In light of the failure of branch platform personnel to explain the bank's services, it would be appropriate for Citibank to use its advertising to inform people of the operation and costs of the bank's services. Citibank's ads, however, serve no such constructive purpose. Instead, the bank's ads, developed by two of the country's largest advertising agencies, J. Walter Thompson and Batten, Barton, Durstine & Osborn, utilize the well-worn technique of making people believe that their dreams will come true if they just buy the product or service. Typical is an FNCB Checking Plus ad, depicting by cartoon a happy scene between a woman and a bank officer, also a woman:

CUSTOMER: First National City?

CITIBANKER: Yes.

CUSTOMER: You have that wonderful checking plus account?

CITIBANKER: Yes.

CUSTOMER: The one that lets me write checks up to $5,000 bigger than my balance?

CITIBANKER: Yes.

CUSTOMER: So if I see a divine pant-suit on sale, I can just write a check and the suit's mine?

CITIBANKER: Yes, yes.

CUSTOMER: Thanks to checking plus I'll look absolutely devastating?

CITIBANKER: Yes.

CUSTOMER: Maybe meet the man of my dreams? Have a June wedding?

CITIBANKER: Yes, yes.

CUSTOMER: Could you be one of my bridesmaids?

ANNOUNCER: First National City hates to say no.

Not only does Citibank fail to disclose the 12% Checking Plus interest rate in its ads, it also omits this information from the descriptive brochure available at its branches.[45] In practice, Checking Plus costs more than 12%. The example cited in the bank's own brochure shows just how expensive Checking Plus can be:

> Let's say you have $250 in your checking account. You see a once-in-a-lifetime buy. Or you have an emergency. And you want to spend, say, $300. Just write a check. Automatically. With no advance notice at all.[46]

As borrowings must be made in multiples of $100, the customer, to overdraw the account by $50 for that "once-in-a-lifetime buy," must borrow and pay interest on $50 more than needed. Citibank thus earns an effective interest rate of 24% a year and still has the other $50 to lend to another customer. Not all checking accounts have the overdraft privilege. Unless the customer has specifically opened a Checking Plus account, the bank will not honor checks exceeding the depositor's balance. Citibank imposes a $3 overdraft charge, which is not mentioned in the "Personal Checking Accounts" brochure.[47]

Because Citibank emphasizes the convenience of Checking Plus, customers assume that Checking Plus loans can be repaid as easily as they are incurred—by a routine deposit in the account. Such is not the case and Citibank's ads and brochures fail to outline the repayment procedure. In order to repay the overdraft, customers must fill out a separate form and mail it in or present it at a special window in the branch office. The failure to spell out the repayment procedure in the descriptive brochure confuses customers and costs them money, as the following statement by one customer shows:

> When my daughter got sick a few months ago, I overdrew my Checking Plus account by $100 in order to pay the doctor's bill. When I deposited my paychecks in the account, I assumed that the loan was repaid. When my first monthly statement arrived and indicated that I was still paying interest on the loan, I assumed that it was due to a lag between the time I deposited the money and the time the bank gave me credit for repaying the loan. When the next statement still showed the loan had not been repaid, I went into the branch and was told for the first time that Checking Plus loans must be repaid separately from normal deposits in the account. Nobody ever told me anything.

While we do not know how many other customers were similarly confused, the number must be substantial, for as Cresap noted in its 1970 Survey, "44% of the platform officers did not clearly explain the rules for making payments on unpaid Checking Plus balances." [48]

FNCB trains its branch office platform personnel to sell each customer as many of the bank's services as possible. If a customer wants to open a checking account, platform workers are supposed to "cross-sell" savings accounts, Master Charge, and other credit services. Although Cresap discovered that FNCB's officers were not cross-selling as much as they could and recommended that the bank increase its emphasis in this area, it is significant that the greatest amount of cross-selling occurs in connection with credit services. [49] To encourage cross-selling, FNCB has devised an employee incentive program. Under the system, each platform employee is motivated to sell as many services as possible to each customer. The most successful employees receive cash awards. This program, however, induces employees to give loans, if not to customers who clearly cannot repay them, at least to marginal applicants. While the platform officer has points added to his total when he books a new loan, he does not have points subtracted for loans that default, although in the long run, each officer's loan loss record is reviewed on a retrospective basis as part of the normal personnel evaluation procedure. [50] The system, therefore, rewards aggressiveness and discourages caution.

FNCB's lead in retail credit is preserved by a policy of giving the Personal Banking Group, which handles Citibank's retail business, as much money for credit as is needed to meet customer demand. As John Reynolds, Senior Vice President in charge of the Personal Finance Department, noted:

> . . . the thing that determines how much in the way of funds we use is the customer. For example, if more people come to us for installment loans, we make more installment loans, and therefore we need more funds. And it's that simple. And we get them. . . . There's never been a limit on the amount of installment loans that we can make for people. . . . So we make as many as we're going to make. They've never done that [cut back on the available money] to us even when funds are short, or when funds are plentiful. . . . The Personal Bank has always had the ability to make those loans which they can make. We've never cut them back, never once in the history of the bank.[51]

Citibank's aggressiveness in the retail credit market leads it to make unprofitably small loans in order to develop a customer relationship that may turn profitable in the future. The bank makes many $200 loans which are unprofitable because they don't bring in enough revenue to offset the $30–$35 fixed cost that the bank estimates it incurs on every loan.[52] Such unprofitable loans are used as loss leaders; they typify the bank's willingness to absorb present losses in the hope that credit customers will use Citibank for all their banking needs as their economic profiles improve.

Loans, according to Citibank, are merely a product to be sold. The unfortunate fact, however, is that Citibank sells its product to thousands of people who simply cannot afford to pay. Citibank extends credit to people whose incomes are relatively low. Though 46% of Citibank's borrowers earn over $10,000 a year, 35% earn less than $8,000 and 11% have incomes under $6,000.[53] John Mosier, Assistant Vice President in charge of Branch Installment Loan Coordination and Training noted that FNCB makes loans that other banks shy away from:

> We can make loans to people in distressed areas and all other areas. . . . And I rather think that by so doing, we may be

making loans—and I know we have, because I've seen it—that some of the competition might not make.[54]

There is some indication that FNCB's retail credit portfolio bears more resemblance to the portfolios of small loan companies than to those of other New York City commercial banks. Comparing the incomes of defaulting debtors sued by FNCB with those sued by small loan companies and other New York City banks, shows a striking similarity between FNCB and the small loan companies.* (See chart that follows.)

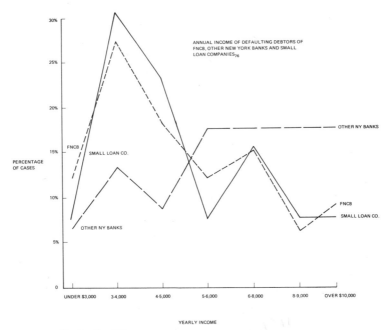

ANNUAL INCOME OF DEFAULTING DEBTORS OF FNCB, OTHER NEW YORK BANKS AND SMALL LOAN COMPANIES[76]

SOURCE: *Caplovitz Files.*

* We are greatly indebted to David Caplovitz, author of *The Poor Pay More* and a professor at the Bureau of Applied Social Research of Columbia University, for making available to us information he gathered for his massive, unpublished report, *Debtors in Default* (1970). The research directed by Professor Caplovitz included more than 330 interviews of defaulting debtors of New York City banks, finance companies, and other creditors. Much of our information came from Professor Caplovitz's files (cited hereinafter as "Caplovitz files").

While the large proportion of low-income debtors sued by Citibank does not prove that FNCB's entire retail credit portfolio has a higher proportion of low-income borrowers, it certainly is consistent with Mosier's assertion that Citibank will extend credit to people that other banks will avoid. While Citibank is to be commended for its willingness to lend money to people of modest means, the fact remains that people earning less than $6,000 a year account for only 11% of Citibank's debtors, but almost 70% of the debtors sued.[55]

The poor should be able to get bank credit. The poor pay more of their incomes for food, clothing, and shelter than do people with higher incomes. With less money left over for "luxuries," it is important for poor people to maximize the value they receive for their purchases. Accordingly, it is important that poor people be able to obtain credit from banks, because their rates are lower than those of the small loan companies. But it is also critical that banks ensure that poor people do not obligate themselves to make credit payments which exceed appropriate debt-to-income guidelines. Unfortunately, the slipshod service disclosed by Cresap's "Third Service Shopping Program" applies to Citibank's implementation of its own credit granting standards.

Although Citibank claims, of course, that credit is granted only after a thorough evaluation of current economic strength, about 30% of its defaulting debtors, according to Professor Caplovitz's research, obtain credit in violation of Citibank's own debt-to-income guidelines.[56] Citibank says that most people have trouble paying their debts if monthly credit payments exceed 20% of their income and that low-income people should not undertake credit obligations that consume more than 15% of their income.[57] The debt-to-income ratios of Citibank's defaulting debtors, however, indicate that these guidelines are violated with distressing frequency. This is not surprising in light of the fact that Citibank approves 85% of all personal loan applications. Of the remaining 15%, more are withdrawn by the customer than are rejected by the bank.[58]

One 69-year-old man, now retired, was earning $5,500 a year when he borrowed $2,500 from Citibank. He obligated himself to make payments of $115 a month, equal to 25% of his monthly income. This is $46 a month over the $69 limit that FNCB considers appropriate at his income level.[59]

Another man, a 44-year-old photographer earning $3,500 a year, already owed $95 a month on an auto loan when he went to Citibank and borrowed $1,200. The $78 a month he had to pay Citibank, equal to 27% of his income, was $34 a month over the $44 monthly limit. Both debts combined amounted to 60% of his income, or an excess of $129 per month.[60]

A 34-year-old automobile salesman, earning $5,500 a year, was already paying $80 a month to General Electric when he obligated himself to pay Citibank an additional $80 a month. The FNCB debt alone was $11 a month over the $69 limit and, together, the two debts were $91 a month over the guidelines.[61]

A 56-year-old restaurant cook, earning $3,500 a year, got a home improvement loan from Citibank which required monthly payments of $60. This amounted to 19% of his income, or $16 per month over the $44 limit.[62]

The examples cited above involve borrowers whose obligations to Citibank alone, without considering preexisting debts, violated FNCB's 15% debt-to-income guidelines for low-income people. In many other cases, though the credit extended by Citibank was within the guidelines, the total amount of the borrower's monthly debt obligations exceeded levels that Citibank deems appropriate.

A 33-year-old lamp decorator earning $3,500 a year borrowed $500 to pay his rent. His total monthly payments of $64—$24 to Citibank plus preexisting obligations of $20 a month to Household Finance Company and $20 to a furniture company—put him $20 over the $44 a month limit for a person with his income.[63]

Another man, earning $6,300 a year, owed $1,200 to Beneficial Finance Company, $800 to Unicard, $150 to Columbia Record Club, and $90 to Manufacturers Hanover, when he received from Citibank a $1,000 personal loan and a credit card that he used to incur another $1,000 worth of debts. His total monthly payments amounted to over $150 a month or nearly twice the 15% limit of $77 and well over the 20% limit of $105 per month.[64]

Altogether, 11 of the 35 FNCB defaulting debtors inter-

viewed for Professor Caplovitz's study obtained credit in violation of Citibank's debt-to-income guidelines.[65] If all of
FNCB's *defaulting* debtors were over the limit with the
same 31% frequency, it would mean that in 1969 and 1970
alone, Citibank sued more than 7,500 people whose debt obligations exceeded the bank's own guidelines. In addition, there
are undoubtedly thousands of other borrowers whose debt obligations are excessive but who avoid being sued by refinancing
their debts when Citibank's collections department starts dun-
ning them. Over 40% of Citibank's retail loans are renewals of
existing loans.[66]

Citibank has little incentive to improve the implementation
of its credit standards. In the first place, liberal credit standards
help attract deposits. According to Cresap, "cross-selling" is
highest when customers apply for credit. This is confirmed by
many customers who reported that they switched their accounts
to Citibank after receiving a loan that other banks had refused. Accordingly, deposit growth probably goes a long way
toward offsetting consumer loan losses. Furthermore, if the
debtor has a deposit account with Citibank, the bank can seize
the funds and apply them to the outstanding debt.

Another factor, to be explored later, is the extraordinary
efficiency of the New York City Civil Court as a collections
device. Default judgments, which constitute over 95% of Citibank's judgments,[67] cost little to obtain. Loan losses are also
a deductible expense for tax purposes; thus it may well be
less expensive for Citibank to absorb its consumer loan losses
—about $7,400,000 (before taxes) in 1969 [68] —than to im-
prove training programs, operating manuals, and salaries for its
hundreds of retail lending officers and reorganize its bureaucracy
to effect tighter management control over its more than 200
branches. Citibank's refusal to accept responsibility for its own
activities shows that more government supervision—not less, as
Citibank is always appealing for—is the only way to make
the bank assume the external costs it presently imposes on
people.

Citibank's aggressive consumer loan policy extends to its
credit card operations. In 1965, Citibank tried to enter the
credit card field by cashing in on the reputation of an established credit card—Carte Blanche. Citibank purchased a con-

trolling interest in the Carte Blanche Corporation to broaden the market for the Carte Blanche card.[69] Due to opposition from the U.S. Department of Justice, however, the plan was never fully implemented. Instead, in 1967, Citibank introduced the "Everything Card" [70] (later switched to Master Charge) and started an aggressive campaign to distribute the card to cardholders and sign up merchants to honor the card. Let's take a look at a typical transaction.

On March 15, John Cardholder buys a $100 suit from Acme Clothing Store, a merchant that honors Master Charge. Let's assume that Citibank signed up both John and Acme into the Master Charge program. It is thus both a "cardholder bank" and a "merchant acquiring bank." Instead of paying for the suit by cash or check, John presents his Master Charge card. Acme uses the Master Charge imprinting machine provided by Citibank to record the transaction on a sales ticket, a copy of which is given to John. Later that day, Acme, which is required to open a checking account with its "merchant acquiring bank," takes the sales slip to its local Citibank branch. The bank credits Acme's account with the purchase price minus the "merchant discount." Citibank's merchant discount ranges from 1.5% to 4.5%, depending on ticket size and volume.[71] A small, neighborhood clothing store must give up a larger portion of the purchase price than, say, a high-volume appliance store with a large average ticket size. Assuming a 3% merchant discount, Citibank would immediately credit Acme's account with $97 ($100 purchase price less 3%).

On April 1, Citibank bills John for the full $100. If John pays the total new balance within 25 days, he avoids a finance charge. But Citibank still earns 24% on the money "loaned" to Acme. Citibank gave Acme $97 on March 15 and got back $100 from John one-and-one-half months later, thereby earning 3% in one-eighth of a year, equal to an annual interest rate of 24%. Additionally, until Acme withdraws its $97, Citibank can use the money for other loans and investments. So Citibank gets its 24% on money that may not have left the bank.

If, however, John fails to pay the total new balance by the end of April, Citibank earns, in addition to the income from the merchant discount, interest income from John. Calculated from the billing date, April 1, this accumulates at 1.5% per month, equal to an annual interest rate of 18% a year. In order to encourage its Master Charge cardholders to go into debt, Citibank gives undue prominence on its billing statement to the *"total* minimum payment due" (emphasis added) and deemphasizes the "total new balance" which must be paid in full to avoid finance charges. By offsetting the "total minimum payment due" in blue and surrounding it with a thick, dark line, Citibank encourages its cardholders to pay only one-twenty-fourth of the total new balance, or the $10 minimum monthly payment, and incur a finance charge on the rest.

FNCB's Master Charge billing statement violates the Truth-in-Lending Act and Regulation Z of the Fed. As the major purpose of the truth-in-lending laws and regulations is to require the clear disclosure of information on credit costs so that people do not obligate themselves inadvertently to needless or excessive finance charges, the Comptroller of the Currency takes the position that ambiguous billing statements designed to encourage customers to go into debt violate the law. As John D. Gwin, Deputy Comptroller, noted in a letter to Chase Manhattan Bank:

> We believe that in order to meet the requirements of the statute and the regulation it is necessary to give equal prominence to the new balance and minimum payment due.[72]

Furthermore, the Comptroller says that the required disclosure of how to avoid the finance charge [73] should be explicitly related to the "total new balance" to clarify what sum must be paid to keep from incurring a finance charge.[74] FNCB has also failed to comply with this requirement.

Like Citibank's Master Charge billing statement, Chase Manhattan has designed a statement that encourages cardholders to go into debt by emphasizing the minimum payment due. In response to a consumer complaint, the Comptroller has been trying to get Chase to redesign its statement to give equal prominence to both the total balance and minimum payment due. We think the Comptroller's office should also get Citibank and all national banks to revise their billing statements to comply with the truth-in-lending laws and regulations, without waiting for individual complaints to be lodged against each national

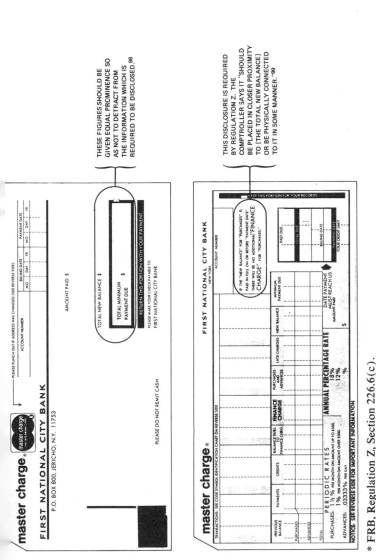

NOTES: * FRB, Regulation Z, Section 226.6(c).

      ** Letter from John D. Gwin, Deputy Comptroller of the Currency, to James H. Harris, Senior Vice President, Chase Manhattan Bank, February 18, 1971. FRB, Regulation Z, Section 226.7(b)(9).

bank. The Comptroller's lethargy in enforcing the truth-in-lending provisions shows why, when the legislation was pending in Congress, the bankers on the National Advisory Committee to the Comptroller expressed a "consensus" that the law should be enforced by the bank regulatory agencies.[75]

There is a significant incentive for banks to sign up as many merchants as possible to honor their credit cards. It is less profitable to be just the cardholder bank without handling the merchant side of the transaction. Suppose that Chemical had signed up Acme and FNCB had signed up John.

On March 15, Acme takes the sales ticket to its local Chemical branch, which credits Acme's account with $97. FNCB, not Chemical, is responsible for collecting from John because FNCB is the cardholder bank. But FNCB has to pay Chemical immediately, and cannot wait until its collects from John. FNCB gives Chemical $98.85—$100 less an "interchange fee" of 1% plus 15 cents per ticket. This fee is designed to cover FNCB's processing costs if John pays within 25 days without incurring any finance charge.

In this transaction, Chemical, the merchant bank, does better than FNCB, the cardholder bank. Chemical paid out $97 on March 15 and got back $98.85 within a day or two (the banks settle their credit card accounts with each other on a daily basis through a clearing house arrangement). Chemical thus earned $1.85 for advancing $97 for a day, without even risking John's nonpayment.

Citibank, on the other hand, receives only $1.15 and it doesn't get its money back for more than a month. Citibank also runs the risk of nonpayment. If John pays within 25 days of the billing date, this $1.15 must cover all administrative costs incurred in collecting, as there will be no finance charge levied against the cardholder. This explains why cardholder banks arrange their billing statements to deceive cardholders into incurring finance charges. It also explains why banks try to sign up as many merchants as possible.

In 1967, when Citibank launched its "Everything Card" and now, since converting the "Everything Card" into the Master Charge card, Citibank's goal has been to sign up more merchants and cardholders than any other bank in New York City.

Citibank did not lose any time. By the end of 1967, there were 1,400,000 "Everything Card" holders and 20,000 business outlets honoring the card.[76] By 1970, FNCB had the largest cardholder base in the New York metropolitan area [77] and over 16,000 merchants [78] operating over 30,000 outlets.[79]

To sign up merchants for its credit card plan, Citibank hired salesmen on a commission basis and assigned each one to a different section of the New York metropolitan area. The salesmen contact the merchants and try to convince them of the advantages to signing up with Citibank. Convenient branch location is one strong selling point in Citibank's favor. Another is Citibank's low merchant discount schedule. The city-wide range for Master Charge discounts is from 1.5% to 7%, depending on average ticket size and total volume. FNCB's maximum discount, however, is 4.5.% [80] Thus by signing up with Citibank, a merchant may be able to keep a higher proportion of the retail price than if he signs up with some other banks.

Another reason for Citibank's success in signing up merchants is that the bank does not thoroughly scrutinize the quality of the merchandise or the selling practices of the merchants it accredits for Master Charge. Though Edward Gottlieb, Vice President in charge of Master Charge, claims that each salesman knows his area and the general reputability of the merchants, Gottlieb also says that there is no systematic method of reviewing the merchandising practices of the merchants in question. The only limits are prohibitions against signing up liquor stores (purchasing liquor on credit is illegal in New York State), food stores ("we in the bank feel that food should not be charged," [81] noted Gottlieb) and door-to-door salesmen (although we did learn of one door-to-door salesman who was selling some sort of "teaching machine" and who had a credit card imprinter accredited to him by Citibank). Though the local Citibank branch must thoroughly examine the merchant's financial condition before accrediting him for Master Charge, no such attention is devoted to the merchant's advertising, selling, and service practices. And salesmen operating on a commission basis are not quick to reject a merchant because of the quality of his goods or his selling and advertising techniques, as the following example of a merchant signed up by Citibank shows.

Between January and May, 1970, thousands of New Yorkers received letters in the mail which read:

> CONGRATULATIONS
> LUCKY TELEPHONE NO. _____
> YOU WERE SELECTED FROM ALL THE PEOPLE IN YOUR AREA TO RECEIVE A 1970 DELUXE TWIN-NEEDLE, ZIG-ZAG SEWING MACHINE IN A HANDSOME PORTABLE CASE WITH BUILT-IN CONTROLS TO MONOGRAM, APPLIQUE, OVERCAST, MAKE BUTTON HOLES, HEM, DARN, EMBROIDER, ETC., AT NO CHARGE! ! !

In the next paragraph, the proverbial catch appears:

> This is part of our advertising program and your only requirement to receive this machine and console is that you purchase our 10-year service and construction contract amounting to only $8.95 a year. This contract also includes sewing machine instructions and annual oiling and cleaning of the machine. Thousands of dollars are spent in National Advertising on the radio, television and magazines.

Finally, the letter concludes with, "As advertised in LOOK, POST, CORONET; Featured on TV Programs, 'Let's Make a Deal,' 'Dating Game,' 'Eye Guess.' "

This was not a genuine contest. The "lucky telephone" numbers were merely selected at random from the telephone book. The Astro Sales Corporation, which was responsible for sending out the letter, could not produce any citations for the national advertisements listed in the letter. In fact, the company signed a Federal Trade Commission consent order agreeing to curtail similar practices.[82] These practices were also enjoyed by the Attorney General of the State of Maryland.[83]

As for the value of the machine, the New York City Department of Consumer Affairs says that the real market value of the machine was in the vicinity of $50, a far cry from the advertised value of $269.50 and even less than the total $89.50 price of the ten-year service contract.

The Astro Sales Corporation will be making no more home service calls, at any price. The company went out of business in May, 1970, having sold hundreds of the machines. One hundred and sixty customers used Master Charge to finance the transaction.[84]

The scheme devised by the Astro Sales Corporation was a classic case of fraud. The New York City Department of Consumer Affairs, after learning of Astro's scheme, called a meeting with the representatives of all the New York banks using Master Charge in order to find out which bank had accredited Astro for Master Charge and to attempt to have the banks refund all or part of the money paid by Master Charge cardholders. Although Citibank was identified as the merchant acquiring bank, it refused, as did the other banks, to make whole or partial refunds or give releases to the deceived cardholders. Their argument was that using a credit card is just like using cash and that therefore, the bank has no responsibility for the deceptive practices of the seller.[85]

FNCB, however, may legally obtain a refund from merchants who use the Master Charge service to engage in fraudulent transactions. Under the Master Charge Seller's Agreement, merchants warrant that each sale is bona fide and legal in all respects.* If the warranty is breached, the bank need not force the consumer to suffer the loss. Rather, it may require the merchant to refund the money to the bank.† Accordingly, Citibank could require the Astros of the marketplace, rather than the bank's cardholders, to bear the cost of fraud and other illegal sales practices.

Citibank's solution to the Astro case was to find another distributor of Riccar sewing machines to honor the service con-

---

* I. "Seller hereby represents, warrants and covenants with respect to each item of indebtedness ("indebtedness") acquired by Bank hereunder: (a) such indebtedness represents a valid obligation of a *bona fide* Buyer who was an adult and competent to contract, (b) such indebtedness arose out of a *bona fide* and in all respects legal sale of Goods made by Seller to such Buyer. . . ."

† IV. "In the event of a breach of any of the representations, warranties, or covenants made by Seller in paragraph I hereof, Seller will, upon demand by Bank, repurchase the Indebtedness in respect of which such breach was sustained; Bank may thereupon charge Seller's regular checking account with Bank (Seller will pay to Bank the amount of any deficiency in such account) with an amount equal to that originally credited to Seller's account in respect of such indebtedness and Bank will reassign such Indebtedness to Seller without recourse or warranty." (FNCB, Charge Service Seller's Agreement, CHS 534 1.70)

tracts of people who had bought their machines from Astro Sales. On the surface this seems like a satisfactory result. But in fact, the company which has promised to honor the Astro Sales contracts, the Allison Distributing Corporation, is run by the same man who was involved in the management of Astro. Citibank, in its eagerness to mollify the Department of Consumer Affairs, accepted at face value Allison's promise to honor the service contracts. Allison claims that postcards were sent to people who had made deposits with Astro Sales, informing them that Allison would honor their contracts. But many purchasers paid in full without making deposit with Astro Sales, so many purchasers will never know of Allison's commitment to honor these "service contracts." [86]

After the sewing machine incident surfaced, Citibank removed Astro's accreditation. But Astro left its imprinter with Allison, an indication of the close relationship between these two outfits. Allison's promise to honor the contracts was motivated by a desire to use Master Charge. The bank, however, eventually took the imprinter away from Allison. Citibank, looking for a way out of the messy situation, jumped at Allison's promise. In effect, the bank merely relied on the same fraudulent merchant operating under a different name.[87]

John J. Reynolds, FNCB Senior Vice President in charge of Branch Administration, indicates that expense is the prime reason behind the bank's reluctance to investigate merchandise and advertising techniques of Master Charge merchants: "The facilities that you suggest are absolutely impossible when you consider the expense that we would have to go through. . . ." Instead, Mr. Reynolds suggests that someone else should do the policing: "I think that those areas that investigate the manufacture of sewing machines and those people who license them to go into business should do a better job. I think they should do a much better job." [88]

Everybody but Citibank should do a better job. But Citibank is in the best position to do a better job. As Fed member George Mitchell noted in 1972, some banks signed up "unscrupulous merchants" who "clearly couldn't meet criteria comparable to those applicable to cardholders." Mitchell recommends that banks "conduct a careful check on the merchant's character and reliability before letting him participate in a bank card system." [89] The Riccars of the marketplace could not operate so easily, if at all, without the assistance of bank credit cards. If Citibank, for example, encouraged its cardholders to complain of shoddy sales practices and publicized its willingness to withdraw accreditation from merchants who bilked their customers, costly fraudulent sales and service practices could be reduced significantly. Citibank, however, is unwilling to lose such merchant/customers to another bank.

Imagine what the impact would be if every monthly billing statement contained a form, to be returned to the bank, on which the cardholder was asked to list Master Charge merchants who failed to live up to their advertising claims or who failed to properly service the products they sold. Encouraging customers to complain about merchants whose sales and service practices are unsatisfactory, compiling the information, identifying to cardholders the names of merchants with a consistent pattern of complaints, and turning the information over to government consumer protection agencies would provide a staggering inducement for merchants to improve their operations. The merchants would know that customer complaints were being centralized on a routine basis and would have a strong incentive to improve their sales and service practices.

Such an operation would not cost very much. Citibank would not have to investigate the validity of the complaints, for a large volume of complaints about a particular merchant would be a significant indication that something is amiss in the merchant's operation. Once the bank had identified such merchants, it could transmit their names to its cardholders and the government consumer protection agencies and threaten to withdraw accreditation unless corrective action were taken.

Citibank's aggressiveness in signing up merchants to honor its credit card was matched by its aggressiveness in signing up cardholders. It launched at least three campaigns to sign up as many cardholders as possible in the shortest possible time. The first of the programs entailed a massive mailing of credit cards to people who were customers of the bank. The people receiving these cards never asked for them. Indeed, the bank's purpose was simply to distribute as many cards as possible into the community, thus providing the bank with ammunition to sign up more merchants.[90]

Citibank says that it screened the recipients under "various criteria," [91] but the criteria must have been fairly ineffective, for our sample study of the 10,000 cases brought by FNCB in Manhattan's Civil Court in 1969, disclosed that 30% were brought to collect on credit card accounts.[92] Many of the cases involved cards that were mailed out in the 1967 unsolicited mailing period, suggesting that the "various criteria" under which the recipients were screened were not very rigorous.[93]

The bank could have screened the recipients if it were really interested in protecting its customers. The most obvious method, of course, would have been for the bank to require a full application and to then run credit checks rather than mail out the cards unsolicited. But the bank was motivated by a desire to develop the market, not protect its cardholders. When FNCB mailed out its unsolicited credit cards, it did not run credit checks to determine the credit position of those who would miraculously discover credit cards in their mailboxes. Eager to circulate as many cards as possible, Citibank was unwilling to incur the expense and administrative burden of a credit check on each recipient's current financial status.

Unsolicited credit cards have cost people a lot of money. A consumer has no way of knowing if an unsolicited card has been stolen from the mails. Consequently, the first time he learns of the theft is when bills arrive for purchases made with the stolen card. Although the intended recipient is not legally responsible for debts incurred on a stolen card, many people have had to go through expensive, time-consuming litigation in order to avoid having to pay, or to protect their credit ratings.[94] The Better Business Bureau has conservatively estimated that during the peak years of unsolicited mailings, which started in 1966, the American people lost $20 million a year.[95]

Skepticism is the only reasonable reaction to Citibank's claim today that it is against the mailing of unsolicited credit cards. On September 1, 1970, a New York law prohibiting banks from mailing unsolicited credit cards took effect. FNCB took an "internal position" on the bill. It supported the new law, according to Edward Gottlieb, vice president in charge of the credit card operation, because "it offers consumer protection." [96] However, in the light of the bank's massive mailings of unsolicited credit cards in the past, this weak support—the bank would not take a public stand and did not testify before the state legislature—is nothing but a cover for the fact that Citibank, having achieved a large lead in the New York City credit card market by unsolicited mailing, would like to keep its competitors from catching up.

A second gimmick used by the bank to distribute its credit cards involved a "sweepstakes" program, which was more concerned with distributing the cards than with giving away prizes. In 1968, the bank purchased a list of names from "name brokers" who are in the business of buying motor vehicle registration lists. A sweepstakes card was then mailed to over a million people in the greater New York area. The recipient could (a) throw the card away, (b) enter the sweepstakes and be considered for a credit card, or (c) enter the sweepstakes and *not* be considered for a credit card. [97]

For a person to refuse a credit card (and still be considered for the sweepstakes) he had to mark a box on the back of the card. If the recipient failed to check any box and mailed back the card, it was considered that he wanted a card. The bank's purpose, of course, was to put the burden of refusing a card on the recipient. A more valid approach would have required the recipient to check a box if he wanted a card, an affirmative act and a conscious choice.

A final solicitation tactic was used in 1968. The bank hired A. J. Wood, Inc., to telephone and offer credit cards to people whose names were taken from the Brooklyn and Queens telephone directories. Although this program was dropped after a month and a half because the number of cardholders signing up was not worth the costs incurred, [98] the fact that that bank based its solicitation on telephone listings is a further indication that Citibank's screening criteria were not very rigorous.

It is clear that no amount of ingenuity and expense was spared to increase the distribution of the bank's credit cards. But expenditures to protect the potential cardholder, such as checking a credit bureau, using a clear and nondeceptive "sweepstakes" program, or using more stringent solicitations standards than a telephone directory or automobile registration list, were never part of Citibank's plan to become the "firstest with the mostest."

Since the prohibition of unsolicited mailings as a result of abuses by First National City and other banks, Citibank now relies primarily on the "take-one" racks displayed in all of the bank's branches and in the offices of the merchants accredited by Citibank for Master Charge. An applicant picks up the brochure, fills out the information requested, and mails the application to the bank's charge plan headquarters in Jericho, Long Island. Some of the applications are immediately rejected if they are void on their face—for example, where the applicant is a minor. If vital information is missing, or if the applicant failed to sign the card, the bank will contact the applicant to obtain the missing data. A credit check may be run through outside credit bureaus. Sometimes, however, the bank omits the credit check, as indicated by Edward Gottlieb:

> Well, if he has a stable job, multiyears on the job, satisfactory income, owns his own home, gets a clear credit report from his employer—you know a good 'pat on the back'—we may not bother checking him out.[99]

The "take-one" rack is only marginally better than the methods formerly used by Citibank to sign up cardholders. Even though an application is required and a credit check may take place, Citibank discloses no information to the applicant about the operation of the plan in the application brochure. By contrast, Chemical Bank and many other banks provide a clear explanation of the operation and costs involved in the Master Charge plan in their application forms.[100]

But Citibank, with the excuse that the truth-in-lending law is new and thus open to many interpretations, refuses to go beyond the minimum. All the minimum requires is disclosure of the interest charges and payment rules before the applicant finally signs up. The bank need not disclose anything when the application is made.

The Master Charge applications of many other banks spell out every cost of using the card to the customer. Complying scrupulously with the spirit as well as the letter of truth-in-lending, Chemical's mailer clearly indicates that the customer can avoid a finance charge by paying the total balance within 25 days of the billing date. Chemical's mailer also spells out the finance charges incurred if the cardholder doesn't pay the full balance within 25 days. A group of 57 banks in Ohio, West Virginia, and Kentucky have even gone so far as to launch an ad campaign describing all the costs of credit cards, including the higher costs of goods to noncardholders who buy at participating merchants (the merchant has to charge everyone more because he has to recover the discount he pays to the bank). The ad campaign even warned cardholders not to be misled by the "minimum amount due" figure on the billing statement. A similar campaign would certainly be in order for Citibank, especially since more than half of Citibank's own platform personnel cannot explain the operation and costs of Master Charge.

What is Citibank's commitment to disclosure? The mailer does not even suggest that costs are involved. On the contrary, in wording that can only be construed as a conscious attempt to mislead the applicant, Citibank's mailer proclaims that Master Charge "Gives you Everything—Costs you Nothing." [101]

Why doesn't the bank disclose more? Mr. Reynolds explains:

> As a result of the new law, and this is the reason that this is the way it is [why we do not disclose more] . . . . you're not permitted—and the new law we're talking about is Regulation Z, or Truth-in-Lending—you're not permitted to give any of the terms if you don't give all of the terms and so on and so forth. [102]

This is nonsense. It is inconceivable that Citibank actually risks a lawsuit if it prints the finance charge and payment procedures on the Master Charge mailer. Again, Mr. Reynolds:

> It's difficult in what is supposed to be a mailer . . . to tell the entire story of every contractual regulation. It's a problem, one that we don't have the answers to, I might add. [103]

Actually, the answer is pretty easy. Like other banks offering Master Charge, it can put its consumer-oriented rhetoric into practice by simply stating the conditions and costs of Master Charge on the mailer. Other banks do it. But Citibank, in its attempts to distribute as many cards as possible, omits the finance charge and the cardholder agreement, and then deceives by claiming that the card "Costs You Nothing." [104]

With all its efforts to sign up as many merchants and cardholders as possible, it is really uncertain whether FNCB's Master Charge operations are profitable. In April, 1969, then Chairman George Moore told FNCB stockholders that its Master Charge operation was just a few months away from the breakeven point.[105] The 1970 Cresap study referred to Master Charge as an important and profitable service." [106] Then in September, 1971, FNCB, plagued by fraud and credit loss problems, found that it had to revise its Master Charge arrangements with 24 of its correspondent banks. FNCB decided that it would no longer carry on its books the accounts receivable generated by those institutions' cardholders, nor would FNCB do their collection work. Immediately three of FNCB's correspondent banks switched to offering the Uni-Card sponsored by Chase Manhattan Bank.[107] By November, 1972, 17 of FNCB's correspondents had terminated their credit card arrangements with FNCB.[108] When FNCB announced its new policy, the question arose why Chase, but not FNCB, could offer its card services profitably. According to Richard Ashley of Fidelity Union Trust Company, "It [Chase] is aware of the importance of being highly selective in deciding to whom to issue cards." [109] Whether Chase is highly selective or not remains to be seen. The point is that FNCB's sloppy credit procedures and lack of selectivity are finally catching up with it.

Credit cards are not the only way in which people can buy merchandise on time. A more traditional method is to sign a retail installment contract which is, in effect, a promise to pay the purchase price, finance charges, and interest over a period of time, generally from one to three years. If the merchant wants his money right away, he can sell the contract to a bank or a finance company and receive cash immediately. The contract, of course, is discounted, i.e., the bank or finance company gives the merchant less than the debtor owes under the contract. The bank or finance company becomes what is known as a holder in due course. A holder in due course is entitled to receive full payment of the debt even if the merchant sold defective merchandise or didn't even deliver the merchandise. The buyer's only remedy in the event that the goods are never delivered, or the wrong goods are delivered, or the goods are defective is to sue the merchant who originally sold the goods. At no time may the purchaser suspend payments to the holder in due course or, as thousands of FNCB's debtors have discovered, he will be hauled into court.

Predictably, FNCB expresses no more concern for the reputability and honesty of the merchants from whom it purchases retail installment contracts than for the reputability and honesty of the merchants it accredits for Master Charge. The bank disclaims any responsibility for ensuring that the underlying sale was performed according to the terms spelled out in the contract.

The holder in due course doctrine—at least its applicability to consumer credit—has been criticized widely by scholars and attorneys as an outmoded holdover from a robber baron age.[110] The doctrine originally grew out of the practice of assigning third-party obligations to pay debts *in commercial transactions.* In the commercial area, the doctrine does not work unfairly because the typical business transaction involves two parties of relatively equal sophistication and bargaining power. In all likelihood, the buyer is capable of preventing fraud and obtaining legal redress if the seller breaks the contract.

In the consumer area, however, the buyer does not have equal bargaining power or access to the judicial process. Consequently, the wholesale application of the holder in due course doctrine to the consumer credit field has victimized millions of people.[111] Although in 1970 New York defeated a bill to abolish the doctrine in consumer credit transactions, the handwriting is on the wall—the holder in due course is dying. It is important, however, to make sure that bank credit cards do not perpetuate the same evils in another form.

The same "we're not responsible" attitude prevails in Citibank's extension of credit to finance companies. Acting here as a wholesaler of money, the bank lends to these retailers of money without a thought to anything except the finance company's ability to repay the bank loans. Citibank looks only at the finance company's "ratios," those magical numbers that are a barometer of the borrower's financial strength. No matter what type of merchant the finance company finances, no matter if the low delinquency figures of the finance company are due to notorious strong-armed collection practices, telephone threats, and harassment, "the main thing I'm concerned with is the soundness of my loan," says Philip Conway, Citibank's Vice President in charge of lending to finance companies.[112] In reality, that's the only thing Citibank cares about. "If there's a social obligation, it's the finance company's obligation, and not ours to police him," says another bank official.[113]

Citibank's typical response, therefore, is to blame someone else and wait for complaints. Most people, however, weaned on the idea that *caveat emptor* "buyer beware" is the immutable law of the market, feel that complaining is rarely worth the time and trouble. Yet, FNCB passively waits for complaints to be made before inquiring about the merchant's merchandise or sales techniques, letting the burden fall on the customer. In the Astro case, the customer had no way of knowing that the contest and advertising claims were fraudulent or that no company existed to honor the service contract. The bank, on the other hand, could have easily prevented such a situation from arising. To weed out Astros before they do their damage, however, takes time and costs money. And Citibank's game plan—to be "the firstest with the mostest"—does not call for any expense or activity that does not further the achievement of that goal. No one at the bank examined the sewing machine offered by Astro to determine its true value. No one at the bank asked to see the national advertisements allegedly run by the company. You don't sign up more merchants than any other bank if you worry about such details as contract performance. As long as the customer pays, the bank is in good shape. And the customer pays—as New York City Civil Court records show.

The one area where Citibank does not lag is the filing of lawsuits—30% of which are brought to collect on credit card accounts.[114] We turn our attention now to the "legal process" and an examination of how New York's largest plaintiff collects from the victims of its aggressive marketing practices and deficient branch credit-granting operations.

3. Collection Practices

Before Citibank resorts to a lawsuit, it tries to collect by sending letters to and telephoning defaulting debtors in an effort to get them to pay. If that fails, the collection department may call the debtor's place of work and try to have the employer convince the debtor to avoid a lawsuit and garnishment of his wages. (Garnishment is a process by which a judgment creditor may require the judgment debtor's employer to deduct and pay over up to 10% of an employee's wages until the judgment is satisfied.) If that also fails, the bank resorts to a lawsuit.

The first stage in the collection process is handled by computer. When the computer determines that a Master Charge debtor, for example, is two weeks late with his payment, it prints out a short notice advising the cardholder that his account is overdue. A week later, the cardholder receives a second notice:

Dear Customer:

A short time ago we mailed you a notice calling attention to the fact that your monthly Master Charge account payment was overdue. We have paid the total charges you incurred. Isn't it only fair that you should pay us the small amount past due? [115]

Please do so as promptly as possible. Thank you.

Two weeks later, a stronger notice goes out if the debtor still has not paid:

Dear Customer:

I'm sure you know how valuable your credit standing is in all your business and personal dealings. *Right now it is in danger.* Your Master Charge account payments are seriously overdue. In fact, we are considering cancellation of your credit privileges. To avoid this—and the resulting damage to your credit reputation, please pay the amount due—*today*.

Illegible signature
COLLECTION DEPARTMENT [116]

After another month, the defaulting debtor receives a STOP CREDIT ORDER:

You are hereby notified to stop using your Master Charge Card. All your charge privileges are cancelled. We are sending notification of this suspension to all our associate establishments.

The full amount of your unpaid balance will be due and payable unless you mail us the amount past due NOW. Additionally, legal steps to collect the amount due are in the process of preparation.

We strongly suggest that you call our Collection Department

at once to discuss this serious matter. The number is shown
above. Office hours: 9:00 A.M. to 9:00 P.M.

COLLECTION DEPARTMENT [117]

At this point, people take over from the computer. The behavior
of the employees in the collection department, like those in the
branches, is very erratic. Some, according to Citibank's defaulting
debtors, are polite and cooperative. Others, however, are abusive
and nasty.

One man, who defaulted on a $2,500 personal loan, said:

> I stopped making payments, then they called me in a nice way.
> They then offered plans to give me more money [apparently re-
> ferring to a long-term bill consolidation loan]. . . . I couldn't
> accept it in good faith.[118]

Many defaulting debtors echoed this man's sentiment, with comments that FNCB's employees were "very nice," offered to refinance the debt and avoided harassment.

Sometimes, however, the collections department fails to follow
through on the offer to refinance. One man, earning $4,500 a
year, couldn't handle the $62 a month he owed Citibank. So he
offered to pay $20 a month: "The bank was very cooperative
and promised to send a new payment book, but before I received it, I got a summons instead." [119] The debtor got his payments reduced to $20 a month, but only after the bank obtained
a judgment, which included court costs and attorney's fees.

For every debtor who described the bank's collection people
as nice, there was another who found them nasty. One man,
who owed $2,000 to FNCB, happened to be out when Citi-
bank's collections department called. His 84-year-old grand-
mother was unfortunate enough to answer the phone and when
she denied that her grandson was home, the collection man called
her "a lying old bastard." The bank continued to harass the
debtor's family, as well as the people listed as references on the
credit application. Finally, the debtor called a vice president at
the bank to complain and threaten a lawsuit. The harassment
stopped.[120]

Another debtor reported that the bank harassed him with
abusive calls as often as two or three times a week when he fell
behind on his Master Charge payments:

Mr. Jones?
No. This is his roommate.
Is Mr. Jones there?
No.
I don't believe you.
Who's this?
This is First National City Bank. Mr. Jones owes us $500 and we want our money or he'll be in trouble. Tell Jones to call us as soon as he gets in.
   Can't you be a little more polite?
Mind your own fucking business. (Click.) [121]

Jones eventually paid after several weeks of similar phone calls from Citibank's collection department.

Although New York State and federal laws prohibit firing an employee because his wages are garnished, the bank frequently threatens to call or actually does call the employer because it is an effective method of getting debtors, especially those with low incomes, to pay. One debtor, earning $3,500 as a factory worker, borrowed $300 from Citibank on top of the $11.50 a month he was paying to Sears and $14 a month owed to Household Finance Company. The debtor ran out of money when he still owed FNCB $100 and stopped paying. When the bank called and threatened to inform the debtor's employer that a lawsuit and garnishment were imminent, the debtor borrowed $100 from a friend and paid the bank because he was afraid of losing his job.[122]

The threat to call the debtor's employer is a potent weapon because many employers prefer to violate the law and discharge the employee rather than bother with the extra bookkeeping involved when wages are garnished. Forty-six per cent of the 332 New York City debtors interviewed for Professor David Caplovitz's massive study of *Debtors in Default* [123] said that their employers had been contacted by the creditor. Ten per cent lost their jobs as a result of garnishment or the threat of garnishment.[124]

Citibank's collection practices are erratic for the same reason that the quality of service varies from branch to branch and from officer to officer—the bank is so large that formulation and implementation of procedures and effective supervision of operating personnel are extremely difficult to achieve. More than

100 people work in the collection department and this makes it difficult to ensure that each of them adheres to the bank's official policy against abusive tactics. Furthermore, threats are effective in getting many people to pay their bills, so there is an incentive for employees who want to get results to continue violating official policy.

Despite the frequent use of threats and abusive collection practices, however, thousands of FNCB's overextended debtors fail to pay. So the bank must turn to the courts, filing 60 lawsuits a day in Manhattan alone, in order to collect its money.[125]

4. First National Civil Court

In light of the frequency with which low-income and overextended debtors obtain credit in violation of Citibank's own credit standards, it is not surprising that Citibank files more lawsuits in New York Civil Court than any other creditor. In 1969, it filed over 10,000 lawsuits—more than all other New York banks combined and more than the ubiquitous telephone company or Consolidated Edison.[126] Compared with other banks and *adjusted for volume of consumer credit outstanding,* Citibank's rate of suit is way out of proportion to the amount of retail credit it extends. Citibank sues six times as often as Chase, three times as often as Chemical, and more than twice as often as Manufacturers Hanover. And the number of lawsuits is rising. In the recession year of 1970, Citibank's lawsuits increased by nearly 50%, to more than 15,000 in Manhattan alone.[127]

Most of Citibank's lawsuits against defaulting debtors—over 60% according to our survey of 100 cases filed by FNCB in 1969—are handled by Robert B. Frank, a salaried attorney employed by the bank. The rest of the cases, including all cases involving credit cards, are handled by three specialized collection law firms, Shenghit, Shenghit, Epstein & Cresci; Sennet & Schultz; and Workman & Stern. Cases are distributed between these firms "strictly on the basis of billing cycles so that each attorney has an opportunity for an equal caseload." [128] Several experienced New York lawyers noted that Shenghit, Shenghit, Epstein & Cresci and Sennet and Schultz are notorious for their strong-armed collection practices, such as calling or threatening

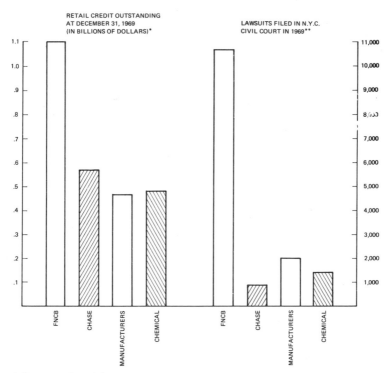

RETAIL CREDIT OUTSTANDING
AT DECEMBER 31, 1969
(IN BILLIONS OF DOLLARS)*

LAWSUITS FILED IN N.Y.C.
CIVIL COURT IN 1969**

* SOURCE: Securities and Exchange Commission
** SOURCE: New York City Civil Court

to call the debtor's employer. Cases involving credit cards are referred to outside attorneys because the law prohibits the creditor from adding on attorney's fees—the maximum is 20% of the amount due—unless the cases are referred to "an attorney not a salaried employee of the seller or holder for collection." [129]

In theory, a lawsuit is an adversary proceeding. *Black's Law Dictionary* defines an "adversary proceeding" as "one having opposing parties; contested, as distinguished from an *ex parte* application; one of which the party seeking relief has given legal warning to the other party, and afforded the latter an opportunity to contest it." Indeed, this is how most Americans envision a lawsuit involving even the smallest of claims. The party seeking relief files a complaint in the appropriate court. Notice of the proceedings is served on the defendant, who files an answer or a counterclaim, and who then hires a lawyer to argue his case. If Manhattan's Civil Court ever approaches the ideal, however, it will be purely accidental. For a large minority of the defendants, around 40% according to most estimates, never receive notice of the legal proceedings.[130]

If, as our survey indicates, Robert Frank handled 60% of the caseload in 1969 and 1970,[131] then his office turned out more than 6,000 lawsuits in 1969 and more than 9,000 in 1970. In any event, he operates an efficient, well-oiled machine, grinding out a fantastic number of lawsuits with only two other lawyers in the office.[132] A look at Mr. Frank's office shows the adversary system in its current state of collapse.

Suit is first requested by one of the bank's collection officers; none of them are lawyers. Mr. Frank exercises little discretion once the decision for suit has been made by a collections officer. He rarely declines to sue as "the determination for suit has already been made." Although Mr. Frank claims that he might decline a case if the amount were too small, we came across one suit which was brought to collect the grand total of $11.72.[133] In fact, few, if any, suits are too small for Citibank. In the words of one lawyer with extensive experience in collections cases, "the bank is very hard-nosed, you know."

Although the adversary system contemplates that both plaintiff and defendant have lawyers to represent them to arrive at a fair adjudication of both parties' legal rights, in fact, neither Citibank nor its debtors are represented by counsel. For only a small fraction of the lawsuits that pass through Mr. Frank's office are ever *seen* by Mr. Frank.[134] According to our survey, only 4% of Citibank's debtors answer the summons and complaint.[135] Once Citibank's officers have decided to institute suit, the case file proceeds not to Mr. Frank or to one of the other two attorneys on his staff, but to the accounting department. The ten to fifteen accountants in this department are not attorneys and are not directly responsible to Mr. Frank, but report to Mr. John Hannon, who is not a lawyer. The accountants calculate the costs and disbursements, penalties, fines, and attorney's fees. From the accounting department, the file proceeds to a typists' pool where all the blank spaces are filled in on the summons and complaint. The 15 to 20 typists are not under the supervision of Mr. Frank.[136]

At this point, an attorney *might* see the case. Complaints that must be "verified" (all suits brought on notes) are handled by Mr. Lawrence, a lawyer in Mr. Frank's office. Verification involves signing a sworn statement that the facts alleged in the complaint are true. Cases filed to collect money owed on Checking Plus, Ready Credit Accounts, and paper purchased by the bank are not signed by an attorney. Where the papers require a signature that must be notarized, a telephone clerk or a typist usually handles this formality, though Mr. Lawrence does this sometimes. Thus, the only contact that a lawyer will have with the case prior to filing suit will come if Mr. Lawrence notarizes or verifies the complaint. Yet even when Lawrence does sign the complaint, he rarely examines the particulars of the case, such as the accounting department's computation of the amount due, collection costs, and attorney's fees.[137]

After the papers are completed, they are forwarded directly to the bank's process serving agency, Aetna Judicial Service. The rates Citibank pays Aetna are negotiated, not by an attorney, but by an officer of the bank.[138]

A plaintiff must hire someone to deliver the summons and complaint to the defendant. The server is obligated under the law to try to effect "personal service." He must use "diligent effort"—make three or more attempts—to effect personal service. If attempts at personal service fail, the server may leave the summons on the door of the defendant's residence and mail a copy of this summons to the defendant, a technique known as "nail and mail."

In New York City, "sewer service" is rampant. Process servers merely throw away the papers to avoid the inconvenience of tracking down the debtor and attempting *bona fide* service. Then, they file false affidavits of service. The New York City Department of Consumer Affairs and many experienced lawyers estimate that 40% of the affidavits of service in Civil Court are false. Because process servers are paid by the piece—currently $3.50 for each set of papers "served"—they have an incentive to file false affidavits. Even though the creditors, debtors, lawyers, judges, and prosecutors know that a large percentage of the affidavits are perjured, the court closes its eyes to this fact and puts the full power of the state behind the creditor's efforts to collect the debts.

Consistent with its refusal to spend money for a credit check on the people to whom it sent unsolicited credit cards, FNCB refuses to spend what's needed to ensure that its defaulting debtors are informed of the lawsuits filed against them. Our 1,000 case sampling of the suits filed by Citibank in civil court during 1969 disclosed that less than 4% of the defendants filed answers. Only 8% of the cases showed activity of any kind. The 8% includes activity that occurred after judgment or garnishment, such as stipulations to discontinue the suit and vacated judgments.

Robert Frank claims that the bank demands "perfect service." [139] This is utterly false. The bank's effort to ensure perfect service is confined, as in other areas of its retail operation, to cases in which people complain. Citibank takes no advance precautionary measures to ensure that the papers are in fact served in accordance with the sworn statements in the process servers' affidavits. The bank assumes that it has perfect service because to deal with the reality of sewer service costs time and money.

When Mr. Frank receives a complaint from a defendant (he refused to estimate the number of such complaints) he contacts Mr. Sapedin, at the Aetna Judicial Service, the bank's process-serving agency. Mr. Frank expects Mr. Sapedin to question the individual server to see what details, if any, he can remember about the alleged service. Mr. Frank claims: "We are unalterably opposed to anything but absolute, perfect service. We have so informed Mr. Sapedin—Aetna—on every occasion possible." [140] Mr. Frank requires a written response from Mr. Sapedin on the server's report. However, Mr. Frank generally accepts the process server's explanation. Mr. Frank claims that Citibank's sewer service rate is "probably" under 1%.[141] This is absurd, and Mr. Frank must know it. For an examination of the affidavits filed in Citibank's cases shows that many of the claims could not possibly be true. And if the affidavits disclose many irregularities on their face, how many affidavits that look okay are really false?

It is impossible to determine precisely how often Citibank uses sewer service. However, it is probably no better than average. Generally, a process server will work for more than one process-serving agency, staking out specific territories and hustling to different agencies for papers to serve. As Citibank uses a commercial agency, it uses the servers everyone else does. Consequently, a thorough study would probably show that the bank does no better—or worse—than anyone else.

Let's examine the claims of Citibank's "perfect" process servers. Mr. Herbert Levitt, a process server for Citibank, claims to have attempted to serve a Miss Carmen Perez,[142] a Mr. Larson,[143] and a Mr. Camus,[144] all at 6 P.M. on July 23, 1970. Miss Perez lives at 557 46th Street, Brooklyn; Mr. Larson lives at 181 73rd Street, Brooklyn; and Mr. Camus lives at 139 Bay 37th Street, Brooklyn. It is, of course, impossible to be all three places at once. He also claims to have attempted service on both Miss Perez and a Mr. Quinones at 10 A.M. on July 27 and on Mr. Camus and Miss Perez at 7 P.M. on the same day. The affidavits must be false.

Marvin Potash is another process server for Citibank. He claims that he tried to serve a Mr. Perry at 707 Marion Street, Brooklyn,[145] and a Mr. McDonald of 1324 Carroll Street, Brooklyn,[146] at 3 P.M. on June 24, 1970. He also claims that he tried to serve a Mr. Williams of 1740 Carroll Street, Brooklyn,[147] and a Mr. Campbell of 249 Hopkins Avenue, Brooklyn at 7 P.M. on June 26, 1970.[148]

Jeffrey Rauch, another Citibank process server, claims that he tried to serve a Mr. Falceto of 306 West 75th Street, Manhattan,[149] and a Mr. Mendelsohn of 175 West 12th Street, Manhattan at 6:30 P.M. on August 8, 1970.[150] Mr. Rauch must drive very quickly.

We could go on and on documenting case after case in which Citibank's affidavits of service contradict each other. It would, of course, be a simple matter for Citibank to ensure that the claims of its process servers were true. It could use its considerable manpower to check the records for irregularities thoroughly, just as we have done on a sample basis. Better yet, it could hire its own salaried process servers, thereby eliminating the financial incentive that exists under the present system to discard the summons and complaint without attempting bona fide service. But this would cost money. And Citibank, as we have seen, is not an innovator when it comes to spending money to protect its individual customers. To hire its own process servers on a salaried basis would cost more than the low rates charged by the commercial process-serving companies. In addition, if more debtors actually learned they were being sued before garnishment, more of them might contest the suits, thereby adding to Citibank's collection costs.

Filing a false affidavit of service is a crime in New York, and filing suit without notifying the defendant violates the due process clause of the U.S. Constitution. So the existing system encourages plaintiffs to sponsor criminal activity and violations of constitutional rights in order to recover civil debts. While this may strike one as absurd, it is not unusual for our legal system to consider the "efficiency" with which creditors can collect from their debtors to be more important than the comprehensive enforcement of *all* criminal laws and constitutional protections. There have been very few prosecutions of process servers in New York City or anywhere else. But of the 10 cases recently brought by the U.S. Department of Justice in Manhattan, the names of two of the defendants appeared in our survey of cases filed by Citibank.

Leo Kaufman, a Citibank process server, was prosecuted for violating the Soldiers and Sailors Civil Relief Act, which requires process servers to make sure that the prospective defendant is not in military service. (Creditors are prohibited from obtaining default judgments against servicemen.) Kaufman was convicted on 90 counts. Judge Dudley Bonsal suspended the jail sentence and imposed no fine.[151]

Bernard Bialo, another Citibank process server, was prosecuted under the Civil Rights Act, on the theory that the failure to notify the defendants of the lawsuit deprived them of their civil rights. Bialo was convicted on three counts. Judge Edward Weinfeld imposed a one-year sentence, which was suspended, and a $500 fine, and placed Bialo on probation.[152]

Robert Wiseman and Herman Rick, two other process servers convicted under the Civil Rights Act, escaped without any punishment. Rick and Wiseman both received one-year suspended sentences, the former from Judge Frederick Van Pelt Bryan and the latter from Judge Weinfeld.[153]

The reluctance of judges to impose jail sentences or meaningful fines on first offenders who are, after all, mere small-time cogs in the "wheels of justice," is understandable. Yet the fact remains, as one prosecutor noted, that these cases will have "minimal impact" because they provide no deterrent to continuing offenders. There are, however, alternative *civil* remedies that would offer meaningful relief by penalizing the prime beneficiaries of sewer service—the creditors.

In 1970, the U.S. Attorney's Office in Manhattan filed a civil lawsuit under the Civil Rights Act and the Soldiers and Sailors Civil Relief Act against Brand Jewelers, one of the most notorious default judgment creditors in New York City.[154] The suit, a class action on behalf of Brand's default judgment debtors, sought to vacate Brand's judgments and require Brand to return the money it recovered from debtors who had not been notified of the lawsuits brought against them. In November, 1972, Brand signed a consent decree wherein it agreed to let the U.S. Attorney write to every Brand debtor who was the victim of sewer service and a default judgment during 1969, 1970, and 1971. The debtors will have the opportunity to reopen their cases and have them tried on the merits. Furthermore, in all future cases in which Brand sues, Brand's attorney will have to send follow-up letters to the defendants asking them if they have been served properly and apprising them of their legal rights.

FNCB, whose default judgment rate of 96%, according to our survey,[155] is only slightly below Brand's, would not go out of business if it consented to similar procedures. We recommend that the Department of Justice bring a similar case against Citibank and the appropriate officers to require the bank to return money recovered through its so-called lawsuits to default judgment debtors who were never served. This would provide Citibank with a substantial economic incentive—the only kind of incentive it really understands—to put its house in order and devise some method of ensuring that its defaulting debtors are notified that they are being sued. If the cost of filing false affidavits of service were made stiffer than the savings achieved by sewer service, Citibank and its other beneficiaries would quickly devise a way to make sure that the law was obeyed.

In a February, 1972, speech, James Farley, Executive Vice President of FNCB, asked: "Isn't there some better way to notify people you plan to sue without relying on an archaic process-serving system?"[156] The question evidences blatant hypocrisy when it comes from an executive of the bank that sues thousands of people a year in just such a manner. During the week after the signing of the *Brand* consent decree, the Project Co-Director called Mr. Farley to ask him if Citibank would consider vacating its old default judgments based on sewer service and whether Citibank would take affirmative action, such as sending follow-up letters to its defendants to check that they had received notice of the suit and that they understood their legal rights. Mr. Farley contended that Citibank already had adequate procedures to protect defendants' rights, although he refused to describe those procedures. When asked the reason for this refusal, Farley replied, "Very simply, I just don't want to describe them to you." [157]

Licensing process servers, the most recent response to this problem, is a needlessly bureaucratic method of dealing with sewer service. New legislation is needed. Defendants whose rights are violated by the manner in which FNCB and other creditors bring their lawsuits should have the right to combine their individual claims into a class-action lawsuit. This would enable them to hire top-flight attorneys to counter those of the creditors.

Unfortunately, the chances for meaningful reform in this area are slim. Eight bills pertaining to service of legal papers were presented to the 1969–70 New York Legislature. Only one passed—a bill allowing service of the notice of entry of a default judgment by certified mail. For some unfathomable reason, Governor Rockefeller vetoed the bill. According to lawyers in the New York Attorney General's Office, which maintains a continuous—if not vigorous—surveillance of the latest legislative developments in this area, the state legislators, many of whom are single-practitioner attorneys who do a lot of collection work themselves, are hostile to measures that would increase their own workload.[158]

After service is accomplished or dispensed with, as the case may be, the complaint and affidavit of service are filed by a Citibank clerk who works full time in the Civil Court record room to do Citibank's filing. To our knowledge, Citibank is the only institution in New York with its own full time file clerk. The other plaintiffs commonly hire commercial filing services.

If "served" personally the defendant has 10 days to file an answer, and 30 days if "served" by "nail and mail." Ninety-six percent of the people sued by FNCB, according to our sampling, do not respond.[159] Although most of the defendants have no defense, many of those who may wish to oppose the bank are prevented from answering because they receive no notice of suit or because they cannot afford a lawyer. Many defendants fail to answer because, as one man noted, "there was no defense; going to court is where you have a defense." [160] Nonetheless, there are situations in which legitimate defenses and counterclaims can be interposed if the defendant receives notice and has a lawyer.

One defendant received an unsolicited Everything Card from Citibank. He and his wife made purchases with the card but after they encountered marital difficulties, they quarreled over who owed what to the bank. The husband made several payments, leaving a balance in excess of $300 for his wife to pay. His wife never paid. To offset this unpaid balance partially, Citibank closed out the husband's checking account—a practice that is legal in cases involving a personal loan, where the set-off right of the bank is clearly stated in the contract. There was no such provision in the credit card agreement, but Citibank sued the husband for the balance, plus $70 in attorney's fees and court costs.

When the man's lawyer contacted the bank for an explanation, he was told "We always do it this way." The defendant filed a counterclaim, alleging that his credit had been defamed since checks drawn on his closed-out checking account had bounced. When the defendant's lawyer called Shenghit to discuss the case, he discovered that it had been turned over to Shearman and Sterling, the 160-attorney corporate law firm that does most of Citibank's legal work. The lawyer handling the case at Shearman and Sterling said that the place was in an uproar because of the counterclaim. He admitted that there was no contractual or statutory support for the bank's action, but again reiterated "We always do it." "Sure," responded the defendant's lawyer, "until some schmuck like me comes along to tell you you can't."

Another argument that might be used by credit card debtors is that the emphasis given the "total minimum amount due" on the billing statement violates the truth-in-lending laws and regulations. The use of the word "total" is particularly misleading. Accordingly, it would be fitting to relieve debtors of the finance charges, penalty payments, and attorney's fees incurred because of credit card defaults.

The Bar Association of the City of New York recently recommended that "a natural person who is sued for collection of a consumer debt who claims to have a legitimate defense, and who cannot afford a lawyer to defend him, should be entitled to counsel." This would help. Caplovitz's study showed that over 50% of Citibank's debtors in default earn less than $5,000. Sometimes defendants can find legal aid or an OEO (Office of Economic Opportunity) sponsored law office to handle the case. But for the vast majority of defendants, the cost of hiring a lawyer is prohibitive.

In all but a tiny fraction of cases, therefore, the defendants fail to answer. After the time to respond has elapsed, Citibank obtains a default judgment and sets off to collect on the judgment, either by getting the judgment debtor to refinance his debt or by garnishing the debtor's wages. The average judgment in our 100 case sample was 24% larger than the amount due.

The threat of garnishment induces many judgment debtors to take out a new loan in order to avoid the possibility of being fired. One debtor, a cafeteria waiter earning $4,500 a year, described his experience as follows:

> When I got myself a new job, I went to the bank lawyer and told him about it. So I told him I was going to continue paying, and he said that he was going to try to send a garnishee to my new job. So I told him if you do that I'm sure I will lose my job, because I have only been there for a week. Then I would not have money for the food for my family or money to pay the loan. So he said what to do, that he will make a new loan for me so I could pay for the late payments, the lawyer's fee and the other expenses. I had to make a new loan. The same bank gave me a new loan. I had been working for about a week then. I had to pay $93.24 in interest by renewing the loan again, $10.08 fine and $85.88 lawyer's fees—altogether $189.20.[161]

Many judgment debtors, however, never learn of the lawsuit until the employer receives the garnishment order, as noted by a clothing machine operator earning $3,500 a year:

> My boss called me one day to the office and told me he got a letter from the court to deduct money from my salary. I don't know how much more I owe them; the way I feel is that I have

had to pay a long time. My boss does not tell me how much more I owe. I just don't know anything on what's going on; all I know is that he is taking 10% off my salary. My boss has all the receipts and the paybook.[162]

Although virtually all of the work in Citibank's "lawsuits" is handled by nonlawyers—collection people, accountants, typists, process servers, and file clerks—the bank routinely adds on 15% to 20% for "attorney's fees." Robert Frank, FNCB's salaried collection lawyer, who also handles small routine mortgages, contracts, and other legal matters, candidly admitted his own limited role (or nonrole):

> I don't see every case that comes in. I don't see one tenth of the cases that come in. If they happen to come to my attention, and I think that I should talk to one of the collections officers about it, I do. *But I would say that 99.9% of these cases I do not see. They go right in.*[163] (emphasis added)

After the cases are filed, Frank and the other lawyers bother only with the few cases in which the defendant answers. If the answered case, as Frank put it, is "open and shut," or if the counterclaim is trivial, then Frank's office will handle it. If it is more complicated or raises novel issues, then the case goes over to Shearman & Sterling. The outside collection firms also refer cases involving unusual activity to Shearman & Sterling.[164] The collection operation, therefore, is really geared up only for default judgments. Cases that threaten to become real adversary proceedings go to Shearman & Sterling.

With a budget of $15,375,388 in fiscal 1969–70, all but $1,200,000 of which was contributed by New York City (the rest comes from New York State), the New York Civil Court handled 183,069 cases in 1969.[165] Each lawsuit thus costs the taxpayers over $80. This money should be viewed, not as a cost in the "administration of justice," but as a government guarantee of loans to marginal borrowers. The efficiency of Civil Court as a collection mechanism enables Citibank to mail unsolicited credit cards, extend credit to customers with marginal ability to repay, and mislead its customers with deceptive monthly statements, secure in the knowledge that when the over-extended debtors default, the court stands ready to put the power of the government behind the bank's efforts to collect.

Recommendation

Buck-passing is Citibank's stock-in-trade. It seeks to escape responsibility for its own actions by placing the blame for every problem at someone else's doorstep. The fact is, however, that Citibank has both the responsibility and the power to act. Its failure to act leaves a vacuum that will not be filled by anyone else.

"Our business is finance," notes John Reynolds. "Our business is not checking the manufacturer of furniture to see that it's properly made. We're not capable of doing that." [166] But Citibank really is capable of doing whatever it sets out to do. Leasing, travel services, and data processing are but a few of the activities it now performs. And it wants to do even more.

The stark fact is that Citibank has no economic incentive to ensure the probity of the merchants it bankrolls. Where a lot of money is at stake, as in a large commercial loan, the bank says that it thoroughly investigates all facets of the borrower's operations because it wants to make sure that it lends to a sound operation. But in the retail end of its business, it has no comparable inducement to similarly examine selling practices because individual buyers are less likely than corporate buyers to enforce contract performance and jeopardize the repayment of the bank's money.

"Government as a manager of the new technology is a failure," declares Walter Wriston, Citibank's Chairman, as he calls "for the centralizers to decentralize and turn back to the private sector to get things done." [167] Yet Citibank's practice of waiting for complaints before taking remedial action and its consistent disavowal of responsibility for what others do with the bank's money, not to mention what the bank itself does, shows Wriston's words for what they are—the rankest hypocrisy.

In a city like New York, where the Department of Consumer Affairs is already working as hard as it can, it would be unrealistic to rely on increased supervision and enforcement by municipal consumer agencies. The Comptroller of the Currency, the federal agency responsible for regulating national banks, has been notoriously lax in supervising banks' compliance with the myriad of laws, regulations, and rulings that affect individuals. It, too, relies almost exclusively on complaints, before taking remedial action. Furthermore, the Comptroller continues to rubber stamp branch applications without any effort to ensure that the ever-expanding banks under its jurisdiction improve the quality of service they provide.

What is needed, therefore, is a broad class-action statute, giving citizens, whose individual claims are generally too insubstantial to justify the enormous cost of litigation against private corporations with their endless legal resources, the right to sue *en masse* to enforce the law.* This would obviate the need to expand existing (or create new) government bureaucracies to enforce the law.

Walter Wriston contemptuously dismisses such proposals as mere "pension funds for lawyers," [168] because the plaintiffs' lawyer in such lawsuits typically retains for himself a substantial portion of the recovery. However, the effectiveness of the class-action lawsuit as a means of controlling widespread illegal behavior hinges on the economic incentive for lawyers to take on such cases. Of course, the real reason for Wriston's opposition is the fact that Citibank would quickly become a major contributor to that "pension fund."

---

* Unfortunately, the banking lobbies have tried to push Congress in the opposite direction and, indeed, in 1972 even succeeded in persuading the Senate (although not the House) to pass a bill (S. 652) that would have drastically reduced the amount of recovery in credit card class actions.

III

Wholesale Banking for Corporations

Introduction

To understand the present incestuous relationship between America's largest banks and largest corporations we have to look back 20 years. During the 1950s, American corporations paid relatively little attention to their bank balances. They put their money into interest-free checking accounts and, in exchange, banks performed a variety of so-called "traditional banking services," such as processing checks, transferring funds, and giving credit information. Bankers were underworked, low paid, conservative, and lacking in initiative. They sat back and relied on their government-granted monopoly over checking deposits to bring in money from corporations, governments, and individuals. By the 1960s, the New York City banks had to work harder for their money. America's major corporations had begun to apply profit-center analysis to their operations. Corporate treasurers began to appreciate the value of their idle funds; they started investing their excess cash in interest-bearing time deposits and became more adept in the use of their funds. They began to demand more services from banks. Furthermore, as major companies encountered increasingly saturated domestic markets for their products, they increased their overseas expansion and looked for banks that could meet their international needs.

To keep abreast of these changes, the large banks were forced to cast off their conservatism. Innovation became the order of the day. Banks developed new and complex services, new money-market devices, new affiliations with domestic banks and acquisitions of foreign banks—all geared to attract more deposits from their increasingly expense-conscious and expanding corporate customers.

In most of these developments, FNCB was the leading innovator. It was first to develop the important negotiable Certificate of Deposits (CD) to attract large corporate interest-bearing time deposits. It doubled the number of its domestic branches within eight years, making its 200-branch network the largest of any New York bank. It rapidly expanded its overseas operations by acquiring foreign banks and opening new affiliates to the point where, in 1972, it has 608 branches, subsidiaries, and affiliates in 85 countries—more than any other bank. It was the first major American bank to form a one-bank holding company to broaden the range of services available to its customers. The other banks waited for Citibank to make the first move and then imitated once FNCB's plans became known. Imitation is a way of life in banking, for the failure to exploit the latest deposit-gathering device can mean billions of dollars in lost deposits and millions in profits.

Rapid expansion of bank facilities and services, combined with greater financial sophistication of corporations who were now demanding interest on their idle cash, pushed banks into a profit squeeze. Banks' profit margins—the ratio of profits to revenues—steadily declined. For example, in 1964, Citibank derived 20¢ of net operating earnings from each dollar of operating revenue,[1] but by 1970, net operating earnings had shrunk to 9¢ on each revenue dollar.[2] To combat this profit squeeze Citibank increasingly worked to raise the yield and volume of its earning assets—loans and investments. Conservative banking principles of the past, which called for a balanced mix of low-risk, low-return but highly liquid (i.e., readily salable) securities on the one hand, and higher-risk, higher-return but less liquid short-term loans on the other, gave way to aggressive, innovative asset management designed to maximize yield. And, as corporations became increasingly involved in long-range planning, banks were called upon to make credit commitments for longer and longer periods of time.

But Citibank's freedom to increase its profits by increasing the yield on its loans is limited. Corporations have alternative sources of credit. If FNCB's price is too high, they can go to other banks; if bank rates in general are too high, they can go to other credit markets. To increase its profits, therefore, Citibank must rely primarily on increasing the *volume* of business it does.

In essence, this chapter will explore some of the implications of Citibank's preoccupation with volume and expansion. After tracing the basic aspects of FNCB's corporate practices —its lending policies, corporate services, and concern for deposits—we will contrast that sector of the economy that can get prime-rate credit, the large corporations, with those sectors of the economy that suffer from near financial strangulation, namely smaller companies and minority businesses. We will show how Citibank's desire to grow larger each year has altered its independence and its ability to evaluate investments on the basis of "good economic sense." As we will see, this has had some unfortunate results. Citibank lends to corporations in violation of the bank's own lending limits; Citibank finances corporate concentration without accounting for social and economic consequences; Citibank accepts "equity kickers" which, if not illegal per se, violate the purpose of the proscription against bank ownership of corporate stock; Citibank has become so involved in the airline industry that it can no longer objectively evaluate airline investment; and Citibank's directors are men whose own corporate interests restrict the bank from using its vast resources to meet the needs of the community.

1. The Basics:
Loans, Services, and Deposits

Loans

Citibank has formal standards and procedures for evaluating the credit risk of the companies that apply for loans. First, the bank lending officer must decide if the purpose or project for which the company wants the loan makes "good economic sense." [3] If the banker determines that the project is not likely to be profitable, he is supposed to turn down the request. He must understand the market in which the customer operates, and assess its management. Of all the factors considered, none is more important than management. Character or, as one banker put it, "the basic sense of the soundness of management," is supposed to be an absolute prerequisite to getting credit.

Once the loan officer has passed this threshold issue, he must analyze the client's entire business to ascertain how much money is needed, as well as when, and for how long. The banker must evaluate the customer's budgets, balance sheets, and future prospects. When this analysis is complete, the banker should be able to determine the client's total needs. If the borrower wants or needs more money than the bank is willing to lend, Citibank's policy is to help the customer raise the money by other means:

> If a proposal inherently makes good economic sense, there should be financing available to fill the need on some terms whether within and/or without the local money market. That portion of the requirement which is not bankable the banker should be able to be of help in trying to fill.[4]

If the customer needs equity capital—common or preferred stock, debentures, etc.—loan officers say they put the customer in touch with the appropriate nonbank financial institutions. In addition, notes Citibank:

> We will provide introductions to investment bankers, insurance companies, pension funds, etc., as well as help in the preparation of a customer's financial story in a manner acceptable and understandable to other segments of the money market.[5]

The size and terms of a loan or credit hinge on three factors: amortization, asset protection, and the overall account relationship. Amortization refers to the company's ability to generate adequate cash flow to repay the loan after taking into account all other expenditures. Asset protection means that the borrower (or a guarantor) should have sufficient assets to ensure repayment in the event that the loan is not repaid from cash flow. If the first two requirements are met, the loan officer is supposed to negotiate a rate of return that takes into account the entire bank-client relationship:

> . . . the rate is set not to maximize the profit on one isolated transaction only, but also with the view that we are looking forward to a mutually constructive and growing lifetime partnership with the borrower.[6]

The officer who manages the prospective borrower's account is responsible for drawing up a short credit memo compiling and analyzing the information on which the bank's decision will be based. In general, "authority for credit extensions should have the joint approval of at least three officers as it is not intended that credit be extended on the judgment of one officer alone." [7] The minimum rank required of the approving officers depends on the amount involved.

When credit is tight and the bank's customers are seeking more money than the bank has to lend, the Money Allocation Committee meets every morning at 11:00 A.M., to approve each loan in the Corporate Banking Group that conflicts with current lending policy or that exceeds $2 million. Robert Rice, the vice president in charge of this committee, decides the policy questions himself. In order to keep flexibility in its loan portfolio, Citibank says it tries to limit loans to five to seven years. Moreover, when money is tight, it is allegedly against policy to make loans for nonproductive purposes, such as mergers and acquisitions, as Citibank claims it wants to channel the available credit into productive investment in plant and equipment. Rice says that when credit is tight, even the best customer with a history of maintaining healthy balances cannot get an acquisition loan. [8]

Rice's committee makes its decisions within the framework of the budget. At the beginning of each year, the bank's Policy Committee slices up the money for the whole bank at the Annual Budget Review. The planning department also takes part in this process and the budgets that are set are reviewed every quarter. In tight money, however, no division is ever satisfied with its share of the budget and consequently Rice must constantly iron out conflicts between the divisions. "Someone is always complaining," says Rice. [9]

Once the Money Allocation Committee gives its approval, the account manager can commit the bank to lend the money to the customer. However, the loan or credit must still go to the Credit Policy Committee, not for approval, because the bank is already committed, but for an *ex post facto* review of the borrower's credit. The account manager fills out a one-page executive committee form which summarizes the terms of the loan or credit. This form is made out for the bank's directors, who are personally liable on bad loans. At the committee's weekly meetings, the senior officers from each division discuss and justify the various credits approved during the week. These meetings give the officers from each section a feel for what the rest of the bank is doing. Also, a certain degree of uniformity in lending policy is achieved by coordinating policy decisions in one committee.[10]

Once agreement is reached, the bank and the borrower sign a written agreement. This spells out such terms as the amount to be borrowed, the period of time during which the money will be made available, the repayment schedule, the interest rate, and the commitment fee. The agreement also requires the borrower to provide the bank with continuing financial information to keep the lending officers informed of his financial condition. The bank is thereby able to compare the company's progress with original forecasts and is more likely to spot in advance difficulties that might jeopardize repayment.

The agreement also provides affirmative and negative covenants whose terms vary from loan to loan, depending on the circumstances. Typical affirmative covenants call for the borrower to pay taxes, maintain insurance, and retain certain subsidiaries as separate corporations. Standard negative covenants prevent the borrower from allowing net current assets to decline below a specified level, paying dividends that exceed certain levels of net earnings, additional borrowing in excess of specified amounts, or merging into another company.

The overall purpose of credit agreement covenants was outlined by FNCB as follows:

> [The covenants] should never be construed as an interference with a management's prerogative to administer its business, but they are utilized for positive reasons in the company's own best interests.
>   Loan covenants are not imposed, but are arrived at through negotiation to provide mutually agreed upon guideposts for the lender and the borrower to follow the financial progress of the business. . . . They attempt to protect the adequacy of the cash flow necessary to amortize the loan, as well as ensuring the existence of an ample equity cushion to weather unforeseen contingencies. Covenants are designed to be flexible. Once made, they are not "in cement," but can be modified as required.[11]

The conditions of the loan are negotiated and tailor-made for each agreement. The covenants, as one banker said, are usually just a safety valve; if the business is any good to begin with they don't really force any change in the company's operation. When strict adherence to the covenants would injure the borrower, banks frequently forego enforcement, as Roy Dickerson, Senior Vice President in charge of the Transportation, Aerospace, and Information Systems Division noted:

> We all live in a real world. And many times you have to rewrite loan agreements; and if the man, the corporation, doesn't have the cash flow that was projected when he contracted for the loan, you try to recast your amortization requirements without too much difficulty to make it possible for him to stay alive and carry on his business in an orderly way. That's been the basic approach of the bank for a long time.[12]

The fact remains, however, that violations of the covenants give bankers the legal right to call their loans, and thereby convert time notes into demand notes. Unless the bankers waive the default, the borrower is given a specified period of time to cure the default. In any event, the default notifies the bank that the borrower's financial position has weakened, enabling it to improve its position by seizing title to or obtaining additional collateral. The ultimate weapon is to force the company into bankruptcy.

However, bankers rarely force defaulting corporate debtors into bankruptcy. Rather, bankers prefer to arrange mergers to maximize the opportunity to obtain full recovery of the debt. One recent, publicized example of banker forebearance involved Mohawk Airlines and Chase Manhattan Bank. Mohawk, losing money and the target of a long pilot strike, defaulted on its loan agreement with Chase and other banks in December, 1970. Chase did not put Mohawk into bankruptcy; it waited for the strike to end and, when Mohawk resumed service in April, 1971, Allegheny Airlines and Mohawk entered a merger agreement, with Allegheny assuming responsibility for Mohawk's debt.

Loans, of course, have always been the traditional function of banks. But, as the next section shows, in the seventies, the services that banks offer to corporate customers are often as important in the struggle to attract and hold business.

Services

Large companies need large banks. Because banks are limited by law as to the amount of credit they can extend to a single borrower—10% of capital and surplus in the case of a national bank—a corporation that measures its bank credit needs in hundreds of millions of dollars would have to borrow from hundreds of regional, midsized banks or thousands of small local banks. Lending syndicates of such size would be impractical, even with today's instant electronic communications. In addition, only large banks have the facilities to handle the huge sums of money and the large number of diversified transactions characteristic of the national and multinational activities of America's largest corporations.

Each large corporation needs many large banks. No bank, not even FNCB with its $90 million lending limit, has enough capital to single-handedly fill the bank credit requirements— often running into hundreds of millions of dollars—of the largest corporations on the *Fortune* 500 list. Accordingly, large corporations typically use many, if not all, of the large New York City banks. In addition, they also patronize dozens, and sometimes hundreds or even thousands, of banks around the country. Metropolitan Life Insurance Company, for example, uses 2,200 banks, not for credit, of course, but to provide collection, deposit, and other banking services throughout the country.

With so many banks vying for large corporate deposits, corporations—at least healthy ones—have a fair amount of leverage in dealing with their bankers. Despite their need for many banks, they can easily dispense with any one bank. This is especially true in light of the growth of the commercial paper market in recent years—an alternative and generally cheaper source of short-term money used by large and well-known companies.

So the banks, whose corporate lending rates are all the same, needed to find new ways to differentiate themselves from each other in order to attract as many corporate deposits as possible. Increasing the number and quality of the services performed became the major way to strengthen existing relationships with, and gather new deposits from, large corporations.[13]

The number of services performed by large banks for large corporations is staggering. Citibank gives equity financing advice; arranges for presentation and clearance of drafts; collects checks, documentary and clean drafts, drafts with securities attached, acceptances, coupons for bills, dividend warrants, etc.; purchases commercial paper and bankers' acceptances for clients; acts as agent for exchange of securities in reorganizations and mergers; collects bond coupons and called and due bonds; gives out credit information; transfers funds by mail, wire and telephone; works with freight forwarders to assist clients in collecting from their customers; acts as escrow agent; does old-line factoring and accounts receivables financing; purchases conditional sales contracts, chattel mortgages, and leases; processes and collects freight bills; collects customers' interest and principal on bonds issued by corporations, states, municipalities, authorities, and foreign governments and subdivisions; registers and transfers bonds issued by corporations, states, municipalities, and foreign governments; maintains bondholders' ledgers; audits and countersigns stock certificates as registrar; provides vault space; documents, prepares, and delivers stock certificates; maintains shareholders' lists and ledgers; prepares and mails cash and stock dividends; prepares and mails proxies; assists at shareholders meetings and mails reports to shareholders; prepares, issues, and forwards subscription warrants to shareholders; buys and lends against receivables; advises on the money markets and issues certificates of deposit; acts as trustee for corporate, state, and municipal securities; transfers and delivers share certificates, maintains shareholder ledgers, etc., for mutual funds; acts as "Special Depository of Public Money" by receiving from corporations manufacturers' excise tax and employees' withholding tax; makes short-term commercial loans, monthly payment loans up to $100,000 to businesses and professional men, construction loans, mortgages, and real-estate loans, revolving credits and term loans; issues commercial and travelers letters of credit; advises on foreign trade and banking; receives deposits and makes loans through overseas branches; quotes exchange rates on foreign currencies; processes requests for suppliers and importers; issues letters of introduction; assists in obtaining sales representatives and distributors; issues travellers checks; provides Post Office Box collection service to speed remittances to bank's customers; reconciles accounts; provides complete payroll services; processes checking-account statements for smaller correspondent banks; acts as a clearing house for capital investors and merger-minded companies; conducts cash flow studies; provides overall financial planning advice and introductions to various sources of capital, including investment bankers, insurance companies, pension funds, etc.; publishes *Monthly Economic Letter* on business conditions, *Foreign Information Service* on overseas business developments, and an *Annual Summary of Exchange and Foreign Trade Regulations;* acts as trustee, investment advisor, and custodian for corporate pension funds; provides corporations with facilities to provide banking services for their employees; purchases and leases aircraft, ships, railroad cars, trucks and other transportation equipment, computers, office equipment and other types of business equipment; makes equity investments in small, growth companies; assists companies in the areas of fringe benefits, training activities, personnel record keeping, and recruitment problems; does research and development for correspondent banks on their organizational procedures; acts as a clearing house for available real estate; and operates a travel agency.

Lending officers with specialized knowledge about their customers' businesses are in the best position to determine which of the bank's services a given company can use. When it is time to make a pitch to the company, the loan officer will bring in the specialist(s) who handles the particular service.

A company must have a checking account to use any of Citibank's services—even those for which a fee is charged.[14] Some services, such as automatic payroll processing, generate their own deposits because they cannot be used unless there is money in the account. Others, such as business consulting and financial engineering, call for compensating balances or fees to cover the costs. The customer decides whether the bank should charge a fee or look to balances for compensation. Pricing, however, even where the bank charges a fee, tends to be something of a shot in the dark, as noted by William Herbster, Senior Vice President in charge of FNCB's Corporate Services Division:

> Pricing is a seat-of-the-pants decision. . . . The bank makes an effort to charge a competitive price, but because of the diversity

of services, we don't always know which are profitable with respect to any one account and which are not. Naturally, the customer tells you if you are not competitive in price.[15]

This is understandable in light of the number of services, the global basis on which they are provided, and the giant, diversified character of today's corporations. The importance of services, however, is in the deposits, not income, they generate.

Deposits

"Deposits," as one Citibank vice president put it, "are like blood." They are the basic raw material that Citibank converts into loans and investments, the bank's most important earning assets, which accounted for 85% of its $958 million gross operating revenue in 1969.[16] Banks are generally ranked by deposits, not by their loans or assets, though there is, of course, a correlation among all three figures. In December, banks strive particularly hard to gather deposits because on December 31 (December 20 for overseas branches) the annual statistics are compiled and each bank must live for another 12 months with its December rank.

So the large banks have developed what the *American Banker* has called the "year-end factor," the practice of holding extra, unneeded funds at the end of December in order to prevent losing ground to a competitor. Though banks deny the practice, the *American Banker* reported on December 11, 1970, that "Euro-dollar deposits in general have risen because of the search by U.S. banks for funds to hold over the year-end." [17] One Chase Manhattan officer claimed that Citibank stole the number two national ranking (after California's 1,000-branch Bank of America) from Chase in 1969 by using a "year-end factor" that was larger than "normal." He may be right, because in 1970, Chase regained the number two spot from Citibank, only to lose it again in 1971.

Most of Citibank's staggering growth came from overseas deposits. Between 1960 and 1970, Citibank's foreign deposits increased by more than 750%, from $1,012,000,000 to $8,702,000,000. Domestic deposits increased "only" 82%, from $6,759,000,000 to $12,311,000,000. In 1970, overseas deposits

TOTAL DEPOSITS AT DECEMBER 31, 1960–71
Comparison of Chase and Citibank

	Chase	Citibank
1960	$ 8,143,000,000	$ 7,771,000,000
1961	8,876,000,000	8,462,000,000
1962	9,632,000,000	9,185,000,000
1963	10,561,000,000	10,425,000,000
1964	11,357,000,000	10,806,000,000
1965	12,913,000,000	11,949,000,000
1966	13,751,000,000	12,940,000,000
1967	15,760,000,000	15,201,000,000
1968	16,709,000,000	16,643,000,000
1969	18,989,000,000	19,142,000,000
1970	21,227,000,000	21,141,000,000
1971	20,373,024,000	24,260,074,000
1972	25,032,034,000	27,704,496,000
1973(3/31)	25,118,234,000	28,577,775,000

SOURCE: FNCB *Annual Reports*, 1965–70. Chase Manhattan Bank *Annual Reports,* 1967–70. Phone conversation with Saul Waldman, Public Relations Officer, Chase Manhattan Bank, April 1, 1971.

accounted for 41% of Citibank's total deposits, up from 13% a decade earlier.[18]

Loan officers keep close tabs on the balances in their corporate accounts, for the most important measure of a good account is the company's average balance. The higher the balances, the better the account. In times of tight money, balances are crucial. When there is not enough money for all who want it, loan officers give preference to the company "that's been treating you right"—and that means the company that has kept up its balances. "In general," says one former FNCB loan officer, "you try and push services in order to get as much of the company's business as possible, but the only thing you absolutely demand is balances." Even companies that need to borrow money must maintain their deposits at certain levels. Banks require all corporate borrowers to maintain "compensating" or "supporting" balances roughly equal to 20% of their outstanding bank loans.

Lockheed Aircraft Corporation, for example, has a $400 million line of credit from Citibank and 23 other commercial banks. Citibank's share is $30 million. Despite Lockheed's desperate need for money, until September, 1970, it drew down only $320 million and left the remaining $80 million on deposit at each of the 24 banks in balances corresponding to each bank's participation in the credit agreement.[19] In September, 1970, as the company's cash shortage reached crisis proportions, the banks consented to let Lockheed draw down an additional $30,000,000, thereby reducing the company's compensating balances to 12.5%, an extremely low level.[20]

Compensating balances raise the banks' yields and enable them to make additional loans. Lockheed was paying the 8% prime rate on the full $400 million for an annual interest cost of $32 million.[21] Before September, 1970, when it drew down the extra $30 million, it had use of only $320 million, so its net effective interest rate was really 10% ($32 million annual interest on $320 million), or 25% higher than the nominal 8% prime rate. Of the $80 million compensating balances maintained in Lockheed's accounts, $66 million was available for loans to other companies ($80 million minus the 17½% demand deposit reserves required to be deposited with the Federal Reserve).

In times of easy money, banks often lend a company more money than it needs; this provides the funds to maintain balances at the agreed-upon level. These are called "Chinese balances" and are frowned upon by some bankers, because a company that doesn't have the cash needed to keep its balances up before receiving credit may be weak.

2. Who Gets Credit—And Who Doesn't?

Who Gets Credit?

Relative to their deposits, corporations get more credit from Citibank than people and large corporations get more than small ones. From the perspective of Citibank's own internal structure, FNCB's Corporate Banking Group, serving national and multinational corporations, is a net *user* of funds; FNCB's Personal Banking Group, serving people and small, neighborhood businesses, is a net *source* of funds; and FNCB's Commercial Banking Group, serving midsized, regional companies, is somewhere in between.

By examining the loan-to-deposit ratios at different FNCB

branches, it becomes apparent that Citibank funnels money
from individuals toward large corporations. Branches serving primarily residential areas make fewer loans relative to deposits than branches serving commercial or industrial customers.
FNCB's branch in the primarily residential Bensonhurst section
of Brooklyn, books $36,000 in loans and generates $3,226,000
in deposits, for a loan-to-deposit ratio of 1.1%.[22] Its branch
in the residential Washington Heights section of Manhattan has
$4,400,000 in loans and $25,700,000 in deposits, for a 17%
ratio.[23] Its Castle Hill Branch, serving a residential community
in the Bronx, has only $587,000 in loans but $28,993,000 in
deposits, a 2% ratio.[24] Its branch serving the residential Luna
Park section of Brooklyn has $32,000 in loans and $747,000
in deposits for a 4.3% ratio.[25]

By comparison, FNCB's branch near Rockefeller Plaza, at
Fifth Avenue and 51st Street, in the heart of the midtown
Manhattan business district, has $126,300,000 in loans and
$222,000,000 in deposits for a 57% ratio.[26] Similarly, its
branch in the J. C. Penney Building at 52nd Street and the
Avenue of the Americas, a commercial location, showed
$58,100,000 in loans and $78 million in deposits, a 75%
ratio.[27] Its branch at 181 Montague Street, housing the headquarters of a regional center of the Commercial Banking Group
(which services the accounts of midsized, regional corporations), listed $49,700,000 in loans and $58,600,000 in deposits, an 85% ratio.[28]

Some residential branches, especially those in wealthy suburbs, show relatively high loan-to-deposit ratios. FNCB's Man-
hasset Branch, in Nassau County, lists $3,600,000 in loans
and $7,200,000 in deposits for a 50% ratio.[29] Its branch in
Harrison, in Westchester County, showed $4,700,000 in loans
and $9,600,000 in deposits for a 49% ratio.[30] By and large,
however, branches serving primarily residential communities
showed ratios under 20%, branches serving mixed residential,
commercial, and industrial areas were in the 20–40% range,
and branches in primarily commercial and industrial areas were
over 40%.

Many bankers defend their lopsided loan-to-deposit ratios on
the ground that the nature of banks' intermediary function—
to attract excess capital and lend it out for productive uses—

necessarily entails borrowing from some to lend to others. The fact remains, however, that the present practice of making credit decisions on the basis of the total account relationship and future growth prospects, excludes from consideration the satisfaction of the credit needs of the community that provides deposits. By thus subordinating, if not completely ignoring, unmet community credit needs—such as local economic development and preserving, rehabilitating, and constructing housing —the banking practices operate like a regressive tax, funneling money of communities with declining economies to those with brighter economic prospects. This merely reinforces existing economic trends, making it increasingly difficult to reinvigorate an area beset by economic blight.

Though Citibank gathers in billions of dollars from individuals and then ignores their urgent need for such credit as home mortgages (see page 154), it is not so insensitive to the needs of its corporate depositors. A corporation that maintains healthy balances at Citibank has "a call at the bank," the right to credit whether money is loose or tight. Corporations—especially large ones—know what to demand and expect from their banks. Because their individual balances are so large and their banking and other borrowing alternatives are so numerous, corporations, in sharp contrast to people, have the leverage to get their way.

A comparison of the relative fluctuation of corporate and individual borrowing costs provides a good example of how corporations command a disproportionate share of the pie. As the recession of 1970 deepened and loan demand dropped off after the summer, most interest rates dropped dramatically. By early 1971, banks had chopped their lending rate for large corporate customers to 5.25%, down from a peak of 8.5% in early 1970. These reductions reduced corporate borrowing costs by 38%. During the same period, the banks made one modest reduction of less than .5% in the cost of borrowing for people. They cut the annual interest rates from 12.59 to 12.02% on two-year personal loans, from 11.58% to 11.08% on one-year personal loans, and from 11.08% to 10.57% on (secured) auto loans. The savings passed on to corporations were therefore eight times those passed on to individuals.

Perhaps one of the best indices of banks' corporate favoritism is the favorable rate at which banks lend money to their biggest corporate clients. The "prime" or "best" rate is the term used to describe a bank's lowest interest charge for loans. In theory, the prime rate is reserved for a bank's most creditworthy customers. In fact, the prime rate is reserved for a bank's largest customers, sometimes irrespective of their creditworthiness.

Many large, weak companies borrow at, or close to, prime. Prime-rate borrowers include Penn Central, Boeing, and Lockheed, to name just three whose financial troubles have recently received public scrutiny. Why are such companies "prime" borrowers? Part of the explanation is that banks—at least until the Penn Central failure—were blinded by the mere fact of size. Size was equated with solvency, even though, as bankers in FNCB's Commercial Banking Group noted, the midsized corporate customers of Citibank have no higher a loanloss ratio than the large corporate customers of FNCB's Corporate Banking Group. Supposedly, the interest paid by a borrower compensates the bank for the use of its money, the degree of its risk, and the amount of work involved in granting the credit. This last factor gives large companies another inherent borrowing advantage, for it takes more work to make 50 $1 million loans than one $50 million loan. Conversely, of course, as one former FNCB corporate loan officer put it, "it takes an awful lot of small bankruptcies to equal one Penn Central."

Another reason why the largest corporations are able to borrow at prime is that banks like to focus on what they call the "total account relationship." As noted by Citibank in its memo on the *Criteria and Philosophy of Bank Term Lending:*

> Yield should be a function of rate together with the earnings to be derived from an active account relationship and the consequent collateral business to be obtained. . . . The rate is set not to maximize the profit on one isolated transaction only, but also with the view that we are looking forward to a mutually constructive and growing life-time partnership with the borrower.[31]

But there is a major fallacy in the "total account" rationale for granting prime rate credit to large customers. Citibank officers themselves admit the difficulty that banks have in determining the overall profitability of their global, multifaceted relationships with giant corporations. Many former account managers from FNCB's Corporate Banking Group asserted that it could take months to ascertain whether a multinational corporation was compensating the bank adequately for all of its services. Large corporations have an advantage because they can overload their banks with requests for many services in return for their deposits and it can take an account manager months to conduct the detailed profitability analysis needed to determine if the company is paying its way. Small companies are at a disadvantage; they use fewer and less complex services. Accordingly, it is easier for account managers to keep track of profits on smaller accounts and make sure that the bank is being compensated adequately, whether by balances, service charges, or interest rates.

Still, Citibank is very serious about seeking collateral business from its largest customers. According to former FNCB officers, corporate loan officers and trust department account managers frequently call on prospective customers together— the corporate banker to try to sell the deposit, loan, and service business, and the trust officer to try to get the company's pension-fund account. Pension-fund business is an important source of deposit growth for a commercial bank and this might be one reason why Boeing, Pan Am, and American Airlines— three troubled companies whose pension funds have been managed by FNCB in recent years—all borrow from FNCB at the prime rate.

Sometimes a large corporation gets a loan at an inordinately favorable rate merely because the bank granting the loan has relied too much on the credit analysis of another bank. According to the remarks of one banker, as reported in the *American Banker:*

> The top lending officer of Manufacturers Hanover Trust Co. [Charles E. Woodruff] says . . . that more than 100 banks had loans, totalling $800 million, outstanding to Penn-Central Transportation at the time it went into receivership last June 21.
> "I think banks as a whole did not analyze in depth the structure of the Penn-Central Corporation," Mr. Woodruff said. "What could happen to a giant of some $7 billion assets?" he asked.
> Some banks went along on the loans because others were making them, Mr. Woodruff said, and there was fear among some of losing balances.

One lesson, in Mr. Woodruff's view, is the necessity for a bank participating in a loan to do its own analysis. "The next time around we should do our own thing, not depend on others," he said.

A bank should also pay far less attention to the possibility of losing balances, Mr. Woodruff said. . . .

Mr. Woodruff said a bank does not have to be large to analyze a credit, and that he knows of many medium-sized banks that turned down Penn-Central.[32]

A final argument given is that the smaller companies allegedly keep less money in the bank and thus must be charged higher borrowing costs to provide comparable return to the bank. Here, too, former FNCB corporate lending officers consistently asserted that the Corporate Banking Group had a higher loan-to-deposit ratio than the Commercial Banking Group. This shows that overall, small companies provide Citibank with more deposits, relative to the credit they receive, than large companies. This is not surprising since bankers say most smaller companies are less sophisticated in cash management and thus leave more idle cash in the bank than their giant, national, and multinational counterparts.

Preoccupation with size, even to the exclusion of creditworthiness, has caused FNCB to favor large corporations. The smaller ones will get credit, but only by paying more for it. As for minority businesses, they belong in the next section, "Who Doesn't Get Credit?"

Who Doesn't Get Credit?

During the presidential election campaign of 1968, President Nixon frequently and emphatically asserted that government and business should seek to improve the economic position of blacks and other minorities by fostering the development of minority owned and operated business. "Black capitalism" thus became the latest attempt to integrate blacks into the American economy and promote grass-roots economic development.

Nixon disclaimed the need for massive government bureaucracies or appropriations, relying instead on the established business community to help blacks and other minorities obtain the financial, managerial, and technological resources needed to open their own businesses. FNCB and the other large New

York City banks warmly endorsed the President's approach and welcomed the opportunity to show what could be done by relying on the private business community to help alleviate racial and economic discrimination.

Soon after the election, the pages of Citibank's 1968 *Annual Report* were glowing with elaborate claims that the bank "has recognized and responded to the enlarged dimensions of its responsibilities as a corporate citizen." [33]

The reverence for growth companies and large corporations that characterizes Citibank's corporate loan activities carries over into the field of financing "black capitalism" and urban economic development. There are, however, some differences between the bank's approach to minority enterprises and its dealings with other corporations. Although Citibank refuses to divulge any information about its relationships with customers of the Corporate or Commercial Banking Groups, it is eager to go into great detail about its transactions with black businesses, underscoring the fact that its activities in this area are primarily geared to public relations. FNCB is neither an innovator nor a leader in the field of "black capitalism." In fact, it's not even a follower.

Thomas Wilcox, who in 1970 was responsible for coordinating the bank's various "urban affairs" programs, summed up the bank's approach very well:

> I think that entrepreneurship, as a practical matter, saw its heyday in the early years of this century. The name of the game now is big corporations and we're going to assume part of the big burden. So why should I emphasize getting blacks in to a form which is appropriate to another time and say the problem is solved. The problem is to get them into the current big mechanism and that's the corporation, to train them to take part in this thing. . . .[34]

This attitude is reflected in the bank's dealings with black businesses.

The investment criteria laid down by FNCB Capital Corporation, Citibank's small business investment company (SBIC), virtually rules out investments in small minority businesses, according to a former employee of FNCB Capital Corporation. The company finances very few businesses that do not have the growth potential to go public within a few years or executives capable of handling $2 million–$3 million in annual sales. Thus, FNCB Capital Corporation's dealings with black enterprises are mostly confined to businesses like "All Pro Chicken," a black-operated chain of fast food outlets and "Zebra Associates," an integrated advertising agency staffed by former employees of J. Walter Thompson, one of Citibank's ad agencies. FNCB's total equity investment in black enterprises is a mere $250,000, most of which is in "All Pro Chicken," a highly successful venture started by football star Brady Keys.[35]

All participants and observers agree on one thing about black capitalism: money, without managerial assistance and counseling, does not go very far in promoting minority businesses. In the words of Sidney Davidson, the FNCB vice president in charge of implementing the bank's "urban affairs" programs, if the businessman is not given advice on how to run his operation, he will become "another black skeleton in the graveyard" deceived by white society.[36]

In light of Davidson's attitude, one would expect FNCB to provide ghetto businessmen with plenty of assistance. Compared with the efforts of other banks, FNCB's endeavors are paltry. While Citibank relies on lending officers to volunteer their services, Chase Manhattan has integrated "economic development" loans into its formal training program for all new officers. The trainees are assigned "economic development" loans during their training period. They spend an average of one day a week working with the recipient of the loan and they are expected to continue working on the loan after the training period ends.[37] Other large New York City banks also devote more personnel to minority development activities. FNCB's Urban Affairs Department has only one nonclerical staff member, compared to three at Chemical [38] and eight at Chase.[39] In addition, Chemical and Chase have assigned responsibility for seeking borrowers of economic development loans to specific branch officers; FNCB sits back and relies on word-of-mouth.

Citibank's *laissez-faire* approach is reflected in a relatively small volume of minority business loans. Its yearly "soft loan" budget of $250,000 [40] is equaled by Chase Manhattan each month. Even Manufacturers Hanover and Bankers Trust, which are roughly half the size of Citibank, put more money into "economic development" loans.

Citibank responds to these figures by deriding the "numbers game" and pointing out that it has always been New York's most aggressive bank in making loans to low-income people. Davidson points out "we've been in this business since 1928," [41] when FNCB entered the personal loan business. Former Vice Chairman Wilcox says that the volume of loans in its ghetto branches is comparable to that in more prosperous areas. The Jamaica branch, he said, is expected to keep up loan volume even though the area around it has changed. As a result, the branches have gotten used to making riskier loans than in the past. In sum, Citibank says it does not need a large special program because its branches accomplish the same results as the special programs of other banks. [42]

This branch argument is nonsense. The highest loan-to-deposit ratios are at FNCB's branches in New York City's business districts. Suburban branches also show relatively high ratios. Branches in lower-income, declining neighborhoods typically show much lower ratios. No one at FNCB headquarters can state definitely how much money the branches are putting into loans to minority businesses. After two or three years of running his own special program through bank headquarters, Davidson did not begin to receive information on the branches' activities in this area until 1970. [43] One economic development specialist who worked for the Bedford-Stuyvesant Restoration Corporation remarked that branch officers in the Livingston Street (Brooklyn) branch were considerably less accommodating than those working in midtown Manhattan branches. "They know," he said, "that they cannot treat the executives who walk into their midtown branches the same way and get away with it." One of his colleagues, though appreciative of bank support of their economic development projects, asserted that the branches had not changed much and that headquarters was responsible for whatever progress had been made.

Even if the other New York City banks are somewhat more involved in ghetto development loans than FNCB, by and large, they are all extremely reluctant to break new ground, as the following experience of a cooperative furniture store demonstrates. In late 1969, Steven Press founded the Cooperative Association of East Harlem, a furniture store located at 116th Street and Lexington Avenue that undersells the neighborhood furniture stores despite the fact that its merchandise is of higher quality than that of its competitors. For the first few months, on the strength of publicity about its opening, the co-op exceeded its breakeven volume of $8,000 in monthly sales.

After a few months, however, sales dropped off to $4,000–$5,000 a month, largely, according to Press, because unlike its competitors, the co-op was not offering credit. So Press approached most of the large New York City banks, including FNCB, Bankers Trust, and Chase, in an effort to have the banks buy the co-op's retail installment credit paper or, alternatively, to lend $25,000 with which the co-op, like most ghetto merchants, could set up its own finance company. At first, Press went to the banks' branches. Receiving no response, however, he soon turned to the "urban affairs" officers at the banks' headquarters.

Bankers Trust Company indicated interest in putting up $5,000–$10,000 if the other banks would provide the balance. Chase Manhattan's officers took Press to four or five lunches in the elegant dining room atop the bank's headquarters in downtown Manhattan, but never agreed to provide any money. Citibank's response was similar.

In July, 1970, Press met with Sidney Davidson, who indicated that FNCB was "greatly interested" in participating in a multibank loan to set up a finance company for the co-op. A few weeks later, however, Davidson told Press that the bank officer who had investigated the project reported that, economically, the operation was not feasible. Press says that the bank reached this conclusion without sending a bank officer to inspect the operation; furthermore, Davidson told Press that the bank did not have anyone available to work with the co-op to help set up the finance company and provide the advice that the bank (but not Press) felt was necessary to ensure the co-op's success.

As of June, 1971, the co-op is still in business—thanks to grants from the New York City Economic Development Administration and Columbia University—but its sales are still $4,000–$5,000 per month and it still has no bank financing.

This lack of branch level cooperation is an important factor behind FNCB's meager involvement in "economic development." Bankers say that many people who want to open a business have no idea of what a bank can do for them and, consequently, never even approach a bank. A Chase official said that one man made and broke several appointments because he did not have a suit and was ashamed to come without one. It seems quite clear, then, that advertising and the aggressive marketing that characterizes the bank's approach to other markets are essential. If FNCB is seriously interested in expanding its activities in this area, branch officers will have to abandon their passive, wait-and-see attitudes and actively seek minority business in the same way that corporate bankers and trust department officers travel all around the country soliciting new accounts.

Most important of all is the need for FNCB to end its volunteer approach and make it clear to the officers of the Corporate Banking Group, who are generally the most able loan officers in the bank, that aggressive and imaginative involvement in financing economic development in the ghettos will be a precondition to advancement. The same talent that is assigned to giant national and multinational corporate accounts must be allocated to minority enterprises on a regularized basis.

The problem is not due to the absence of able and willing loan officers. Former FNCB officers frequently asserted that there are many talented FNCB officers who are eager to tackle urban economic development problems but who are convinced that senior management is not willing to make a significant commitment of resources. As one former Corporate Banking Group loan officer noted, "if you read Citibank's *Annual Reports,* you'd think they're a part of OEO. The truth of the matter is that they don't give a damn."

3. Some Unfortunate Results

Citibank's preoccupation with size and growth has led to some unfortunate results: (a) various pressures on loan officers result in their exceeding the bank's own loan limits; (b) ignoring all the social factors, FNCB continues to fuel mergers; (c) shunning the principle that credit decisions should be completely objective, FNCB still accepts equity kickers; (d) involving itself with the airlines beyond the bounds of "good economic sense," has now forced the public to bear the brunt of FNCB's and the other banks' errors; and (e) Citibank's directors force the bank into a perspective that can only be called "corporate myopia." This section will discuss these results.

Exceeding Lending Limits

Lending officers are under a variety of pressures and incentives that often lead them to make loans against policy and commit the bank without careful analysis of the borrower's finances.

That "the official lending limits don't mean a damn thing," is a frequently heard remark. One former FNCB corporate lending officer put it this way:

> If the assistant cashier doesn't have the authority, it becomes a selling job to his superiors who have to sign the sheet. One morning, the financial officer of an old corporate customer called at 11 A.M. and said he needed $3 million immediately. The company sent over some statements and then I went over with the note. The guy signed it and only then, after committing the bank, did I go to my superiors for their authority. I suppose I could have been fired, but I didn't think anything of it because it's very common.

Bankers sometimes circumvent formal loan policies to further their own careers. Many corporate loan officers view their years with a bank as a stepping stone to more lucrative jobs with the banks' corporate customers. These officers often try to impress corporate financial officers with their ability by doing something difficult for a customer—such as granting a loan against policy.

In early 1969, when the Federal Reserve Board shifted to a tight monetary policy, FNCB formally instituted a policy against loans to finance mergers and acquisitions in order to preserve the limited amount of credit available for more productive purposes. However, one customer wanted more than $100 million from FNCB and other banks to finance the acquisition of a controlling interest in another company during the summer of 1969. If the customer had labeled its request an acquisition loan, Citibank says it would have had to turn down the loan for being against policy. But as FNCB had been lending to the customer on a regular basis for working capital purposes, the loan went through, even though the loan officers knew that they were, in effect, making a disguised acquisition loan.

One FNCB officer working on the customer's account at the time now works for the customer. This type of occupational mobility from bank to customer—characterized by one banker as "akin to generals going to work for defense contractors"—is extremely common. In fact, most of the former corporate loan officers contacted by project members are now working for FNCB customers.

If FNCB were seriously interested in stopping this revolving door and the conflict of interest it poses, it could require its loan officers to agree, as a condition of employment, not to become employees of companies on whose account they have worked. Banks feel, however, that having their loan officers move into the financial departments of their corporate customers is a good way to strengthen the bank-corporation relationship. Furthermore, the knowledge that loan officers have frequent contact with senior officers of America's major corporations is a significant factor in attracting many talented business-school graduates to large banks in the first place. So FNCB undoubtedly feels that the benefits of stronger customer ties and easier recruitment outweigh the adverse impact of policy violations.

Financing Corporate Concentration

Primary and legal responsibility for the failure to stop galloping corporate concentration rests with the government. For all intents and purposes, however, the large banks are also responsible, for without them, the merger movement of the 1960s could never have gone as far as it did. Loan agreements include covenants that give bankers the power to veto mergers. Control over credit also gives banks the power to grant or withhold the funds needed to consummate many of the mergers and acquisitions. As a practical matter, therefore, banks could have stemmed the concentration more effectively than the government could through drawn-out investigations and court proceedings.

Is corporate concentration in itself bad? Congress has determined that concentration that inhibits competition is harmful. We will also focus on the broader social implications of concentration.

The passage of the Sherman Act of 1890, outlawing agreements in restraint of trade, monopolies, and monopolistic activities, was Congress's first effort to prevent power over America's productive resources from becoming unduly concentrated. In 1914, Congress enacted the Clayton Act to outlaw mergers that substantially lessened competition but fell short of creating outright monopolies. In 1950, Congress passed the Celler-Kefauver antimerger amendments to plug some of the loopholes, such as the failure to prohibit anticompetitive asset acquisitions.

Despite these laws, American corporations during the 1960s, and especially the late 1960s, acquired and merged with each other at an unprecedented rate. Between 1955 and 1959, mergers and acquisitions averaged 1,162 per year, but by 1969, the average had jumped to 3,605 per year.[44] The size of the mergers and acquisitions also increased. Between 1962 and 1968, 110 of the 500 largest industrial corporations were taken over by other corporations.

The most striking result of this trend has been to bring a greater share of the nation's manufacturing assets under the control of large corporations. America's 100 largest corporations today control a greater *percentage* of the nation's assets than the top 200 did in 1950, the year the Celler-Kefauver antimerger law was passed in an attempt to stop the increasing concentration. And the top 200 today control the same share that was divided among the top 1,000 companies in 1941, the year the Temporary National Economic Committee recommended an investigation into the concentration of economic power. Most of this growth—75% during the 1960s—has come from mergers and acquisitions rather than internal growth.[45]

Unfortunately, antitrust legislation and enforcement policies have focused almost exclusively on the anticompetitive advantages accruing to the combining companies, and on the economic impact in the combining companies' markets. There are, however, many dangers of corporate concentration that cannot be reduced to narrow competition-oriented terms. The following dangers have been ignored in most merger analyses:

1. Expansion into hundreds of thousands of different markets has made it increasingly difficult for those who formulate corporate policy to keep informed of trends affecting all of the company's global activities.

2. The enormity of the corporate bureaucracies and the size of their investments in existing modes of production reduce the flexibility of large companies to respond to changing conditions.

3. As corporations grow larger and larger, the federal government becomes less willing to chance the unforeseen consequences of major bankruptcies; this fosters a tendency to bail out large corporations that get into trouble and undermines the efficiency that the threat of bankruptcy should bring.

4. Concentration of decision-making power into fewer corporations reduces the ability of local communities to influence, much less control, the decisions that vitally affect their economies and environments.

5. Use of resources to finance mergers and acquisitions diverts funds from the productive investment in plant, equipment, goods and services, and the credit-starved segments of the economy such as home mortgages.

The failure to analyze corporate concentration in terms of these social factors has meant that companies in unrelated or tangentially related markets have been free to combine into huge "conglomerate" complexes virtually without government interference. The banks in turn have provided the essential fuel to the merger movement. Like other large banks, FNCB played an important role in financing and encouraging the merger mania of the 1960s. FNCB performs a function somewhat similar to that of a marriage broker; its Corporate Advisory Department maintains a list of acquisition-minded companies in order to match up companies that want to buy with those that wish to be bought.

The bank also finances acquisitions—especially in times of easy credit. Citibank has been so aggressive in financing acquisitions that one former vice president said that the bank "financed mergers of clients almost with a rubber stamp." Former FNCB officers said that the Extractive, Energy, and Process Industries Division, for example, helped finance Kennecott Copper's acquisition of Peabody Coal ($315,600,000 in assets), Continental Oil's acquisition of Consolidation Coal ($446,000,000 in assets), Atlantic Richfield's acquisition of Sinclair Oil ($1,851,300,000 in assets), Martin Marietta's acquisition of Harvey Aluminum ($286,300,000 in assets), and Hess Oil's acquisition of Amerada Oil ($491,000,000 in assets). Citibank claims that in order to preserve credit for productive purposes, it stopped making acquisition loans after the Fed switched to a restrictive monetary policy in 1968. But this claim cannot be valid since the acquisitions of Harvey Aluminum, Amerada Petroleum, and Sinclair Oil all occurred in 1969.

Merger services help attract new customers and retain old ones. As one banker put it, "if you help put together a successful merger, the company is not likely to forget you." Though deposits may initially decline because the parent and subsidiary can manage their cash more efficiently, the size and scope of the account increases in the long run as the corporation's overall business grows larger. The acquisition may enable FNCB to displace the acquired company's "lead bank" and become "lead bank" for the entire corporate family. Accordingly, FNCB sees the merger movement as a good way to strengthen its own relationship with the ever-expanding giants of the American economy.

Mergers also help FNCB when one of its borrowers gets into trouble. One former officer in the Corporate Banking Group said that he tried to arrange a merger for a customer with doubtful loans. The bank was successful and got another company to take over the borrower and pay off the loans. Another former Citibank officer described his approach to an ailing company as follows:

> Look, be realistic. Your past forecasts have been no good. We know you think you can pull yourself up but we're not so sure. Here's a merger that will get everybody off the hook. We want you to take it or we'll call the loan.

The trouble here is that it's not easy to find a willing buyer. "It's very difficult to unload a dog," the banker noted.

The impact of corporate mergers on competition in the banking industry has not received the detailed study it deserves. Antitrust analysis focuses exclusively on the impact of a merger on competition in the industries and markets in which the marriage partners are engaged. Mergers, however, often increase the amount of concentration in the field of commercial banking as well.

In 1969, Teledyne, Inc., which made more than 100 acquisitions during the 1960s,[46] bought out the Monarch Rubber Company of Hartville, Ohio. Because Monarch was a cash-heavy company, Citibank wanted to obtain its account and sent an officer to visit Monarch. When the FNCB officer arrived in Hartville, he was surprised to learn that Teledyne had just agreed to buy out the company. He called New York to check out the information and was told, "Forget it, Teledyne just picked them up and we'll get the deposits." Sure enough, after the acquisition was consummated, the First National Bank of Canton lost most of Monarch's deposits and the Harder Bank and Trust Company of Canton lost Monarch's $2.5 million pension fund.

Harder Bank and Trust had a similar experience when Gulf and Western picked up another local concern, the Bliss Company. Bliss had maintained $200,000–$300,000 demand-deposit balances in Harder B&T, a substantial account for the $180 million deposit bank. When Gulf and Western moved in, the bank lost "practically all of Bliss Company's money." [47]

Officers at other small local and midsized regional banks indicate that similar incidents have occurred at hundreds, if not thousands of banks around the country. As one top officer of a midsized Connecticut bank noted, "as soon as a national company picks up some local outfit, the money just shoots down to New York."

The Antitrust Division of the U.S. Department of Justice should broaden the scope of its merger investigations to include a detailed appraisal of how corporate mergers affect competition in commercial banking. All corporations use banks and thus every merger or acquisition potentially affects competition between the banks of the acquiring company and the acquired company. Citibank does not just compete with Chase, Morgan, and the other large banks in New York City and other money markets. It competes in virtually every city in the country, including, as the Monarch Rubber Company incident shows, cities as small as Canton, Ohio (1970 population, 108,872, down from 113,631 in 1960).[48] When local businesses are bought up by national companies, the local banks are effectively foreclosed from competing for the local deposits.

In addition to the antitrust implications of the merger movement, the redistribution of local money into money center banks raises a broader issue of national banking policy. Is it desirable to have the bank deposit assets of a local company removed from the local economy? We think not. Monarch Rubber Company's bank deposits came from its profits on local operations. Monarch's profits were made possible by the people of Ohio, who put in their labor, and the state and local governments of Ohio, which provided their services. We think, therefore, that the profits represented in the form of bank deposits, ought to remain available to meet the credit needs of Ohio's economy.

"Equity Kickers"

An important factor in Citibank's credit evaluation is growth potential. As one former senior credit officer noted, "Sometimes loans will be made to companies with low cash positions if their prospects for growth are good." Loans to "growth companies," especially those that are growing by merger and acquisition, often carry an "equity kicker."

In one form or another, an "equity kicker" increases the bank's profit on a loan by giving the bank additional compensation that is tied to an increase in the price of the borrower's stock. A kicker works like this: The bank says, "Yes, we'll lend you the $25 million, but for every point your stock rises, you pay us $50,000 additional." In the recent tight money period, when banks were in a strong negotiating position, equity kickers increased in popularity, especially on loans used to finance mergers that were virtually certain to increase the borrower's stock price once the merger plans were announced.

The most direct form of equity involvement, stock investment, is not available to commercial banks. The banking laws
and regulations of the Comptroller of the Currency prohibit
national banks from owning corporate stock and making "investments which are predominantly speculative in nature." [49]
There are, however, several ways that banks can cash in on
the rise in corporate stock price that usually follows announcement of a merger or other corporate plans.

Some banks, like Chase Manhattan, take kickers in the form
of stock warrants.[50] A warrant is the right to purchase a
stated number of stock shares at a set price. Since the price
of a warrant varies directly with the price of the stock, warrants can be bought and sold like stock. A bank that holds
warrants cannot exercise them by converting into stock. That
would violate the prohibition against bank ownership of corporate stock.[51] But Chase apparently feels that it is legal to
cash in on the appreciation in stock price through the warrant.

With uncharacteristic conservatism, Citibank shuns warrants. One former Citibank officer who worked in the Commercial Banking Group and tried to set up a straight warrant
deal, said that Shearman & Sterling, Citibank's law firm,
advised the bank not to take warrants in connection with loan
agreements on the ground that it would pose a conflict of interest to enter a loan agreement where the bank stood to earn
money from appreciation in the company's stock. There is also
a practical problem. If the bank takes warrants, an investment officer must watch the stock prices to make sure that
the bank sells the warrant at the right time.

So Citibank takes its kickers in cash. If the borrower's stock
is traded publicly, the amount of the kicker is often computed
according to the price of the borrower's stock. If the stock
is not traded publicly, the kicker may vary according to the
increase in the borrower's gross sales. Citibank loses, however,
one great advantage of the warrant—favored capital gains tax
treatment—because a cash kicker is taxed at the higher ordinary income rate. "The theory," according to John C. Slagle,
a Citibank vice president who sits on the Credit Policy Committee, "is that if you could take a warrant, you would." But
the bank feels it can't, so it takes the cash "shadow warrants"
instead.[52]

FNCB is lead bank for City Investing Company, a diversified holding company that has rapidly expanded by acquisition
to more than $1 billion in assets. Edward Sheridan, a former
vice president in FNCB's Corporate Banking Group is City
Investing Company's treasurer. When FNCB lent City Investing
$25 million in 1968 to acquire Rheem Manufacturing Company,
FNCB was given a $50,000 kicker for every point that City
Investing's stock increased in price.[53]

In another deal, FNCB had been financing the operation of
a young, modular housing company, Stirling Homex. In 1969,
the company went public and Citibank made what one former
officer called "a killing" through "floating" or "shadow warrants"
tied to the company's stock price increases. FNCB reportedly
earned approximately $250,000 on the transaction.

FNCB also bankrolled the expansion program of Extendicare, Inc., a Louisville, Kentucky company that bought up dozens
of nursing homes in the late 1960s.[54] Citibank lent money to
Extendicare and received an "equity kicker" in warrants or
shadow warrants. Extendicare's stock, which was selling over
the counter at $8 in 1968, climbed to a high of $125 after it
was listed on the American Stock Exchange in 1969.[55] The
kicker accounted for most of the bank's income from the transaction, according to a former FNCB loan officer. FNCB set
up a similar deal when it financed the D. H. Baldwin Company (of piano fame) acquisition of Central Bank and Trust
Company of Denver, Colorado.

Many former Citibank officers said that kickers were "common," especially on merger loans and that they were often set
up to give the bank an extra ½ % on the loan for every point
the price of the borrower's stock increased. Time and again,
the bankers noted that the bank's ability to obtain a kicker
was a function of bargaining power. Thus, kickers are more
common in periods of tight money and when loans are being
made to smaller companies. They were also most common in the
so-called "growth" fields, such as radio, television and communications, modular housing, and small computer companies.

The kicker is part of the total compensation package to the
bank and can affect other terms in the loan agreement. Several
former Citibank officers noted that officers sometimes recom-

mended a larger loan if a kicker was involved. One former Citibank officer said that "lots" of loans with kickers were written for growth companies with potentially large balances even if their current cash positions were poor. Another banker, however, said that the bank was not adamant about kickers and if the company was firmly opposed to giving up part of its equity, the banker could be persuaded not to insist. Still another banker, a former senior credit officer, said he never knew that FNCB took kickers at all. He felt that the practice constitutes a "conflict of interest" in that the lending officer might lose sight of his "public trust" and make unwarranted credit extensions to bring in a lot of kicker income.

Kickers violate the purpose, if not the terms of the statutory prohibition against bank ownership of corporate stock by inducing banks to give preference to companies that will surrender "a piece of the action." Credit decisions are supposed to be characterized by complete objectivity, not by a desire to make a "killing" on stock price fluctuations. To require a company with limited alternatives for credit to surrender part of its equity, whether by straight warrant, shadow warrant, or cash kicker, is an abuse of credit granting power that ought to be prohibited.

Flying High With No Money Down—A Case Study of the Commercial Aircraft and Airline Industry

The nation's largest banks, with billions of dollars in credit and lease-financing arrangements, extensive interlocking directorates, and substantial holdings of stock and other securities by bank trust departments, are deeply involved in the commercial aircraft and airlines industry. Because modern jets take years to research, develop, and manufacture and because each unit is so expensive, much coordination and planning between the manufacturers, subcontractors, airlines, and financial institutions is required for the successful production and operation of the new $15 million–$23 million jumbo jets. The financial decisions required to make these projects successful are inordinately complex. They require detailed analysis of the long-range trends in the economy and the market. To make these decisions intelligently, independence and objectivity are crucial. This must include a willingness to say no to important customers if the future looks uncertain.

But the bankers have lost their objectivity and independence. Because they are devoted to the idea that giant corporations are more efficient and more creditworthy, they overestimate the ability of corporate managers to understand and control their ever-expanding, interdependent, multinational companies. They minimize the uncertainties in planning and fail to scrutinize adequately the underlying assumptions on which the success of the projects depend.

The most important component of the banks' relationship with the aircraft industry is credit agreements and other financial arrangements. This is especially true today, as many of the borrowers have suffered contracting markets and declining income. These have led to defaults under various covenants of the credit agreements.

In 1970, a 17-bank syndicate, including the 10 largest banks in America, entered into a $650 million prime-rate revolving credit agreement with McDonnell-Douglas to finance construction of the wide-bodied DC-10 airliner. The 10 largest banks also participate in a $400 million prime-rate credit line to Lockheed Aircraft Corporation and a $200 million prime-rate credit line to Boeing. FNCB and the other large banks also finance major aircraft suppliers. FNCB is lead bank for United Aircraft Corporation and participates in the company's $350 million prime-rate credit line. FNCB and/or the other large banks also finance various aircraft subcontractors such as LTV Aerospace, General Dynamics, North American Rockwell, Rohr Corporation, Northrop Corporation, Collins Radio, Lear Siegler, and Avco.[56] As far as the airlines themselves are concerned, FNCB participates in the syndicate credit agreements shown opposite with airlines.[57]

The latest relationship to develop between the banks and the airlines grew out of the leasing technique. The growth of aircraft leasing has been phenomenal. In 1960, only 4% of the aircraft operated by American domestic trunk lines were on lease. By 1970, that figure had climbed to 19%, and Pan Am and the domestic trunk airlines were operating leased aircraft valued at more than $2.5 billion.[58]

AIRLINE CREDIT SYNDICATES IN WHICH FNCB PARTICIPATES

Borrower	Amount	FNCB's Participation	Interest Rate	Term
Pan American	$300,000,000	18,000,000	prime	8 years
T.W.A.	250,000,000	N.A.*	prime	8 years
American	200,000,000	N.A.	prime	6 years
United	300,000,000	9,600,000	¼% over prime	8 years
Eastern	100,000,000	9,750,000	½% over prime	1½ years
	80,000,000	15,360,000	prime**	6 years
	50,000,000	3,900,000	5.25%	9 years
Delta	210,000,000	37,250,000	½% over prime	8 years
National	250,000,000	N.A.	½% over prime	8 years
Northwest	250,000,000	N.A.	5%	6 years
Braniff	36,000,000	6,080,000	¼% over prime	3 years
	60,000,000	5,400,000	5%	5 years

NOTES:
* Not available.
** Not below 5% or above 7%.

103

Banks are attracted to leasing because of its tax advantages, like the investment tax credit and accelerated depreciation, which flow to the banks as owners and lessors of the aircraft. Since the banks had record-breaking earnings in 1969 and 1970, they were in an ideal position to utilize these tax breaks. The airlines too love leasing; in 1969 they had outstanding commitments to buy $4.7 billion of new flight equipment,[59] which they could hardly afford in light of the large losses they were experiencing. Leasing, therefore, supposedly was the panacea; it permitted the banks to get the tax advantages—which the money-losing airlines could not use—and it permitted the airlines to meet their commitments to buy the planes. The banks, however, failed to consider what later proved to be the most important aspect of the arrangement: whether buying the planes, which were the 747, DC-10, and L-1011 jumbo jets, made any sense at all. According to the 1969 Civil Aeronautics Board (CAB) staff study, *Impact of New Large Jets on the Air Transportation System, 1970–1973,*

> the economies inherent in these [wide-bodied] aircraft will not be realized to a meaningful degree until 1974 and beyond [60] . . . the manufacturers may have minimized the significance of past and future indirect cost trends and are optimistic in predicting potential fare reductions within the study time-frame.[61]

Nonetheless, FNCB was the first major bank to make a substantial commitment to leasing. It formed a specialized leasing department within the bank, a subsidiary company for domestic leasing (FNC Leasing, Inc.), and a subsidiary company for international leasing (Citicorp Leasing International, Inc.). Departing from the traditional banking practice of staffing new departments with bank officers, FNCB hired proven experts from independent leasing companies because of the complex nature of this field.

FNCB's various leasing operations own $815 million of leased assets and control another $185 million.[62] FNCB owns more Boeing 747 aircraft than any other company in the world, except for Pan American World Airways. It owns five 747s operated by Pan Am,[63] two 747s operated by TWA,[64] five operated by American Airlines, and has agreed to buy and lease another five for American.[65] As Reuben Richards, Executive Vice President in charge of FNCB's Corporate Banking Group noted, "it's said that, after the Russian and American governments, we have the biggest air force in the world." [66]

The tax-reducing effect of Citibank's extensive leasing activities substantially diminishes the bank's incentive to purchase tax-exempt state and muncipal securities. As Brian Livsey, FNCB's leasing specialist noted, "the cash flows of the entire investment come from the investment tax credit and accelerated depreciation and some part of the cash rent paid from the lessee. . . ." [67] This is one reason why FNCB's holdings of tax-exempt state and municipals as of March 31, 1971 dropped to 3.1% of assets, an all-time low, and well below Chase's 6.2%, Manufacturers' 5.4%, Morgan's 5.2%, Chemical's 7.2%, and Bankers Trust's 5.3%. In fact, FNCB has a lower percentage of its assets in state and municipal securities than any one of the 100 largest banks in America. [68]

Another component of the relationship between the banks and the aircraft companies and airlines comes from the common stock holdings of the banks' trust departments. A 1968 report by the House Banking and Currency Committee disclosed that Chase had exclusive voting power over 4.5% of United Aircraft's common stock, 6.4% of Pan Am, 7.4% of TWA, 6.1% of Eastern, 9.9% of Northwest, and 6.6% of Western. Chemical had exclusive voting power over 4.7% of General Dynamics, and Morgan had 6% of United Airlines and 6.4% of American Airlines. [69]

Interlocking directorates provide still another link between the banks and the aircraft industry. There are many interlocking directorships between the ten largest banks and the aircraft manufacturers, major subcontractors, and their airlines customers. Boeing shares directors with FNCB and Morgan Guaranty Trust, as does Lockheed with Security Pacific National Bank. United Aircraft shares three directors with FNCB and one with Chase. General Electric shares three directors with Morgan and one each with FNCB and Chase. General Dynamics shares directors with Morgan and Chemical, Fairchild Hiller, and North American Rockwell. [70]

Among the airlines, TWA shares directors with Manufacturers Hanover, First National Bank of Chicago, and Continental Illinois National Bank & Trust (Chicago). Pan Am, until recently, shared a director with FNCB. American is linked to Morgan and Continental Illinois Trust, Eastern to First National Bank of Chicago and to Continental Illinois.[71]

This deep involvement cannot be considered sound business when one considers the large losses all segments of that industry have experienced. As the CAB's staff study on the jumbo jet market showed, these losses were by no means unforeseen. And the CAB was right. In 1970, seven of the lines lost a total of $200,000,000 (Pan Am—$48 million; American—$26 million; Braniff—$3 million; Northeast—$11 million; TWA—$65 million; United—$40 million; National—$6 million).

By now, most of the airlines have fallen below the net worth and/or working capital requirements specified by their credit agreements. At the end of 1970 Pan Am's net worth fell to $422 million, more than $10 million below the minimum required by its $300 million credit agreement. The working capital positions of TWA ($4 million), American ($7 million), Eastern ($30 million), and United ($17 million) have dropped well below the levels specified in their credit agreements.[72]

Lockheed too, has had its own problems, its losses from the C-5A, in particular. Lockheed's $400 million credit agreement required the company to maintain a net worth of $320 million in 1970 and $340 million thereafter,[73] but its losses on the C-5A program reduced the company's net worth to $240 million, despite a government rescue package estimated at $747 million.[74]

The defaults of the airlines and Lockheed give the banks the right to call their loans and force the companies into bankruptcy. Despite this right, the banks claim that they are stuck because of their other collateral commitments. To force Lockheed into bankruptcy, for example, would jeopardize far more than the continued existence of Lockheed. It would also pull the rug out from under many of Lockheed's 35,000 suppliers [75] that are experiencing their own financial difficulties and can hardly afford to lose the millions of dollars in work that Lockheed provides. Because many of the banks with money out to Lockheed are also bankrolling these subcontractors, Lockheed's failure would have a multiplier effect and jeopardize repayment of loans by its suppliers. Furthermore, Lockheed's airline customers, notably TWA and Eastern, cannot afford to lose the millions of dollars in prepayments they have already made to Lockheed on their L-1011 aircraft. The total impact of a Lockheed bankruptcy would make the Penn Central failure look small by comparison. The large banks are understandably anxious to avoid a second consecutive jump in loan losses such as the 500% increase they experienced in 1970.[76]

So the banks continue to subsidize the aircraft and airline industries with prime-rate credit and attractive lease financing arrangements even though, relative to other industries, their creditworthiness is not very good. The banks expect that their help will be sufficient to see the airlines through the end of the recession when it is anticipated that accelerating passenger growth levels will restore the industry to profitability.

This back scratching between banks and big business hurts the consumer and taxpayer most. The airlines have refused to accept the fact that their losses from jumbo jet innovation were due to a poor risk that failed. Rather, they are appealing for rapid fare increases; and Lockheed's response was to ask for the public dole. The airlines' creditors have gone along with them by complaining to the CAB chairman that the CAB takes too long to process the carriers' applications for higher fares.[77] However justified the complaints of bureaucratic inefficiency may be, they should not be allowed to obscure the fundamental responsibility for the current state of the airlines. Private manufacturers, not the CAB, are responsible for building the jumbo jets. Private airlines, not the CAB, are responsible for ordering the new aircraft. And private lenders, not the CAB, are responsible for not having examined the economic feasibility of the jumbo jets. Representative William Moorhead of Pennsylvania aptly likened Lockheed's plight to "an 80-ton dinosaur who comes to your door and says, 'If you don't feed me I will die. And what are you going to do with 80 tons of dead stinking dinosaur in your yard?' "[78] Break it up and cart it away.

The unemployment consequences and domino effect of a Lockheed bankruptcy pale by comparison with the irreparable damage that will be done by continuing to encourage corporate and banking slovenliness. If Lockheed and the banks get assistance, there's hardly a company in the country that does not deserve similar welfare payments. Citibank's Chairman, Walter B. Wriston, is fond of noting that risk is part of life:

> Where we have gone wrong is to expect government to manage in order to build a riskless society. What the people of the world

are really asking for is a return to risk. They want the education
and opportunity to take risks. They want to participate in a
system that is built on risks.[79]

Wriston concluded with a call for "the centralizers to decentralize and to turn back to the private sector to get things
done . . ." [80] Now's the time. FNCB, the other large banks,
Lockheed and its airline customers took their risks—and lost.
The "private sector" should rescue the Lockheeds or let them die
a natural death.

If the banks' credit decisions really depend, as FNCB's credit
officers contend, "on the basic sense of the soundness of management," why were all the airlines given credit, and on substantially similar terms? How did Lockheed, whose mismanagement
has been chronicled for years, get the prime interest rate? One
answer lies in the growth fetish—the compulsion to grow larger
each year. "Citibank hates to say no" because it doesn't want to
lose customers to a competitor. Another factor is the increasing
focus on profit centers. If the customer's balances are high, the
company has "a call at the bank" and the bank will do everything possible to meet its credit needs. Another factor is the community of interest that develops out of interlocking directorates.
If Citibank had not been represented on the boards of Boeing,
United Aircraft, and Pan Am when the jumbo jets were being
developed, it might have been in a better position to analyze all
the implications of these enormous corporate projects objectively.
In the next section we examine the composition of Citibank's
board to determine just how independent the directors are, or
can be.

First National City's Board of Directors

The disparity between FNCB's billion dollar investment in the
aerospace-airline industry and its paltry support of minority business enterprises reflects the fact that Citibank's board of directors is composed almost exclusively of the same men who direct
America's giant multinational corporations. A look at the primary affiliations of the men who were elected to the board at
FNCC's 1971 annual meeting shows that, except for the senior
partner of the bank's law firm and two other men, the directors
are businessmen or bankers: [81]

Lord Aldington	Chairman, National & Grinlays Bank, Ltd.
William M. Batten	Chairman, J. C. Penney Co.
Milo M. Brisco	President, Standard Oil Co. (N.J.)
Fredrick M. Eaton	Partner, Shearman & Sterling
Louis K. Eilers	Chairman, Eastman Kodak Co.
Lawrence E. Fouraker	Dean, Harvard Business School
J. Peter Grace	President, W. R. Grace & Co.
William P. Gwinn	Chairman, United Aircraft Corp.
John G. Hall	President, The Anaconda Co.
Amory Houghton, Jr.	Chairman, Corning Glass Works
John R. Kimberly	Chairman, Kimberly-Clark Corp.
Arthur E. Larkin, Jr.	President, General Foods Corp.
C. Peter McColough	President, Xerox Corp.
Charles B. McCoy	President, E. I. duPont de Nemours & Co.
Roger Milliken	President, Deering Milliken, Inc.
Robert S. Oelman	Chairman, National Cash Register Co.
Edward S. Palmer	Chairman, FNCB Executive Committee
William I. Spencer	President, FNCB
Franklin A. Thomas	President, Bedford-Stuyvesant Restoration Corp.
Thomas R. Wilcox	Vice Chairman, FNCB
Walter B. Wriston	Chairman, FNCB

The top executives of giant multinational corporations typically sit on the boards of many such corporations. Thus, in 1970, First National City was interlocked with 40 of the 300 largest industrial corporations in America, including 7 of the top 10, 6 of the 15 largest life insurance companies, 2 of the 4 largest retailing companies and the 2 largest utilities.[82]

Companies with Director Interlocks to FNCB

Rank	*Company*	*Rank*	*Company*
	Industrial Corporations		
1.	General Motors	3.	Ford Motor
2.	Standard Oil (N.J.)	4.	General Electric

Companies with Director Interlocks to FNCB

Rank	Company	Rank	Company

Industrial Corporations

5.	IBM	99.	Olin
7.	Mobil Oil	103.	Colgate-Palmolive
9.	ITT	108.	Borg Warner
12.	United States Steel	111.	Kennecott Copper
15.	E. I. duPont	116.	Martin Marietta
	de Nemours	132.	Bristol-Myers
16.	Shell Oil	133.	St. Regis Paper
17.	Westinghouse Electric	134.	Kimberly Clark
26.	Boeing	160.	Ingersoll-Rand
28.	Procter & Gamble	164.	National Distillers
29.	Atlantic Richfield	168.	Phelps Dodge
36.	United Aircraft	187.	Johns-Manville
43.	Monsanto	204.	Magnavox
46.	General Foods	209.	Koppers
50.	W. R. Grace	210.	Corning Glass
56.	American Can	266.	City Investing
71.	Xerox	284.	Potlatch Forests
76.	Anaconda	314.	Bell & Howell
81.	Allied Chemical	343.	ACF Industries
82.	American Standard	475.	F & M Schaefer
87.	National Cash Register		

Life Insurance Companies

1.	Prudential	10.	Mass. Mutual
2.	Metropolitan	11.	Mutual of New York
4.	New York Life	13.	Conn. Mutual

Retailing Companies

1.	Sears, Roebuck	4.	J. C. Penney

Transportation Companies

1.	Southern Pacific	13.	Union Pacific
5.	Pan American World		
	Airways		

Utilities

1.	AT&T	12.	Consumers Power
2.	Consolidated Edison		

The men on Citibank's board are primarily concerned with the affairs of their own giant multinational corporations, to which Citibank already assigns its most talented loan officers and directs most of its money. The directors, therefore, have no incentive to initiate changes that would alter the bank's present policies. On the contrary, there is every inducement for the directors to continue business as usual, hoping to minimize any change in bank policy that might pose new priorities to conflict with those of their own organizations.

Because many economists, including those who write Citibank's *Monthly Economic Letter,* have predicted a shortage of capital in the 1970s, the multinational corporate executives on Citibank's board would be making their own expansion plans more difficult and expensive if they effected substantial changes in Citibank's orientation. Every dollar that goes into a home mortgage or municipal bond is one dollar less for commercial loans.

National bank directors have a much greater responsibility than the directors of most business corporations. The importance of their responsibilities is underscored by the fact that they are liable, under civil law, for violations of the restrictions against excessive loans and investments,[83] loans on the security of the bank's stock,[84] and loans to affiliates.[85] They are also liable for violations of the prohibitions against filing false reports,[86] against improper dividends,[87] and against the payment of interest on demand deposits.[88]

The board is responsible for the "initiation and maintenance" of "an effective internal audit and control program." [89] The board or a committee of the board must examine all cash items, suspense accounts, overdrafts, correspondent bank accounts, investment securities, loans and discounts, bank property, certificates of deposit, cashier's checks, savings accounts, dormant accounts, contingent liabilities, fidelity bond insurance, income and expense accounts, and the capital accounts.[90]

Because stockholders elect directors to represent their interests, it is appropriate to examine the identity of FNCC's stockholders. FNCC's major stockholder is FNCB. On February 16, 1970, Citibank's trust department, through various nominees, owned 1,232,198 shares of FNCC stock. This works out to

4.5% of the outstanding shares, more than any other single stockholder holds: [91]

Nominee of FNCB Trust Department	Number of Shares Held
Dwyer & Company	25,891
Gerlach & Company	132,627
Hurley & Company	76,446
King & Company	387,586
Stuart & Company	52,034
Thomas & Company	302,590
Weber & Company	255,024
Total	1,232,198

Altogether, the trust departments of the six largest New York City banks owned 4,523,659 shares of FNCC stock, or 16.6% of all outstanding shares: [92]

Bank	Number of Shares Held	% of Outstanding Shares
First National City	1,232,198	4.5%
Chase Manhattan	954,486	3.5
Chemical	698,783	2.6
Morgan Guaranty	664,274	2.5
Bankers Trust	501,598	1.8
Manufacturers Hanover	472,320	1.7
Total	4,532,659	16.6%

Although there are more than 65,000 FNCC stockholders owning an average of 415 shares, large stockholders own more than half of FNCC's outstanding stock. As of July 30, 1970, 360 holders of 10,000 shares or more held 16,025,804 FNCC shares, or 58.7% of the outstanding stock. FNCC is one of the most popular investments among institutional investors, such as bank trust departments, insurance companies, and mutual funds. In September, 1970, FNCC stock was held by more institutional investors than all but 12 listed companies: [93]

1. IBM
2. General Motors
3. AT&T
4. Standard Oil (N.J.)
5. Texaco
6. General Electric
7. Eastman Kodak
8. Xerox
9. Mobil
10. Sears, Roebuck
11. Gulf Oil
12. General Tel. and Elec.

13. FNCC
14. Ford Motor
15. Atlantic Richfield
16. Dow Chemical
17. 3-M
18. Goodyear Tire
19. DuPont
20. Standard Oil (Ind.)
21. Merck
22. Texas Utilities
23. American Electric Power
24. Standard Oil (Cal.)
25. Westinghouse
26. ITT
27. Southern Cal. Ed.
28. Phillips Petroleum
29. American Home Products
30. Southern Co.
31. Chase Manhattan
32. RCA
33. Union Carbide
34. General Foods
35. J. C. Penney
36. Commonwealth Ed.
37. Caterpillar Tractor
38. Polaroid
39. Warner Lambert
40. Florida Power & Light

Traditional antitrust analysis of interlocking directorates focuses on the possible anticompetitive effects of these directorships. If General Motors and Citibank share a director, so goes one theory, Ford, Chrysler, and American Motors will be hurt because Citibank will be inclined to refuse them credit. But Citibank, as we have seen, does not operate this way.

The overwhelming majority of all giant national and multinational corporations are customers of Citibank. A few years ago, Citibank boasted that its customers included "99 of the 100 largest U.S. industrial corporations.[94] This is confirmed by responses to a questionnaire sent to 300 of the largest industrial, transportation, utility, retailing, and life insurance companies in the country. Of the 80 companies that responded with information, 75 (93%) were Citibank customers. Citibank has interlocks with many competing companies in the same industry. In 1970, it shared directors with the two largest automobile companies, four of the six largest oil companies and two of the four largest retailers. Citibank, ever anxious to increase its own size, is not likely to turn down a customer merely because that company's competitor shares a director with the bank.

The significance of interlocks is more subtle. Interlocking directorates are, as one FNCB corporate loan officer noted in a comment endorsed by many others, one more way of tying the bank to its customers, of strengthening the bond and increasing the identification between the bank and its large corporate customers. They cement existing relationships with major corporate customers. The interlock means that the corporation has a friend at the bank and vice-versa.

In some cases it may mean avoiding a loss of business or gaining more business. As another banker put it, "If First National City Bank refused a directorship and another bank took it, that might signify a loss of business for FNCB." The corporation and the bank usually have a long-term preexisting relationship that the directorship merely confirms.

Though an interlocking directorship may help solidify a bank's relationship with a customer, it cannot singlehandedly turn a poor relationship into a good one. One large industrial company, that used to have a director on Citibank's board, never had any collected funds in the bank. The bank's relationship with the company deteriorated so badly that the bank finally turned down a request for credit, even though there was an interlock.

Some of the directors said they were personal friends of bank executives who asked them to be on the bank's board. One director, asked why he went on the board, replied, "It's a great bank with a fine group of directors."

Though the board is nominally responsible for formulating policy, information and initiative resides with management. The outside directors are successful, busy executives with many responsibilities to their primary employers and the other companies on whose boards they sit. Their only preparation for the semimonthly board meetings, which generally last about an hour and a half, involves examining a pamphlet of background materials that management distributes when the meeting is scheduled to take up important policy questions.

The directors themselves characterize their responsibilities in nebulous terms: "To see that the bank is well-run," "to appraise management," "to make sure that the bank is not misrepresenting any information to the public," and "to insure that the bank is a good corporate citizen," are phrases used by the outside directors to describe their own responsibilities. Citibank's officers see the directors' roles in similar terms. As one senior vice president noted, board members, with their broad business knowledge, can keep the management abreast of the market. Citibank's Chairman, Walter Wriston, says he likes to sound out the board members' opinions on new ideas.

Asked whether the board in essence "defers" to Wriston's superior knowledge, one director begged the question by retorting, "Of course not. Walt wouldn't dare override a majority of the board." The director, however, refused to say how often the board does not "see it Walt's way." Directors insist that policy questions are hotly debated but would not say how often, if ever, the board vetoed something that Wriston favored. All we got was "Wriston makes sense."

In fact, the policy decisions are made by the bank's top executives through a 17-man committee that is called, appropriately enough, the Policy Committee. This committee, which meets every Thursday, usually for the whole morning, is composed of the top bank executives and representatives of the six operating groups plus the men in charge of important departments such as personnel and the money-market operation. The Policy Committee has the expertise, information, opportunity, and time to consider carefully all the factors that go into formulating policy for a $25 billion world-wide bank. The board then "hotly debates" the issue and ratifies the Policy Committee.

FNCB made its first move to diversify the board of directors when it selected Franklin Thomas, President of the Bedford-Stuyvesant Restoration Corporation, to become a member of the board in the fall of 1970. Although the board remains overwhelmingly composed of business executives from large corporations, the appointment of Franklin Thomas is at least token recognition of the fact that the bank must increase its responsiveness to capital-starved sectors of the economy that compete for funds with the bank's primary constituency—the large corporations. Let us hope that Franklin Thomas, who is also a trustee of Columbia University, Robert F. Kennedy Memorial, Carnegie Corporation of New York, and John Hay Whitney Foundation, and a director of the New York Urban Coalition, the City Center of Music and Drama, Inc., Lincoln Center for the Performing Arts, and the Urban Design Council of New York, can devote the time necessary to lead Citibank into applying more of its resources and innovation to the problems of urban rot and environmental pollution.

At a minimum, we think that Citibank's board should include at least one director chosen by each of the following constituencies: employees, individual customers, small and/or midsized corporate customers, individual trust customers, beneficiaries of pension funds managed by the bank, and New York City. These directors should be selected, not by management with the approval of stockholders (who put up less than 10% of the bank's funds) but by the people whose lives are affected by the bank's policies. Each constituency should have complete autonomy to select its own director in order to increase the bank's responsiveness to needs other than those of national and multinational corporations.

IV

Banking For Government

Introduction

Governments, like people and corporations, depend on banks; this chapter will explore the ramifications of that dependence. We will examine Citibank's role as a financier for New York City that provides long-term and short-term credit. We will also look at the other financial services FNCB provides to New York, such as checking accounts, income-tax processing, welfare check distribution and pension fund management, and we will evaluate the costs and benefits of having FNCB provide such services.

FNCB and New York's other banks do more than supply financial services for government. With representation on important public bodies, such as the Metropolitan Transportation Authority (MTA), and through civic associations, such as the Downtown-Lower Manhattan Association (DLMA), bankers are responsible for formulating public spending policies that directly influence the lives of the millions of people who live and work in New York City. We will present four case studies —a) New York State's purchase of the Long Island Railroad, b) the State's purchase of the New Haven commuter line, c) the financing of the World Trade Center, and d) the effort to have automobile tolls subsidize mass transit—to show how FNCB and its executives use positions of public trust to reap private profit for the bank.

Given that FNCB, as a major bank for governments, has the opportunity to make private profit from public moneys, we must ask what FNCB does for the community that supports it. By looking at the amount of taxes FNCB pays to the city, we will question whether the bank is paying its fair share. By examining FNCB's residential mortgage policies, we will see if FNCB has returned to the community what it has taken out.

1. First National City Creditor

Like other cities, New York often has to borrow. To raise money,
to raise long-term funds, New York City issues bonds. To raise
short-term funds, New York issues notes. In both endeavors, the
city relies on its banks who, as we will see, sometimes prove to be
fair-weather friends.

State and Municipal Bonds

New York City reserves $832 million, or 10% of its 1970-71
budget, for servicing its debt. This is 35% more than the total
budget for the Police Department and 3.5 times the total budget
for the Fire Department. Of the $832 million, more than $300
million, or 36%, constitutes interest payments.[1]

States, municipalities, and other governmental subdivisions,
like corporations, do not issue bonds and sell them to the
investing public themselves because they lack the expertise and
contacts with buyers to unload their bonds quickly. So they sell
their bonds—generally on a competitive basis—to underwriting syndicates that act as middlemen. The winning syndicate
pays the issuer in one lump sum and assumes the burden and
risk of finding buyers for the bonds. The underwriters' profits
come from underwriting fees and the difference between the
underwriters' purchase and selling prices.

The Glass Steagall Act of 1932 prohibited banks from underwriting corporate securities. They may, however, underwrite the
securities of states, municipalities, and other governmental subdivisions. Accordingly, commercial banks play a leading role in
underwriting these securities.

Commercial banks are in an excellent position to market the
tax-exempt securities of states and municipalities. Banks are
substantial investors in tax-exempt securities for their own investment portfolios. With low risk and a ready market, tax
exempts are quickly salable if a bank needs to raise cash
quickly to satisfy loan demand or meet an outflow of deposits.
For this reason, bank holdings of tax-exempt securities are
sometimes called "secondary reserves."

Although banks do not necessarily buy the securities they
underwrite for their own portfolios, the large money-market

banks have correspondent relationships with thousands of local and regional banks around the country for which they provide a wide variety of services, including bond analysis. These relationships provide the money-market banks with an outlet for the tax exempts they underwrite. Insurance companies also buy tax-exempt securities from commercial bank dealer departments. Bank trust departments are another important outlet for state and municipal securities.

Because of their ready access to tax-exempt investors, banks do most of the underwriting for local governments. Citibank's bond underwriting department is one of the most aggressive and well-run in the country, according to experts at investment banking houses that participate in syndicates with all the major banks. The vice president in charge of FNCB's underwriting effort carries a lot of weight at syndicate meetings because, backed by the bank's enormous capital, he can take on tremendous participations if some of the underwriters drop out because they are not pleased with the terms.

In 1969, New York City sold $648 million worth of bonds. Four times the City Comptroller held public biddings at which he awarded the bonds to the underwriting syndicate submitting the lowest bid. Syndicates led by Citibank and Chase split the business; two bids totaling $325 million went to Citibank's syndicate, and two others totaling $323 million went to Chase's syndicate.[2] In 1971, it cost New York City about $20 per $1,000 bond, or $10-$13 million a year to sell its securities, up from $7.50 a bond in 1969.[3]

Although competitive bidding reduces long-term borrowing costs, many states and municipalities pay more than they should because of the tremendous weight that underwriters and investors give to the Moody's and Standard and Poor's ratings. Despite all the scare talk in the financial community about state and municipal financial problems, the fact remains that governments with general powers of taxation are good risks and defaults on their bonds are virtually unknown. Relative to the risk of corporate securities, state and municipal obligations backed by the full faith and credit of issuers possessing general powers of taxation should all be rated AAA.

New York City, for example, is required by law to pay its debt service before any other expenses, including salaries. Rev-

enues from real-estate taxes alone are twice the size of the
total debt service obligations. Total city revenues amount to
more than nine times its debt service obligations.[4] Despite the
safety of its bonds, however, in 1970 New York's rating was a
marginal Baa, which decreased the marketability of its bonds and
increased the interest cost to city taxpayers by a substantial
amount. In 1966, when New York City's rating was dropped
from A to Baa, the cost of borrowing rose by ¼–½ of 1%. Because New York City each year issues over $500 million of
new serial bonds with an average maturity of eight years, the
total extra interest cost to the city is $10-$20 million per year.[5]

State and municipal borrowing costs come under particularly
heavy pressure in tight money, as the Federal Reserve Bank of
New York noted in its *1969 Annual Report:*

> The banks responded to the pressures of monetary restraint and
> continued strong loan demand by liquidating securities on a
> major scale. By the end of 1969, the banks' holdings of United
> States Government securities had fallen to the lowest level in at
> least twenty years. And for the first time in ten years they
> liquidated tax-exempt state and local issues on balance adding
> to the pressures in the municipal securities market.[6]

In 1970, when credit loosened up again, commercial banks
resumed their investment in state and municipal securities,
increasing their holdings by nearly $10 billion (17%) to
$67,409,727,000.[7]

Citibank, however, continued to give preference to its corporate customers. Although its dollar volume of state and municipal security holdings was unchanged between 1969 and
1970, FNCB's holding in its own investment account actually
dropped by $40 million, which was offset by a comparable in-
crease in the trading account of its dealer department.[8]

Walter Wriston explained that the bank "needed every dollar
that we could raise to lend to the corporate customers during
the money squeeze last year. We had no investment money left
over to increase our portfolio."[9] Thus, in 1970, Citibank's
holdings of state and municipal securities dropped to 4.3% of
assets, an all-time low. In the first quarter of 1971, FNCB's
ownership of state and municipal securities plummeted another $270 million, to 3.1% of assets, a smaller percentage
than that held by any one of the nation's 100 largest banks.[10]
By the end of 1971, FNCB's holdings of such obligations

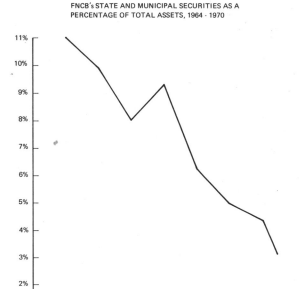

FNCB's STATE AND MUNICIPAL SECURITIES AS A
PERCENTAGE OF TOTAL ASSETS, 1964 - 1970

(BILLIONS OF DOLLARS)

	1964	1965	1966	1967	1968	1969	1970	1971
STATE AND MUN. SECURITIES	1.4	1.4	1.2	1.6	1.3	1.1	1.1	.8*
TOTAL ASSETS	12.5	14.0	15.1	17.7	19.6	23.1	25.8	27.1*

* First quarter, 1971.
SOURCE: FNCC-FNCB *Annual Reports,* 1965–66.

equaled only 2.64% of its total assets, still the smallest percentage of any of the 100 largest banks.

New York City's tax-exempt bonds were among those that
Citibank decided to liquidate. According to James Allen, vice
president in charge of the bank's municipal bond portfolio,
Citibank's holdings of New York City bonds, which amounted
to $95 million in 1968 [11] did not increase during 1969 and
1970.[21] In every year since 1964, more than 10% of the nation's commercial bank assets have been in state and municipal
obligations and on December 31, 1970, the figure stood at
11.8% [13] If the six largest banks put 10% of their assets into
state and municipal bonds, it would mean an additional

$4,300,000,000 of demand and lower borrowing costs for states and municipalities.

One reason for Citibank's relatively small investment in state and municipal securities is its extensive involvement in aircraft leasing. Due to huge losses, the airlines do not have the strength to borrow money and buy the billions of dollars in new aircraft, parts, and associated ground equipment to which they are committed. Nor can they take advantage of the investment tax credit or depreciation tax benefits accompanying the purchase of their new equipment because the losses have wiped out their tax obligations. So Citibank (and to a lesser extent, a few other banks) purchased many of the aircraft and leased them to the airlines, obtaining for itself the investment and depreciation tax benefits. The tax benefits thus reduce the banks' tax bills and are passed on to the airlines in the form of lease payments that are 3% to 3.5% below what it would cost the airlines to borrow and buy the equipment themselves.[14] The banks' reduced tax liability, however, diminishes their incentive to invest in tax-exempt obligations. This adds to the pressure on the tax-exempt markets, reducing demand and increasing borrowing costs.

States and municipalities are extremely dependent on commercial bank purchases of their securities. As opposed to corporations which can sell stock in the stock market, bonds in the bond market, or commercial paper in the commercial paper market, states and municipalities must go to the banks for both long- and short-term credit. Unfortunately, however, the municipal bond market is a residual user of funds; banks, especially the large ones, invest in state and municipal securities only after they have met the loan demand of their corporate customers. In 1967 and 1968, commercial banks absorbed over 90% of the state and municipal bonds issued. When money got tight in 1969, their participation collapsed to 17.%[15] As a result, state and municipal borrowing costs skyrocketed even higher than borrowing costs for corporations, despite a 30% drop in the number of new issues.[16]

The limited demand for tax-exempt securities has boosted state and municipal borrowing costs to more than 70% of corporate borrowing costs, despite the existence of the tax exemption, as the following figure illustrates:

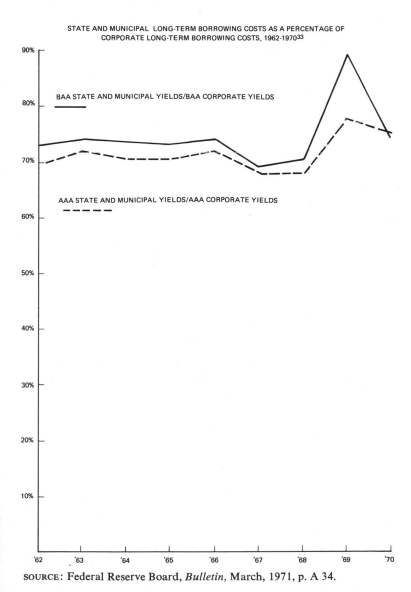

STATE AND MUNICIPAL LONG-TERM BORROWING COSTS AS A PERCENTAGE OF CORPORATE LONG-TERM BORROWING COSTS, 1962-1970[33]

SOURCE: Federal Reserve Board, *Bulletin,* March, 1971, p. A 34.

One recommendation, aimed at expanding the demand for state and municipal securities and reducing the borrowing costs for the issuers, has been proposed by Professor Stanley Surrey of the Harvard Law School and Frank E. Morris, President of

the Federal Reserve Bank of Boston.[17] They recommend that
issuers have the option of selling fully taxable securities, subsidized by the Federal Government. The existing subsidy generated by the tax exemption is inefficient—that is, the tax
exemption costs the federal government more in lost income-
tax revenues than it saves the states and municipalities in
lower interest costs.[18] Therefore, if the federal government
paid the states and municipalities 50% of their interest costs
directly, it would recoup most, if not all, of this money by increased revenues from income-tax collections on the investors'
interest income.

Higher, taxable interest rates would make state and municipal securities attractive to many savers and investors who now
have no incentive to consider them. Tax-exempt pension funds,
for example, which currently shun state and municipals, would
find higher yielding state and municipal securities an attractive,
low-risk investment, with predictable payouts. State and municipal pension funds, which already invest heavily in tax exempts
because of legal restrictions on their investment freedom, would
obtain higher income. Individuals would also obtain a high return, low-risk alternative to bank time deposits at the same time
that their money would be used to help their own communities,
rather than some distant, multinational corporation. It is thus
essential to develop a method of issuing high-yield, taxable state
and municipal obligations in small denominations and a marketing device to make them readily available to all citizens.

Replacing tax-exempt bonds with subsidized, fully taxable
securities would save New York City at least $40 million a
year. Over the past decade, Baa-rated corporate bonds and
Baa-rated state and municipal bonds have carried average
yields of about 6% and 4.5%, respectively.[19] If fully taxable
Baa state and municipal securities carried roughly the same
yields as Baa corporate securities and half of the interest costs
were subsidized by the federal government, Baa-rated state
and municipal issuers would lower their interest expenses by
at least 1%, which would save New York City $40 million a
year (assuming $500 million of 16-year serial bonds issued
each year).

In all probability, the savings would be higher because Baa-
rated securities of states and municipalities with general powers

of taxation are better risks than the securities of Baa-rated corporations. Thus, once state and municipal securities were made attractive to the broad spectrum of investors that currently have no incentive to consider tax exempts, state and municipal securities would probably carry lower interest rates than comparably rated corporate bonds. In light of the financial crisis that grips the nation's state and local governments at the very time that huge, long-term capital expenditures are needed to improve schools, hospitals, mass transit, sanitation, pollution control, courts, and the prisons, it is imperative that Congress do everything possible to encourage such investments by reducing the onerous burden of borrowing long-term funds.

Short-Term Debt—BANS, RANS, and TANS

New York City also depends on banks for short-term funds. In the fiscal year which ended June 30, 1970, New York borrowed more than $3 billion for short periods of time because it couldn't wait for the proceeds of its bond sales, tax collections or state and federal revenues.[20] The city borrows short-term funds by issuing notes backed up by anticipated revenue from these three sources. The notes are called Bond Anticipation Notes (BANs), Tax Anticipation Notes (TANs), and Revenue Anticipation Notes (RANs). Until November, 1970, the six largest New York banks handled 84% of the TANs and RANs, according to a formula dating back to 1933: [21]

Participating Bank	Percent
Chase Manhattan	22.62
First National City Bank	22.06
Manufacturers Hanover Trust Co.	11.13
Chemical Bank	10.34
Morgan Guaranty Trust Co.	9.68
Bankers Trust Co.	8.27
All other banks	15.90
	100.00

In the 1969–70 fiscal year, the city issued TANs 41 times. These borrowings totaled $2.2 billion at tax-exempt interest rates of 6.2 to 7.1%. In the same period of time it also issued RANs 28 times, for a total of $1.2 billion.[22]

Unlike their abandonment of the long-term municipal bond market when money is tight, the banks have not ignored New

York City's short-term credit needs in times of money market stress. City officials said that the large banks continued to meet New York City's short-term credit needs throughout the tight money period of 1969 and early 1970, even though many of the bankers asserted that they had better uses for their money and didn't need any more tax-exempt income. The *Perotta Report* agreed:

> The banking relationships . . . have proved crucial to the City in times of financial crisis such as in 1933 and 1966. In view of the obvious financial problems facing the City in the '70's, it would be unwise to endanger these relationships.[23]

In November, 1970, after New York City had been following the 1933 formula for 37 years, Comptroller Abe Beame switched to competitive bidding. The first test of the competitive bidding procedure for short-term borrowing involved the largest borrowing in the city's history, $515 million worth of 92-day TANs, offered on November 5, 1970, with six bank syndicates submitting bids. The city paid interest of $4,800,000 equal to an annual interest rate of only 3.72%, down from the 4.8% the city had to pay on TANs two months earlier. With extra funds on their hands due to weak loan demand, the banks turned to tax-exempt securities as a profitable short-term use for their money. The Comptroller's Technical Advisory Committee on Debt Management prevailed upon Beame to open up TANs and RANs to competitive bidding—thus giving more banks an opportunity to participate in the short-term tax-exempt market.[24]

Even accounting for the fact that the lower borrowing cost on the 92-day TANs was due largely to the general decline in interest rates during the fall of 1970, the competitive bidding procedure definitely saved New York City over $1,500,000 in interest payments on the 92-day TANs.

Surrey and Morris's idea for federally subsidized fully taxed municipal bonds, and Comptroller Beame's program of competitive bidding in short-term markets are examples of how greater financial savvy can be applied to public financing. The following section shows that similar expertise as well as constant supervision are also needed to ensure that New York City's other banking needs are met.

2. At Your Service—For a Fee

Like individuals, New York City needs a bank in which to keep a checking account. Like many corporations, New York turns to banks for help with its paper work, such as income-tax processing and welfare check disbursement. And also like corporations, New York City has banks provide investment advice for its employee benefit funds. FNCB is among the banks that provide these services to the city—usually for a fee. Sometimes the fee is exorbitant, as we will see was the case with the city's checking account. Sometimes there are also hidden costs, like the risk that FNCB will make use of the private information contained on citizens' tax forms or the risk that a large bank will be so careless as to cash $400,000 of fraudulent checks. Sometimes there is no outright charge; instead the bank merely uses its investment discretion indirectly, to make friends and attract deposits.

New York City's Checking Accounts

The New York City Charter prevents the city from depositing its money in banks that do not meet certain capital requirements.[25] This restriction, designed to ensure the safety of government deposits, effectively prevents all but the largest New York banks from handling the large and profitable clearing account. Since 1965, the clearing account has rotated on a quarterly basis between Chase, FNCB, Manufacturers Hanover, and Bankers Trust; Chemical, and to a much lesser extent, Morgan Guaranty, have some of the city's other checking accounts.

The city's funds are supervised by both the New York City Finance Administration and the New York City Comptroller. The finance administrator, a mayoral appointee, administers the city treasury bank accounts. In 1970–71, the annual receipts of these funds amounted to approximately $15 billion. The city comptroller, an elected official, administers certain trust funds relating to payroll deductions, such as federal withholding taxes, state withholding taxes, social security, and so on. In 1970–71, the annual receipts of these funds came to about $883 million; in addition there were sinking-fund receipts amounting to $444 million and pension fund receipts of $2.8 billion.[26]

New York City's checking accounts have been exorbitantly profitable for the banks. In 1970, the Finance Administration

PROFITABILITY ANALYSIS OF NEW YORK CITY ACCOUNTS AT FNCB, 1969

EARNINGS
Average Collected Balance $58,442,000
Average Investable Balance (average collected balance minus 17½% reserves) ... 48,214,000
Earnings (average investable balance times 6½% Treasury Bill interest rate) ... $ 3,134,000

Expenses	Number of Items	Charge per Item	
Checks cashed	2,054,832	$.15	$ 308,255
Checks paid	2,396,947	.06	143,816
Checks reconciled	1,205,021	.03	36,157
Items deposited	143,195	.03	4,296
Real estate bills processed	225,162	.13	39,271
Frontage bills processed	504,245	.225	113,230
Corporate tax bills processed	237,157	.66	156,523
Other			78,057

Total Expenses .... $ 879,575

PROFIT
Earnings .... $ 3,134,000
Expenses (rounded off by Finance Administration) 880,000

Profit (earnings minus expenses) .... $ 2,254,000
Profit/Expense Ratio 256%

EXCESS PROFIT
Total Profit .... $ 2,254,000
Fair Profit (50% of expenses) 440,000

Excess Profit (total profit minus fair profit) .... $ 1,814,000

SOURCE: Fiorvante G. Perotta, New York City Finance Administration, *Profitability Analysis of New York City's Checking Accounts at FNCB, Chase Manhattan, Manufacturers Hanover, Morgan Guaranty, Chemical, and Bankers Trust,* April 14, 1970.

conducted a detailed profitability analysis of all New York City checking accounts. According to their figures, a fair profit for the banks is a profit equal to 50% of the bank's expenses. Based on this guideline, $8,071,000 of the banks' 1969 profit from the city's accounts was excessive. FNCB's share of the excess profit was $1,814,000.

The profitability analysis for FNCB's handling of New York City's accounts is shown opposite.

One city official who worked on the report said that the banks inflate the number of services they actually provide, for instance, by counting every check that is not deposited as cashed, even though other banks frequently absorb this cost. The Finance Administration surveyed city employees and discovered that most of the employees cash their checks where they have their own accounts, not at the bank on which the check is drawn. Thus, the check cashing charge, which constitutes a substantial cost in servicing city accounts, is often absorbed by the bank that handles the payee's account, not by the city's bank.

According to the finance administrator's guideline for fair profit (50% of expense) more than half the city's average balance available for investment was excessive (see page 130).

Although meaningful changes in the city's business dealings with the banks involve, in the words of former Finance Administrator Perotta, "long and difficult negotiations with the banks," New York City did restructure its money management policy to save the taxpayers money. In August, 1971 the Finance Administration adopted a balance reduction program to lower the profits that the banks can earn on New York City's accounts, to reasonable levels.

This is the way the "zero balance" system works. Checks drawn on bank accounts are not presented immediately for payment. From the time the city writes the check until the check is deposited, processed by the back office of the depositor's bank, and presented for payment, the city, rather than maintaining idle funds in its account, invests the money in interest-bearing overnight repurchase agreements. The "zero balance" account is funded as the checks are presented for payment—a process that can be predicted with fair accuracy.

The Finance Administration also maintains a separate "pool"

PROFITABILITY ANALYSIS OF NEW YORK CITY ACCOUNTS AT SIX LARGEST BANKS, 1969

	Average Investable Balance	Earnings	Expenses	Profit	Profit/ Expenses	Excess Profits	Excess Balances
FNCB	$ 48,214,000	$ 3,134,000	$ 880,000	$ 2,254,000	256%	$1,814,000	$ 33,831,000
Chemical	21,954,000	1,427,000	488,000	979,000	219%	755,000	14,080,000
Man-Han	78,553,000	5,105,000	2,177,000	2,928,000	134%	1,840,000	34,316,000
Morgan	3,278,000	214,000	63,000	151,000	240%	119,000	2,220,000
Chase	65,800,000	4,277,000	1,116,000	3,161,000	283%	2,603,000	48,546,000
Total	$246,222,000	$16,006,000	$5,290,000	$10,717,000	203%	$8,071,000	$150,525,000

SOURCE: *Perotta Report.*

account at each bank with compensating balances geared to the cost of processing items on the "zero balance" account. The Finance Administration figures expense costs by averaging all the banks' cost estimates. It maintains a balance in each "pool" account sufficient to compensate each bank for services rendered based on the three-month U.S. Treasury Bill rate.

A few of the large banks expressed displeasure over the new system and some of them, in the words of one city official, "keep asking us not to talk to anyone else." Apparently, they hope that other government money managers will not adopt the same system. Their unhappiness is not difficult to understand.

In 1970, the average daily amount that the Finance Administrator was able to withdraw from bank demand deposits (i.e., checking accounts) to use to produce income for the city was $67 million. After the zero balance method was put into operation, in August, 1971, the average daily amount available for investment shot up to $305 million. In the first nine months of 1972, the Finance Administration was able to raise this average daily investable balance to $400 million.[27] Assuming a conservative constant rate of return of 5%, adoption of the zero balance method promises to save the city at least $16 million annually. If all governmental units were to adopt such a system, the aggregate savings would be staggering. On June 30, 1970, commercial banks held $17,218,413,000 of interest-free demand deposits of states, municipalities, and other political subdivisions.[28] $1,244,873,000 of this money was held by the six largest New York City banks and $466,418,000 by Citibank.[29] Widespread adoption of the "zero balance" system would save American taxpayers hundreds of millions of dollars each year.

New York City Personal Income Tax Processing

When New York City instituted a personal income tax in 1966, it sought assistance in processing the returns from the banks, which had traditionally helped collect water, sewer, cigarette, sales, and real-estate taxes. Because the city didn't have the resources to gear up the administrative machinery needed to process the returns in less than six months, and because it anticipated difficulty in scheduling the enormous variations in manpower needed to handle this extremely labor-intensive operation, the city got Chase Manhattan to do the processing for the first three years.

Chase received $1,850,000 for the first year and lost money, $2,750,000 the second year and earned about $110,000 profit, and $3,700,000 the third year and earned about $370,000.[30] In 1969, the city asked for competitive bids on the income tax processing contract. Citibank, the lowest bidder, offered to do the job for three years starting at $4,240,000 and ranging up to $4,750,000 the third year. Chase Manhattan's bid was 15% higher, and Bankers Trust was 30% higher.[31]

City officials have been trying to get the state to process the city returns by "piggybacking" the city return onto the state return—a procedure that would entail little additional expense to the state while saving the city at least $5 million per year. Governor Rockefeller, however, anxious to avoid any increase in the amount of money taxpayers have to send to Albany, has refused to support the city's request.

Taxpayers send their returns and checks to a post office box maintained by the bank. The bank collects the returns on a daily basis, opens the mail, examines the checks to make sure that the amount corresponds to the return and that the checks are properly made out to the city. It enters an identification number on each check keyed to the taxpayer's return, deposits the checks in New York City's FNCB account, and informs the city daily of the balance in the account. It keypunches information from the returns onto computer cards, which are then fed into Citibank's computers. The information is thus transferred onto tapes which are sent over to the Finance Administration for further processing on the city's own model 360 IBM computers. The bank retains a backup copy of each tape.[32]

Although Citibank's role in the processing of personal income tax returns is somewhat analogous to the lock box collection service it performs for corporate customers, the job entails much more detailed, labor-intensive work. It is, in the words of J. Howard Laeri, FNCB vice chairman, "one of the toughest jobs we've ever undertaken." [33] The forms from which the information must be extracted, the data processing, and the training required are detailed and complex. Most important of all is the fact that the volume of paper processed varies tremendously from month to month. In October, November, and December, the bank processes about 60,000–70,000 forms per month. In April, it does 40,000 *per day* and at the peak, receives as many as 200,000 forms per day.[34] This variation makes it very difficult to schedule manpower requirements.

Initially, Citibank tried to automate part of the work by using optical scanning machinery to extract the information from typewritten returns, but this scheme didn't work out as planned. Although Citibank had submitted its bid on the assumption that the optical scanners would reduce some of the manpower requirements,[35] the bank had to abandon this procedure and hire additional personnel. When Citibank fell behind schedule in 1970, New York City Finance Administrator Perotta met with FNCB's Chairman, Walter Wriston, and told him that the city wanted the bank to put more resources into the job and try to remedy the deficiencies. Wriston assigned a new team to manage the job, headed by Larry Small, an extremely capable young vice president whose diversified seven-year experience at the bank (credit officer in International Banking Group, head of Santiago, Chile branch network, international development of Master Charge, Operating Group) marks him as a man on the way up. Small streamlined the operation so well that city officials say that FNCB's performance is now better than Chase Manhattan's. But it has cost money. The bank told city personnel that it lost about $1 million the first year. Small told us that the bank "had a difficult time of it the first year. From a business standpoint, it wasn't one of the best deals we ever got into." [36]

The bank got into the project for a number of reasons. One is the fact that the city is an enormous customer of the bank, and, as the original bank supervisor of the project noted, "when New York City asks you to bid, you bid." [37] Also, the bank may have been moved by a sense of social obligation to help tackle a difficult problem for the city. Another reason may have been the opportunity to use the information from the income tax returns in its credit files.

Despite the supervisory involvement of city officials, there is no way that the city can ensure that the information from the returns does not end up in the bank's credit files. As Robert H.

Aten, a Finance Administration official, noted in a memo to Jay Kriegel, one of Mayor Lindsay's top aides: "The income tax information . . . is on computer tape and banks could misuse the information in any way without our knowledge." [38]

Citibank clearly has a strong incentive to transfer the credit-related data from the returns into its credit files. The income information on the tapes is well-documented, up-to-date, and of obvious use to New York's number one retail creditor. Citibank has the opportunity to use the information for credit purposes, because it retains a back-up copy of the tapes.[39]

We think that the potential for abuse of this information far outweighs the administrative benefit to the city in having the returns processed. We reach this conclusion despite the fact that city officials say FNCB has been doing an excellent job, despite the fact that city officials monitor the bank's activities in processing the returns, and despite the fact that the contract beween FNCB and the city prohibits the bank from using the information extracted from the returns for purposes unrelated to the scope of the contract.

Accordingly, we recommend that the city resume its efforts to have the state process the city returns and, if unsuccessful, do the job itself. The city should exercise as much caution as possible to prevent any misuse of the sensitive information that citizens submit on their income tax returns, especially in light of the growing threat to individual privacy from the ever-burgeoning numbers of computerized data banks. The city could have avoided the problem by contracting with a data processing company that has no incentive to use the information and the city could have retained the back-up tapes itself. By failing to take these elementary precautions, the city has breached its responsibility to maximize the protection of the data submitted in confidence by its citizens.

The state legslature should repeal the exemption that allows Citibank access to personal income tax returns and require the state to assume responsibility for processing the city returns along with the state personal income tax returns. In any event, the city should conduct a thorough examination of the credit files of Citibank and Chase, in order to ascertain whether the banks abided by their contractual obligation not to use the data for their own private purposes.

New York City Welfare Checks

Stolen and forged welfare checks have posed a continual problem for New York City. In 1972, a pilot program designed to reduce welfare check fraud was begun in Nassau County, Long Island. Welfare recipients were issued identification cards with their photographs, and they could go to the six participating banks to pick up their money. FNCB's Rockville Center branch was one of the participating banks.[40] According to the Social Services Commission the program is working quite well. The banks too are happy; they get the benefit of a two-day float on the welfare funds.

While FNCB has been doing a good job on the other side of the city line, the same cannot be said of its performance in Brooklyn. In March, 1972, it was revealed that owners of a Brooklyn candy store had illegally cashed 7,500 welfare checks, totaling close to $400,000, at FNCB and National Bank of North America. According to New York City Social Services Commissioner Jule M. Sugarman, these were two-party checks; when they were cashed by FNCB and NBNA they had been endorsed by only one of the two parties to which they were made out and these signatures may themselves have been forged.[41] The question—still unanswered—is why FNCB cashed checks that, lacking the second signature, were on their face invalid.

The New York City Employee Pension Plan

In 1969, the New York City Comptroller solicited bids to select advisors to help invest $5 billion of municipal employee pension funds. Citibank was selected as the exclusive advisor on the corporate bond portfolio—$2.7 billion at June 30, 1970 [42] — and was advisor on half of the common stock portfolio—$210 million on June 30, 1970.[43] Irving Trust Company and Moody's Alliance Capital Corporation provided advice on the other half of the stock portfolio. All the winning bidders offered to give their advice gratis, but they retained the right to select which securities dealers would execute the investment transactions.[44]

Pension funds are sent to the advisory banks each month. The banks immediately invest the funds in U.S. government securities until they are later put into a wide variety of corporate and government securities. The cash accounts of the pension funds are not handled by Citibank and Irving alone, but are spread out among many different New York City banks. FNCB and Irving make investment recommendations, which must be approved by the Comptroller's Bureau of Investments. In practice, the Comptroller's personnel rarely disagree with the banks' advice. As of July, 1970, only one suggested investment had been vetoed.[45]

Personnel in the Comptroller's Bureau of Investments feel that Citibank and Irving have been doing an excellent job restructuring the pension fund portfolio into higher yielding securities. The Bureau of Investments estimates that income has been increased by about $15 million per year as a result of these changes.[46]

Citibank congratulated itself in the "Human Environment" section of its 1969 *Annual Report* for acting as pension fund advisor for the city. We wonder, however, whether Citibank wanted the job to use the power to choose brokers as a device to attract deposits from those brokers. This practice, known as "broker reciprocity" is discussed more fully in the trust chapter. Our suspicion that FNCB used New York City's pension fund account to attract deposits is based on observations by personnel in the New York City Comptroller's office,[47] statements by responsible persons in one brokerage house that FNCB chose to handle corporate bond transactions, and aggregate statistics compiled by the SEC. Without identifying the brokerage house it uses, and without stating the amount of deposits FNCB holds of those houses, FNCB denies that it directs brokerage to obtain deposits.

It seems clear that when a major bank provides its home city with financial services, it should do so at a reasonable price, with respect for citizens' privacy, with care, and with regard for the law. The exorbitant fees charged to handle New York City's checking accounts, possible misuse of private tax information, careless check cashing procedures, and probable broker reciprocity all illustrate how FNCB's relationship with the city is subject to abuse. Similar abuses are found when FNCB is represented on public commissions.

3. Public Trust for Private Profit

There are subtle and blatant forms of influence that a bank and its employees can exercise. A blatant form might exist if a Citibank employee conspired with a dance studio to give customers loans so that they could sign up for costly lessons. The banker would presumably get kickbacks from the dance studio which, in turn, would be able to saddle customers with lessons costing over $2,000. A more subtle form of influence would exist if Walter Wriston, Chairman of Citibank, went to the White House and argued with President Nixon to exempt interest rates from Phase II controls. With frozen wages and prices but unfrozen interest rates, FNCB would have the best of both worlds: it could increase its profits by raising rates on loans and consumer credit while not having to worry about rising expenses such as wages.

True, such influence peddling sounds highly unlikely. Maybe not however. New York's Department of Consumer Affairs is presently suing Dale Dance Studios and FNCB, alleging exactly the kind of conspiracy described above.[48] William Finn, a Citibank employee who also gave lessons for Dale, reportedly arranged $130,000 in loans from FNCB to Dale students for dance courses. In November, 1971, Walter Wriston was among the 11 businessmen who met with President Nixon to discuss ideas for Phase II of the President's economic policy. At the meeting Wriston argued against freezing interest rates, although he did favor some wage and price actions.[49] His arguments apparently were successful, for under Phase II interest rates and consumer finance charges remained exempt from price controls while wages of service industries, like banks, were subject to the controls. It might be presumptuous for us to ascribe the exemption of interest rates from controls to Mr. Wriston's influence at the White House. On the other hand, we can only surmise what Mr. Wriston himself meant when he wrote in his confidential "state of the bank" message:

> . . . through government relations and public relations, we now have in place a very delicate information gathering system to alert us to developing pitfalls. And through low-key selective and determined efforts in both areas, we believe that we are

beginning to develop a more sophisticated anticipatory approach to some of the public problems that will have a substantial effect on our future.[50]

Four case studies—the takeovers of the LIRR and the New Haven Commuter line, the financing of the World Trade Center, and the effort to have auto tolls subsidize mass transit—will show just how "sophisticated" Mr. Wriston's "anticipatory approach" can be.

"A New Long Island Railroad"

In addition to providing New York City with credit, Citibank and other banks influence how the City's funds will be spent. One way of affecting City policy stems from the banks' representation on various public and civic groups.

"The bank makes available a vast number of officers for various, what we consider civic obligations," notes Donald Colen, Citibank's vice president in charge of public relations.[51] A close look at Citibank's performance of these "civic obligations," however, shows that the bank's interest in the public welfare is tempered by a large amount of self-interest. New York City mass transportation provides a good example of just how profitable these "civic obligations" can be for FNCB.

In 1964, when the Long Island Railroad, a subsidiary of the Pennsylvania Railroad (which merged with the New York Central in 1968 to form the Penn Central) was threatening to go into bankruptcy, Citibank held $65 million of Pennsylvania's conditional sales agreements.[52] The LIRR was heavily in debt to its parent; if it were to go under, Pennsylvania's creditworthiness would have been affected. The public interest was also involved since the LIRR was (and is) the only rail line on Long Island, carrying over 250,000 passengers each day and serving as a major line in New York City's commuter rail network.

In 1964, New York's Governor, Nelson Rockefeller, appointed a Special Committee "to look into the condition of the Long Island Railroad and make recommendations . . . as to its future."[53] The Governor, whose brother, David Rockefeller, was President of the Chase Manhattan Bank and whose cousin, James Stillman Rockefeller, was Chairman of FNCB, appointed Citibank Senior Vice President, Eben W. Pyne, to the Special Committee to represent the creditors' interests.

The report of the Special Committee, *A New Long Island Railroad,* recommended that New York State purchase the LIRR from the Pennsylvania Railroad "if a reasonable price could be obtained," [54] In 1965, the LIRR was a near wreck. The tracks were falling apart and 70% of the cars were more than 30 years old. The Special Committee's report recognized that more than $200 million in improvements were needed to restore safe, reliable service. New York State Comptroller, Arthur Levitt, questioned whether the LIRR had any value at all.

> In reviewing the proposed agreement it is apparent that if fair market value were the only consideration, it might be that the railroad had no market value since its total operations have become uneconomic and are only continued as a public service. . . .[55]

Nevertheless, the state, following the Special Committee's recommendations, bought the LIRR from the Pennsylvania Railroad for $65 million.

In 1965, the LIRR owed Citibank's debtor, the Pennsylvania Railroad, $76.1 million. Of the $65 million paid by New York to the Pennsylvania Railroad, $60 million was given "in consideration for cancellation of (LIRR) debt." [56] The Special Committee defended these terms by comparing the cost with the cost of building a superhighway to replace the LIRR if service were discontinued, or to the cost of a drawn-out court proceeding if a negotiated settlement could not be reached.[57] As Comptroller Levitt noted, these are spurious arguments. For years, the Pennsylvania had been trying to dump the LIRR. In 1965 alone, the railroad lost $2.5 million. Eben Pyne, Citibank's representative on the Special Committee, felt, however, that New York State needed the railroad and was "willing to pay the price." [58]

The Takeover of the New Haven

Citibank also stands to gain from the recent public takeover of another Penn Central operation, the commuter service from

New Haven to New York City. In April, 1970, the Penn Central
entered a $250 million loan agreement, with Citibank as lead
bank in a 73-bank syndicate. This loan was secured by all the
outstanding common stock of the Pennsylvania Company, Penn
Central's real-estate subsidiary. Six months later, New York and
Connecticut agreed to lease and purchase the aged ailing commuter line which registers an annual loss of $6 to $8 million.[59]
Eben Pyne, as a Director of New York's MTA, approved the
agreement which provided that:

1. New York and Connecticut would assume all Penn-Central
losses on the commuter service;
2. New York and Connecticut would pay for new rolling
stock, electrification, station platforms, and signal system improvements;
3. Penn Central would continue its freight service, obtaining
the benefits of the publicly paid improvements on the line with
little cost to the railroad;
4. New York State would pay $7 million to buy the right of
way from the New York City line to the Connecticut border;
5. New York State and Connecticut would pay an annual
rental charge for use of Penn Central's tracks from 59th Street
in Manhattan to the New York City line;
6. Penn Central would retain the valuable real-estate assets
associated with the line (this includes the land under such prime
real estate as the Waldorf, Biltmore, Barclay, Roosevelt, and
Commodore Hotels, and the Pan Am Building);
7. New York State and Connecticut would pay $3.9 million
to Penn Central for old rolling stock; and
8. New York State and Connecticut would pay all annual expenses for Grand Central Terminal, except for the annual credit
of $2 million and the net revenues from terminal concessions.[60]

According to the Association of the Bar of the City of New
York:

The central conception of conflict of interest regulation is that
an official should not act for the government where his private
economic interests are involved.
    The evil is not only the possibility or appearance of private
gain from public office, but the risk that official decisions,
whether consciously or otherwise, will be motivated by something other than the public's interests. The ultimate concern
is bad government, which always means actual harm to the
public. . . .

Eben **Pyne**, a Senior Vice President at the Pennsylvania Railroad's major creditor, was placed in an untenable position when he was appointed to the Special Committee to examine the LIRR. His directorship on the MTA placed him in a similar position. Pyne should never have been appointed to positions of public trust which required him to choose between the interests of his employer and those of the taxpayers and commuters of New York. The law should prohibit such conflicts of interest unequivocally.

The World Trade Center

The World Trade Center being completed in lower Manhattan is a good example of comprehensive, private city planning, with the banks at the helm. The banks, through the Downtown-Lower Manhattan Association (DLMA), conceived the World Trade Center, ostensibly to preserve New York City as a center of world trade. The banks, through a $210 million loan agreement and millions of dollars of investments in bonds, are financing the center's construction. The banks, with branches and office space for their international departments, will inhabit the World Trade Center. And the banks, through the DLMA and their representatives on the Metropolitan Transit Authority, have accelerated the construction of additional subway facilities—at taxpayers' expense—needed to carry the 130,000 people who will travel to the center daily.

Independent public authorities combine many powers of government with the autonomy of private corporations. They have the government's powers to condemn private land and borrow money at low, tax-exempt interest rates. But like private corporations, authorities effectively have the autonomy to invest capital as they see fit, without regard to the overall impact on the millions of people whose lives their activities affect. A 1921 compact between the states of New York and New Jersey and ratified by the Senate of the United States created the bistate Port of New York Authority to promote "a better coordination of the terminal, transportation and other facilities of commerce in, about and through the port of New York," which was defined as "a territory with a radius of approximately twenty-five

miles from the Statue of Liberty." [61] The compact explicitly gave
the authority broad powers to implement its goals:

> The Port Authority shall constitute a body both corporate and
> politic with full power and authority . . . to purchase, con-
> struct, lease and/or operate any terminal or transportation fa-
> cility within said (port) district.[62]

Armed with the power to borrow money at low, tax-exempt
interest rates, the Port Authority built or acquired a wide variety of transportation facilities to serve the New York-New
Jersey metropolitan area. The authority operates six toll bridges
and tunnels, four airports, various bus, truck, and marine terminals, and a commuter railroad (called PATH) which operates
between Newark, New Jersey, and New York City. These operations, with the exception of PATH, are enormously profitable.
In 1969, the Port Authority earned tax-exempt *net* operating
revenues of $108 million on a gross of $240 million.[63]

The World Trade Center is the largest project that the Port
Authority has ever undertaken. When completed, the project's
$650 million will represent 25% of the Port Authority's total
invested assets—more than all of its tunnels and bridges put
together.

The World Trade Center was conceived by the DLMA and
financed by its members. The directors' list of this association
reads like a "Who's Who" of Wall Street:

Rank In New York City	*DLMA Director And Position At Bank*
1. First National City Bank	Richard S. Perkins, Chairman Executive Committee
2. Chase Manhattan Bank	David Rockefeller, Chairman
3. Manufacturers Hanover Trust	R. E. McNeill, Jr., Chairman
4. Morgan Guaranty Trust	Ellmore C. Patterson, President
5. Chemical Bank	Hulbert S. Aldrich, Vice Chairman
6. Bankers Trust	Edmund F. Ebert, Senior Vice President

Rank In New York City	DLMA Director And Position At Bank
7. Irving Trust	George A. Murphy, Chairman
8. Marine Midland Grace	Ralph S. Stillman, Chairman Executive Committee
9. Bank of New York	Elliott Averett, President

The DLMA's "primary purpose" is "to provide a sound foundation for the expansion of Lower Manhattan as the dominant center of finance, world trade and shipping." [64] As the DLMA itself noted, "we recommended the development of the great World Trade Center, now under construction by the Port of New York Authority." [65] The World Trade Center is to serve as headquarters for all sectors of the export-import business and associated industries concerned with international trade. With overseas markets growing faster than those in the United States, large corporations and banks are expanding their overseas operations at an extraordinary rate. The World Trade Center was designed to ensure that New York City retained its importance in international trade at a time when electronic communications and centralized management information systems make geographical proximity to a port less important.

In 1961, the Port Authority studies showed that the World Trade Center project was economically feasible. In 1962, plans were begun. The location for the center was chosen above the terminals of the PATH commuter railroad, which the authority had been directed to take over and rebuild in 1962. To make sure that the Port Authority would not have to subsidize additional mass-transit operations that were in the red, the authority and its bondholders obtained the passage of legislation that prohibits the Port Authority from operating additional transit facilities. In the words of the Port Authority:

> The 1962 statute adopted by the Legislatures of the two States, which authorized Port Authority acquisition of the interstate Hudson and Manhattan Railroad, specifically recognized and met the fundamental need of protecting the credit of the Port Authority to insure that it could continue its vital self-supporting

programs. The Legislatures recognized that the credit of the
Port Authority would be impaired if the Authority undertook
responsibility for the operation of such a perpetual deficit
facility, unless the States entered into *an enforceable contract
with the Authority bondholders,* [i.e., the banks] which gave
assurance against dilution of already pledged revenues by any
additional commuter rail deficits beyond those of the basic
PATH systems.[66] (Emphasis added.)

The Port Authority was thereby protected from having to use
some of its tax-exempt revenues to alleviate the additional burden that its World Trade Center would cause to the already over-
taxed mass transit facilities of New York City.

The banks also favored the World Trade Center because they
expected to make a lot of money in financing the project.

In 1968, the Port Authority raised $600 million worth of long-
and medium-term funds. Thirteen banks (ten DLMA members
plus the giant Franklin National Bank of suburban Mineola,
New York, the largest bank in western New York, and the
largest bank in New Jersey) loaned the authority $210 million,
participating in the following amounts:

First National City Bank	$39,900,000	19.0%
Chase Manhattan Bank	39,900,000	19.0
Bankers Trust Company	23,100,000	11.0
Manufacturers Hanover Trust Co.	23,100,000	11.0
Morgan Guaranty Trust Co.	23,100,000	11.0
Chemical Bank	19,950,000	9.5
Irving Trust Co.	19,950,000	9.5
Marine Midland Grace Trust Co. of N.Y.	7,350,000	3.5
Franklin National Bank	5,250,000	2.5
Fidelity Union Trust Co. (of N.J.)	2,100,000	1.0
Marine Midland Trust Co. of Western N.Y.	2,100,000	1.0
The Bank of New York	2,100,000	1.0
United States Trust Co. of New York	2,100,000	1.0
	$210,000,000	100.0

The banks earn 4.25% tax-exempt interest on this loan, which
is being paid back in seven annual installments of $35 million.
Approximately 15% of the proceeds of the loan were redepos-
ited as interest-free compensating balances in the participating
banks (see facing page).

These compensating balances are reduced as the loan is repaid.
The proceeds of the loan were invested in U.S. government se-
curities until they were needed to pay construction costs on the
World Trade Center.[67]

First National City Bank	$ 6,000,000
Chase Manhattan Bank	6,000,000
Bankers Trust Co.	3,500,000
Manufacturers Hanover Trust Co.	3,500,000
Morgan Guaranty Trust Co.	3,500,000
Chemical Bank	3,000,000
Irving Trust Co.	3,000,000
Marine Midland Grace Trust Co. of N.Y.	1,150,000
Franklin National Bank	800,000
Fidelity Union Trust Co.	325,000
Marine Midland Trust Co. of Western N.Y.	325,000
The Bank of New York	325,000
United States Trust Co. of New York	325,000
	$31,750,000

In addition to the $210 million bank loan, the Port Authority also sold three issues of tax-exempt bonds totaling $300 million in 1968, carrying interest rates ranging from 4.8% to 5.6%. $224 million, or 75% of the money raised by the bond sales was invested in time deposits at the same banks that participated in the $210 million bank loan. The banks paid the Port Authority 5.75% to 6.25% on these deposits, about 1% more than the Port Authority paid on the bonds. The rest of the bond proceeds were invested in U.S. government securities.[68] Citibank, the Port Authority's lead bank for over 20 years, handling all receipts and payrolls,[69] received the largest share of the bond proceeds—$66 million in addition to the $45 million of Port Authority time deposits received in 1967.

At the end of 1968, the Port Authority's $297 million in bank time deposits was divided up as shown on page 146.[70]

James C. Kellogg, III, Port Authority Chairman, brags of "the confidence placed in the Authority by the financial community." [71] This confidence is due, first of all, to the extraordinary profits enjoyed by the Authority's operation of its various monopoly enterprises. Owning every bridge and tunnel crossing between New York City and New Jersey and all of New York's air and bus terminals, the Port Authority, unlike most business enterprises, need not worry that competitive enterprises might attract some of its business. Additionally, the Port Authority's earnings are free from income taxation—further increasing its extraordinary income. In view of this financial strength, it is not surprising that the $210 million loan was handled by only 13 banks—a relatively small number of banks for so large a loan.

146 CITIBANK

* First National City Bank	$111,000,000
* Chase Manhattan Bank	39,000,000
* Morgan Guaranty Trust Co.	35,000,000
* Bankers Trust Co.	20,000,000
* Irving Trust Co.	17,000,000
* Marine Midland Grace Trust Co. of N.Y.	17,000,000
* Manufacturers Hanover Trust Co.	15,000,000
* Franklin National Bank	11,000,000
* Fidelity Union Trust Co.	6,000,000
* Bank of New York	5,000,000
American Bank & Trust Co.	4,000,000
County Trust Co.	3,000,000
First National State Bank of N.J.	3,000,000
New Jersey Bank & Trust Co.	3,000,000
National Bank of North America	2,000,000
National Bank of Westchester	2,000,000
Kings County Lafayette Trust Co.	2,000,000
Community National Bank & Trust Co.	1,000,000
Republic National Bank of New York	1,000,000
Total	$297,000,000

* Participant in $210 million loan agreement

Another important reason for the authority's popularity with the banks is that the interest income on its loans and bonds is tax exempt. The tax exemption is the key that enables both the Port Authority and the banks to make money with money. The banks loaned the Port Authority $210 million for seven years (actually, only $179,250,000, because the banks retained 15% as compensating balances) and received 4.5% in tax-exempt interest income. They also loaned the Port Authority long-term funds by buying the Authority's bonds at slightly higher interest rates. While we do not know how much of the Port Authority's $300 million 1968 bond issues were bought by the 13-loan syndicate banks, according to James H. Allen, vice president in charge of Citibank's municipal bond portfolio, Citibank "owns fair holdings" of the Authority's bonds.[72] When the Port Authority deposited the proceeds of its bond issues in bank time deposits, the banks paid about 6%, more than they were receiving in interest income from the Authority. However, because the banks can deduct this interest cost as a business expense, the 6% the banks paid to the Authority on the time deposits only cost them about 3%. So the banks earn the difference between the tax exempt 4¼% or 5% they receive on the loan and bonds, minus the 3% after tax costs of paying the Port Authority interest on the time deposits. In addition, the $31,750,000 compensating balances could be used for more loans and investments. And the Port Authority nets the difference between the 6% it earned on bank Certificates of Deposit (CDs) and U.S. government securities, minus the 4¼% or 5% it pays on the loan and bonds. Everybody comes out ahead—except the individual taxpayers.

If the banks took an income-tax deduction for the interest paid on the Port Authority's time deposits, in our opinion they violated Internal Revenue Service (IRS) laws, regulations, and rulings in effect in 1968. IRS regulations state that "no amount shall be allowed as a deduction for interest on any indebtedness incurred or continued to purchase or carry obligations, the interest on which is wholly exempt from tax . . ." [73] A 1967 ruling held that

> interest deductions are disallowed on indebtedness incurred by a bank through the issuance of certificates of deposit to a State in exchange for the receipt of State and Municipal obligations, the interest from which is exempt from federal income tax.[74]

James Allen, Citibank's vice president in charge of the municipal bond portfolio, said that "this is very definitely frowned upon by [New York State Comptroller Arthur] Levitt, the tax people and everybody else. So people don't do it." If "people don't do it" now, it would appear that FNCB nonetheless did it in the past.

On December 31, 1968, the Port Authority had $276 million, or 93% of its time deposits in the same banks that were receiving tax-exempt interest on the $210 million loan. Citibank, and probably the other banks as well, was also receiving tax-exempt interest on the bonds issued by the Port Authority. The Authority deposited the proceeds from its bonds in the same banks that were receiving its tax-exempt interest payments. If the banks took tax deductions for the interest they paid on the Port Authority's time deposits, then they were violating the law.[75]

Theodore Kheel, the labor mediator who has done extensive research into the Port Authority's affairs, says that he told the Authority that he felt it was illegal for the banks to deduct their interest expenses on the Authority's CDs while the same banks were investing in tax-exempt Port Authority bonds. This prompted the Port Authority, according to Kheel, to convert its bank CDs into U.S. government obligations. Thus, in 1969, the Port Authority slashed its bank deposits from 50% of its surplus funds to 10%: [76]

Assets	December 31, 1968	December 31, 1969
Investment in Securities	$341,417,000	$504,515,000
Cash and Time Deposits	339,644,000	48,308,000
	$681,061,000	$552,823,000

We believe that the IRS should investigate the financing arrangements for the World Trade Center to determine whether or not the banks took illegal income-tax deductions for the interest paid to the Port Authority on its time deposits.

There is much opposition to the World Trade Center. Real-estate interests do not like it because of the extraordinary competitive advantages that the Port Authority enjoys over private real-estate developers. As financing constitutes about 40% of real-estate construction costs, the Port Authority's ability to generate massive amounts of capital from its tax-exempt income and sales of tax-exempt bonds constitutes a huge competitive advantage. The Port Authority is also exempt from New York City and State sales taxes—an exemption that saves millions of dollars on building materials costs. The $6 million in real-estate taxes that the Authority pays—the same low taxes that owners of the site paid before construction was begun—is less than half of what a commercial owner would have to pay. No wonder, then, that real-estate men are angry.[77] As one developer noted, "We had a shipping company lined up some time back to take space at $10.50 a square foot in New York Plaza (a downtown commercial office building). The Trade Center came along and offered $6.50. Naturally, we lost out." Real-estate interests have sued to block the center but the courts have rebuffed their efforts.

The small merchants who had been located on the site prior to construction also opposed the project and sued to block it. They too were unsuccessful.

Also opposing the project were transit experts, such as labor mediator Theodore Kheel:

> The World Trade Center is rising despite the fact that private builders have demonstrated a unique capacity to build office buildings in Manhattan without government assistance. The real

needs of the people in the Port District which private industry
cannot satisfy include housing, education, community services,
medical care, park lands, environmental protection and, of
course, transportation . . .[78]

The Port Authority estimates that the World Trade Center will
bring an additional 50,000 employees and 80,000 business and
other visitors to lower Manhattan each day.[79] Eighty percent of
the 500,000 people who work in the downtown area rely on subways to get them to work.[80] The city's subways, which have not
had a major addition since 1935, are already overcrowded and
inadequate.[81] Thus, the 130,000 people who will travel to the
World Trade Center each day will further add to the city's subway crisis.

The banks that proposed and financed the World Trade Center realize that the capacity of the subways must be expanded
to transport the increasing numbers of people who staff the offices in the downtown business district. However, support for
mass transit, a money-losing endeavor, would reduce the Port
Authority's profits and the size of the reserve funds available
to pay back the loans and bonds held by the banks. So the banks
and the financial community, through the DLMA, lobbied for
the MTA to accelerate—at taxpayer's expense—the construction of a new subway line into the downtown financial district.[82] After getting the MTA to accelerate the expansion of
subway capacity into Lower Manhattan, there remained the
problem of ensuring that the route chosen for the new subway
line would efficiently transport people to the Wall Street area.
This goal, however, would have been frustrated if the new line
had been routed, as many people suggested, through the pov-
erty-stricken Lower East Side—a decayed slum whose 300,000
inhabitants are without any subway service at all. So the DLMA
retained a management consulting firm "to devise routings
which would provide through trains from the [Wall Street area]
to the regions which generate the greatest volume of potential
passengers." [83] The consultant's report argued against a detour
into the Lower East Side contending that very few of the Wall
Street area employees who traveled to work by subway lived
in that area. One reason for the low incidence of subway travel
from the Lower East Side, of course, is that there's no subway
into the area.

The MTA agreed with the DLMA and its hired consultants and routed the new line from the Bronx and Queens directly into the Wall Street area without any detour into the Lower East Side. Eben Pyne approved this plan. Not surprisingly, the MTA, seven of whose 11 members are officers or directors of banks, was more responsive to the bank-dominated DLMA than to the residents of a slum. The New York City Board of Estimate, however, forced the MTA to include a modified loop which will meet, to some extent, the needs of the Lower East Side residents.

The Metropolitan Transportation Authority

In 1967, the MTA was created by New York State as an umbrella agency to coordinate rail, subway, and highway transportation in New York City. The Transit Authority (buses and subways), the Triborough Bridge and Tunnel Authority (seven toll bridges, two tunnels, two parking garages, an airlines terminal, and the New York Coliseum), and the LIRR, were placed under the MTA's jurisdiction. One reason for the reorganization was to offset the bus and subway deficit with the surplus revenues derived from bridge and tunnel toll receipts.[84]

Seven of the MTA's 11 members are affiliated with commercial banks:

Dr. William J. Ronan, Chairman—Director, Security National Bank and Metropolitan Savings Bank;
Leonard Braun—Director, Security National Bank;
William A. Shea—Director, Security National Bank and Metropolitan Savings Bank;
William L. Butcher—Chairman, County Trust Company;
Mortimer J. Gleeson—Vice President, Morgan Guaranty Trust Company;
Frederic Powers—Director, First Westchester National Bank;
Eben W. Pyne—Senior Vice-President, First National City Bank.

Additionally, banks, as holders of Triborough Bridge and Tunnel Authority (TBTA) bonds, have a veto power over many policy decisions of the MTA.

For example, in 1967, Chase Manhattan Bank, as trustee

for TBTA bondholders, sued to block the transfer of surplus TBTA revenues to cover bus and subway operating expenses. The city calculated that by the end of 1969, the TBTA would have accumulated $106 million of surpluses which, according to a 1967 law, were to be applied to the subway deficit.[85] Governor Nelson Rockefeller, representing New York State, his brother David Rockefeller, representing the Chase Manhattan Bank, and William Ronan, representing TBTA, reached an out-of-court settlement which provided that $74 million of TBTA surpluses could be transferred to offset transit deficits if two-thirds of the bondholders, largely commercial banks, including Citibank, would give their consent. Moreover, the bondholders received an extra ¼ of 1% per year interest on their bonds— equal to $12 million over the lifetime of the $300 million in bonds. The banks thus had the leverage to exact the extra interest income even though, according to Pyne, "there was enough security for the bondholders . . ." without the extra ¼ of 1%.[86]

Despite the additional compensation, the bondholders* took their time in granting approval to the transfer of surplus TBTA funds. Their approval was not granted until June, 1970, demonstrating the banks' effective veto power over municipal efforts to rationalize overall transportation policy. When representatives of Mayor Lindsay met with Dr. Ronan to try and increase the amount of surplus funds to be transferred, Ronan indicated that the bondholders objected to transferring more than the $74 million agreed to by Governor Rockefeller, David Rockefeller, and himself.[87]

Another source of bank influence is that the same bank-af-

---

* They included, according to William Ronan's notice to Bondholders of TBTA, printed in the *Wall Street Journal* on March 6, 1969:
  Citibank
  Bankers Trust Company
  Chemical Bank
  Manufacturers Hanover Trust Company
  Marine Midland Trust Company
  Morgan Guaranty Trust
  U.S. Trust Company
  Travelers Insurance Company
  Fireman's Fund Insurance Company
  American Express Company
But not Chase Manhattan.

filiated MTA members are members of the MTA's constituent authorities such as the TBTA. Shortly after the state legislature passed the law requiring the transfer of TBTA surplus toll receipts to support mass transit, the TBTA embarked upon a new $92 million capital spending program. Instead of financing the program by the traditional means of selling long-term bonds, TBTA earmarked its surplus funds for capital spending in order to reduce the amount of money it would have to transfer to mass transit.[88]

Business depends on mass transit to get its employees to work, as Citibank noted in its transit report:

> An efficient, well-run transportation system can contribute greatly to the smooth functioning of business and to life in general in a major metropolitan area such as New York.[89]

But how are the increasing costs of mass transportation to be financed? The banks do not want the city to pay for the transit deficits out of its revenues because, as bondholders, they want to preserve as much protection for debt service as possible. As noted by the Transit Fare Committee, a group of New York City financial experts that has been exploring methods of financing the deficit, "the banking community considers using municipal revenues to pay transit operating costs as fiscally irreponsible, lacking political guts." [90]

Banks are also opposed to having the beneficiaries of mass transportation services pay for those services. Eben Pyne says businesses are already paying their "fair share." [91] Whether or not Pyne's claim is true for businesses in general, it is certainly not true for banks, which receive preferential corporate income-tax treatment.

Opposing transit support from city revenues and the business community, it is not surprising that Pyne endorsed the one alternative that doesn't cost Citibank anything—the January, 1970 fare increase from 20¢ to 30¢. This raised—by $50 to $100 per year—each employee's cost of getting to work and had, as the bank's own transit report noted, "a seriously regressive effect on low-income residents who have no alternative to mass transit." [92] Despite the fact that passengers were already paying for 90% of the transit system's operating expenses,[93] Pyne exercises his public responsibilities as a member of the MTA in a manner that consistently serves the interests of FNCB.

In our opinion, Governor Rockefeller should replace the bankers and bank directors on the MTA with men whose employment responsibilities do not conflict with their ability to consider alternative sources of money for mass transportation objectively.

Converting public positions of trust, such as those on the MTA and DLMA, to private profit are examples of how FNCB drains the confidence and funds of New York City. We turn now to an analysis of what FNCB contributes and, more importantly, to what it could contribute, if its resources were directed toward helping the city.

4. Quid Pro Quo

FNCB derives a great deal of private profit from the community. It holds hundreds of millions—$729,463,000 as of June 30, 1970 [94]—of interest-free demand deposits of federal, state, and local governmental units. It benefits from police, fire, sanitation, transit, and other municipal services. It depends for its existence on a community that can supply adequate manpower, and on citizens and corporations who can and will avail themselves of its services.

How does Citibank reciprocate? To answer this question we will focus on bank taxes and Citibank's residential mortgage policies. Taxes represent a bank's financial dues to its community. Providing housing is one index, perhaps the most important index, of a bank's long-term commitment to its community.

Bank Taxes

Prior to 1966, banks paid no business taxes to New York City and since 1966, when the Financial Corporation (income) Tax was put into effect, the tax on banks has been 18% lower than the rate applied to other businesses under the General Corporation (income) Tax.

New York City used to tax businesses by their gross receipts —a method of taxation from which national banks are exempted by federal law.[95] State banks were accorded the same exemption to provide "neutrality" in taxation (i.e., equality among banks). Consequently, before 1966, the only city taxes that banks paid were real-estate taxes and commercial occupancy taxes. Taxes paid by banks to the city amounted to only 2.3% of their net income attributable to their New York City operations, compared to 8% and 18% paid by securities dealers and wholesalers, respectively.[96] This worked out to less than $20 million per year, or 2.2% of the total business tax receipts, despite the fact that banks generated about 17% of the total net income originating from all businesses in New York City.[97]

In 1966, New York City abandoned the old gross receipts tax in favor of business income taxes. However, banks continue to receive preferential treatment. Although the General Corporation Tax rate is 5.5% of net income that can be attributed to New York City activities, the Financial Corporation Tax rate applied to banks is only 4.5%. Thus, despite the fact that the banks' New York City business taxes have increased to $43 million a year,[98] banks still pay about $10 million per year less than they would if they were taxed at the 5.5% rate applied under the General Corporation Tax.

When asked why the tax on banks is discriminatorily low, city officials noted that the New York City taxes were patterned on the state business tax structure, which also gives banks special treatment. There is, however, no justifiable reason for such favoritism.

With more than 100,000 employees,[99] $95 billion in deposits,[100] and hundreds of branch offices in New York City, banks require and receive considerable services and protection from the city (and state) of New York. At a time when the state and local governments are suffering from a severe shortage of funds, it is absurd that one of the fastest growing and most profitable industries in the nation [101] should receive preferential tax treatment. New York City and New York State should amend their tax laws to remedy this inequality.

"The Only Bank Your Family Ever Needs"— Unless You Need A Mortgage

Like the market for state and municipal securities, the mortgage market is a residual user of funds that suffers whenever money is tight. Even when money is relatively plentiful, however, Citibank avoids residential mortgage loans, allegedly because it doesn't want to get locked into long-term, illiquid loans. The reluctance of Citibank and other banks to provide sufficient residential mortgage money has made mortgage loans scarce and has been an important factor in the deterioration of existing buildings and the failure to construct new housing in New York City.

Reasonably priced, long-term mortgage credit is prerequisite to residential construction, preservation, and rehabilitation. Thomas Wilcox, who was FNCB Vice Chairman in 1970 and the man responsible for coordinating Citibank's so-called urban affairs programs, notes that the cost of borrowing accounts for 40% of construction costs.[102] Dr. Frank Kristoff, Director of Housing Programs for the New York State Urban Development Corporation, says that it is generally agreed that each 1% increase in interest rates adds $4 per room per month to residential rents.[103]

Professor George Sternlieb, of Rutgers University Institute of Urban Studies, author of *The Tenement Landlord* and a detailed study of New York City's housing stock commissioned by Mayor Lindsay, concludes that the absence of mortgage financing severely limits the landlord's capacity to preserve or rehabilitate his property. "Most of the return on residential real estate," notes Sternlieb, "comes not from the operations of the building *per se,* but from the capacity of the owner to remortgage his building." Without mortgage financing, there is insufficient cash flow to finance maintenance or rehabilitation. Dr. Michael Tietz, Director of the RAND Corporation Urban Affairs Institute, which studied the city's housing problems for the New York City Housing and Development Administration (HDA), agrees, noting that the unavailability of mortgage financing has accelerated the abandonment syndrome that has developed in parts of New York City.[104]

Savings and other time deposits provide commercial banks with funds well-suited to long-term mortgage lending. Unlike volatile checking deposits, which rise and fall at FNCB each week by as much as several hundred million dollars, savings deposits are extremely stable.[105] The cost of attracting savings deposits is also comparatively stable. Fed Regulations Q limits the maximum interest payable to 4.5% on passbook savings accounts up to 5.75% on special deposits left with the bank for more than two years.

Accordingly, savings deposits are ideally suited to long-term investment in residential mortgages. Indeed, Congress's desire to direct savings deposits into residential lending is the major reason for the existence of the Regulation Q interest-rate ceiling—a provision that commercial banks have long sought to eliminate. Regulation Q, designed to channel individuals' savings into residential mortgages, prevents commercial banks from outbidding mortgage-lending savings banks and savings-and-loan associations in the competition to attract funds.[106]

Even though commercial banks pay less interest on savings deposits than savings and loan associations and savings banks (the difference varies from .25% to .50%), commercial banks attract huge amounts of consumer savings deposits because of their greater branching powers and because they provide checking and other services not available at competing financial institutions. Commercial banks hold nearly $100 billion in passbook savings deposits[107] and FNCB has about $1.4 billion more than any other commercial bank in New York City.[108]

Relative to their savings deposits, however, commercial banks do little residential mortgage lending. The $45 billion of residential mortgages held by all commercial banks[109] is less than half of the $99 billion in savings deposits that they attract.[110] Citibank's $450 million residential mortgage loan portfolio[111] is only one-third the size of its $1.4 billion in passbook savings deposits.[112] As a percentage of assets, the gap between FNCB and other banks is greater. Residential mortgage loans account for less than 2% of Citibank's assets,[113] compared to 13% for all commercial banks.[114]

The aggressive marketing that is Citibank's hallmark in most areas is absent from the residential mortgage field. Its Residential Mortgage Department has only three officers and is headed by a man whose rank after 24 years is assistant vice president. Citibank's lack of interest in residential mortgage loans is underscored by the fact that Cresap's study (discussed in Chapter I) ignored platform officers' handling of mortgage loan inquiries.

The little residential mortgage lending FNCB does do is for

housing that is relatively unsuited for much of New York City. "Our program," notes William Gavin, head of the Residential Mortgage Department, "is for single-family, owner-occupied, all-year-round houses." [115] By comparison, Chase Manhattan finances, in addition to single-family houses, two- to four-family homes, which are becoming more common in the New York City area. Chase's residential mortgage lending volume, however, is not significantly different from Citibank's.[116]

Citibank refuses to disclose the distribution of its residential mortgage loans between 1–4 family dwellings and multiple dwellings. It is safe to estimate, however, that a relatively small proportion of its residential mortgage portfolio is in multiple dwelling mortgages. At Chase Manhattan, for example, mortgages on multiple dwellings (five or more families) constitute only one-fifth of the $550 million residential mortgage loan portfolio.[117]

Occasionally, Citibank participates in special programs to rehabilitate some of New York's worst slums, but by and large, Citibank makes very few apartment house mortgage loans. Thus it has a small part of the $50 million multibank mortgage pool for the Bedford-Stuyvesant section of Brooklyn [118] and another piece of a similar pool for the low-income Lambert Houses in the Bronx.[119] But it lends very little to the thousands of landlords whose deteriorating buildings could be preserved and rehabilitated economically if long-term mortgage money were available.

Even in the short-term construction loan area, FNCB does little lending on multiple dwellings. Robert Graham, FNCB Senior Vice President in charge of the Real Estate and Construction Industries Division, says that the bank finances "very few" apartment houses.[120] Occasionally, Citibank provides short-term interim funds for special housing projects. It put up $11,500,000 to help finance the construction of housing projects in the Bellevue South and West Side sections of Manhattan. And it participated in the construction loan for the Waterside Housing Development in Manhattan.[121] But it refused to provide long-term mortgage financing for the Waterside project, even after the insurance companies pulled out when the developer refused to surrender part of his equity to sweeten the deal.[122]

Despite its occasional participation in special projects to re-habilitate certain areas of the city, FNCB by and large avoids lending in the areas of the city that are most in need of money. Except for the well-publicized special programs, it avoids lend-ing mortgage money in the slums as well as in neighborhoods that are on the verge of deteriorating. Robert Graham, Senior Vice President in charge of the Real Estate and Construction Industries Division, explains:

> . . . we will tend to try to put our money, to make loans, in the areas that are actually moving in the direction of people and in terms of economics.[123]

With such a timid attitude on the part of New York's leading bank, there is, of course, little hope of arresting decay in de-clining middle-class neighborhoods, not to mention restoring slums.

One reason for Citibank's primary orientation toward single family homes is that its mortgage lending is largely an "ac-commodation" business for employees of corporate customers. As one former FNCB corporate lender put it, "if an employee of a corporate customer needs a mortgage and the company wants him to have it, he'll get it." William Gavin, Assistant Vice President in charge of the Residential Mortgage Depart-ment, confirmed the preferential treatment given to corporate employees: "Well, I think you have to understand," Gavin told a project member, "that mortgages today are an accommoda-tion. . . ."[124]

FNCB excuses its niggardly participation in residential mort-gage lending on the ground that the New York State Usury Law—which limited home mortgage interest to 7.5% in 1970 —makes mortgage lending uneconomical.[125] It also claims that because its major source of funds is short-term demand de-posits, it would be inappropriate for the bank to lend long-term. These are spurious arguments. FNCB could obtain a higher yield than the New York State maximum by participating, as did other banks, in the Federal Housing Administration (FHA) program, which allowed rates of 8.5%, during 1970, a legal way of avoiding the New York ceiling. But FNCB, claiming that too much red tape is involved, does not make FHA mort-gage loans.[126] Mortgage lending is clearly profitable. Residen-tial mortgage loans provide a healthy markup over the cost of attracting consumer savings deposits and, as the chart opposite shows, during four of the last five years, their yields were actually higher than FNCB's overall domestic loan portfolio.[127]

The availability of long-term mortgage money directly affects the housing market because apartment houses and one-to-four family homes cannot be carried economically without reasonably priced long-term funds. Mortgage loans, however, take a back seat to other, more profitable uses of funds, as the following passage from FNCB's *Monthly Economic Letter* shows:

> Commercial banks and insurance companies find that the demands of their industrial customers press against available supplies of loanable funds. Tighter terms for mortgage credit discourage potential home-buyers.[128]

Citibank's economists argue that "the seesaw in home construction probably is inevitable in a free market economy . . ." [129] The residential mortgage market, however, should not—and need not—be a residual user of funds.

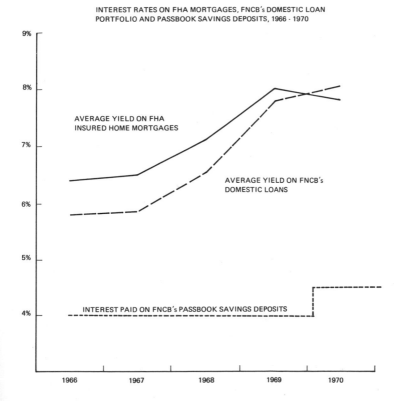

INTEREST RATES ON FHA MORTGAGES, FNCB's DOMESTIC LOAN
PORTFOLIO AND PASSBOOK SAVINGS DEPOSITS, 1966 - 1970

AVERAGE YIELD ON FHA
INSURED HOME MORTGAGES

AVERAGE YIELD ON FNCB's
DOMESTIC LOANS

INTEREST PAID ON FNCB's PASSBOOK SAVINGS DEPOSITS

The myriad of government programs designed to encourage residential mortgage lending has failed—especially in tight money—to provide enough mortgage money to meet the nation's housing needs. Mandatory controls therefore are the only effective way to get the large money market banks into a significant amount of residential mortgage lending. This could be done without new legislation.

The Federal Reserve Board's broad authority to regulate maximum interest rates payable on time deposits, plus its power to set reserve rates, could be used to make Federal Reserve member banks—which hold 80% of the nation's commercial bank deposits—increase their residential mortgage lending.

The law gives the Fed extremely broad authority to adjust time deposit interest rate ceilings in the public interest.[130] Accordingly, the Fed could establish a minimum standard of residential mortgage lending—we think it should be at least two-thirds of passbook savings deposits—enforced by requiring non-conforming banks to reduce their passbook savings account interest rates to noncompetitive levels. If Citibank were faced with the choice of boosting its residential mortgage portfolio by $500 million or reducing to 1% the interest it pays to attract passbook savings, it is safe to predict that it would rather make the mortgage loans than lose the business to other banks.

In addition, the Fed has the power to set member bank reserve requirements.[131] The Fed could require higher savings deposit reserve requirements for banks that failed to meet the minimum mortgage lending standards. This would force non-complying banks to deposit additional funds into nonearning reserves.

We are not suggesting that commercial banks be required to put volatile checking account deposits into long-term mortgage loans. But to the extent that commercial banks hold the savings of the community, those funds should be channeled into expanding, preserving, and restoring community housing. There are still tens of billions of dollars of untapped savings deposits that could and should be used to support the mortgage market. The $45 billion in residential mortgage loans held by all insured commercial banks (98% of all banks) on December 31, 1970 [132] amounted to less than half of their $98 billion in passbook savings accounts.[133] If commercial banks were required to maintain a residential mortgage loan portfolio equal to two-thirds of passbook savings deposits, it would mean a staggering $20 billion of additional mortgage credit.

That the Fed possesses the power to channel these stable, long-term funds into residential mortgages does not mean that the necessary regulations will be promulgated. The Fed has strongly opposed all suggestions that it directly influence bank lending policies, preferring to adopt an aggregate approach to the supply of money and bank credit. Congress, however, has the power to enact mandatory legislation on this subject and should exercise that power.

Conclusion

Years of building World Trade Centers while housing crumbled for want of mortgage financing, years of minimal taxes, years of exorbitant profits in New York City accounts, and years of using membership on public bodies to bail out bank customers have helped generate huge profits for Citibank and a crisis of enormous dimensions for New York City. We think that Citibank must make a massive commitment of resources to help solve the crisis. This is not a plea for charity, but for recognition of Citibank's responsibility for the legacy of neglect that the people of New York City have inherited.

Applying the bank's enormous experience and resources to tackling problems within its own area of expertise is more important to the people of the city and the country than charitable contributions and "urban affairs" projects. "Urban affairs" should not, as it is at present, be relegated to a small, under-staffed department that links top management and public relations with respectable "urban affairs" groups. Rather, a routine part of each banker's career pattern should include continuous on-line responsibility for dealing with the extraordinary needs of those sectors of society that are starved for capital, technology, and management. Such changes will not occur by themselves. Citizens, governments, and bankers themselves, many of whom express frustrations at the banks' limited commitment to solving urban problems, must apply pressure, especially publicity and economic pressure, to bring these changes about. "Business as usual" with a sop to "urban affairs" is just not good enough.

If New York City is becoming increasingly uninhabitable for many people—and most Citibank officers seem to think that this is so since they live in the suburbs [134]—the banks have played a substantial role in the decisions and nondecisions that have made it so.

V

In Citibank We Trust

1. Size and Scope

Bank trust departments are big, powerful, and usually ignored. Most people are familiar with the commercial side of a bank; the trust department, located on a quiet upper floor to permit trust officers to confer softly with widows and moguls alike, is off the beaten track. However, any bank department that handles upwards of $14 billion cannot remain unexamined forever. A study of Citibank's commercial banking activities must be accompanied by a study of its trust activities.

In 1971, FNCB's trust department, known as the Investment Management Group (IMG), managed $14,257,000,000 in over 10,000 accounts. Of this sum, $7.4 billion was held in employee benefit accounts, $4.9 billion was in personal trust accounts, $1.7 billion was in investment advisory accounts, and $179 million was in estate accounts.[1]

In terms of amount of assets managed, in 1970 Citibank's trust department was fourth largest in the nation, ranking behind Morgan Guaranty, Bankers Trust, and Chase Manhattan.[2] Although over 3,000 banks have legal authority to operate trust departments,[3] the top six New York bank trust departments manage close to 27% of the $292 billion total held by trust departments across the nation.[4]

Citibank's Investment Management Group provides several kinds of services. IMG's personal services include serving as executor of estates and acting as trustee under living and estate trusts. The bank also serves as agent and custodian of securities, allegedly providing investment and bookkeeping help. For corporations, Citibank serves as trustee and investment advisor to benefit plans, providing investment and management advice to pension and profit-sharing plans.

During the initial examination of FNCB conducted in the summer of 1970, the Study Group was permitted to interview only a few senior vice presidents from IMG. When, in 1971, an attempt was made to study Citibank's trust activities specifically, Walter Wriston, Chairman of the Board, sent a memo (dated October 4, 1971) to every employee of the bank dictating that no employee was to speak with members of the Study Group.

In light of Citibank's lack of cooperation, the closed-door policy adopted by other New York banks (e.g., Bankers Trust, Morgan, and Chemical) and the shortage of publicly available information about trust department investments and operations, this chapter cannot be comprehensive. Our goal is to indicate where abuses appear to exist and to ask the banks either to provide evidence to the contrary or to embark on a course of self-reform. We also call upon the Comptroller of the Currency, the Federal Reserve System, the FDIC, and the SEC, to assert their jurisdiction,* especially where other studies, such as the SEC's own *Institutional Investor Study,*[5] have already exposed violations of the law.

FNCB's trust department is divided into three main divisions: the Personal Investment Division, the Institutional Investment Division, and the Securities Administration Division. The Personal Investment Division is responsible for managing personal estates and for acting as trustee under living and testamentary trust agreements. The Institutional Investment Division handles the employee benefit plan work of the trust department. The Securities Administration Division performs stock transfer and security custodial services.

The entire work and performance of the trust department is the responsibility of FNCB senior vice president Thomas Theobald. There is, however, a committee which oversees the investment policies of the Personal and Institutional Investment divisions. This committee, known as the Investment Policy Committee, is "responsible for the coordination of investment policy among the various investment units within the Investment Management Group and generally for matters of long-range invest-

* The Comptroller of the Currency regulates trust departments of national banks (e.g., FNCB), the Federal Reserve Board regulates trust departments of state banks that are members of the Federal Reserve System, and the FDIC regulates trust departments of state banks not members of the Federal Reserve System. The SEC enforces the Securities Acts, parts of which affect trust departments in their securities dealings.

ment policy." [6] As of 1970, Messrs. Walter Wriston, William Spencer, Edward Palmer, Howard Laeri, and Thomas Wilcox— all names that should be familiar from FNCB's commercial side —were among those who sat on the Investment Policy Committee.

This chapter will focus on the work of the Personal Investment Division and the Institutional Investment Division since they have the greatest influence on the lives and security of individuals. It is first necessary, however, to have some understanding of trusts themselves, the reasons persons create trusts, and the reasons banks are chosen as trustees.

2. Citibank's Personal Trusts

In terms of disposing of property, one has a basic choice: either to give the property outright or to create a trust. Those who give property outright appoint executors to carry out the terms of their wills. Executorships are usually short-term positions, lasting for two or three years and involving the collection and sale of assets, the payment of debts and taxes, and the distribution of property to beneficiaries. Creating a trust means that the owner of the property, the settlor, places the property in the hands of another, the trustee, who in turn manages it according to the settlor's directions for the benefit of designated persons, the beneficiaries. A person can create a trust that will take effect while he lives; this is an "inter vivos trust" or "living trust." A person can also create a "testamentary trust" to take effect after his death.

Why create a trust? There are several reasons. If a person wants to give large sums to children not old enough to manage money, he can name a trustee to manage it until the children are older. The trust device also permits a settlor to divide his wealth into two convenient parts: principal, and income generated by that principal. The settlor can ask the trustee to distribute the income to the settlor's spouse for the duration of his or her life, and then to distribute the principal to the settlor's children. This common practice is known as creating a life estate for one's spouse and a remainder interest for one's children. Some sense an egotistical reason for creating a trust. While "you can't take it with you," a trust does permit one to reach from the grave to control wealth long after death.

An additional and more concrete incentive for creating a trust is the tax advantages. There are three main tax breaks in the trust device. First, if one creates an irrevocable trust, the money placed in it is taxed at gift tax rates, considerably lower than the estate tax rates that would otherwise apply. Second, if one is in a high tax bracket, one can create trusts for persons in lower tax brackets, such as children, so that income from the trust will be taxed at a lower rate. Third, by creating trusts with life interests that pass through several generations (e.g., from children, to grandchildren, to great-grandchildren), one can im-munize family wealth from estate taxes for several generations. In their book, *Halfway to Tax Reform,* Messrs. Ruskay and Osserman explain this "generation-skipping" advantage:

> For example, John J, Sr., desiring to provide for the welfare of his son, his grandchild, and even his great great grandchild, not yet born, may by his will create a trust which provides that the trustees are to pay the income first to his son John J, Jr., during the latter's lifetime, and thereafter to his grandson John J III as long as he lives. After John J III dies, the income is to be paid to his great grandchild, John J IV; and on his death the trustees will continue to pay the income for twenty-one years to John J V, the great great grandchild. Only at the end of the twenty-one-year period will they distribute the property held in trust to John J V.
>
> Under our laws an estate tax is incurred when the creator of the trust dies, but no estate tax is due thereafter as beneficial ownership passes from one generation to the other, not even when the trust finally terminates. Only when John J V, five generations removed from the creator of the trust, eventually dies, sixty or seventy years after the trust ends, will a second estate tax have to be paid. Thus one hundred and fifty years may pass without any estate tax being paid on a family's fortune. Moreover, by his will, John J V may start the process all over again by creating trusts for his descendants which will exempt the family fortune from estate taxes for another one hundred and fifty years.[7]

A 1969 U.S. Treasury Department study examined genera-tion-skipping trusts and found that, for the most part, only families of considerable wealth created them. The Treasury De-partment recommended that:

A special tax would be imposed on "generation skipping" transfers of property which would serve as a substitute tax for the tax that would have applied if the property had paid estate tax successively through each generation.[8]

The Treasury Department estimated that if their proposal for a substitute tax were adopted, revenues to the public treasury would have been increased by $72 million in 1970, and by 1980, projected tax revenues would be increased by $264 million.*

With the possible exceptions of charitable trusts and trusts created to provide for persons legally declared incompetent, it is difficult to see any public policy arguments for providing a tax incentive to encourage trusts. It is our view that the funds could better be used in the public treasury than as a tax incentive for the rich and a subsidy to bank trust companies.

Your Lawyer Has a Friend at Citibank

When it comes to the choice of executor and/or trustee, banks enter the picture. Banks want the fees paid to executors and trustees. To get them, banks compete against individuals and nonbank trust companies. New York State, however, refuses to charter nonbank trust companies,[9] which means that for trust business New York banks have only to compete against individuals, usually friends and relatives of the settlor and/or testator. As part of its marketing strategy, Citibank distributes elaborate brochures explaining the need to set one's financial affairs in order and the folly of appointing a friend or relative as sole fiduciary; indirectly, Citibank sells its trust wares by catering to the legal profession. Since it is almost always an attorney who draws a will and trust agreement, the legal instru-

---

* The Treasury Department, in summarizing the impact of its transfer tax provisions, estimated that if their generation-skipping proposal was adopted, revenues would be increased by 2% of the total estate and gift tax paid in 1980. (See U.S., Congress, Senate and House, Senate Committee on Finance and House Ways and Means Committee, Joint Publication, *Tax Reform Studies and Proposals U.S. Treasury Department,* 91st Cong., 1st Sess., 1969, Table 1 (Part 2), p. 48.) The total estate and gift tax paid in 1970 was $3.6 billion, 2% of which is $72 million. (See the IRS Commissioner's *Annual Report to the Secretary of the Treasury,* 1971.) Assuming the same rate of growth of estate and gift tax revenues for the 1970-80 period as the 1960-70 period, the total estate and gift tax revenue for 1980 will be $6.6 billion, 4% of which is $264 million.

ments which name the executor and trustee, Citibank and other banks provide attorneys with form books for will and trust agreements, and provide a host of other favors for lawyers who refer business to the bank. According to several attorneys the Study Group spoke to, lawyers almost invariably use the form books when drafting wills and trust agreements and the suggested phrasing is accepted with few or no changes.

Citibank's forms, as well as the forms of most other major banks, contain "boilerplate" or standard clauses that name Citibank as executor or trustee and give Citibank full powers over estate and trust assets. Such powers include retaining property for investment; selling property; investing and reinvesting in any kind of property; retaining and investing in FNCC obligations and stock; exercising all conversion, subscription, voting, and other rights pertaining to such property; consenting to reorganizations and foreclosures; exercising rights and granting proxies; managing real estate; lending and borrowing; and exercising stock options.[10] Thus Citibank's free forms help to ensure that the bank will have full control over the estate assets. Some of the above powers are powers ordinarily entrusted to fiduciaries, but other powers, such as the right to invest and vote FNCC's stock, actually gives IMG the authorization to use trust monies to further the bank's own interests.* Commenting generally on the use of boilerplate and specifically on the authorization of a corporate fiduciary to vote its own stock, the *Columbia Law Review* states:

> . . . a provision giving the trustee the right to vote shares of its own stock may be overlooked by the settlor or considered unimportant. Settlors are usually more concerned with the mechanics of the estate plan than with particular rights of the trustee. Thus, there may be created an authorization to vote shares which creates a risk of harm to the beneficiaries without serving any real desire of the settlor.[11]
>
> A corporate trustee's practice of voting its own stock seems a clear example of such prohibited self-dealing; management can

---

* If the trust instrument authorizes it, national banks can vote their own stock held in a fiduciary capacity on all matters except the election of directors. (See 12 USC 61 [Supp II, 1966]). State banks are not even subject to this one restriction; see *Cleveland Trust Co.* v. *Eaton* 21 Ohio St. 129, 256 NE 2d 198 (1970) and *Graves* v. *Security Trust Co.* 369 SW 2d 114 (1963).

be expected to vote its stock for management, and such a vote may not always be in the best interests of the beneficiaries.[12]

Some may ask: Why do lawyers cooperate with the banks, what's in it for them? Citibank states as its policy: "The bank will retain the attorney who prepared the Will or trust agreement as counsel for the estate or trust"; [13] by suggesting a bank executor, or trustee, the lawyer guarantees that he will be appointed counsel to the estate. If a lawyer suggests that one of the client's relatives or friends should be executor, the relative or friend might later choose his own lawyer.

This system places the attorney in a position where it could work to his own advantage to suggest a bank, though that might not be in the best interests of the client. Possibly, a client's relative or friend might waive the right to executor fees. In some cases it will be less expensive to appoint an individual instead of a bank, such as FNCB, which insists on a minimum fee. For instance, if the client has an estate of $100,000 an executor would be entitled to a fee of $3,625 under New York State's statutory rate of compensation.[14] If an attorney advised his client to appoint Citibank trustee, it would cost the client's estate $5,000, because Citibank insists on a $5,000 minimum fee.

If a client wishes to appoint more than one executor and his estate is less than $100,000, the law allows only one executor's fee which must be apportioned among the executors.[15] Therefore, if *two individuals* were appointed coexecutors and each did the same amount of work, each would receive $1,812.50, half of the statutory fee. But if *an individual and Citibank* were appointed coexecutors and each did the same amount of work, the individual would receive $1,812.50 and Citibank would receive $5,000. Citibank makes sure that the will specifies that it will receive at least $5,000 by including the following provision in its standard will form:

> First National City Bank shall be entitled to receive for its services as Executor hereof the commissions to which *a sole Executor* is entitled under the laws of the State of New York. . . . The minimum commission to First National City Bank shall be Five Thousand Dollars ($5,000).[16]

It seems clear that lawyers should be given the affirmative duty of informing their clients of any adverse consequences, such as higher fees, that might result from the appointment of a corporate fiduciary and that national and local Bar associations should study the extent to which collusive arrangements exist between trust departments and local attorneys. Banks should also be required to disclose the list of lawyers they recommend to their trust clients and the number of clients referred to each lawyer.

Why Trust a Bank?

Because a bank holds itself out to be a professional, some might think that it is preferable to appoint a bank as a fiduciary; after all, one reasons, as a professional, a bank will be held to a standard of care higher than that of an individual. Such is not the case in New York State.* Discussing the standard of care to which City Bank Farmers Trust Company, FNCB's predecessor, was to be held, Justice Shientag of the New York Supreme Court stated, "Generally speaking, and in the absence of any agreement to the contrary, a corporate trustee has no greater duty or responsibility than an individual acting in the same capacity." [17]

Even though, in the courts' eyes, banks and individuals are equal, there will always be some customers who naturally gravitate toward a bank's trust services. Some will do so because of a long standing close association with the bank. For others, less intimately related, Citibank furnishes a list of reasons why it should be appointed fiduciary in its brochure entitled "Reasons for Naming a Bank an Executor of Your Estate." FNCB describes itself as an organization:

a) Which strives to provide a certain quality of compatible highly personalized service.
b) Whose people are here when you need them.
c) That can and will act promptly, impartially and wisely to protect your interests.
d) That has extensive foreign domestic facilities of all types available at all times.
e) That combines a tradition of competence and experience.

By examining each of these claims, the Study Group hopes to illustrate what kind of service and performance one can expect

* In a few other jurisdictions, such as New Jersey and California, corporate trustees are held to "exercise a skill greater than that of an ordinary man," *Liberty Title and Trust Co.* v. *Plews,* 141 N.J. Eq. 493, 60 A.2d 630, 642 (1948). See *Coberly* v. *Superior Court,* 42 Cal. Rptr. 64 (1965).

from the trust department of a major commercial bank like First
National City.

Our Procedure—Personal Trusts

To determine what sort of job Citibank was doing as a fiduciary
for personal trusts and estates, the Study Group interviewed current and former Citibank trust officers. Our interviews with current Citibankers were all highly structured and subject to the
strict ground rules described in the preface to this book. Interviews with former trust officers were more helpful; those men
gave less standardized answers and were less hesitant both to
praise the bank and to criticize it.

Since the Study Group realized that bankers provided only
one side of the picture, we thought it was also important to hear
what beneficiaries thought. We therefore spent months searching
the files at the Surrogate's Court in Manhattan, listing every
estate since 1956 in which Citibank (or its predecessor, City
Bank Farmers Trust Company) was appointed trustee. We chose
at random every fifth estate, a total of 66 estates, for further
analysis. The estate files provided the names, addresses, and respective interests of the trust beneficiaries. We wrote to some
200 beneficiaries enclosing a questionnaire asking their opinions
of Citibank as fiduciary. Sixty of our letters were returned because the beneficiaries had moved and could not be traced. Of
the 140 beneficiaries who presumably received our questionnaire,
we received 30 responses, five from family members who explained that the beneficiary had died, and 25 from the beneficiaries themselves. Of these 25 substantive replies, 22 persons
indicated that they were dissatisfied with Citibank's performance,
and only three replied that Citibank was doing satisfactorily.

It is hard to know why some beneficiaries did not respond to
the questionnaire. By chance, a member of the Study Group met
a beneficiary who did not answer the questionnaire. She explained, "I really did not know what to look for or how to judge
what the bank was doing. Besides, I do not want to get anybody
in trouble. That trust fund is all I've got now—I have to rely on
the bank for my money, you know." The Director of the Study
Group met a woman whose father had left her a substantial
sum in trust with Citibank. She began to rattle off a litany of

complaints against the bank—late checks, poor investments, un-caring trust officers—until her husband stopped her, suggesting that his business connections with Citibank might be impaired by her remarks. Others presumably did not want to spend the time filling out the questionnaire.

Our sample is small. The complaints we received, however, were consistent and they focused on specific issues, indicating the problems were representative, not unique. The responses we received also were in accord with the conclusions reached by other studies of trust departments, specifically the SEC's *Institutional Investor Study* [18] and the 1968 staff report for the House Banking and Currency Committee, *Commercial Banks and Their Trust Activities*.[19]

Some Claims and Some Findings

One way to evaluate Citibank's role as fiduciary is to examine Citibank's own claims about itself and compare those claims to views of beneficiaries and trust officers, and the aggregate conclusions of other trust department studies. Following is a summary of our findings:

"Citibank strives to provide a certain quality of compatible, highly personalized service." Citibank trust officers apparently ignore the investment needs of beneficiaries. Trust officers have difficulty managing trusts with unique assets. Although Citibank promises individualized investment advice, the bank has a history of investing all portfolios in the same manner irrespective of investment needs. The lack of any activity in 44% of all personal trust portfolios (for 50 large trust departments) indicates that quite a few accounts are being ignored completely.

"Our people are here when you need them." In fact, personnel turnover at Citibank prevents continuous or personal service.

"Citibank will act promptly, impartially and wisely to protect your interests." In fact, Citibank is late in mailing checks and tax information; cash is left idle in trust portfolios; trust funds are used to promote the interests of the commercial side of a bank rather than the interests of the trust beneficiaries.

"Citibank has extensive foreign and domestic facilities of all types available at all times." Obviously—but the law forbids a trust department from using material inside information obtained from the bank's commercial activities; any representation or implication that the bank uses the expertise of its commercial side is deceptive.

"*Citibank combines a tradition of competence and experience.*" In absolute terms, the value of units in three out of four of FNCB's Common Trust Funds actually declined during the period examined. Comparatively, three out of four of Citibank's common trust funds were able to beat the market averages but Citibank's Common Trust Fund D did not perform as well as the comparative market index.

Remarking on the quality of Citibank's "personalized service," one gentleman noted: "The bank refuses to invest in anything but the most conservative and lowest-interest fixed income bonds when no beneficiary is in need of a fixed income from the trust. This policy is callous in its inflexibility." Another beneficiary explained, "We paid for investment advisory service— yet all monies were automatically put into U.S. government bonds. Over the years, the asset value of the trust decreased."

A common situation where a bank trustee must be especially sensitive to the personal needs of beneficiaries is when the settlor leaves portions of his trust to successive generations. For example, if a settlor gives his wife a life interest in the income of the trust and gives his children a remainder interest in the principal, the bank must choose whether to invest for income, thereby benefiting the wife, or to invest for growth, thereby benefiting the children. As Howard Scribner, a Vice President in Chase Manhattan's Trust Department, put it, "This forces the bank to do a juggling act, juggling between the conflicting needs and wishes of the life tenants and the remaindermen." [20]

Thomas Theobald, head of Citibank's Trust Department, told the Study Group how Citibank does the juggling:

> The account officer, the trust officer, tries to meet with everybody in the family and determine what the needs are. If the widow needs a high income, they manage to produce a high income. . . . On the other hand, if the widow says, "I don't need any income, and I'd rather that you accumulate more for my children;" then they decide, well, we'll put it more into common stocks that have more growth potential and less yield. It's done by an interview with the parties involved.[21]

Citibank apparently does not always succeed in acquainting itself with the needs of life tenants and remaindermen. A midwestern woman, herself a remainderman of a trust in which her mother was given a life estate, explained:

The bank kept on investing in tax-exempt bonds, although my mother's income level did not justify this. They refused to invest in higher income securities, although we [the children who were remaindermen] told them we wanted mother to get as much income as possible from the trust. They seemed to have no idea of the family situation at all.

One way to resolve the inherent conflict between life tenants and remaindermen is to require settlors to specify which generation of beneficiaries shall receive primary investment consideration. This would provide trustees with some guidance in their investment decisions.

Such guidance seems especially necessary for corporate trustees like banks, who apparently cannot familiarize themselves with the needs of their beneficiaries. One veteran Citibank trust officer, who worked for seven years at FNCB, reflected:

They [Citibank] overload their people with so many accounts that accounts are not handled properly. Some men were asked to manage between 300 and 400 trust portfolios. The accounts were by no means given adequate review.

With over 10,000 personal trust accounts and only 60 portfolio managers, the average Citibank manager is responsible for continually monitoring over 160 portfolios. Another Citibanker told the Study Group that he was in charge of the investment decisions for 80 estates (where FNCB was an executor) and 30 trusts, although he had no investment expertise and originally was hired to do administrative rather than investment work. "It was a farce," he reminisced.

Instead of giving personalized service, the bank has a built-in incentive to create overall investment policies for its trust accounts. If all the accounts contain the same portfolio mix, the bank can buy stock in large blocks and parcel out shares to various of its trust accounts. Because a favorable price sometimes can be obtained when purchasing a large block, such a purchase can benefit a trust account—but only if the stock also meets the needs of that account. Block purchases can be a disadvantage, especially to smaller trusts. In a large trust department, for example, a group of portfolio managers might be eager to purchase a certain stock for some favored clients. Knowing that they will obtain an advantageous price by buying a large block, they will submit a large order. The trust department purchases the block and divides it to the extent needed among the accounts that submitted the order originally. The leftover shares are placed in some of the smaller trust accounts, even though, on purely financial grounds, the stock would not have been bought for those accounts.

Thomas Theobald explained Citibank's procedure regarding block purchases:

> . . . for a discretionary account, the portfolio manager has the opportunity of picking whichever he thinks are the best stocks for that customer's needs from this list of say 200. And a typical account may have say only 20 stocks, so he selects. . . . In what I might call a run-of-the-mill stock like IBM or General Motors, and so on, the portfolio manager might put an order in for 100 shares, or 50 shares, or whatever, and, as I understand the process, on any one day, if there are a lot of orders together, the trader tries to coordinate them. But you're still not going to get a lot of shares in one of those companies on any one day. However, if there is a new stock recommended and many of the portfolio managers indicate interest in that stock, which is done by a telephone canvas, then they can accumulate a fair order at any one time and then the trader knows that he's looking for a block, which is 10,000, 20,000 or maybe even 50,000 shares, in which case he then goes down and tries to buy that as a block.[22]

Citibank's practice of having a list from which portfolio managers must select investments guarantees that all the accounts managed by the bank will contain pretty much the same stocks. A randomly selected group of 25 trust portfolios over which FNCB had full investment discretion, indicated that those portfolios contained common stocks of only 65 different companies.*

Standardized investment policies and impersonalized treatment especially harms beneficiaries when an estate or trust contains assets that require specialized attention, like real estate or a family business. Rather than retaining the unique asset, the bank will be anxious to liquidate it so that all the bank's portfolios can be invested similarly. The rationale is that the bank will be less prone to criticism for having bought blue chips, even if the market goes down, than if the bank had retained the unique asset that later proved to be a bad investment.

---

* Similar standardization will be shown in the portfolios of pension funds where FNCB serves as trustee.

Citibank claims, "Another assignment which Citibankers handle regularly is the sale of cooperative apartments. . . . Liquidating unusual estate assets is no unusual assignment for the bank either." [23] But according to the daughter of a Citibank beneficiary:

> The bank makes a point of telling my mother that the trust is theirs—not hers. The apartment she lives in is part of the trust. She has had to yield to the bank's desire not to become involved in renting a room out off from the rest of the apartment—even though renting it could have profited her more than selling it, as the bank forced her to do.
>
> Also in selling another apartment owned by the trust, the bank's real estate department grossly underpriced it—by the opinion of many people knowledgeable in New York City real estate—meaning a considerable loss in income to my mother.

Small closely-held family businesses are another kind of asset not amenable to wholesale investment policies of corporate fiduciaries. They present problems for a bank, especially if the bank is not anxious to manage the business left in trust. John C. Sutherland, Vice President of Irving Trust Company's Investment Administration Division, has written about small businesses left as part of estates:

> We manage such holdings with scrupulous care, though *whenever trust instruments permit us to do so we endeavor to turn a concentrated holding of a family corporation into a diversified list of marketable securities.*[24]

Sometimes, however, such family businesses are supporting many of the settlors' relatives; liquidation, while perhaps expedient for the bank, might not have been the desire of the settlor or in the best interests of the beneficiaries. The fault in such cases lies less with the bank (although it does impugn a bank's pledge of personal treatment) than with lawyers who permit settlors to sign trust agreements that give banks full investment discretion instead of providing instructions for the handling of unusual assets.

To prove that Citibank was not giving trust accounts individual attention but was rather creating similar portfolios regardless of investment needs or the kinds of assets originally in the estate, one would have to compare several personal trust portfolios. To prove that the bank was engaging in block trading to the detriment of the trust accounts, one would have to look at a large group of trust portfolios. Access to this information was denied to the Study Group. Not even the Comptroller of the Currency, the regulatory agency charged with supervising trust departments of national banks, examines trust departments for block trading and collective investment practices.[25] However, complaints we received from beneficiaries raise the suspicion that Citibank does not give individualized treatment to personal trusts. So does Citibank's history of similar practices, specifically its 1970 encounter with the Securities and Exchange Commission.

In 1970, the SEC challenged Citibank's Special Investment Advisory Service (SIAS), a service that Citibank provided to investors with between $25,000 and $200,000 to invest. In advertising SIAS, Citibank made the following representations, in language rather similar to that used to promote its executor and trust services:

> Here is an organization . . . with the tradition, talent, and time to give your financial affairs the sort of close personal attention that is required in this fast moving age.[26]
> Personal full-time portfolio management by an officer dedicated to accomplishing your objectives. . . . This is a complete financial service on a personal basis.[27]

According to the SEC, Citibank failed to reveal the following facts:

> Citibank and the SIAS have publicly stated that the investment of each investor in the SIAS will receive personalized or individual attention; whereas, the following facts are not disclosed to investors:
> (i) After SIAS receives funds from investors, such funds are invested in a virtually identical manner in one of two groups of securities, one for investors whose objective is a long-term capital growth and the other for investors whose objective is income.
> (ii) Generally, the initial investment for investors whose objective is long-term capital growth is in eight common stocks in accordance with predetermined percentages which are uniformly applied to all new investments.
> (iii) As of at least October 20, 1969, the funds of all such SIAS investors were being initially invested in general in accordance with the following percentages: 20% in each of 2 stocks; 15% in each of 2 stocks; and 7½% in each of 4 stocks.
> (iv) Approximately 47% of the assets held by SIAS for such

investors are invested in securities issued by companies affiliated or controlled by persons who are also directors of Citibank.

(v) After the initial investment has been made, for such investors, all decisions by Citibank to buy or sell a security for SIAS are generally applied uniformly to the entire fund.

(vi) Pursuant to instructions from defendant Citibank, defendant Merrill Lynch executes all transactions for SIAS.

(vii) Because of the structure and operation of SIAS, the transactions described in paragraph 13 (a) (vi) of this complaint are not executed in the best manner for both SIAS and the investors.[28]

In short, Citibank was charged with providing no individualized investment advice when the bank advertised that it gave personal investment attention to each account. Citibank did not contest the SEC suit. The bank filed a Stipulation and Undertaking, denying the charges but stipulating that it would not engage in any of the activities complained of by the SEC.

Sometimes beneficiaries worry not whether they are getting personal treatment but whether their account is getting any notice at all. One man wrote, "the bank paid little or no attention because it was not a large trust and the fees were small." Another gentleman observed, "You know you are just a number to them."

When we asked a former Citibanker how closely the Personal Investment Division watched their trust accounts, he gave the following historical insight:

> In the days before Hoguet [Theobald's predecessor] the tendency was for the bank to aggressively seek out trust business. Then, once the money was in the bank, since it was stuck there, the bank forgot about it. Hoguet, however, was more actively oriented—he made sure that there was a regular policy of portfolio review.

When a bank is appointed a testamentary trustee, there is the temptation for the bank, once it has gotten the business, to ignore the trust altogether since the settlor is dead. In theory, the beneficiaries will have a sufficient interest to police the bank. All beneficiaries, however, are not adept at financial affairs; often they do not know their rights under the trust. To challenge a trustee often requires a court proceeding, something that few persons have the courage, or resolve, or time, or money to bring. Some beneficiaries also assume that money they receive from the

trust is money from heaven, a bonus one would be wise not to
question.

Some states protect beneficiaries by requiring trustees to file
periodic accountings; Citibank guards against such inconveni-
ences by including this provision (which might not be legally
enforceable) [29] in its standard forms: "Any law to the contrary
notwithstanding, the Trustee shall not be required to file periodic accounts in any Court." [30] This provision can work both
for and against the beneficiaries. It saves the estate the expenses
that such accountings entail. However, it also makes it harder
for beneficiaries to measure the trustee's performance.

To determine if a trust account has been ignored, one might
look to see if any changes have been made in the trust portfolio;
but if the portfolio has been well invested, there might not need
to be changes. Too much activity can also indicate mismanagement, either poor initial investment or "churning," a practice
whereby the bank buys and sells securities just to general commissions for brokers who reciprocate with deposits in the bank.
According to Yates Eckert, Vice President of the Fidelity Union
Trust Company of Newark, New Jersey: "The present state of
the art would indicate that a correlation between turnover and
performance does exist; however, the determination of an opti-
mum rate of turnover . . . remains to be established." [31]

With that caveat in mind, it is still useful to examine the SEC's
findings on portfolio turnover.

In 1970, the SEC's *Institutional Investor Study* studied the
turnover and activity rates of the personal and employee benefit
accounts of the 50 largest bank trust departments.* The SEC
study noted that there was significantly greater activity in pension
funds than in personal trusts. In 1969, 44% of the personal trust
accounts in the SEC's sample had no turnover at all; 8% had
turnover rates greater than zero but less than 1%, which the SEC

---

* The SEC defined the turnover rate "as the lesser of cash purchases or
cash sales of equities during the year divided by the average of holdings
of equities at the beginning and end of the year." (See *Institutional Investor Study Report of the Securities and Exchange Commission.* H.R.
Doc. No. 64, 92nd Cong., 1st Sess.; 1971, Vol. 2, p. 459.) The SEC defined
the activity rate as "the average of the sum of purchases and sales in the
period divided by average holdings. The activity rate reflects all trading,
including trading results from net accumulation or liquidation of stock."
(See *Institutional Investor Study,* Vol. 2, p. 460.)

attributes to accounts which have done nothing more than dispose of rights.[32] According to Yates Eckert:

> No discussion of common stock turnover would be complete without mentioning the hopefully rare phenomenon of non-turnover. Such instances can and do occur and may be attributed to excessive workloads on Portfolio Managers which led them to merely monitor rather than manage their accounts.[33]

Citibank was unwilling to provide us with the activity and turnover rates for its personal trust portfolios. Morgan Guaranty Trust Company does publish its annual activity rates of the employee benefit funds for which it serves as trustee (16.5% in 1971, 10% in 1970), but Morgan, like the other New York banks, does not reveal the activity rates of personal trusts. Frank Barnett, a member of FNCB's Trust Board, and Chairman of the Executive Committee of Union Pacific Railroad, told a member of the Study Group, "I don't think there is a lack of activity in Citibank's personal trust accounts," [34] but Mr. Barnett was unable to substantiate his opinion. Howard Scribner of Chase Manhattan's trust department estimated that there was no activity in 20% of Chase's personal trust accounts. "More mistakes are caused by activity for activity's sake," Mr. Scribner explained. "There are also tax considerations why we would leave a trust alone." [35] The tax consideration is the desire to avoid capital gains that are chargeable to the trust account. The SEC's study analyzed the influence of taxes on activity rates and concluded that in 99% of the cases, the low activity rates for the personal trust accounts could *not* be so justified.[36]

Citibank also strives to liquidate personal trust portfolios and invest the proceeds in the bank's own common trust funds, further refuting the bank's claim of "highly personalized service." Traditionally, banks have maintained separate trust portfolios for each of their accounts, thereby providing each account with a unique portfolio mix, supposedly tailored to the particular needs of the beneficiaries involved. Like several other commercial banks, Citibank has established common trust funds. These are essentially mutual funds where the participants are the trusts managed by the bank. Citibank has four common trust funds, each with a different investment objective: growth, income, balanced growth and income, and tax-exempt income. According to one bank, the advantages in common trust funds include:

They simplify the task of diversification, especially for smaller accounts. A given amount of money can be spread more economically over a given variety of stocks, say, by being used to purchase units in a common trust fund than by being applied directly to the purchase of the stocks themselves . . . common funds also provide an equitable way for all participating trusts to share in a desirable investment which may not be available in sufficient quantity to permit efficient allocation among a large number of trusts.[37]

Another advantage of common trust funds, according to Reese Harris, formerly of Manufacturers Hanover Trust Co., is that common trust funds are used as "showpiece accounts." Since national banks are required annually to publish the performance of their common trust funds, trust departments give special investment attention to them, which should mean that they are better managed than other accounts.

There are two important disadvantages to the common trust funds: first, before a trust portfolio can be invested in a common trust fund, its holdings must be converted to cash, often causing the beneficiaries to incur untimely capital gains taxes; second, since common trust fund units cannot be redeemed in kind, when a trust portfolio is distributed, its common trust fund units must be converted to cash, again causing beneficiaries to incur inopportune capital gains.

Thus, one has to measure the relative advantages of having a share of the bank's showpiece account (especially when, on average, 44% of the bank's other accounts are ignored) against the two tax disadvantages. The bank, of course, prefers to have as many accounts as possible participating in the common trust funds. It greatly simplifies the bank's job and increases its profits if it only has to manage four common portfolios instead of 10,000 separate ones.

A bank really concerned with the best interests of the beneficiaries would not force any account to realize capital gains in a year when those gains could not be otherwise offset. One approach is to liquidate personal accounts over several years so that taxes will be spread out and reduced. Yet, according to a former Citibank trust officer, many FNCB portfolio managers were so anxious to get their accounts into the common funds that they liquidated the portfolios all at once, completely ignoring the adverse tax consequences to the beneficiaries. Unlike

other New York banks, FNCB did not consult the trust beneficiaries before it started shoveling the trusts into the bank's
common funds. The Study Group asked beneficiaries: "Has the
bank ever suggested putting the trust assets in a common trust
fund?" One replied:

> They didn't suggest, they just did it—in their own money-los-
> ing Investment Fund 'D' . . . which depreciated in value by
> approximately 35% since its original purchase by the trust on
> July 19, 1965.

Mrs. R., a 74-year-old widow, sent us copies of her correspon-
dence with the bank, precipitated by the bank's placing her trust
assets into their common trust funds without her knowledge. Citibank put the widow's trust into the bank's Common Trust "C"
and "D" Funds on March 31, 1970, not informing her of this
action until nearly a month later. The bank wrote:

> We apologize for not having consulted you before taking this
> action, but we believe you will feel constructively toward our
> action as you begin to derive benefits from this new invest-
> ment.[38]

Mrs. R. wrote back that very week:

> As you know, my portfolio is marked by a notation requiring
> that I be consulted before any changes are made. Several years
> ago, you may recall, I was asked to make this very change in-
> vesting in the common trust funds. After analysis of the com-
> position of the Trust Investment Funds I ruled against it. I do
> not now "feel" any more "constructively" toward it, nor can I
> discern any benefits to be derived from it.

Mrs. R. went on to inform the bank that her original portfolio
was divided almost equally between tax-exempt bonds and common stocks, but the bank had altered that ratio so now she had
40% tax-exempt bonds (Common Fund "D") and 60% common stocks (Common Fund "C"). She then concluded: "Accordingly, I request that the bank dispose forthwith of the Trust
Investment Funds and repurchase the securities that it sold without consulting me." [39] The trust officer handling her account
was in Europe. Finally, Arthur B. Mittwoch, head of Citibank's
Personal Trust Investment section, responded:

> . . . as noted in your letter, there was a mathematical error in
> our computation of the degree by which your income would be

improved by virtue of investing in a combination of Fund "C"
and Fund "D" units, for which I apologize . . .

We will certainly bear in mind your desire for increased income rather than growth potential and may, under certain circumstances, liquidate a portion of your Fund "C" units to add
to Fund "D." However, as sole trustees charged with the legal
responsibility of managing the trust, we can not honor your request that the entire program be reversed.[40]

The bank finally got around to correcting its error and sold some
of the widow's C units to buy D units, but the trust lost over
$13,000 in the process. Mrs. R. told us "Why does the bank
think a 74-year-old woman is interested in growth stocks any-
way? They ought to realize that if they took any personal interest." Since she has the right to dispose of the trust funds herself upon her death, the bank cannot hide behind the excuse that
it had to preserve principal.

As this story illustrates, a major reason why banks provide
impersonal and incompetent treatment of personal trusts is that,
practically speaking, once the settlor is dead, the beneficiaries
have little recourse. This situation differs from that of pension
trusteeships where the employer is at least free to move the pension trust to a different bank. If trust beneficiaries had more
leverage against a corporate trustee, the trustee might be more
responsible. Trustees might be more responsible, too, if they
had the kind of long-term commitment to their accounts that
the bank implies exists but that, as we shall see, is in fact very
rare.

A bank's chief calling card for its estate and trust business is
the fact that it can provide continuity of service, something
which an individual trustee allegedly cannot. This argument is
persuasive. Often, those planning the disposal of their wealth
are old, and their contemporaries are also old or deceased. They
feel that only a bank can perform the long-term job of trustee.
Testators and settlors, however, should be aware that choosing
a bank will not ensure continuity, at least not at Citibank.

One beneficiary wrote: "They change trust officers so often,
one can never count on talking to the same man from year to
year." Another Citibank beneficiary wrote from California:

We have had to deal with one bank employee, then another, then
another. Since we are at a distance from the bank, this is dis-
concerting because no continuing relationship can be set up.

We talked with a woman living in the Midwest who, along with her mother, are beneficiaries of a trust run by Citibank. The woman explained that her father had been a senior officer at Citibank and naturally chose the bank as trustee. However, the woman explained the troubles that her mother had as a beneficiary: "Every time she went to the bank, she was handled by a new person who knew nothing about her needs or the family situation. . . . There is no continuity whatsoever."

Why do banks have a hard time keeping the same man on an account? Richard Johnson, a former executive at Morgan Guaranty's trust department who is now working for an independent money manager, gave the Study Group this view:

> Portfolio managers in banks are frustrated and underpaid. The tendency is for investment researchers to get promoted to administrative work, which they are not interested in. Overall, there is limited opportunity in the trust department of a bank. Since many men leave, customers rightfully complain that there is little continuity for their accounts.[41]

FNCB refused to furnish the Study Group with the personnel turnover figures for its trust department. If turnover in Citibank's trust department approximates the turnover rate for the bank as a whole, each year one-third of the trust accounts change managers.

The one study on the subject confirmed that trust men are not particularly happy with their lot. In 1970, Don Howard Personnel, Inc., sent a questionnaire to 2,800 senior trust men, of whom 636 responded. Of those respondents, 51.8% complained of inadequate compensation, 20.9% noted the limited opportunity for advancement, 13.5% felt that insufficient use was being made of their ability, and 13.3% expressed dissatisfaction with management policies.[42]

Trust departments, when advertising their fiduciary services should be required to disclose their average annual personnel turnover and the average number of years the same manager can be expected to supervise an account. Trust departments should also consider assigning at least two administrative and investment men to each account so that if one leaves the bank, the beneficiaries will still be able to deal with someone familiar with their particular needs. Banks should also consider ways of restructuring the role of trust officer so that men do not try to leave as soon as other positions become available.

Impersonal service, as reflected in the high turnover of account managers and the scanty attention paid to the individual needs of beneficiaries, would be at least partially compensated for if Citibank acted, as it claims, "promptly, impartially, and wisely." Some beneficiaries feel that promptness is certainly not one of Citibank's fortes. One wrote:

> I have had to write to receive my annual check as ordered under the will for two years. This year I did not receive a check until December, although it was due in July. I have also not gotten a statement telling me what amount of this income is taxable. I have had to write also for this information. I do know that a six months overdue check costs me six months interest.

The above beneficiary enclosed a letter which an Assistant Trust Officer at Citibank wrote her in December, 1971:

> I apologize for not sending you at an earlier date the enclosed $1,300 which was due you during the middle of July of this year. I am sorry for the inconvenience and assure you that the check due July of 1972 will be remitted to you timely.

Polite apologies aside, it is significant that the bank's letter made no mention of the lost interest which its error cost the beneficiary, nor did FNCB offer to pay for its mistake.

Some of the other responses we received included such comments as: "Bank has been somewhat slow about information necessary for tax reports," and, "Checks arrive late, once unsigned. Tax information is inadequate," and, "Particularly irksome are late tax letters."

Another beneficiary described her lengthy battle with the bank:

> The money from the above trust was not distributed as requested and was allowed to lie idle. It, the income, was not reinvested. Income taxes for 1969–70 had to be amended. First National City admitted error, but hoped it wouldn't happen again.
>
> The custodial account under First National City failed to keep my securities in order. They lost some securities in a vault transaction and this resulted in a substantial loss to me. They admitted their error in writing but once again hoped it wouldn't be repeated. A letter was written to Mr. Moore, then Chairman of FNCB, more letters to assistants, trips to the bank, etc., but the same reply—they were sorry. I then contacted a lawyer.

> Last week my lawyer who I had engaged after getting nowhere myself, informed me that the bank would settle out of court. I am very pleased that all the time and effort wasn't in vain. Why though, when they clearly were in error, would they not assume responsibility?

When it comes to impartiality, banks have an indisputable advantage over relatives of the settlor, since a relative might be prejudiced toward or against particular beneficiaries. The Study Group spoke to a woman who explained that her husband definitely wanted a bank trustee because he was leaving money to both his first and second wives and he did not feel that any relative could be impartial. Banks are nevertheless prone to a different kind of partiality—partiality to their own interests. A detailed description of the conflicts of interest that face bank trust departments will be found later in this chapter; at this point it is more appropriate to discuss another kind of conflict of interest—that between the trust department and the commercial departments of Citibank.

Citibank claims that trust beneficiaries can gain from the bank's "extensive foreign and domestic facilities of all types available at all times." It is not entirely clear what this means in the context of promoting Citibank's fiduciary services. If the bank is merely stating that it has many branch locations, both in the New York area and abroad, then the claim is valid. If, however, the bank is implying that by virtue of its overall commercial banking facilities it will provide better estate and trust services, such an implication is misleading. Although a bank might want customers to infer that the trust department benefits from investment information obtained from the commercial side of the bank, by law, persons and institutions are not allowed to trade on the basis of such inside information.[43] In the words of William Cary, former Chairman of the SEC, "insiders, having access to material information available for a corporate purpose, may not take advantage when it is not yet known to the public." [44] Inside information about a company obtained by a bank in the course of its commercial relationships with that company must therefore be kept secret from the bank's trust department. According to the SEC's recent study of the Penn Central failure:

> As a lender to corporations, a bank is obviously entitled to non-public information. As a manager of trust accounts, a bank seeks

out information to advance the interest of these accounts. It is clear, however, that no confidential information gathered in a commercial banking capacity may be used to benefit the trust accounts.[45]

Citibank agrees:

> . . . analysts and portfolio managers in the Investment Management Group are specifically prohibited from seeking confidential customer information which may be provided to the commercial banking areas of First National City Bank in conjunction with lending activities, just as lending officers are prohibited from providing such information to IMG employees. The Bank scrupulously maintains complete isolation of the IMG investment activities from the traditional banking functions.[46]

While a bank trust department cannot take advantage of the bank's commercial contacts, a bank's commercial relationships might actually disadvantage a trust department. This anomaly might result if a bank trust department with access to inside information did not trade in the company's stock for fear of being accused of acting on inside information. As Arthur Fleischer, an attorney and securities law expert, put it: "If an insider does indeed have inside information, he has only one alternative and that is not to trade." [47] The problem is that a bank trust department under the same umbrella as the commercial department will invariably have access to inside information, whether or not the trust officers use it. Fleischer goes on to state, "there is undoubtedly a concept of constructive information"; under that theory, the possession of inside information would be imputed to those with access even if the information was never actually obtained.[48]

The courts have not finally settled the issue.[49] The SEC, in the *Cady, Roberts* case,[50] has determined that a fiduciary cannot trade on the basis of inside information and then excuse itself on the grounds that as a fiduciary it was obliged to use all the information available to it. What needs to be resolved is the extent to which a trust department must refrain altogether from trading in companies with director interlocks to the bank. In Citibank's case, the trust department invests heavily in companies like Monsanto, Phillips Petroleum, Allied Chemical, Exxon, etc., while officers of those companies sit on Citibank's board. If these persons make their information available to the rest of Citibank's board, Citibank's trust department presumably would not be able to trade in those stocks. Otherwise, the trust department might be held accountable for any short-swing profits realized through the investment.

A legal theory, known as "deputization," might in the future have important consequences for bank trust departments. Essentially, deputization refers to the deputizing by one company of one of its officers to sit on another company's board so that the first company can obtain inside information about the second company. Thus, if any Citibank officer sat on a corporation and Citibank bought that company's stock, Citibank might have to give up any short-swing profits the bank made. Many Citibank officers serve on boards of directors of companies in which Citibank invests heavily. For example, Walter Wriston, Chairman of the Board of FNCB, also sits, or at one time sat, on the boards of General Electric, General Mills, and J. C. Penney—which rank among Citibank's 100 largest investments. If courts begin to apply the deputization theory, beneficiaries of trusts managed by Citibank may be affected adversely; conceivably their trusts could be surcharged for profits resulting from trading in "tainted" companies' stock.

In light of the proscription against trading on inside information and the deputization theory, bank trust departments clearly are obliged not to imply that their trust investment decisions can benefit from the bank's commercial contacts. Should a trust department, however, be required to tell trust beneficiaries that it is investing trust funds in companies that have commercial dealings and interlocking relationships with the bank? We feel it should. Other fiduciaries, such as broker-dealers, must tell their customers whenever they buy for their customers' accounts securities of companies which the broker dealers "control." The Securities and Exchange Act defines control as:

> the possession, directly or indirectly, of the power to direct or cause the direction of the management and policies of a person, whether through the ownership of voting securities, by contract, or otherwise.[51]

The SEC has ruled that common control exists "whenever both corporations are controlled by individuals united by several factors tending to create and maintain community of interest among them." [52]

The 1968 Congressional staff study [53] indicated that interlocks between banks and major U.S. corporations were widespread. In 1968, Citibank's trust department held 15% of the common stock of Blue Diamond Coal, 6.3% of Consolidated Cigar, 23.4% of Doubleday and Co., and 8.5% of Corning Glass.[54] Some of these holdings, like Corning Glass and Doubleday, represent family holdings. But Citibank's trust department also held 5% of the total common stock of Xerox at a time when there were two director interlocks between Citibank and Xerox.[55] Whether such holdings and interlocking directorships constitute "control" will be a matter for the SEC and the courts to determine. Whether trust departments in this context so resemble broker-dealers as to require disclosures of transactions between a bank and commercially related companies is also in need of determination. When the Study Group asked Frank Barnett, Chairman of the Board of Union Pacific Railroad and a member of Citibank's Trust Board, whether Citibank should tell beneficiaries when the trust department purchased stock in companies commercially related to the bank, Mr. Barnett replied, "No, it would raise undue questions." [56]

There are many ways to measure the competence of a bank trust department. Sensitivity to personal needs, ability to mail checks out on time, awareness of market trends—all are indices of competence. In the last analysis, however, many consider financial performance to be the most important criterion.

With the sole exception of its common trust funds, which by law all national banks must make available to the public, Citibank does not make public the performance of its trust accounts. Citibank's four discretionary common trust funds, as the chart below shows, generally did better than the market. Nevertheless, the value of Citibank's A, B, and D funds declined during the period examined. Most of this negative performance can probably be ascribed to the overall downward trend in the market; comparing the performance of Citibank's common trust funds to the performance of the market as a whole, three out of four of the bank's funds outperformed the market, by as much as

PERFORMANCE OF CITIBANK'S PERSONAL COMMON TRUST FUNDS

Name of Fund	Period Examined	Percent Change in Fund	Percent Change in Appropriate Index*	Change in Fund Compared to Change in Appropriate Index (III–IV)
Discretionary Common Trust Fund "A" (Balanced)	Jan. 31, 1969 May 28, 1971	— 1.6%	—13.7%	+12.1%
Trust Investment Fund "B," Taxable Fixed Income (Income)	June 28, 1968 May 28, 1971	—13.7%	—17.8%	+ 4.1%
Trust Investment Fund "C," Common Stock Portfolio (Growth)	April 30, 1969 May 28, 1971	+ 2.2%	— 3.8%	+ 6.0%
Trust Investment Fund "D," Tax-exempt Bond Portfolio	June 28, 1968 May 28, 1971	—21.6%	—20.0%	— 1.6%

* The Balanced and Income Funds (Funds A and B) have been compared to Moody's High Grade Bond Index; the Growth Fund (Fund C) has been compared to the Standard and Poors 500 Index; and the Tax-Exempt Fund (Fund D) has been compared to the Bond Buyer's Municipal Index. These are the comparable indexes recommended by Edwin M. Hanczaryk in his analysis *Bank Trusts: Investments and Performance.*

12% in the case of Citibank's A Fund. On the other hand, Citibank's D Fund, the tax-exempt bond portfolio, not only declined 21.6% over the period, but also declined 1.6% more than the comparable market index.

The Power of the Personal Trust Portfolio

Citibank serves as trustee for over $4 billion worth of personal trusts and the bank acts as executor of $150 million in personal estates.[57] When the Study Group suggested to Citibank officials that the bank could wield a lot of economic leverage by virtue of these large sums, we were told that the trust monies are separated into many accounts and there are so many restrictions upon their use that the bank could never use the money in a block sum. The Study Group decided to test the bank's argument by checking the 66 randomly chosen wills and trust agreements described earlier. The sample showed:

> In 16 out of 66 cases, or 24% of the time, Citibank was chosen sole executor with full investment powers.
> In 24 out of 66 cases, or 36% of the time, Citibank was chosen sole trustee with full investment powers in 22 cases.
> Life estates are most often given to a spouse or children.
> Remainder interests usually go to children, relatives, or charities.
> The right to determine how the trust eventually will be distributed, i.e., the so-called power of appointment, is almost invariably given to a spouse.

Apparently, although testators and settlors have an infinite variety of ways to dispose of their estate, they create fairly predictable arrangements; for example, they give a life interest to a spouse and name children as remaindermen, and when they appoint a corporate fiduciary usually it is given full investment powers.

In only two cases did the trust agreements restrict the investment of funds by the sole bank trustee; both required the trustee to hold blocks of stock in closely held companies for a specified period of years after the death of the settlor. Based on our sample, it appears that Citibank has complete investment and voting control over approximately 30% of the assets in its personal portfolio, or about $1.3 billion. Corroborating our study is the SEC's finding that the 50 largest trust companies have full investment and voting discretion over 30% of the assets in their personal trust portfolios.[58] Ed Ryan of Chase's trust department estimates that Chase has full power over 40% of its $2.4 billion personal trust assets.[59] Any claim, therefore, to the effect that a bank has little investment control over the personal trust assets it manages is dubious indeed.

If a cofiduciary has been appointed, the bank trustee will in theory have to share investment decisions with the cofiduciary and will therefore not have complete discretion. However, the experience of being a cofiduciary with Citibank was described by one man.

> The bank likes to act on its own even if you are a cotrustee. They sell rights without asking if they should be taken up. They

don't accept suggestions on investments other than their own. Many times I've suggested good income stocks but they wouldn't go along, so I finally had to accept their choices. Our trusts have gone back in value more than they should have.

Citibank does not equivocate about its own preference: "If a co-trustee is named to act with the Bank we prefer all investment powers to be lodged with the Bank alone." [60] This means that Citibank's power over its personal trust portfolio includes not only actual control over one-third of its accounts but also includes virtual control over the holdings in the accounts where FNCB is cotrustee with sole investment discretion.

As will later be shown, this control, combined with the even greater control the trust department has over pension accounts, places a large commercial bank like FNCB in a position to wield considerable influence over the companies whose stock is held in its trust department.

Does It Pay?

New York is a state with a statutory rate for fiduciary services. Thus, if a will or trust does not specify the fees to be paid fiduciaries, the statutory rate will be applied. The statutory fees for executors are based on the assets, including income, received and paid out from the estate.[61] The statutory fee for a trustee consists of both an annual fee, measured by the value of principal, and a paying-out fee, measured by the value of the sums of principal paid out.[62] Irrespective of the statutory rates, Citibank always insists on certain minimum fees, $5,000 for serving as executor and $750 annually for serving as trustee. Despite the statutory fee schedule and provisions for minimum fees, trust departments allegedly do not make ends meet. According to Reese Harris, retired Executive Vice President of Manufacturers Hanover Trust Company, the fees do not always cover the costs of managing an account, particularly the smaller accounts.[63] When the Study Group asked Thomas Theobald, present head of Citibank's Trust Department, whether fees covered costs, he replied: "It is certainly our intention that they [the fees] do so. . . . We strive to cover our costs with the fee schedule." [64]

Messrs. Voorhees, Dobosiewiscz, and Sampson, all officers in the Personal Investment Division of Citibank's Trust Department, refused to answer the question; Mr. Raymond Sampson finally stated, "This is highly competitive, strictly confidential information." Mr. Sampson's argument is nonsense. There is nothing inherently confidential or competitive about the profit or loss statement of a particular bank department. Indeed, Citizens and Southern National Bank of Atlanta, Georgia, in its report of its trust department (the 38th largest in the nation) published a complete breakdown of the operating income and expenses of all its trust activities.[65]

According to the Federal Reserve Bank of New York, for "ten large" New York City Banks (the Fed was unwilling to get more specific), personal trust work has not been profitable for

TEN NEW YORK CITY BANKS
NET OPERATING INCOME BEFORE INCOME TAXES*
(in thousands)

	Net Operating Earnings before Income Taxes	Allowed Credits for Deposits	Trust Department Net Earnings
Estates			
1966	6,195.8	2,550.3	8,746.1
1967	5,027.0	2,667.5	7,694.5
1968	3,675.3	2,952.5	6,627.8
1969	3,621.4	3,920.8	7,542.2
1970	3,813.8	3,861.8	7,675.6
1971	4,911.0	2,777.0	7,688.0
Personal Trusts			
1966	7,248.0	9,823.9	17,071.9
1967	5,258.8	10,695.3	15,954.1
1968	2,640.8	13,400.9	16,041.7
1969	−724.4	12,905.4	12,181.0
1970	−376.7	17,300.2	16,923.5
1971	744.0	14,030.0	14,774.0

* For smaller banks as well, the story is the same: trust departments, overall, post net losses. According to the Federal Reserve System the trust department of the average bank with deposits up to $50 million, has $22,000 in total income but $34,000 in total expenses. The trust department of the average bank with deposits between $40 and $200 million, has a total income of $210,000 but total expenses of $373,000. The trust department of the average bank with deposits over $200 million has a total income of $1.89 million but total expenses of $1.93 million. This information is based on the *Functional Cost Analysis 1970 Average Banks,* based on data supplied by 951 participating banks in 12 Federal Reserve Districts, p. A20.
SOURCE: Annual Survey of Trust Department Income and Expenses 1970, Federal Reserve Bank of New York, Table III.

two out of the past three years; and for estate work, net operating earnings before income taxes has, with the exception of 1971, been declining for the past several years.

Robert Hoguet, former head of Citibank's Trust Department, said that until 1969, Citibank's Trust Department broke even; it took in fees of about $3 million a month and its expenses were $3 million a month. Hoguet explained that the bank's profits came from the $250 million in demand deposits maintained by trust customers (both individuals and corporations) in the commercial side of the bank.[66] Hoguet's statement points to one important truth. The only way trust departments have been able to show a profit for their personal fiduciary work is by adding to their earnings so-called "allowed credits for deposits." This is a credit for bank revenues produced by uninvested cash balances generated by the trust accounts and deposited with the commercial side of the bank.

A serious question arises as to the propriety of including "credits for deposits" in computing trust department profits. A basic fiduciary principle, embodied in Section 170 of *Restatement of Trusts 2d,* is that except for his fee, a trustee may not profit from a trust at the expense of the beneficiaries. If a corporate trustee can earn income from uninvested trust funds deposited in its commercial banking department, the temptation will always exist for the trustee to maintain high balances. As Reese Harris states:

> One of the most important reasons for a bank to have a trust department is to benefit by its inevitable cash balance. But here, fiduciary duty and self-interest most obviously conflict.[67]

Traditionally, the American Bankers Association (ABA) has taken the position that the earnings of a trust department should include earnings on deposits, though its latest official statement, released in 1949, appeared to modify the ABA position:

> After careful study the Committee on Costs and Charges concluded that the *gross earnings* of the trust department should be considered as being comprised solely of compensation received for services rendered and should include neither interest earned on trust department deposits nor earnings from the investment of the capital funds of the bank.[68]

Yet, when it came to the matter of the bottom line, the American Bankers Association did an about face and stated:

However, it is recognized that bank management should be informed of the full earning power, both direct and indirect, of the trust department in relation to other bank functions, and for this reason provision has been made in the trust department cost and earnings statement for the net earnings on trust departments deposits to be added to *net income* from operations.[69]

In our opinion, to allow trust departments to include credits from deposits as part of their net earnings is a dangerous practice that encourages self-dealing by banks. The very practice of permitting commercial banks to earn money from deposits generated by their trust accounts appears to us to violate even the ABA's own Statement of Principles of Trust Institutions, which reads:

It is the duty of a trustee to administer a trust solely in the interest of the beneficiaries without permitting the intrusion of interests of the trustees.[70]

Trust departments should either be efficient enough to earn a profit from fees charged or should cease operations. Trust business can be profitable without relying on credits from the commercial department; there are 49 trust companies existing separate from commercial banks in the U.S. According to C. Arthur Weis, Comptroller of St. Louis Fidelity Trust Company, one of the 49 unaffiliated trust institutions: "We manage to stand on our own two feet and come out with a profit. We have to because we have no big brother to lean on." [71]

The Study Group asked Citibank board members Richard Furlaud and Frank Barnett why FNCB engaged in the trust business if it was not profitable. Both replied, "Citibank wants to be a full-service bank." [72] Howard Scribner of Chase's Trust Department felt, "it's all part of the 'get 'em cradle to grave' philosophy." [73] Helmut Andresen, Executive Vice President of U.S. Trust Company, gave another view, reflecting the attitude that a trust department can be used as a loss leader to attract business for the commercial department and to enable the commercial department to benefit from the cash deposits of trust accounts:

A trust officer . . . should automatically offer checking accounts as an additional facility. In this way, the income that is accumulated by the trust department from one quarterly remittance day to the next stays with the bank even after distribution.[74]

Whatever reasons bankers give for maintaining trust departments, the fact remains that unless the department will pay for itself and return a profit, the pressure will also be there to use trust funds to further the bank's own gains rather than to benefit the beneficiaries. Banks should be required to disclose the profitability of their trust departments and the computation of profitability should not include any credit for earnings on cash deposits in the commercial side.

3. Pension Trusts

Pensions are a major feature in American life, and bank trust departments play a major role in the private pension system, managing over 70 per cent of private pension fund assets, some $100 billion. It is estimated that by 1980 bank trust departments will manage more than $200 billion in pension assets.[75] Of this vast sum, by far the largest portion is managed by five New York banks—Morgan, Bankers Trust, Chase Manhattan, FNCB, and Manufacturers Hanover—which in 1970 served as trustee for close to $40 billion in employee benefit funds. FNCB's share was $4.8 biilion.[76]

If only in terms of the amount of money managed, the role of banks as pension trustees warrants examination. Paul P. Harbrecht, author of *Pension Funds and Economic Power,* notes:

> The pension trusts are currently buying nearly as much common stock as all individual purchasers together, and their acquisitions of corporate bonds are even greater in amount than their stock purchases. These trusts are even now in a position to affect the balance of forces in our economy by their influence on the level of savings, the capital markets, and the buying power of millions of workers.[77]

Even more importantly, since over 30 million employees are presently enrolled in private pension plans, the way that these plans are managed affects the future security of half the American work force.

Our Procedure—The Right to Know

Since Citibank closed its doors to any inquiries about its pension trusteeships, the Study Group went to the bank's customers, writing to some 400 companies whose pension funds are managed in whole or part by Citibank.* Among other things, we asked the companies to describe their pension plans and to evaluate Citibank's performance as trustee.

It soon became apparent that Citibank's corporate clients were much more reluctant to discuss their relationships with the bank than individuals were. Many personal trust clients welcomed the opportunity to comment about the bank. One beneficiary wrote:

> My experience with the bank has been like a mouse battling a lion. *Bless you* Nader Raider for taking an interest.

On the other hand, some of the responses we received from corporate pension fund clients included:

> *Allied Chemical Corporation:* As a matter of policy our Management is unwilling to incur the expense of responding to detailed surveys or questionnaires about our business from well-meaning individuals or groups who act independently and in an unofficial capacity.[78]
>
> *Wild Heerbrugg Instruments:* We wish to advise you that we feel the information you have requested is confidential and we therefore do not wish to divulge any details of our plan for an outside project.[79]
>
> *Kaar Electronics Corporation:* I am returning your request of November 8 without response. Most of your queries are of a confidential nature which we do not care to divulge.[80]
>
> *Pan American World Airways:* While we recognize the role your group is playing, the Company, having just laid off another 1200 employees, is busy trying to create a profitable airline and at the moment is unable to provide the resources to furnish all the information you requested.[81]

One surprising result of our questionnaire was a memo that Towers, Perrin, Foster & Crosby, a Philadelphia management consultant firm, sent to all its pension fund clients:

---

* See Appendix, p. 367, for copy of letter sent to FNCB's pension clients.

DATE November 17, 1971

TO CONSULTANTS
SUBJECT TRUST QUESTIONNAIRE—DONALD ETRA
FILE
REFER QUESTIONS TO BASSETT

1. Mr. Donald Etra, of _____ 5th Avenue, New York, is writing to a number of companies asking for basic data in regard to their pension trust operations. He is doing this project for The Center for the Study of Responsive Law. Several of our clients have probably already received this questionnaire and may ask us about it.

2. The Center for the Study of Responsive Law is one of the branches of the Nader Operations. Ralph Nader is looking into pension plans, problems of the aged and other facets concerned with their problems. The purpose of this study is to collect data on the operations of the trustees of pension funds.

3. A copy of the questionnaire is attached.

4. My personal feeling is that Mr. Etra has asked a lot of questions which may not be any of his business. I feel it is the employer's responsibility to hire the trustee and retain him as long as he feels the trustee is doing a satisfactory job. I question whether it is Mr. Nader's prerogative to survey and analyze this relationship. There are also many practical reasons why I believe our clients will not want to complete the questionnaire, such as lack of information and difficulty in obtaining answers to several of the questions.

While Towers, Perrin, Foster & Crosby feels that public inquiry into pension plans is none of our business, that was not the feeling of the President's Committee on Corporate Pension Funds. The committee, in its 1965 report, *Public Policy and Private Pension Plans,* explained that there are four main reasons for public interest and concern: first, pensions have a direct impact on the security of 25 (now 30) million covered employees and their families; second, pension plans are subsidized by means of the tax laws; * third, pension assets play a vital role in our savings process; and fourth, pension plans influence labor mobility and structural unemployment.[82]

The Study Group was not alone in having difficulty soliciting information about pension funds. The Senate Subcommittee on

_____

* Contributions made by an employer to a qualifying pension plan are tax deductible (see Section 404 of the Internal Revenue Code). Also, income and capital gains accruing to a qualified pension plan are not taxed (see IRC § 501).

Labor recently held hearings on pension plans. During his opening remarks at the October 1971 hearings, Senator Jacob Javits stated:

> . . . it was most disappointing to learn that the testimony of some of those witnesses actually had to be compelled through use of subpoena. In effect, this subcommittee was told that the pension plan was none of their business.
>
> Let me set the record straight. Private pension plans are this subcommittee's business; they are the Congress's business; and they are the public's business. The private pension system has been fostered directly by the collective bargaining policy of the National Labor Relations Act, and it is a tax-sheltered industry estimated by some to be subsidized at the rate of $3 billion annually.[83]

Not only does the public have difficulty obtaining information, the employees covered by pension plans are often left in the dark. Even when employees are given more information about their pensions, that information is not always correct:

> Only 84 out of 188 plans analysed for this purpose clearly stated that pension benefits were not promised or guaranteed. Contrary to the facts, 70 plans out of 188 expressly stated or implied that the benefits were guaranteed or promised without reservation. An additional 34 plans were completely silent on the conditional nature of the pension "promise." [84]

If all were well with the private pension system, then perhaps no pressing need would exist for disclosure of the mechanics and the financing arrangements of pension plans. But all is not well. The Senate subcommittee examined a sample of 6.9 million retirement plan participants and found that since 1950, 70 per cent of the participants left their plans without benefits.[85] Arbitrary qualification requirements and inadequate financing are principal reasons why workers' expectations are dashed when they near retirement. The problems exist; continued secrecy can only perpetuate what has become an intolerable situation.

The Role of the Pension Trustee

In a typical pension plan, the employer decides what kind of pension benefits he wishes to provide, hires an actuary to compute how much the employer (and sometimes employees) must contribute into the pension fund each year, then appoints a bank to manage the pension fund. Of course, banks too, anxious for the business, actively solicit pension trusteeships. The bank's duties as trustee are specified in the trust agreement between the employer and the bank. These duties usually, but not always, include investment power over the pension fund.

What is the role of a pension trustee? Is a bank, when it assumes the trusteeship of a pension fund, a true trustee, subject to all the fiduciary duties of trustees, or is the bank a trustee in name only? Does a bank trustee have any responsibilities for the mechanics of a pension plan, or is the bank merely an investment advisor? As a 1956 Senate report observed: "The application of well-established doctrines of trust law to the field of employee benefit funds is a most difficult task." [86]

The Study Group asked several bankers what they felt to be the role of a bank as pension trustee. We specifically asked whether bankers felt any obligation to ensure that pension plans were adequately funded. According to Kevin Keenan, a vice president at First Pennsylvania Banking and Trust Company, "We, the bank, have nothing to do with the funding of a pension plan or the adequacy of the pension benefits." [87] The Study Group asked Frank Barnett of Citibank's Trust Board if First National City ever suggests to a company whose pension plan it trustees that the plan is underfunded. Barnett replied, "No, that is none of the bank's business." [88] Robert Hoguet, former head of FNCB's Investment Management Group, explained, "The bank's responsibility is just an investment responsibility. The bank is not in the traditional sense a trustee." [89]

Even if we accept the bankers' own restrictive view of their role, that of investment advisor, because investment advisors are also fiduciaries,[90] banks cannot and should not disclaim responsibility for the solvency of the pension fund and the adequacy of benefits.

The bank trustee should take responsibility for protecting the employees' interests because when plans are managed without union or employee representatives, no one else can. The employer might not want to protect the employee: the fewer employees get pensions, the less the employer will have to contribute to the fund. The actuary's role is restricted to mathematical computations. Nor can the employee protect himself because, unless he becomes "vested" (i.e., obtains a nonforfeitable right to his pension regardless of whether or where he continues working), he is not recognized as having enough interest to contest the pension plan.

A few pension plans, such as those created under the Taft-Hartley Act,[91] are managed by a board of trustees that includes representatives of employees, but pension plans that are employer administered rarely give employees or unions any say in management. A New York State Insurance Department report indicated that only 5% of the 271 plans studied provided for union representation.[92]

Rather than accept responsibility, banks do their utmost to limit it, by writing various exculpatory clauses into the trust agreement with the employer. For example, to assure that the bank is never bothered by challenges from employees, their standard form of trust agreement includes clauses such as:

> No person other than the Company or the Committee may require an accounting or bring any action against the Trustee with respect to the Trust or its actions as Trustee.[93]

The whole system produces a situation in which, in Harbrecht's words, "the so-called trustee has all the prerogatives of property management with none of the obligations to account to the beneficiary for his stewardship." [94]

The Problems—What Banks Are Not Doing to Solve Them

As highlighted by the recent hearings of the Senate Subcommittee on Labor and by *You and Your Pension,* by Ralph Nader and Kate Blackwell, the three main problems facing the private pension system today are funding, self-dealing, and vesting.

The subcommittee uncovered many instances of underfunded pension plans—plans that do not have enough funds to pay all the accrued pensions due. Among the plans described in the Senate hearings was Anaconda Company's pension plan, trusteed by Morgan Guaranty and FNCB. Anaconda's pension fund had assets of $68 million and accrued liabilities of $176 million.[95] Thus, should Anaconda go out of business, there will not be enough money to pay the pensions that employees have already earned. As explained in *Pension Funds and Economic Power:*

The security of a pension expectation under a noninsured [i.e., managed under a trust agreement plan] thus depends on the solvency of the pension trust. And this, in turn, will depend on whether or not the pension trust has been fully funded and well administered during the active employment period of the pensioner.[96]

The pension plan of Studebaker workers was also underfunded. When Studebaker shut its plant in 1963, "4000 workers who had a promise of a private pension witnessed it vanishing before their eyes." [97] Although some of Studebaker's workers had accumulated more than 20 years of service toward their pensions, all they received was one lump-sum payment of $350.

The Senate subcommittee also examined many pension plans whose investment policies permitted the trustees to invest the plan's assets in the employer's own stock or in employee-related enterprises. One hazard of investing a major portion of the plan in the employer company's assets arises when the employer company fails.* At that time the fund's assets become almost worthless. Simultaneously, workers are laid off, making their need for a pension more urgent than ever. As of 1968, at least 34 employee benefit funds trusteed by Citibank were invested in the securities of the employer establishing the fund,[98] although in some of those plans, only an inconsequential sum was so invested (see chart, page 243). According to a 1969 SEC sample of 91 bank-managed pension plans, on average, 4.4% of the total common stock of each fund was invested in the stock of employer affiliated companies; "on the other hand a very substantial portion (up to 80%) of the common stock holdings of profit-sharing plans consists of the shares of affiliated companies."† [99]

---

* The Studebaker and Penn Central failures and the near collapse of Lockheed make this possibility less remote than once might have been the case.
† The SEC study distinguishes between a pension and profit sharing plan by noting: The essential difference between a pension plan and a profit-sharing plan is in the nature of the employer's commitment. In a profit-sharing plan the employer does not undertake to provide defined benefits upon retirement or other separation from service. Instead, the employer agrees or undertakes to contribute on a reasonably regular basis from the profits of the enterprise to the fund. The interests of employees in the fund are generally definitely ascertainable by the language of the plan, and as in the pension plan, employees may be permitted (or required) to contribute. Again a range of possibilities exists for the management of such plans, but generally a trustee will be used.

Vesting was a third problem discussed in the subcommittee hearings. If a plan has no vesting provision, a worker who does not remain with a company until retirement receives no pension at all, even if he works for 30 or 40 years for the same company. The subcommittee heard testimony from a shoe salesman who was enrolled in the Retail Shoe Employees Retirement Fund, a pension plan trusteed by Citibank. The man labored for 19 and one-half years before the shoe store in which he was working closed. As he explained: "We don't have any vested rights whatsoever after twenty years. Everything goes down the drain." [100]

Underfunded plans, self-dealing by employers, and inadequate vesting requirements—all problems that rob an employee of his pension benefits and all problems for which banks disclaim responsibility. The underlying cause of these problems is the present structure of the private pension system; we would favor separating control of pension funds from the employers who sponsor them and from the banks who have commercial ties to those employers. A proposal for independently managed pension funds will be outlined later in this chapter. If the present system is retained, however, pension trustees should at least accept the fiduciary duty to manage pension funds solely for the benefit of the participants and accept the affirmative duty of informing plan participants of all the mechanics of their plan, the financial status of the fund, and the conditions under which employees might lose their benefits.

Profile of Pension Portfolios

To determine the investment policies of Citibank's trust department, the Study Group analyzed the portfolios of 52 of the larger pension funds managed by Citibank in 1967. The smallest fund analyzed was the $500,000 Chrysler Industrial Pension Plan, and the largest was the Western Electric Company Pension Fund, valued at $584 million. Only four of the funds totaled less than $1 million; 33 funds had assets of between $1 million and $50 million, and five funds had assets over $100 million. The total assets of the 52 funds in the sample were $2 billion,* which appears to be slightly more than half the total employee benefit

* Market value as of August 15, 1967.

assets trusteed by Citibank. Common stock accounted for 50%
to 60% of each pension trust's total value in all but five cases.
In four of these five, common stock accounted for just below
the 50% mark. The only exception was the Western Electric
fund, with only 28% of its holdings in common stock. Real-estate
mortgages and corporate and government notes and bonds comprised the remainder of the assets in the portfolios. Preferred
stock holdings were small—1.3% of the total assets.

The table below indicates that there is a fairly standard pattern of investing for trust portfolios; common stock is by far
the largest asset held both in Citibank's trust department and
trust departments nationwide.

Trust Department Holdings by Asset Type

	Citibanks' Total Trust Department			All Trust Departments	
	1969*	1970**	1971***	1969†	1970‡
Common Stock:	61.0%	58.0%	63.8%	64.7%	62.2%
Corporate Bonds and Notes:	18.0	18.7	14.4	13.5	14.8
Government and Agency Obligations:	10.3	10.6	9.5	6.2	6.3
State and County Obligations:	3.8	4.3	3.7	5.6	5.8
Real-Estate Mortgages:	2.7	2.8	2.3	2.2	2.2
Preferred Stock:	2.3	2.0	2.1	2.0	2.0
Other Assets:	2.0	3.0	3.9	6.0	8.0

* FNCB, "The Anatomy of an Investment," pp. 26–7.
** Ibid.
*** "The Investment Management Group of First National City Bank,
Review of 1971," pp. 28–9.
† Trust Assets of Insured Commercial Banks—1969, Board of Governors,
Federal Reserve System, Federal Deposit Insurance Corporation, Office of
the Comptroller of the Currency, p. 6.
‡ Trust Assets of Insured Commercial Banks—1970, op. cit., p. 6.

The 52 pension funds invested in 183 common stocks. While
this appears to be a broad diversification, a closer inspection reveals just the opposite—a high degree of concentration in a few
stocks. Sixty-two of the 183 different stocks were held by only
one fund. But two stocks, IBM and Monsanto, were held by every
one of the trusts. Another five stocks (Avon, Sears, Exxon,
Texaco, and Xerox) were held by 51 of the 52.

Looking at this distribution by market value of the securities
further emphasizes the concentration of investments. The five

largest holdings of common stock (IBM, Xerox, Avon, Kodak, and Merck) accounted for more than one quarter of the total invested by the 52 funds in common stocks. The 20 largest holdings of common stock made up approximately 55% of the total —more than half the common stock held by the 52 pension funds.

IBM, held by every single trust account, was the largest single common stock investment for 44 pension trusts and was the second largest in the other eight. In terms of percentage of common stock held, IBM accounted for between 8% and 12% in 49 pension funds. Fairchild Camera's and Seagram's pension funds had almost 20% of their common stock total invested in IBM. Xerox was the second largest common stock holding of the 52 funds. It was held in every portfolio save one (Hess Oil). For 48 of the trusts, Xerox accounted for between 6% and 8% of the common stock investment. In every case, the leading ten holdings (IBM, Xerox, Avon, Eastman Kodak, Merck, Sears, Coca Cola, Texaco, General Electric, and General Motors) accounted for at least 35% of total stock investments. In most cases, the top ten holdings accounted for more than 45% of the total common stock.

That this sample of 52 pension portfolios is representative is shown by the fact that the ten largest common stock holdings of those funds correspond almost exactly to the ten largest stock holdings of FNCB's whole trust portfolio:

Ten Largest Common Stock Holdings in 52 Pensions (1967)	*Ten Largest Common Stock Holdings— Whole Department (1970)* **	*Ten Largest Common Stock Holdings— Whole Department (1971)* ***
IBM	IBM	IBM
Xerox	Xerox	Xerox
Avon	Avon	Eastman Kodak
Eastman Kodak	GM	Avon
Merck	Kodak	Coca Cola
Sears	Merck	GM
Coca Cola	Coca Cola	Merck
Texaco	Phillips Petroleum*	Sears
GE	Exxon	GE
GM	Sears	MMM

* Indicates that a major portion of the holding is not under the bank's control.
** FNCB, "The Anatomy of an Investment," p. 28.
*** "The Investment Management Group of First National City Bank, Review of 1971," p. 23.

Two features of FNCB's investment policies have become evident: the major portion of each account is invested in common stock, and the portfolios concentrate on only ten stocks. These two features are significant in that they (a) reveal the way Citibank handles individual accounts, (b) have implications for the liquidity of Citibank's trust portfolios, and (c) indicate the kind of power the bank has over companies in which it invests.

(a) Our analysis reveals that almost every pension fund was invested in the exact same manner. For example, if a pension fund held total assets of $100, on average, $60 would be invested in common stocks, divided approximately as follows: $6 in IBM, $4.20 in Xerox, and $16.80 divided among Avon, Kodak, Merck, Sears, Coca Cola, Texaco, General Electric, and General Motors. Despite this finding, Citibank, consonant with its public policy of claiming that it gives each account personalized attention, contends, "portfolio managers, however, do a lot more than stick to a formula and pick stocks from an approved list." [100] Irrespective of what FNCB writes in its public-relations brochures, the fact is that at Citibank there is a list that restricts a portfolio manager's investment freedom. According to Thomas Theobald, "it is one individual who approves or disapproves the name going on the list and then it is up to the portfolio manager to act or not to act." [101] The Securities and Exchange Commission has already once challenged First National City Bank for promising individualized investment management but investing all funds alike. It appears that Citibank practices this policy for its pension funds accounts as well, and an investigation by the SEC is clearly in order.

(b) A heavy concentration in the common stock of a limited number of companies might make it difficult for a trust department to sell some of its larger holdings without depressing the market price of the stock. Professor of Finance Eugene Lerner recently completed a study to determine how liquid the market is for securities an institution might purchase. He concluded:

> . . . it is difficult to buy and sell even a modest size block of stocks and that in [sic] the process of accumulating or disposing of the shares the seller may have an impact upon the price at which the stock trades. Moreover, since more and more shares are being accumulated by institutions because of the savings habits of the country, the problem associated with block trading

and the lack of liquidity in the securities market is likely to increase rather than diminish in the years to come.[102]

Roy Schotland, law professor at Georgetown University and for a short while Chief Counsel for the SEC's Institutional Investor Study, also noted that:

> The relative homogeneity of the money managers, and their impacts on market stability and corporate action, are such serious problems because of the size and concentration of institutional portfolios.[103]

And Paul Harbrecht observes:

> . . . it is inevitable that heavy selling or buying by these institutions will have an effect on general market levels. Thus, if a trustee begins to sell or ceases to purchase shares on the basis of his prediction of a market decline he may succeed in making his own prediction come true. Conclusions now must be tentative, but these possible effects will become increasingly real as the pension funds increase their equity holdings.[104]

If bank trust departments do depress the market price of stock when they sell off large holdings, and if the same stocks are held by each pension portfolio, then certain pension funds can receive favored treatment. In a declining market, the first account to sell has a distinct advantage—it sells the stock with the least loss. In theory, the SEC tries to monitor such situations; one former Citibank trust officer explained:

> A few years ago we decided to sell off a stock that was held by every one of our trust portfolios. We had the damnedest time with the SEC. We even had to go to the extreme of selling off fractional shares from some of the trusts just so everything would be fair.

The same officer, however, admitted that when the decision to sell is not clear-cut, accounts that have threatened to move to other banks have been put on top of the pile, so that they sell at the least loss. "There's always got to be a pile," the former Citibanker noted.

(c) The large and concentrated equity holdings of trust departments like Citibank's enable banks to exercise considerable control over the corporations in which the trust departments invest. Roy Schotland described this concentration with some awe to the Joint Economic Committee:

By the end of 1968, total assets of $283 billion were managed by insured commercial bank trust departments. This represents growth of $30 billion per year for at least the preceding 2 years. Of the $283 billion, $188 billion is in stocks and that is over 20 per cent of the outstanding stock in the United States; and close to another $39 billion is in corporate bonds. This growth is being fueled in substantial part by private pension funds: almost three-quarters, or $84.3 billion of 1968's $115.3 billion in private pension assets, were bank managed.

Not even the size and growth of bank trust departments are as remarkable as the concentration of control of that $283 billion. Five banks, all in New York City, managed $67.4 billion, or almost 25 per cent. If we add the next five banks, we have 10 banks managing $102.1 billion, or over one-third of all trust department assets in the 3,317 banks.[105]

Robert Soldofsky, Professor of Finance at the University of Iowa, goes so far as to predict:

. . . by 1980 or before, an increasing number of companies will come under the control of four to eight financial intermediaries; by "control" is meant that 50 per cent or more of their voting stock will be held by four to eight individual organizations. By the year 2000, under present legislation, almost half or more than half the voting stock of hundreds of corporations will be held by ten or fewer organizations.[106]

Not all of the stock held by a trust department is under its complete investment and voting control. Custodian accounts, for example, give the bank merely the job of holding the stock for the true owner. However, the larger bank trust departments do have full control over about 30% of the assets in their personal trust accounts and 89% of the assets in their employee benefit accounts.[107] In 1970, Citibank served as trustee for $4.8 billion in employee benefit accounts and $4.1 billion in personal trust accounts.[108] With about 60% of these amounts invested in common stock, and with complete discretion over 89% of the employee benefit funds and 30% of the personal trusts, Citibank had total investment discretion, including voting power, over almost $3.3 billion in common stock.

What does this mean on a company-by-company basis? According to a 1968 study Citibank held 18.5% of the common stock of Boise Cascade, with sole voting rights over 13.7%.[109] Citibank and Morgan together held 14.7% of Xerox's common stock, retaining voting power over 8.4.%[110] Similarly, Morgan and Chase held 12.8% of Pennsylvania Railroad's stock, with voting power over 11.6%; [111] they also held 15.2% of TWA's stock, with voting control over 13.5%.[112]

Stock ownership is only one of the ways in which a trust department can exert influence; FNCB's trust department also invests in long-term convertible debentures (corporate bonds) of several of the airlines:

Company	Total Issue	FNCB Holdings	Interest Rate	Term
American	N.A.	1,000,000	4½ %	25 years
Braniff	60,000,000	4,375,000	5¾ %	20 years
Eastern	50,000,000	1,155,000	4¾ %	25 years
T.W.A.	150,000,000	3,485,000	6½ %	17 years
	100,000,000	1,551,000	4%	25 years
United	175,000,000	1,025,000	5%	20 years
Pan Am	100,000,000*	2,000,000	5¼ %	25 years
	175,000,000	2,500,000	4½ %	20 years

* Loan agreement
SOURCE: Civil Aeronautics Board, Form B-46, December 31, 1969.

The bank's influence is even greater, however, because Citibank's commercial department invests in the very companies whose stock and debt obligations are held by Citibank's trust department. In the airline industry, for example:

First National City Bank has an investment of $538 million in air carriers in the form of long-term debt and ownership in 114 jet aircraft that are leased to those carriers. The Bank's ownership interest in *American*'s 37 aircraft ($121 million) constitutes 7.2 per cent of the carrier's assets or 14.68 per cent of the net value of the carrier's flight equipment. Similarly, the Bank's ownership interest of $87.5 million in *TWA*'s 33 jet aircraft constitutes 6 per cent of the carrier's assets or 11.5 per cent of the net value of its flight equipment. The Bank's aggregate investment of $50 million in *Braniff* amounts to 11.7 per cent of the carrier's assets, and the Bank's interest of $33.5 million in aircraft is equivalent to 17.5 per cent of the net value of the carrier's flight equipment. 5.8 per cent of the net value of *Pan American*'s flight equipment is owned by the Bank as it owns 4.5 per cent ($85 million) of the carrier's assets. First National City owns 8.4 per cent of the assets of *North Central*, and 4.3 per cent of the assets of *Delta*. Further, the Bank's ownership interest in *United*'s 31 aircraft exceeds $31 million.* [113]

* This passage is excerpted from a complaint filed before the CAB. The complainants, Aviation Consumers Action Project, have alleged that FNCB violated Section 408 and 409 of the Federal Aviation Act by ac-

It is clear that the banks have considerable influence because of their commercial and trust investments.

Once banks concede that they have the influence, the question is: how do they use it? A former Citibank trust officer described what used to be FNCB's policy:

> We always felt that if the bank thought highly enough of a company to invest in its stock, the stock should be voted for management. If we didn't have confidence in management, then we felt we shouldn't be holding the stock at all.

Today, the policy of "vote for management or sell" is no longer standard operating procedure, at least according to Thomas Theobald: "For accounts where we are the sole trustee and have the legal responsibility to vote, our Investment Policy Committee decides on contested matters." [114]

In a statement of its policy, Morgan Guaranty Trust Company asserts:

> Just as with investment decisions, officers of the [Morgan Guaranty Trust and Investment] Division consider proposals in terms of the best interests of the party or parties for whom the shares are held. Not surprisingly, since the holding of a company's shares as an investment reflects confidence in the management, most of our votes on proposals have coincided with the recommendations of company managements. But not all.[115]

It is enlightening to look at the way Citibank, Morgan, and other bank trust departments reacted to one recent challenge. In 1970, the Project on Corporate Responsibility launched its Campaign General Motors. Campaign GM formulated three shareholder proposals and asked all GM shareholders, especially large institutional shareholders like trust departments, to support them. The first proposal dealt with shareholder democracy and called for nomination of directors by shareholders themselves rather than by management. The second proposal called for constituent democracy whereby three additional directors would be elected, one each by GM employees, GM dealers, and owners of GM vehicles. The third proposal asked GM to disclose in its annual report information about its minority hiring practices, its air pollution controls, and its auto safety policies.

---

quiring substantial properties of air carriers and by establishing interlocking relationships without prior CAB approval.

Campaign GM solicited the support of all the major bank trust departments holding GM stock. The responsiveness of the banks is perhaps best shown by quoting from Campaign GM's "Scoresheet," which summarized the reactions of the banks:

> Banks, with their strong desires for commercial accounts and their frequent interlocks with corporate management, typically vote unquestioningly for management.
>
> One notable exception this year was the *First Pennsylvania Banking and Trust Company,* the twentieth largest bank in the nation, which voted the approximately 750,000 General Motors shares it holds in trust in favor of our proposal on disclosure. This was an important breakthrough, for the First Pennsylvania Banking and Trust Company became the first bank to recognize that it can selectively disagree with management.
>
> Most banks not only failed to give our proposals open-minded consideration but also refused to send out the Project's proxy materials to cotrustees and custodial clients who can vote their own stock. Only the *Fidelity Bank and Trust Company of Philadelphia* and the *Bank of America* agreed to send out our materials.
>
> The banks that refused our request were the *Chase Manhattan, Bankers Trust, National Bank of Detroit, Morgan Guaranty Trust, First National Bank of Chicago, Girald Trust of Philadelphia, First National City Bank of New York City,* and *Manufacturers Hanover Trust Company.*[116]

FNCB's failure to respond or even cooperate with consumer groups does not inhibit the bank from contending:

> . . . we now weigh investment on a social responsibility basis as well. Specifically, we are interested in how companies are responding to environmental issues, to the consumer movement, and to pressures for social reform.[117]

In 1971, FNCB's trust department's third largest purchase (by market value) was 843,000 shares of GM stock.[118]

What is most surprising about Citibank's investment policies is that the bank itself commissioned a survey of investors which concluded that most shareholders were willing to take a 10% reduction in returns in order to clean up the environment.[119] Thus, the bank cannot use as an excuse the fact that beneficiaries are concerned with profit to the exclusion of all else.

The situation was summed up well by James Byrne of *The American Banker.* Byrne interviewed some of the bankers who had attended a May, 1972 meeting sponsored by the Project on

Corporate Responsibility (Campaign GM's progenitor). According to Byrne:

> One banker more cynically observed that trust officers are like everyone else—"we give lip service to the issues but we don't do anything about them. We vote our pocketbooks.[120]

Pension Performance

One indisputable criterion for evaluating banks as pension trustees is how well bank-trusteed pension funds have performed. According to Richard Cantor, former head of the Investment Advisory Service at Chase Manhattan's trust department:

> My conclusion is that as a class pension fund investors have been unsuccessful, which is really a great shame, since their less than successful practices raise the costs to corporations of providing benefits and through the bargaining process must ultimately affect what workers receive.[121]

Cantor went on:

> How good has performance in pension funds been? During the period 1957–65 the appreciation of all noninsured pension plans has averaged about 7¼ per cent. Even allowing for the rather sizable amount of assets invested in fixed income securities, the implied return on the equity portion of the investments of these corporate pension funds appears to barely approximate that of the Dow Jones industrial average. A recent study of 77 equity trust funds covering the period of 1961–68 indicates that *the performance of these funds almost exactly equals the Standard & Poor's 500 index.* It should not be surprising to anyone that the common trust performance and pension fund results—now I am talking just about the equity portion—are so similar, since *the assets are all handled by bank trust departments which despite much recent publicity, handle them in essentially the same manner.* (emphasis added) [122]

A recent study of the performance of employee benefit funds, conducted by A. S. Hansen, bears out Cantor's observations.[123] Hansen examined 58 bank-managed commingled equity funds, (including FNCB's). The results of his study, presented below, show that, except for the last three-year period, bank-managed funds were not able to outperform the market. For the five-year and seven-year periods examined, mutual funds outperformed the banks. For the seven-year period examined, bank and insurance company managed funds had the same rate of return, 5.9%, while the Standard & Poors annual return was 6.1%.

Equivalent Level Annual Time-Weighted Rates of Return

Multi year Periods	58 Bank Regular Equity Funds	16 Insurance Company Regular Equity Funds	45 Growth And Income Mutual Funds	27 Growth Mutual Funds	Standard & Poors 500
Last 3 years (1969–71)	3.0%	0.9%	1.6%	1.7%	2.8%
Last 5 years (1967–71)	7.8	7.3	8.7	9.4	8.4
Last 7 years (1965–71)	5.9	5.9	7.5	10.1	6.1

Another study of pension fund performance, conducted by William Dreher, shows that for the five-year period ending December 31, 1969, bank managed funds averaged a total return of only 5.5%, and close to half of the bank managed funds were not able to outperform the market. Dreher sums up his findings by stating: "It is simply indefensible that a pool of tax-exempt equity capital has barely a 50 per cent chance to outperform the S&P 500 over a five-year period." * [124]

Since a pension fund is a pool of capital where contributions paid in by employers remain in the fund several years before they are paid out in pension benefits, performance over the life of the fund is especially important. Good performance throughout the life of the fund will exponentially increase the returns to the fund by the time pensions are paid out. Based on the two studies that Dreher conducted, he remarks:

> When a one per cent gain in performance achieved over the life of the fund can produce 15 to 25 per cent more benefits or reduced contributions, the implications of this spread are enormous.[125]

To determine the performance of pension funds trusteed by Citibank, the Study Group asked each of the companies whose funds were managed in whole or in part by FNCB "what was the

---

* Dreher is referring to the fact that the IRS exempts from taxation income earned by a pension fund. Because money managers do not have to worry about tax considerations (e.g., capital gains, etc.) when they manage pension funds, they have greater investment leeway and therefore should do a better job.

rate of return from your pension fund over the past five years?"
Some of the responses we received included:

> *Pennzoil United, Inc.:* As you know, there are many ways of measuring rates of return, none of them universally acceptable. Suffice it to say that our rate of return has compared reasonably well with the standard indicators such as the S&P 500.[126]
> *Tennessee Valley Authority:* TVA's pension fund, trusteed in part by Citibank, had from 1966 through 1970 a cumulative annual (internal) rate of return of 3.35% and a cumulative annual (time weighted) rate of return of 3.2%.[127]
> *Exxon:* For the five years ended June 30, 1971, the account at FNCB earned a rate of return significantly above what it

Citibank's Common Trust Funds for Pension Trusts

A Name of Fund	B Period Examined	C % Change in Fund	D % Change in Appro- priate * Standard Index	E (C-D), i.e., Fund's Performance Compared to Appropriate Standard Index
1. Bond Fund (I)**	June 28, 1968– May 28, 1971	— 5.9%	—17.8%	+11.9%
2. Bond S (I)	Dec. 31, 1968– Aug. 31, 1971	+ 2.0%	—20.7%	+22.7%
3. Common Stock Fund (G)	June 28, 1968– May 28, 1971	+ 4.7%	0.0%	+ 4.7%
4. Foreign Securities Fund (I)	June 28, 1968– Oct. 15, 1970	— 4.3%	—21.9%	+17.6%
5. Mortgage Fund (I)	June 28, 1968– May 28, 1971	+ 2.2%	—17.8%	+20.0%
6. Private Placement (I)	June 28, 1968– May 28, 1971	— 7.6%	—17.8%	+10.2%
7. Supplementary Common Stock Fund (G)	June 28, 1968– May 28, 1971	+ 5.0%	0.0%	+ 5.0%
8. Self-Employed Employees Fixed Income Fund (I)	June 28, 1968– Dec. 31, 1970	+10.8%	—17.8%	+28.6%
9. Self-Employed Employees Equity Fund (G)	June 18, 1968– Dec. 31, 1970	—11.5%	— 7.4%	— 4.1%

* The Growth funds have been compared to the Standard & Poors 500 Index and the Income funds have been compared to Moody's High Grade Bond Index.
** (I) = Income
   (G) = Growth

would have earned had the money been invested in the securities comprising the S&P stock index.[128]

Mutual Marine Office, Inc.: Mutual Marine stated that its pension fund trusteed by Citibank "had very little growth due to market." [129]

Corning Glass Works: Corning explained, "A number of the questions request information on data which we have not made public and hence will not reply directly to them." Corning also refused to tell us whether they made the performance data of their pension fund available to workers covered by the fund.[130]

One index of Citibank's investment performance for pension funds is the performance of its pooled funds. As already noted, banks tend to use pooled accounts as "showpiece accounts," thus the performance of the pooled accounts is not necessarily representative of overall performance.

Eight out of the nine pooled pension funds managed by Citibank beat the market over the period examined. In doing so, Citibank's funds performed at least better than half of the other bank-managed funds, which, according to Dreher's study, were not able to outperform the market. Citibank's good performance record for its pooled pension funds, however, is only in terms of comparative performance. It still must be noted that four out of the nine funds managed by the bank lost money; in three other funds, the growth was under 5%; thus in seven of the nine funds employers during this period would have done better had they put their pension funds into savings accounts.

The Move Away from Banks

An increased concern with the mediocre overall performance of many trust departments has persuaded many employers to move part or all of their pension fund business away from banks to independent money managers.

According to Business Week, "The new managers are capitalizing on the widespread impression that banks are too stodgy or simply too big to care." [131]

Some of Citibank's clients have participated in the move away from exclusive bank management of funds. John Masten, Vice President and Secretary of Phelps Dodge Corporation, told the Study Group that Phelps Dodge will keep the pension money presently managed by Citibank with Citibank, but will invest all new contributions to the fund with an independent money manager. "We want to try out the theory that competition will enable us to get better performance," Masten explains.[132]

In November, 1971, the Study Group spoke to Alan Brightman, Assistant Treasurer at Charles Pfizer & Company. Brightman explained that in 1968, Pfizer switched about half of its pension fund from Citibank to the investment advisory services of Donaldson, Lufkin & Jenrette, hoping to get more aggressive money management. In general, Brightman thinks that bank investment policies are too conservative. As to Donaldson, Lufkin & Jenrette's performance, "We're not too thrilled." By June of 1972, Pfizer had advised the firm that they would probably end their relationship. "But," Mr. Brightman explained,

> we would not take our fund to another bank. The big banks are so large that it is very difficult for them to react to the market, especially when they should sell. We also like the more personal contact that an independent manager can offer us. We can't get that where an account manager handles fifty to a hundred accounts.[133]

Some Recommendations

We recommend that pension trustees be held to strict fiduciary principles, and that they be held responsible for ensuring: that no self-dealing occurs, that the fund is invested for the sole benefit of the participants, and that the participants are fully informed of all aspects of the plans. When plans are not fully funded, the pension trustee should inform participants of the contingent nature of the pension benefits. Although sometimes the pension trustee is not appointed until after the plan is drawn up, pension trustees should, wherever possible, encourage employers to provide early vesting and portability provisions in their plans.

The SEC should investigate the investment policies of pension trustees to determine if, as claimed, individualized attention is being given to each plan. The SEC may already have this information from its 1970 study; if so, it should be disclosed publicly on a bank-by-bank basis.

The increasingly large holdings held by bank trust departments and the concentration of these holdings in the securities of few companies cannot help but affect the whole securities market. We have already discussed the implications the situation has for the liquidity of the market and the fact that some portfolios might suffer when more favored ones are given first benefit of market fluctuations. The control that trust departments have over their holdings, especially when considered along with the influence that the commercial side has over the same companies, raises several antitrust questions. If, as predicted, bank pension and personal trust holdings continue to grow, so too will bank control over the companies whose stock is held.

If no money manager were permitted to manage more than a fixed sum, and if that sum could not be invested in more than a fixed percentage of any one company's stock, many of the liquidity problems now facing the larger trust departments would be solved. If pension management were divorced from commercial banks, antitrust problems would be lessened. But there are more basic problems—inadequate vesting, lack of portability, underfunding, and self-dealing—inherent in the present private pension system, and there are broad market problems—liquidity and antitrust—equally inherent; to deal with them we propose an alternative to the present pension system.

We suggest a system whereby employers would pay pension contributions directly to employees. The employees would be required to invest this money in funds established specifically to manage pension money. The funds would be private, competitive, insured financial institutions, licensed and regulated by the SEC. The SEC would determine the maximum amount that any one pension fund administrator could manage. The SEC would also fix a limit on the percentage of voting stock that any one fund could hold in any one company. Pension fund administrators, investment managers, actuaries, and other persons with the necessary expertise who joined together to form corporations would be eligible to apply for licenses. It would be possible for a bank's pension trust department, if it were spun off and all connections with commercial banking severed, to qualify as an independent retirement fund.

The majority of a fund's directors would be elected by its members, i.e., its contributors. Where investment decisions raise questions of social policy, the directors could poll members to ascertain their investment and proxy voting preferences. This policy would enable members to help decide how to invest their funds—whether to invest in companies who are notorious polluters or who flagrantly violate civil rights or labor relations laws; or whether to accept possibly slightly lower return on their fund investments in order to foster the construction of moderately priced housing, or to build schools or hospitals—investments that might have compensating indirect benefits in their daily lives.[134]

Since each year an employee would be paid a portion of his pension money, in effect, there would be immediate vesting. Because an employee would lose none of his accrued payments when he changed jobs, his benefits would be completely portable. The annual payout would eliminate the problem of an employee losing his pension due to an underfunded plan of a bankrupt employer. Because pension fund management would no longer be in the hands of banks and employers, there would be no opportunity for banks and employers to use the funds for their own benefit. SEC regulations concerning size and concentration of holdings would guarantee liquidity for the funds and would prevent pension managers from obtaining control of companies held in their portfolios.

4. A Question of Conflicts

A trustee is held to something stricter than the morals of the marketplace. Not honesty alone, but the punctilio of an honor the most sensitive, is thus the standard of behavior.[135]

—*Justice Benjamin Cardozo*

However we ultimately judge the performance of a bank trust department, we must also look at the reasons why commercial banks should or should not accept fiduciary appointments.

The fact that bank-managed funds have had only mediocre returns provides reason to question whether these funds have been invested solely to benefit plan participants. This inquiry leads us to consider the kinds of conflicts that can, and apparently do, arise when banks serve as trustees.

Essentially there are three potential conflicts inherent in the role of a corporate fiduciary. The first is between the interests of the trust department clients and the interests of the commercial bank itself. The second arises when a bank, as trustee of a pension fund, must choose between the interests of an employer and the interests of employees. The third arises among trust accounts in a commercial bank as they vie for investment attention.

1. *Type One Conflict: Trust Beneficiaries Versus the Bank*

The principal ways the bank trust department can utilize trust funds for its own benefit are (a) to engage in "broker reciprocity"; (b) to maintain large uninvested cash balances; (c) to invest trust funds to support companies with commercial ties to the bank; and (d) to use trust funds to invest in its own stock.

Broker reciprocity is the practice of directing brokerage business to those brokers who reciprocate by maintaining deposits in the bank. Bank trust departments manage close to $180 billion in common stock,[136] and banks have complete discretion to buy and sell some $63 billion of it.

When they play the market, bank trust departments generally use stockbrokers, just as private investors do. And stockbrokers, like all other businesses, maintain bank accounts. It would be natural for a bank to "reward" a stockbroker who maintains an account in the bank by directing business to that stockbroker. It might even seem natural for a bank to allocate its brokerage business in proportion to the amount of money various brokers maintain in the bank. Natural—but illegal, and potentially damaging. Illegal because it violates the antitrust laws and the proscription against a trustee's personally profiting from a trust. Potentially damaging because the broker is not chosen on the basis of his ability to execute the transaction or the quality of his research. Broker reciprocity can lead a trust department to transact all of its trust business through brokers, and not deal directly with a purchaser or seller on the so-called third market, thereby saving trust clients brokerage fees. It can also lead to "churning," whereby securities are bought and sold for no purpose other than to generate commissions for brokers. Even if a reciprocal arrangement results in no monetary harm to trust beneficiaries, broker reciprocity enables a trustee to profit personally from trust funds; this in itself is a breach of fiduciary duty.

Speaking in September of 1970, Donald Baker of the Department of Justice's Antitrust Division warned bankers:

> It has long been customary . . . for banks to allocate securities brokerage service on the basis of deposits maintained by the broker at the bank. This is plain old-fashioned reciprocity . . . we regard such reciprocity as illegal.[137]

Despite the stated illegality of broker reciprocity, the 1970 SEC study found it to be prevalent. Based on information obtained from 50 bank trust departments, the SEC concluded:

> The analysis indicates that an increase of $1 in commissions paid by a bank and received by a broker is accompanied, on the average, by an increase of $4.26 in the broker's deposits at the bank. . . . Some persons interviewed by the SEC Study have suggested that the average ratio of deposits to commissions was 10:1 rather than 4.26:1.* [138]

In light of the SEC's findings, one might hope that the appropriate regulatory agencies would take steps to stop broker reciprocity. The Justice Department, however, believes that, since its 1970 warning, the larger banks have eliminated reciprocal arrangements with brokers. Donald Baker wrote the Study Group in July, 1972:

> We have brought no suits for injunctive relief, believing that our prior reciprocity suits in other industries would cause counsel for banks and brokerage firms to recommend voluntary elimination of any illegal practices. To the best of our knowledge, our approach has been successful.[139]

It is hard to understand the Antitrust Division's inaction when, as documented by the SEC, broker reciprocity was widespread.

Direct jurisdiction over trust departments of national banks rests with the Comptroller of the Currency and most directly

---

* The [SEC] study sought to determine whether there is typically a relationship between the amount of commissions paid by a bank to brokers and the amount of brokers' deposits in the bank. Since some of the brokers' deposits are at particular banks for the brokers' convenience or because of the banking services received by the brokers, the study sought to separate the portion of brokers' total demand deposits attributable to these factors from the portion attributable to the brokerage paid the banks.

with his Deputy Comptroller for Trusts, Dean E. Miller. The Study Group Director (DE) interviewed Mr. Miller:

> DE: The SEC Institutional Investor Study noted that widespread broker reciprocity exists. . . . In your examination of trust departments, does your office find this broker reciprocity to exist?
>
> MILLER: No, the SEC statistics are not valid.
>
> DE: Do you have figures to prove otherwise?
>
> MILLER: No.
>
> DE: When your examiners go into a bank, do they look to see what brokers the bank uses and if those brokers maintain reciprocal balances with the bank?
>
> MILLER: No, we do not do that type of analysis.
>
> DE: Then how could your examiners ever tell if broker reciprocity is taking place?
>
> MILLER: Well, our examiners ask the bank on what basis the bank is choosing its brokers. If the bank tells us they are choosing brokers because those brokers are the ones with deposits with the bank, we tell them that is illegal.
>
> DE: I can't imagine that a bank would come right out and admit that they were using brokerage to obtain deposits; do you think they would admit that?
>
> MILLER: No.[140]

In a speech delivered two months after the above interview, Miller expressed continued confidence in the Comptroller's present procedures:

> As you who are national bankers are aware, we have had an interest in this area for some time. Currently our examiners request a statement of the policy of the bank as to allocation of brokerage commissions. This does not satisfy the professional critics, who assume that bankers will willfully give false statements in writing to examiners. This has not been our experience, and until it is, we believe that the procedure is a meaningful check.[141]

All is not as hopeless as it may seem in the Comptroller's office. In February of 1972 Miller admitted that he was considering a change in the Comptroller's regulations to broaden the scope of trust department examinations to determine the basis for the bank's allocation of brokerage business and to investigate whether violations of the law have occurred.[142] As of August 1972, however, the Comptroller's office had not progressed to the point of publishing this as a proposed rule-making even though the President's Commission on Financial Structure and Regulation had made this same recommendation in its December, 1971 report.[143]

The Study Group spoke to some of the men who worked on the SEC Study, especially those who wrote the chapter about bank trust departments and broker reciprocity. One of the SEC men explained that he was assigned to interview trust officers at ten New York banks. He interviewed officers at nine banks but had no time to visit the tenth bank, which turned out to be Citibank.

Thomas Theobald told the Study Group:

> We [FNCB] have no deal with any broker, nor have we ever made one with any broker whereby we say, "You keep so much in deposits with us and we will reward you on a formula basis or any other kind of explicit or unexplicit arrangement." [144]

According to FNCB's Corporate Policy Manual:

> In selecting brokers, no recognition will be given to the fact that a broker maintains deposit balances with the Bank or transacts other business with IMG [i.e., FNCB's trust department] or other departments or branches of the Bank. IMG may, however, take account of research and statistical services provided by brokers, assuming that they also provide the best execution available.[145]

Interestingly, this paragraph was inserted into the Corporate Manual in November, 1970, just two months after banks received the broker reciprocity warning from the Justice Department.

When the Study Group spoke to a former executive from Citibank's trust department, he stated that brokers were usually chosen on the quality of their investment research, although it was not an unbreakable rule. The former executive recalled a case where a brokerage firm received a letter stating that because of the research furnished by your Mr. X in the past year, we (FNCB) are giving your firm $10,000 in commissions in the coming year. Mr. X had been dead for two years. The same executive remarked that the prevalent philosophy at

Citibank was, "We'd rather do business with our friends than those who are not our friends."

A request by the Study Group to Citibank for the information the bank furnished to the SEC about the bank's procedures for choosing brokers was denied. Raymond Sampson, head of FNCB's Personal Investment Division and an attorney, explained, "That's all confidential information." [146]

Those members of the Trust Board at Citibank who would talk with the Study Group were also asked whether reciprocal agreements ever existed between FNCB and specific brokers. The following exchange took place between the Study Group Director (DE) and William C. Greenough:

> DE: Does the fact that the broker might have commercial relationships with the bank influence the bank's choice of that broker?
> WCG: I doubt it, but I don't know.
> DE: Does the Trust Board discuss this sort of question?
> WCG: No.[147]

Richard Furlaud, another Trust Board member, believes that a strong effort is made to choose brokers on the basis of their ability to transact deals at the best price and also on the basis of the research they furnish to the bank. Mr. Furlaud asked the Study Group Director why he was suspicious about broker reciprocity. After hearing the SEC's statistics, Furlaud stated that he was not aware of a problem at Citibank.[148]

FNCB board member Frank Barnett was also interviewed about broker reciprocity.

> DE: Is broker reciprocity taking place?
> FB: This does not exist at Citibank.
> DE: Would you be in favor of requiring the bank to disclose to the public the names of those brokers with whom it deals and the amounts of deposits maintained by those brokers with the bank?
> FB: No.
> DE: Why?
> FB: That would be confidential information.
> DE: Suppose we look at it this way: the broker receives the *privilege* of getting the commissions, and therefore has the concomitant *responsibility* to disclose its balances at the bank.

FB: I would still not favor disclosure.

DE: Then how will the public ever really know whether or not reciprocity is taking place?

FB: They will just have to take the bank's word for it.[149]

The Study Group approached some of the other New York banks to determine what their procedures were. When Samuel Calloway, executive vice president in charge of Morgan Guaranty's $18 billion trust department, was asked if his bank engaged in broker reciprocity, he shouted, "Of course not, it's illegal." Mr. Calloway refused to provide the figures as to how much in brokerage commissions Morgan directed each year and how much in deposits the favored brokers maintained with the bank. By way of explanation and before hanging up the telephone, Calloway replied, "I did not call you to have you ask me questions. I just called to say that we are sorry Morgan will be unable to cooperate with the Nader study." [150]

C. W. Farnam, senior executive vice president at Bankers Trust, was asked if his bank engaged in broker reciprocity; in measured tones, he replied, "I am not in a position to answer that." Mr. Farnam, asked for a copy of that part of the questionnaire Bankers Trust filled out for the SEC relating to broker reciprocity, refused, saying, "We are not in a position to discuss the answers with organizations other than the SEC." [151] Because Chemical Bank was engaged in litigation with a trust beneficiary who charged that Chemical practiced broker reciprocity to her detriment,[152] Chemical explained that it could not answer any of the questions the Study Group had asked about its trust activities. Trust officers at Chase Manhattan Bank emphatically deny that their bank's trust department practices broker reciprocity, but refused to supply the SEC information on the grounds that it "contained a great deal of competitive information as well as detailed information concerning individual trust relationships." [153]

Helmut Andresen, Executive Vice President of the United States Trust Company, expressed his views for the record by writing in *Trusts and Estates* magazine:

> Take the matter of stock brokerage commissions which a trust department, any trust department, necessarily generates in the ordinary course of business: the volume only reflects the value

of the assets it has in its care. It is entirely proper, it seems to me, and would not fall within the definition of conflict of interest, if this leverage were used to attract reciprocal brokers' deposits or were used to compensate brokers for making available to your investment officers the fruits of their firm's independent research; I see no breach of trust in so recognizing a community of interest.[154]

Andresen wrote that in 1968, two years before the Justice Department's warning. In June, 1972, the Study Group asked Mr. Andresen if he still felt that broker reciprocity was entirely proper. He replied, "Oh, I don't know; I haven't given it much thought since I wrote that article." We asked Andresen if U.S. Trust Company still uses brokerage business to obtain time deposits. "No," Andresen replied. "When did U.S. Trust change its policies?" the Study Group asked. "That's really not my province," Mr. Andresen answered.[155]

Because of the lack of cooperation by the New York commercial banks, because of the lack of publicly available information about trust department procedures, and because even the Comptroller does not examine for reciprocal agreements, the future of broker reciprocity remains uncertain. The SEC unequivocally found it to exist; but the alleged perpetrators deny vehemently that it does.

We therefore asked the SEC for the data the banks submitted to the 1970 study. The SEC replied:

> The Institutional Investor Study Data to which you request access, were collected on a confidential basis. Therefore, disclosure of individual reports cannot be permitted.[156]

If the SEC's findings had been negative or even if they had been equivocal, one could understand its reluctance to release its data. But the SEC found that the banks were blatantly violating the law. The SEC's position amounts to concealing conclusive evidence of a crime. This posture is unpardonable, especially for an agency charged with protecting the public from the very abuses uncovered in the study.

Fortunately, the courts are a last resort for an individual; at present, two people have taken their cases to court.[157] Perdita Schaffner, a beneficiary of a trust managed by Chemical Bank, and Sophie Ruskay, a beneficiary of a trust managed by Morgan Guaranty, are suing those banks, alleging that the banks have engaged in broker reciprocity to their detriment. The gist of both actions, as explained in the Schaffner complaint is:

> Since 1938 and before, defendant [Chemical Bank] has entered into understandings with several broker-dealers, the names of whom are to the plaintiff [Mrs. Schaffner] at this time unknown. The essence of these understandings has been and is "reciprocal business," that is, that defendant agrees to allocate the securities purchase and sale business of its beneficiaries to broker-dealers to the extent that they place their deposit and brokers' loan business with defendant. This "reciprocal business" really amounts to "mutual back scratching." [158]

The complaint charges that the practice of broker reciprocity is:

> In restraint of trade and as such violates the Sherman Antitrust Laws.
>
> A material fact which must be disclosed in connection with purchase and sale of securities. In that the practice was not disclosed to Mrs. Schaffner, Chemical Bank violated the Securities Exchange Act of 1934.
>
> A device used to pay interest on demand deposits, in violation of the law that banks which are members of the federal reserve system shall not directly or indirectly pay interest on demand deposits.
>
> A practice by which Chemical breached its fiduciary duties and warranties not to make profits for itself from the trust other than administration charges.
>
> A practice by which Chemical breached its fiduciary duties to preserve the assets of the trust and not to convert for its own sums charged against the trust.

Both Mrs. Schaffner and Mrs. Ruskay seek to enjoin Morgan and Chemical from engaging in broker reciprocity and to recover damages. These damages include the extra expense of a broker commission instead of a commissionless deal on the third market and the profits made by the banks on the reciprocal deposits.

Win or lose, the Schaffner and Ruskay cases may force banks to be more open about their trust investment procedures.* How-

---

* On April 4, 1973, both the Schaffner and Ruskay cases were discontinued by stipulation of the parties (i.e., the parties agreed to drop the suits). This was prompted by the fact that class-action status had been denied and also by the threat that if the beneficiaries lost the suit they, or possibly the trusts themselves, might be subject to exorbitant charges by the banks for costs the banks incurred in defending the suits. The discontinuance of these cases is unfortunate; it undoubtedly will delay public

ever, especially in light of the SEC's findings, the burden of proof should no longer be on individual plaintiffs who must enter into expensive litigation to uncover facts that the SEC already has in its possession. Banks should now have the affirmative duty publicly to report which brokers they use for trust transactions, how those brokers are chosen, and what deposits those brokers maintain with the bank.

A trust department can also convert trust monies to its own use by leaving some trust funds uninvested. The leftover money is at the disposal of the bank's loan department. Throughout the course of a year, every trust portfolio will have idle cash —dividend checks coming in and awaiting distribution or new cash contributions from employers awaiting investment, for instance.

In big bank trust departments, the amount of idle cash is enormous. According to the Federal Reserve Bank of New York, in 1971 ten large New York banks realized profits of $114,062,000 attributable to these balances. The banks use this money, in effect making short-term, interest-free loans to themselves. Without these credits, the trust departments at those banks would not have been profitable.[159]

Six-Year Trend of Trust Department Income and Expenses
For Ten Large New York City Banks
(in thousands)

Whole Trust Department	Total Commissions and Fees	Total Expenses	Net Operating Earnings Before Income Taxes	Allowed Credits for Deposits	Trust Department Net Earnings
1966	215,096.1	180,947.6	34,148.5	66,543.2	100,961.7
1967	237,047.3	209,925.7	27,121.6	77,345.5	104,467.1
1968	266,942.7	260,180.4	6,762.3	106,889.5	113,651.8
1969	307,194.0	320,402.6	—13,208.6	137,083.4	123,875.8
1970	332,455.1	364,724.0	—32,268.9	155,972.1	123,703.2
1971	360,471.0	378,811.0	—18,340.0	114,062.0	95,722.0

George Lingua, head of FNCB's Institutional Investment Group, asserts that "Fees are the way we make our bread," [160] and contends that Citibank earns nothing more than the fixed

---

exposure of an illegal banking practice that the SEC unequivocally found to exist on a wide scale. The discontinuance emphasizes the need for strong class-action legislation and vigorous prosecution by public regulators when illegalities are uncovered.

management fees from trust accounts. The aggregate statistics compiled by the Federal Reserve Bank of New York belie Mr. Lingua's conclusion. The Federal Reserve Bank refused to give us a breakdown on the profits and losses of each of the ten bank trust operations it examined, and Citibank refused to provide us with the average daily amount of uninvested cash maintained in its trust portfolios; nevertheless, it is extraordinarily unlikely that FNCB varies much from the pattern of the ten banks together.

A former portfolio manager at Citibank told the Study Group that Citibank tried to be careful about letting idle cash accumulate in trust accounts:

> Every two weeks each portfolio manager would receive a computer print-out listing the amounts of uninvested cash in the portfolios under his supervision. But if a manager was lax about investing extra cash, no one pushed him too hard to do it.

In the view of one investment manager: "It is obviously both bad investing and unethical to let cash balances sit around in any account when there is something you can do with it." [161] The point is that there are things that can be done with these balances. For instance, part of the money can be used to make one-day broker call loans, which in 1971 had average yields of close to 5.5%. At least one bank, the Citizens and Southern National Bank of Georgia, uses idle cash to buy shares in short-term loans to corporations.[162] Certainly part, if not all, of the uninvested cash balances that resulted in the $114 million credit to the large New York bank trust departments could have been invested for the benefit of those banks' trust clients.

That the banks used the money for their own ends instead is, in our opinion, a violation of their fiduciary duty. The law on the subject is clear:

> Funds held in a fiduciary capacity by a national bank awaiting investment or distribution shall not be held uninvested or undistributed *any longer than is reasonable* for the proper management of the account. (emphasis added)
> Funds held in trust by a national bank . . . awaiting investment or distribution may, unless prohibited by the instrument creating the trust or by local law, be deposited in the commercial or savings or other department of the bank, provided it shall first set aside under control of the trust department as collateral security [U.S. bonds or other approved securities].[163]

The Comptroller of the Currency's office claims that it scrutinizes cash balances in trust departments to ensure that this regulation is complied with. But the adequacy of the examinations is doubtful. Question D-8 on the Comptroller's examination form asks, "Are cash balances eligible for investment held uninvested for an unreasonable length of time?" [164] But that question need not be answered; it is intended to serve merely "as a form of outline or guide." As of February, 1972, the Comptroller was considering a requirement that "Such reviews shall include the amount of uninvested cash in each account and a justification of the retention of any balances," [165] but as of November, 1972 no action had been taken to implement it.

The courts are still undecided as to what constitutes a "reasonable time" for cash to be left uninvested. The United Mine Workers Pension Fund was sued successfully, but that was an extreme case:

> When they say that the most important benefits are the ones you don't know about, just try to figure out the ones that belong to the *United Mine Workers.* For some 20 years, the UMW Pension & Welfare Fund assets have been *sitting in a checking account* with the National Bank of Washington, doing nothing, *not collecting a cent in interest.* Nobody knows why or how, and nobody ain't telling . . . not even the actual amount, which has been estimated at about $50 million. Now that the courts have ordered the pension fund money withdrawn and put elsewhere where it can earn a dollar, the big question is *what will National Bank of Washington do about the $11.5 million that the courts insist must be added to the pot* to make up for what the money would have earned if invested all those years.[166]

Other courts have held trustees liable for leaving $104,000 uninvested for 14 years,[167] leaving $100,000 uninvested two years,[168] failing to invest dividends adding up to $47,000 for more than five years,[169] and letting $20,000 lie fallow for eighteen months.[170] The courts, apparently, have not decided whether professional trustees are liable for keeping smaller sums uninvested for shorter periods, when short-term investments are available. For example, what of the trust that receives dividends of $400 on January 10, although money is not paid to the beneficiaries until February 1 (the beginning of the next month) or even April 1 (the beginning of the next quarter)? It is from these relatively small sums that the New York banks realized $155 million in 1970 and $114 million in 1971.[171]

According to common law, a trustee may not use trust funds for his own benefit and must return all private profit (excluding trustee fees) made from such funds. Thus, banks should return to trust beneficiaries all profit made from uninvested trust money.

A third way a bank uses trust funds for its own benefit is by investing them in companies that have commercial ties to the bank—loans, deposits, or interlocking directors. According to the SEC:

> The fact that an institution has a business relationship—as creditor, depository or employee benefit plan manager—with a company whose shares it holds may simply reflect a mutually advantageous arrangement. On the other hand, such a situation presents an inherent conflict of interest, however innocent its origin.[172]

There is nothing wrong per se with a trust department's investing in companies commercially related to the bank if the investment is a purely financial one, based on objective financial criteria and designed to achieve maximum returns with minimum risk. As for the returns that banks have achieved, according to William Dreher's study, most bank-managed pension funds do not outperform the market average. Richard Cantor offers one explanation:

> America's largest companies have pension funds which they invest through America's largest banks, which in turn buy shares in America's largest companies, which offer less than the most attractive returns in the marketplace.[173]

A recent challenge to such relationships has been brought against Bankers Trust Company, former trustee of the Bakery Drivers Local 816 Labor and Management Pension Trust Fund.[174] The present trustees allege that Bankers Trust invested the fund in "private offerings of some of its customers with whom the trustee had business relationships"; to purchase "low grade stocks and bonds in companies with which the trustee had business relations"; and to make loans to its commercial clients at low interest rates. The administrators contend that the fund had an average annual rate of return of less than .7% while similar funds were earning between 6% and 10%.[175] This case has not yet been tried on the merits.

Sometimes the conflict of interest arises not with the decision to buy a commercially related company's stock as with the decision not to sell it. As the SEC describes the situation:

> A large institutional shareholder may have the economic power to compel a portfolio company to do business with it; at the same time, its concern for the maintenance of good business relationships with a company might tend to deter the institution from using its shareholdings—by voting or otherwise— to oppose corporate management *or from disposing of portfolio company shares.* Such business relationships may also have anticompetitive impacts. (emphasis added) [176]

This problem recently arose with some stocks that Chase Manhattan Bank, as investment advisor, was holding for its pension trust accounts. Allegedly, Chase recommended Villager Industries stock to three pension funds. Chase at the time was a creditor of Villager and a participant in its financial affairs. It is contended that despite the decline of the stock, Chase never advised the funds to sell. Now the three pension funds are suing Chase for $301,739, the difference between the value of the Villager stock when it was purchased and the value when it was sold.[177] The funds allege that Chase, as a creditor of Villager, acted in its own interest contrary to the interest of the pension fund, and that Chase had a duty either to disclose its interest in Villager or to tell the pension funds that it was disqualified from advising them with respect to Villager stock.

Banks refuse to disclose the extent of their commercial relationships with their corporate clients, making it all the more difficult for trust clients and the public to assess whether trust departments are investing to obtain maximum returns or whether they are investing, say, to bolster the stock price of debtor corporations or to finance loans to favored commercial clients. However, one kind of commercial tie that a bank cannot keep secret is its interlocking directorships.

The men who have recently served and who are presently serving on Citibank's Board of Directors, include:

Albert L. Williams	Chairman of the Executive Committee, IBM
Joseph C. Wilson	Former Chairman of the Board, Xerox

Dr. Louis K. Eilers	Chairman and Chief Executive Officer, Eastman Kodak
Milo Brisco	President, Exxon
Gordon M. Metcalf	Chairman of the Board, Sears, Roebuck and Company
M. Cabell Woodward, Jr.	President, ITT Continental Baking
Amory Houghton, Jr.	Chairman of the Board, Corning Glass Works
Charles B. McCoy	President, E. I. Dupont de Nemours & Company
Robert S. Oelman	Chairman, The National Cash Register Company
John D. deButts	Chairman, AT&T
William M. Batten	Chairman, J. C. Penney

Among the 50 largest holdings of Citibank's trust department, one finds: [178]

IBM (1) *
Xerox (2)
Eastman Kodak (5)
Exxon (9)
Sears, Roebuck and Co. (10)
ITT (14)
Corning Glass Works (15)
E. I. Dupont de Nemours & Co. (26)
The National Cash Register Co. (30)
AT&T (37)
J. C. Penney (46)

According to the SEC's 1970 report:

> To the extent that an institution might otherwise be in a position to influence corporate policy, the existence of personnel interlocks will tend to increase the opportunity to exercise such influence.[179]

---

* Number in parentheses refers to rank of holding in trust department.

In an attempt to discover how a chief executive officer of a company whose stock constitutes a major holding of a bank's trust portfolio views his position as a director of that bank, the Study Group tried to contact each man personally. We were especially anxious to reach Albert Williams because he chairs Citibank's Examining Committee, but Mr. Williams answered neither the letter nor the questionnaire the Study Group sent him.*

A similar letter and questionnaire were sent to Joseph Wilson, but Mr. Wilson died before the letter was received.

A similar letter went to Dr. Eilers, whose office replied:

> I wish to acknowledge your December 23 letter because it arrived while Dr. Eilers is away from the office. Your letter will be held for Dr. Eilers to read when he has the opportunity but, in the meantime, I thought I should advise you that it is unlikely that Dr. Eilers will want to take the time to respond to the questions enclosed in your letter.[180]

Dr. Eilers never replied.

On December 14, 1971, the Study Group Director (DE), who himself is a shareholder and depositor of the bank, called Milo Brisco's office. His secretary said that Mr. Brisco was not in and asked the purpose of the call. DE explained the nature of this study and the need to obtain the views of FNCB board members on the bank's trust activities. DE then left his name and the telephone number of the office he was working from, nine blocks from Mr. Brisco's. Three days later DE called again; the secretary said she had relayed the message and Mr. Brisco had told her to reply, "Mr. Brisco does not have any views on banking and does not see any reason why he should." The secretary suggested writing to Mr. Brisco. On December 23, DE wrote Mr. Brisco a letter similar to those written to the other directors. A month later, the following reply came from Terry A. Kirkley, Executive Assistant to Mr. Brisco:

> Mr. Brisco asked that I acknowledge receipt of your letter of December 23, 1971. I have referred your letter to Mr. C. W. Desch of the First National City Bank.

* See Appendix, p. 363, for copy of letter and questionnaire sent to FNCB Directors.

On January 31, 1972, DE wrote Mr. Brisco:

> Thank you for having your executive assistant, Mr. Kirkley, acknowledge receipt of my letter of December 23, 1971 to you, asking your views of First National City Bank's trust activities.
>   I was surprised to note that Mr. Kirkley referred my letter to Mr. C. W. Desch of First National City Bank. It is *your* views, from your perspective as a Citibank Board member, that I am seeking, not the views of Mr. Desch.
>   . . . I would greatly appreciate your answering the questions about Citibank's trust activities. If you would prefer our meeting together and discussing your ideas, it would be my pleasure to arrange such a meeting at your convenience. I have already spoken at length with Messrs. Greenough, Furlaud, and Barnett and I feel all parties concerned learned much from those discussions.

One week later DE received the following (somewhat familiar) reply from Mr. Kirkley:

> Mr. Brisco asked that I acknowledge receipt of your letter of January 31, 1972. I have referred your letter to Mr. C. W. Desch of the First National City Bank.

On February 17 DE again wrote Mr. Brisco:

> Please explain to me why you continually ask your executive assistant, Mr. Kirkley, to refer letters I send you to Mr. Desch at Citibank. As I mentioned to you in my last letter, it is *your* views, not those of Mr. Desch that we are interested in . . . .
>   My offer to meet with you at your convenience of course remains open.

Mr. Brisco did not reply.

DE also wrote Messrs. Gordon Metcalf and Cabell Woodward, who never replied.

On December 17, 1971, DE called Mr. Amory Houghton, Jr. Mr. Houghton expressed a sincere desire to meet with Study Group members but a convenient time could not be arranged since he spends much of his time in Corning, New York. However, Mr. Houghton's position differs somewhat from that of other directors we tried to contact: much of the Corning Glass stock that Citibank's trust deparment holds consists of stock owned and controlled by the Houghtons themselves, not the bank.

DE wrote Robert Oelman, who answered, "because of an extremely busy schedule, it is necessary for me to make a general response to the detailed questionnaire which you sent me." Mr. Oelman wrote:

> ... In summary, during the nine years I have served as a director of the First National City Bank, all evidence that has come to my attention indicates that the Bank's trust division conducts its business entirely independent of the commercial banking activities. Insofar as I am aware, these trust division operations are handled in a highly competent manner.[181]

On the fourth try, DE reached Mr. John deButts on the telephone. Mr. deButts refused to be interviewed because our preliminary report (on Citibank's commercial activities) allegedly contained "many inaccuracies." DE asked Mr. deButts if he had read the report and Mr. deButts said that he had. DE asked Mr. deButts to specify some of the inaccuracies. DeButts refused. DE contended that if deButts were unwilling to specify inaccuracies, perhaps that was because there were none.

DeButts replied, "That is just the sort of stuff your report is made of. I refuse to point out a mistake and you accuse me of not being able to." DE asked deButts to what extent, as Chairman of AT&T and as a director of Citibank, he felt responsible to the public. DeButts answered, "I am responsible only to the shareholders of the bank, and even they have no right to question bank policies and look at bank records." DeButts concluded by saying that he did not feel any need to answer further questions. He said goodbye and hung up.[182]

On December 14, 1971, DE called William Batten's office and left his name and phone number after being told by a secretary that Mr. Batten was out of the office that day and would "return to a very busy schedule." On December 21, DE called Mr. Batten's office, was told "Mr. Batten is out of the building today," and left his name and number. On January 11, 1972, Mr. Batten was "in a meeting." On January 20, DE spoke to Mr. Batten. Mr. Batten said,

> It would be a waste of time to talk to you because I don't feel that I have anything to contribute. I am not a knowledgeable person about what goes on at the bank. My views are not worth much because they are not informed views.

"If you are not knowledgeable about the bank's activities," DE asked, "what role do you play on Citibank's Board of Directors?"

"That is a different question, one which I do not wish to be interviewed about over the phone," Batten stated.

"Then let us sit down together at your convenience and discuss it," DE suggested.

Mr. Batten declined the offer.

DE suggested to Mr. Batten that potential conflicts of interest existed between the trust activities and the commercial activities of the bank.

"I am not aware of any conflicts," Mr. Batten asserted.

DE gave Mr. Batten a hypothetical: "Suppose the trust department owns stock in a company with director interlocks and commercial ties to the bank—"

"Look, Mr. Etra, I told you that I do not want a hit-and-miss interview over the phone," Mr. Batten interrupted.

"Then let us meet together and discuss some of these things," DE again suggested.

"No," said Batten.

Batten suggested that if any studies were to be made of the bank they should be made by the proper regulatory authorities.

"In your opinion, are those agencies doing a good job?" DE asked.

"I really haven't the slightest idea," Batten replied. "I do not want to hang up on you, Mr. Etra, but I believe that I have explained my position to you."

DE asked Mr. Batten that if he changed his mind and decided to become more actively interested in the bank on whose board he sits, he should call. Mr. Batten never called.

The responses that we received raise serious questions about the directors' own qualifications. If, as two directors put it, they truly are not knowledgeable about banking or the bank, then those directors have violated their legal duty as directors of a national bank "to diligently and honestly administer the affairs of such association," [183] and should be removed.

According to First National City's *Policy Regarding Conflicts of Interest:*

A possible conflict of interest exists whenever a director, officer or employee or a member of his immediate family has an interest, direct or indirect, in an entity dealing with the Corporation and the interest is of such an extent or nature that his decisions might be affected or determined by it.

Each of the directors the Study Group tried to contact is (or was) an executive officer of his respective company. The stock of those companies are among the largest holdings of FNCB's trust department; those companies also have other commercial ties to the bank. According to the bank's own policy, in each case "a possible conflict of interest exists." In light of these "possible conflicts," we recommend that such directors either resign or disclose every commercial relationship their companies have with the bank and the nature of every vote they cast in director meetings. The public has a right to know if the conflicts are truly only "possible."

A fourth way a bank can use trust funds to its own advantage is by investing them in the bank's own stock. Both laws and commentators discuss this practice. The *Comptroller's Manual for National Banks* states:

> Unless lawfully authorized by the instrument creating the relationship or by court order or by local law, funds held by a national bank as fiduciary shall not be invested in stock . . . of . . . the bank. . . .[184]

However, we have already seen that Citibank's boilerplate trust forms explicitly authorize the retention and investment in FNCC stock, thus bypassing the Comptroller's regulations. *The Restatement of Trusts* reiterates the rule that investment by a corporate trustee in its own stock is improper without authorization, and goes on to state:

> If, however, because of circumstances which are known or ought to be known to the trustee the retention is or becomes imprudent, it becomes the duty of the trustee to dispose of the shares within a reasonable time.[185]

Scott, in his treatise on trusts, provides the following commentary:

> It is quite true that under ordinary circumstances there is in fact no actual conflict of interest; but there is a possibility that circumstances may arise in which there is a conflict of interest. The rule of undivided loyalty is based upon this possible conflict. The trustee and its officers and directors are in a position where in determining whether to sell or to retain in the trust the stock of the trustee they cannot approach the problem with the same detachment with which they could approach the problem of selling other securities.[186]

In 1970, Citibank's trust department, through various nominees, owned 1,232,198 shares of FNCC stock. This works out to 4.5% of the outstanding shares, more than any other stockholder. Altogether, in 1970 the trust departments of the six largest New York City banks owned 4,523,659 shares of FNCC stock, or 16.6% of all outstanding shares.[187]

Even if these extensive holdings by Citibank's trust department are not enough to enable the bank to hold virtual control of FNCC, it still must be asked at what point to draw the line— how much of its own stock can a trust department hold before a real conflict arises? In answer, we feel Scott's observation is the best guideline; fiduciaries must not only avoid actual conflicts, but the rule of undivided loyalty applies to potential conflicts as well. Thus we would recommend that a bank not be permitted to have any voting control whatsoever over its own stock held in its trust department.

2. Type Two Conflict: Bank and Employer Versus Employee

In theory, employer and employees want the same thing from their pension fund—maximum return with safety. The employer wants a good return to keep his own contributions to the fund down. The employees want a good return to ensure that there will be enough assets in the fund to pay pensions and even to increase them. As long as this community of interest exists, a bank has no difficulty as a pension trustee. Problems arise when the employer makes demands on the bank inconsistent with the best interests of the employees: an employer asks the pension trustee for a loan out of the pension fund at a low interest rate; an employer, concerned about the declining price of its stock, asks the bank to invest part of the pension fund in the employer's own stock to boost its price; an employer wishes to sell a piece of realty and, finding no buyer, asks the pension fund to buy it, for an inflated price. Faced with such demands, the bank must choose whether to accede to the employer, thereby sacrificing the return and the safety of the pension fund, or whether to refuse the employer, thereby risking the loss of the fund as a trust client and the loss of the employer as a commercial client. The bank's position is further complicated by other relationships it may enjoy with the employer, such as common directors, outstanding loans, and holdings of the employer's stock in other trusts. The 1968 congressional staff study strikingly revealed that if a large bank serves as pension trustee for a major corporation, it almost invariably has other commercial ties with the firm. The SEC's 1970 study confirmed this relationship.[188] According to the chart on page 240, this holds true for Citibank as well; for the most part, when FNCB acts as trustee for a major company's employee benefit fund, FNCB either has a director interlock with the company or holds the company's stock in its trust department.

A closer look at the relationships between pension trustees and employers reveals that where there are director interlocks and large stock holdings, there are often substantial loans as well. While FNCB was serving as pension trustee for two Anaconda pension funds Anaconda was borrowing up to $19.2 million from FNCB.[189] At that time, among Anaconda's directors were James D. Farley, an executive vice president of FNCB, and Robert L. Hoguet, who was then head of FNCB's trust department and an executive vice president at the bank. While FNCB was managing Allied Chemical Corporation's pension plan, Allied was indebted to FNCB for various amounts ranging up to $23 million, and Richard Perkins, a member of Allied's board, was also Chairman of FNCB's Executive Committee.[190] While FNCB was investment manager for part of two Monsanto pension funds, Monsanto was borrowing up to $45 million from FNCB.[191] Sitting on Monsanto's Board of Directors at the time were Charles Sommer, a Director of FNCB, James S. Rockefeller, former Chairman of FNCB, and Frederick Eaton, a partner in Shearman & Sterling, FNCB's law firm.

The very fact of such corporate interlocks is significant. It shows that the people in charge know one another and are likely to make deals and direct business in each other's direction. The key question is whether this situation hurts anyone. Is influence exercised to anyone's detriment? Do companies choose pension trustees on the basis of objective investment considerations or on the basis of which bank they do business with? There are no definite answers, but the fact remains, as evidenced by Dreher's, Hansen's, and Cantor's studies, that banks have not produced

Company	Employee Benefit Funds Managed By Citibank	Director Interlocks	Percentage of Outstanding Stock Held By Bank (when in excess of 5%)
Blue Diamond	1	—	15.0–C*
Panoil Company	1		5.2–C
General Foods Corporation	2	2	—
National Distillers and Chemical Corporation	2	1	12.4–P
Wyomissing Corporation	2	1	—
St. Regis Paper Company	1	2	—
Monsanto Company	2	2	—
Allied Chemical Corporation	1	1	—
Colgate-Palmolive Company	2	1	—
Exxon	1	1	—
Phillips Petroleum Company	6	1	6.6–C
Sinclair Oil Corporation	1	2	—
Corning Glass Works	**4**	**2**	**8.5–C***
Anaconda Company	2	2	—
Phelps Dodge Corporation	1	1	—
Scovill Manufacturing Company	1	—	15.8–P
American Can Company	1	2	—
National Cash Register Company	1	2	—
Westinghouse Electric Corporation	2	1	6.6–P
International Telephone & Telegraph	4	1	—
Borg-Warner Corporation	1	1	—
ACF Industries, Inc.	1	1	—
Oneida, Ltd.	1	—	5.5–C
Merchants Refrigerating Company	3	—	10.2–C
Pan American World Airways	2	1	—
Consolidated Edison Company of New York, Inc.	1	2	6.1–P
Panhandle Eastern Pipe Line Company	4	—	9.5–P
Intermountain Gas Company	1	1	—
Consumers Power Company	4	1	—
Mercantile Stores Company, Inc.	1	2	—
Jewel Companies, Inc.	2	—	6.0–C
City Investing Company	1	1	—
Foote, Cone & Belding, Inc.	1	—	6.6–C

* C=Common Stock
P=Preferred Stock

SOURCE: U.S., Congress, House, Banking and Currency Committee, *Commercial Banks and their Trust Activities,* 1968.

impressive returns for pension funds. The most important consequence of poor pension fund performance is the decreased likelihood that employees will obtain increased pension benefits.

One healthy sign in the whole pension business is that more and more employers are parcelling out their pension business, often to independent money managers. This trend presages a renaissance in competition for the pension fund market. One continuing unhealthy sign is the presence of bank-trusteed pension plans invested in securities of the employer.

On the face of it, there appears to be nothing wrong with investing a benefit plan in the employer's own enterprise, especially if the employer is solvent and profitable. However, the danger of the practice becomes apparent when the rationale and the mechanics of a pension plan are more closely examined.

A pension fund is established to provide money in the future for employees who have qualified for pensions. The employer could have chosen a pay-as-you-go plan, paying pensions out of current income each year. But the tax advantages of a separately funded plan, and employee pressure to be secure in the knowledge that they will receive pensions, usually induce the employer to set up a pension fund. As long as the assets in the pension trust are adequate to meet present and future liabilities, the vested employees are entirely assured of getting their pensions even if the employer goes out of business. If the trust is underfunded, i.e., the assets are less than the accumulated liabilities, the vested employee still has a good chance of receiving his pension as long as the employer himself is solvent. But the employee runs severe risk of losing out if his pension fund is underfunded *and* his employer is insolvent. In that situation, the employee's earned right to a pension is worthless. According to Paul Harbrecht, "it is not mere alarmism to point out that pension expectations depend on the solvency and continued existence of the employer," [192] especially since most pension plans are underfunded.

To protect pensions, common sense dictates that the fortunes of the pension fund not be tied to the fortunes of the company:

> When you buy the company stock you are, in effect, undoing the funding the company has done, because you're putting the employees back in the situation where they are dependent entirely on the future of the company. [193]

Bank trustees do not always follow this advice. After hearing a description of a plan whose assets were partially invested in real estate of the employer (its own office building), Senator Javits reflected,

> . . . think of the barn door it opens when the assets of the pension fund go down the drain at the same time with a company. And most of them are materially under-funded and the worker is left holding the bag.[194]

A further problem with the above pension plan was that the real estate mortgaged to the pension fund was alleged to be greatly overvalued. The president of the employer company sat on the board of the bank trustee.

As long as the trust agreement does not specifically prohibit it—and few FNCB-managed plans do—the trustee is free to invest the fund in the employer's assets. The trustee must merely be able to justify his investment as one which a reasonably prudent man would make.[195] Even a provision in a trust agreement prohibiting investments in the employer's stock does not deter some pension trustees. The Senate subcommittee noted that a large communications company, whose plan's assets exceeded $229 million, had $11 million of those assets invested in the employer's subsidiaries' securities, despite a provision in the plan itself prohibiting such related investments.[196]

The large New York banks are also prone to investing pension funds in employer-related enterprises. F. W. Woolworth Company's pension fund, managed by the Irving Trust Company of New York, has $115 million in assets, 26.7% of which is invested in real estate and mortgages of F. W. Woolworth Co. itself.[197]

Added to the potential disaster to employees' pensions is the continual problem of self-dealing. Even when the trustee is used as a conduit to purchase employer assets for the pension, since the transaction is not an arm's length one, there is no guarantee that the pension fund will not be charged a higher-than-market price for the assets or that the pension fund will be forced to accept a lower-than-market rate on the mortgage.

As of 1967, the following companies whose employee benefit plans were trusteed by Citibank had the following amounts of their funds in the companies' own securities: [198]

CITIBANK-MANAGED EMPLOYEE BENEFIT FUNDS INVESTED
IN FOUNDING CORPORATIONS SECURITIES

Name of Corporation Establishing Trust	Number of Employee Benefit Trusts	Trust Investments in Founding Corporation Securities
Allied Chemical Corporation	1	11,016 common
American Maize Products Company	1	23,564 common
American Natural Gas Company	4	120,711 common
American Sugar Company	2	$300,000 note at 5.30%
		$200,000 note at 5.30%
		20,000 preferred
American Tobacco Company	3	434,438 common
Boeing Company	3	215,109 capital
Caterpillar Tractor Company	1	9,000 common
Colgate-Palmolive Peet Company	1	363,468 common
Commonwealth Oil Refining Company	3	510 common
Consumer Power Company and Michigan Gas Storage Company	2	125,821 common
Corning Glass Works	3	986 common
Diamond International Corporation	1	98,178 common
Discount Corporation of America	1	650 capital
Ethyl Corporation	6	193,159 common
Exxon	1	41,986 capital
FMC Corporation	4	9,000 common
Foot, Cone & Belding, Inc.	1	113,752 common
General American Investors Company	1	8,597 common
IT&T Corporation	4	4,887 common
Lehman Corporation	1	21,755 common
McGregor Donizer, Inc.	2	3,700 common
Merchants Refrigerating Company	2	27,859 common
Monsanto Company	2	17,985 common
National Tea Company	1	15,028 common
Oneida, Ltd.	1	2,800 preferred
		72,998 common
Owens-Corning Fiberglas Corporation	1	71,539 common
Pan American World Airways	1	Convertible debenture reg., $60,000 at 4½%
Panhandle Eastern Pipe Line Company	2	119,181 common
Phillips Petroleum Company	6	2,131,022 common
Safeway Stores, Inc.	1	465,994 common
Sarco Manufacturing Corporation	2	302 preferred
Tidewater Marine Service	1	188 common
Wickes Corporation	1	129,600 common
J. R. Wood & Sons, Inc.	7	2,500 capital

SOURCE: *Trust Assets of Insured Commercial Banks—1970,* Board of Governors of the Federal Reserve System, Federal Deposit Insurance Corporation, office of the Comptroller of the Currency, Table 27, p. 524.

The list illustrates that Citibank, too, will invest employee benefit funds in employer-related assets. Sometimes these investments will be dictated by the employer himself; in that case, Citibank can try to disclaim responsibility. The crucial question is, however, whether such a disclaimer should be permissible to a bank trustee. It is not surprising that many of the companies (e.g., Allied Chemical, Corning, ITT, Ethyl, Monsanto, and Exxon) also have director interlocks and outstanding loans with the bank.

One added advantage to the employer in coopting the pension trustee to invest in employer stock is that the fund-owned stock will be captive stock. The banks themselves admit that they almost always vote for stock they hold for management. Especially if the bank holds employer stock in an employer pension fund, it would be rare for a bank to vote against management— after all, it's the same management that decided to give the bank its pension business in the first place.

Those involved in the operation of pension plans disagree on whether pension monies should be allowed to finance employer-related activities. Richard Furlaud, a member of Citibank's Trust Board, told us that while he did not favor investing pension funds in the employer company's stock and believed that Citibank did not do so, he said he would see nothing wrong in such an investment if the stock in question were a well-known stock with sufficient liquidity.[198]

Preston Bassett, a management consultant who serves as an advisor to many pension funds, contends that an overall proscription against the use of pensions to finance employers would hurt some pension funds; they would miss out on some good investments. Bassett illustrated his point by citing the case of Litton Industries, which recently sold $500,000 of its bonds to Prudential Life Insurance and this sale served to establish the going price for the bonds. Litton then proceeded to sell the rest of its bonds to its own pension fund.[199] The wisdom of Bassett's reasoning is somewhat marred by the fact that now Litton itself is on the verge of collapse.

Some employers ask: Why use someone else's money if you can use your own? The trouble with that kind of thinking is that an employer who uses his company's pension fund is not borrowing from himself; he is using what is rightfully the property of the employees.

Fortunately, this seems to be one area that evokes a strong re-action from the Comptroller's office. In a recent speech Deputy Comptroller Dean Miller asserted:

> . . . the philosophy held by some of them [lawyers and pension fund consultants] that a company may freely make use of its employee benefit trusts as sources of capital, to the full extent permitted by tax laws, is a continuing source of difficulty for all of us . . .[200]

The occasion for this speech was the annual Mid-Winter Trust Conference of the American Banking Association. Most of the speech related to proposed revisions of trust regulations. At one point, however, Miller squarely faced his audience, and said:

> Speaking personally, *I would hope that there be enacted abso-lute prohibitions on the investment of funds of employee benefit trusts in any employer-related media*—its stock, property leased to it, loans to it—whatever. Our experience with direction trusts and the continued efforts of some of you to get absolution for closing your eyes to them, have contributed to this conviction. *Some day a large number of employees are going to have their retirement expectations dashed because our tax laws do not sufficiently prevent the use of employee benefit funds by employ-ers as an additional source of capital.* I hope banks don't get tarnished in the process, but I'm afraid that it will happen as long as you keep accepting these trusts and whining that your only course of action is exculpation.[201]

The one way to eliminate conflicts between the interests of the bank and employer and the interests of the employees is to entrust pension funds only to managers who have no commer-cial ties to the employer. Essentially this means giving pension management to independent money managers, to trust depart-ments not affiliated with commercial banks, or to bank trustees with no other business with the employer. As we have already urged, the best solution is to create new institutions, federally regulated and insured, whose sole responsibility is pension fund management. Under our proposed system, where employees would select their own pension managers, there would be no op-portunity for an employer to coopt a pension fund for his own use.

As long as pension funds continue to be managed by banks, they and other pension trustees should be held to a strict fiduciary standard; any investment in employer-related enterprises should be deemed a breach of that standard.

3. Type Three Conflict: Trust Client Versus Trust Client

A bank can pick and choose among its trust accounts to ensure that favored accounts get better treatment. Such a problem is impossible to prove without complete access to the activity records of all trust portfolios managed by a bank. Bankers contend that they treat all trust accounts equally, although sometimes biases do appear; at least one trust officer has remarked, "Small accounts have few virtues in themselves and a profit margin is bound to be nearly nonexistent." According to a former Citibank portfolio manager, attached to each portfolio is an index card, listing not only the investment needs of the client, but also the other relationships the client has with the bank and some indication of the relative importance of the account to the bank. Citibank refused to affirm or deny this.

Ways in which a bank can favor one client over another include giving one client the first opportunity to purchase new offerings or to benefit from advice to sell. As noted earlier, while the SEC tries to monitor such situations to make sure no one is allowed to bail out first, trust officers still concede that one account always has to be placed on the top of the pile. One such officer admits:

> When we've got an account that's performing poorly, it suddenly becomes a first-class account in comparison to the rest, so the rest become second-class accounts. So, if a hot issue comes along, you stick it in that account and pull its performance up a little bit. It can raise a lot of ethical questions.[202]

When, as in Citibank's case, its trust portfolio exceeds 10,000 accounts, there will also be ample opportunity for a bank to buy and sell from accounts under its management. Thus, if one trust account contains a hard-to-sell asset, the bank can sell it to another trust it manages. Although this practice seems shady, the Comptroller permits it, if it is "fair":

> A national bank may sell assets held by it as fiduciary in one account to itself as fiduciary in another account if the transaction is fair to both accounts and if such transaction is not prohibited by the terms of any governing instrument or by local law.[203]

That trust departments seem unable to make a profit without credits for deposits exacerbates the conflict among accounts. Rather than suggesting that trust departments become more efficient and that service and performance be improved for all accounts, Peter Prior, Senior Vice President of the Hartford National Bank and Trust Department, recommends:

> It would seem logical that more service should be given to the larger, profitable accounts and either less service, higher minimum fees, or a combination of the two must be applied to the relatively small accounts if we are, in fact, going to have a truly profitable cost oriented Trust Division.[204]

Under the present structure of bank trust departments, there is no sure way to prevent this kind of favoritism. If trust departments were separated from commercial banks, the trust department would no longer be able to favor a client because of the size of that client's business with the commercial bank; even unaffiliated trust companies, however, face having to choose among their clients.

We do feel that some of the recommendations we made earlier will minimize favoritism. Requiring trust companies to publish the performance statistics for all accounts, including activity and turnover rates, will better enable a client to assess the performance of his own account. Giving the beneficiaries of personal trusts the option of moving their accounts to another corporate fiduciary gives them the same leverage that pension clients now have; unless the trustee performs, it will lose the business.

Our pension proposal, since it divorces the management of pension funds from employers and banks, will eliminate favoritism towards any one fund. Under our proposed system, pension fund managers will no longer individually manage the funds of several employers. Rather, newly-created financial institutions will manage collectively the passbook pension accounts of employees and an employee will always retain the right to move his account to another institution.

The Wall

Bankers contend that the conflicts their critics find are only *potential* conflicts and that there are adequate safeguards to ensure that they never materialize. To a man, trust officers publicly state that commercial information never leaks to the trust side and that the commercial side never influences trust decisions. Bankers talk about an "impermeable wall" between trust and commercial departments.

This wall, if it does exist, is of recent construction. One trust officer who used to work at Citibank recalls:

> Six to eight years ago, any trust officer could order the credit files of any corporation from the commercial side. Those documents were not very illuminating, however.

Another former Citibanker reminisced:

> The officers of the investment group had relatively easy access to the credit files of the bank. There was some kind of "need to know" criterion that was easily circumvented, although it might have prevented some lowly clerk from having access. . . . The reports were not of great value, because the kinds of useful information there could be found in aggregate information published elsewhere, and this kind of cross-check, usually over the telephone, never was the influencing factor. Sometimes we would call up the loan department and ask for their impression of the management. However, the buy and sell decisions were not influenced by whether the company had loans outstanding with FNCB. . . .

Frank Barnett, asked if Citibank's commercial relationships influenced its trust department investments, replied:

> No—categorically—at National City there are efforts to prevent this. There is a segregation of the commercial credit files. There aren't even common lunches with commercial and trust men.[205]

Denials notwithstanding, in 1970 among those sitting on FNCB's Investment Policy Board, which coordinates the investment policies of the whole trust department, were Messrs. Wriston, Spencer, Palmer, Laeri, and Wilcox, the same men who sit on the committees which supervise major loan commitments and other commercial activities of the bank. Even close observers like Henry Harfield, one of Citibank's lawyers, agree that it is impossible to construct an "impermeable membrane" between a bank's commercial and trust departments.[206]

Courts too have found the wall to be a myth, especially when they find banks placing banking interests above the interests of the trusts. A prime example is presented by Denver U.S. National Bank. The bank sold Denver Post stock to Helen Bonfils instead of S. I. Newhouse, even though Newhouse was willing to pay a significantly higher price.[207] According to one description of the case:

Denver U.S. National had been involved with these trusts for many years and had strong ties with the Bonfils family. There- fore, it would be natural for the bank to favor a sale to Miss Bonfils to preserve their present and possible future relationships rather than to sell this stock to the Newhouse publications, with which they had no relationship. This would also tend to sour relations between the bank and some of its customers.[208]

The sale to Bonfils rather than Newhouse resulted in a loss to the trusts of $2,655,697.30, the amount the court surcharged the bank when it held the bank in breach of fiduciary duty.

In another recent case, the Cleveland Trust Company at- tempted to use its fiduciary status to intervene in a lawsuit.[209] It was found that the bank's motive was to thwart competition which threatened its own banking operations. Commenting on these cases, the House Banking and Currency Committee staff study concluded:

These cases illustrate quite well how a bank trustee with conflict- ing interests and pressures is either unwilling or unable to act strictly in the best interests of the beneficiaries.[210]

Most recently, investigation into the Penn Central failure re- vealed that large blocks of Penn Central stock were sold by bank trust departments before the railroad's impending collapse be- came known to the public. A 1972 study by the House Banking and Currency Committee staff showed that during the two-and- one-half months before the railroad filed for bankruptcy, five in- stitutions, including three bank trust departments, sold almost 1.5 million shares of Penn Central stock, more than 28% of the Penn Central stock sold during the period.[211] There were no publicly known events that could have caused the banks to sell at that time. According to the 1972 study:

It becomes apparent that the trust departments of such banking institutions as Chase Manhattan conducted their massive sales of Penn Central stock on the basis of either great clair- voyance or inside information.[212]

Focusing on Morgan and Chase, which sold the most Penn Cen- tral stock during the two-and-one-half months, the committee staff noted that the banks had other relationships with the rail-road. Chase held about $50 million of the railroad's outstanding debt, the railroad and its subsidiaries maintained deposits of about $5 million with Chase, and Stuart Saunders, Chairman of the Board of Penn Central, was a director of Chase Manhattan.[213] Morgan Guaranty Trust Company held about $35 million of Penn Central debt and over $6 million in deposits. John T. Dorrance and Thomas L. Perkins, of Penn Central, were also directors of Morgan.[214] In light of all these interlocks, the House Committee staff study concluded that it would be impossible to dismiss the timing of the stock sales to mere coincidence.

In August of 1972 the SEC released its own study on the collapse of the Penn Central. According to the SEC, on the morning of May 28, 1970, Kenneth MacWilliams and G. K. Crowther, two officers from Morgan's commercial department, attended a meeting where they learned "a good deal of information about the financial and operational condition of Penn Central which at that time had not been publicly disclosed." [215] After the meeting, MacWilliams wrote a confidential memo describing what they had learned; this memo had "normal distribution in the credit department."

The next morning, May 29, 1970, three men from Morgan's trust department, Samuel Calloway, Executive Vice President; Harrison Smith, Senior Vice President; and Carl Hathaway, Senior Vice President, held a meeting which according to Smith lasted "two to three minutes at the most." [216] At this meeting the three trust officers issued an order to sell all Penn Central shares from pension accounts managed by Morgan. That day, Morgan sold 45,930 shares of Penn Central; this amounted to 21.6% of the total exchange volume for that stock that day. Smith testified that Morgan sold the stock because of an article in the *Wall Street Journal* of May 29th announcing the postponement of Penn Central's proposed debenture offering. According to the SEC, Smith and Hathaway testified that when they issued the order to sell they were not then aware of what Morgan's commercial bank officers had learned the day before.

The SEC refuses to provide the Study Group with the complete testimony of Messrs. Smith and Hathaway. According to Stanley Sporkin, Deputy Director of the SEC, "the Commission has a continuing interest in the matter including the consideration of possible enforcement action." [217] When the Study Group requested copies of the testimony directly from Smith and Hathaway, Morgan Guaranty's legal counsel replied:

> As you know, the testimony was taken as part of a private investigation and, as such, is confidential except to the extent already released by the Securities and Exchange Commission. We see no reason to depart from that principle of confidentiality and accordingly must decline to comply with your request.[218]

On November 30, 1972, Beverley C. Moore, an attorney, filed suit against the SEC to obtain this testimony. The District Court ruled against Mr. Moore in July, 1973; he promptly filed a notice of appeal.

The SEC study also described Morgan's lack of meaningful procedures for separating trust and commercial departments. Until the end of May, 1970, the same research department served both Morgan's trust and commercial departments. During April and May of 1970, James Holschuh, who worked in Morgan's research department as its railroad specialist, met on several occasions to discuss the Penn Central with officers of both the commercial and the trust departments. According to Harrison Smith, Senior Vice President of Morgan:

> Of course, I am also aware that while the research and corporate research personnel had seemed to be able to handle problems of potential conflicts of interest arising from their working for more than one part satisfactorily, it put us in a position that somebody might say that this was a hole in the wall that existed between us [the Trust Department] and the commercial bank.[219]

The wreck of the Penn Central is just beginning to engender litigation of bank trust clients. In October, 1972, two union pension funds filed suit against Continental Illinois National Bank and Trust Company in Chicago. The funds allege that Continental Illinois, as a major creditor and depositary of Penn Central, had inside information of the railroad's deteriorating financial condition before Penn Central filed for bankruptcy in June, 1970.[220]

The Denver U.S. National Bank case, the Cleveland Trust case, and the Penn Central saga all raise the presumption that trust departments are quite prone to influence from the commercial side of the bank. The broker reciprocity cases pending against Morgan and Chemical banks will determine how real the wall is. The pension fund suits against Bankers Trust, Chase, and Continental Illinois will also test whether the rights of employees have been sacrificed to the interests of bank trustees. A handful of cases—some of which have not yet been tried—does not necessarily indicate widespread abuses; but the handful is growing, and the plaintiffs are alleging only what the SEC and congressional staff studies have already found to exist. It seems probable that breaches in the figurative wall are frequent. Only the deep secrecy surrounding bank operations prevents beneficiaries and the public from seeing more than the tip of the iceberg.

In light of the mythical nature of the wall and because of the actual and potential conflicts that arise when a commercial bank accepts a personal or pension trusteeship, we recommend that trust departments be separated completely from banks. By complete separation we mean total severance of all financial and corporate connections; merely making the trust department a subsidiary of the bank or the bank holding company would not eliminate the temptation to favor the bank's interests over the interests of settlors and beneficiaries. We are not persuaded by arguments that trust departments could not survive without a commercial bank to share some of the overhead; the existence of profitable unaffiliated trust companies refutes such claims.

Recommendations

Based on our study of FNCB's trust department and corporate fiduciaries in general, we offer seventeen specific recommendations. Since the proposals concerning disclosure (No. 16) and the use of trust funds (No. 17) have been the topics of much current debate, we have elaborated our positions on those subjects. Our recommendations follow:

1. Tax Subsidization. Trust departments should no longer be subsidized by a tax structure that encourages generation-skipping trusts. A tax should be imposed on generation-skipping transfers of property to substitute for the tax that would have applied if the property had paid estate tax through each generation.

2. Trust and Estate Bar. Attorneys should inform their clients of any adverse consequences, such as higher fees, that might result from the appointment of a corporate fiduciary. National and local Bar associations should study the extent to which collusive arrangements exist between trust departments and local attorneys. Bank trust departments should be required to disclose the lists of lawyers they recommend to their trust clients and the number of clients referred to each lawyer.

3. Truth in Trust Advertising. A trust department should not be permitted to advertise that it is providing individualized investment services unless it actually is. The SEC, as it has examined FNCB's Special Investment Advisory Service, should now examine FNCB's personal trust investment services to see if, as it appears, the accounts are being managed in an assembly-line fashion. The other regulatory agencies, in their examinations of trust departments, should monitor individual accounts to ensure that there has been periodic review. Trust departments should be required to disclose the average activity and turnover rates for their personal trust portfolios.

4. Common Trust Funds. Trust departments should not be permitted to liquidate trust portfolios for the purpose of investing them in the banks' own common trust funds without first obtaining the informed, written permission of settlors and/or beneficiaries.

5. Unique Assets. Settlors should be warned, both by banks and by attorneys, of banks' proclivity to dispose of unique assets and small closely-held businesses.

6. Beneficiaries' Rights. Upon a showing of due cause, beneficiaries should have the option of moving testamentary trusts to another corporate fiduciary.

7. Continuity of Service. When advertising their fiduciary services, a trust department should be required to disclose the average number of years the same manager can be expected to supervise an account. Trust departments should consider assigning at least two administrative and investment managers to each account so that beneficiaries will be able to deal with someone familiar with their needs. The role of trust officer must be restructured so that it does not remain merely a stepping stone to other positions.

8. Candor Regarding Conflicts. If a trust department invests a customer's account in a company that has commercial dealings with the bank, the bank should inform the customer of the existence and extent of those commercial dealings.

9. Profitability. Banks should be required to disclose the profitability of their trust activities along with breakdowns of the profitability of each fiduciary service offered. Computations of trust department profitability should not include "credits allowed for deposits" generated by uninvested cash deposited in the bank's commercial department.

10. Fiduciary Standard for Pension Trustees. As long as the present private pension system is maintained, pension trustees should be held to strict fiduciary standards; they should be held responsible for ensuring that no self-dealing occurs and that the participants are fully informed of all aspects of their plans. Where plans are not fully funded, the pension trustee should affirmatively inform participants of the contingent nature of the pension benefits. Wherever possible, pension trustees should encourage employers to provide early vesting and portability provisions in their plans.

11. Pension Investment Policy. The SEC should investigate the investment policies of FNCB and other banks that serve as pension trustees to determine if individualized attention is being given to each plan. If the SEC has this information from its 1970 study, it should make it public on a bank by bank basis to enable employers to choose pension fund trustees prudently.

12. New Institutions to Manage Pension Money. The present private pension system should be restructured to separate control of pension funds from employers and commercial banks. Each year employers would directly pay an employee a portion of the employee's salary; the employee would be required to invest this money in funds established specifically to manage pension money. The funds would be private, competitive, cooperative, insured financial institutions licensed and regulated by the SEC. Each would have a board of directors that would represent the participating employees' investment interests and social concerns.

13. Profits from Uninvested Cash. All profits resulting from trust funds left uninvested in the commercial side of the bank should be distributed pro rata to the beneficiaries of the trusts that generated the deposits.

14. Voting Bank's Own Stock. A bank should not be permitted to exercise any voting control over its own stock held in its trust department.

15. Separate Trust Departments from Commercial Banks.
Trust departments should be completely separated from commercial banking institutions.

16. Additional Disclosures. Until trust departments are separated from commercial banks, and until new institutions are created to manage pension monies, each trust department should be required to disclose the following:

a) its 20 largest stock holdings; *
b) all holdings over $10 million;
c) all holdings constituting more than 5% of the outstanding voting stock of publicly listed corporations; *
d) all holdings of the bank's own stock or of the stock of other financial institutions;
e) the dollar value of (a), (b), (c), and (d) above, also broken down by sole, shared, and no-voting responsibility;
f) common directors, officers, and senior employees of, and outstanding loans to, all companies in which the trust department holds stock;
g) performance data and portfolio composition of the common trust funds and commingled pension funds managed by the bank, and similar data for representative personal and pension accounts not managed collectively;
h) names of all brokers used for securities transactions and respective amounts of commissions paid to those brokers and amounts of deposits maintained by those brokers with the bank;
i) average daily balance of uninvested cash held by trust department as a whole and average time cash remains in different accounts between accrual and distribution.

17. Use of Trust Funds. Without necessarily sacrificing the investment performance of trust funds, trustees should use their investment powers and exercise their stock voting responsibilities to engage our nation's pressing social problems.

More on Disclosure (Recommendation No. 16). In our study of trust departments, several abuses are indicated which, because of lack of publicly available information, are not amenable

---

*except if this holding is stock held by a family trust in a family-controlled corporation and the stock is not subject to voting control by the bank.

to absolute proof. The question rightfully is asked whether mere disclosure of additional information would prove anything. In answer, it can be shown that where information has been obtained, by subpoena or otherwise, trust departments have been found in breach of their fiduciary duties. The prime example is the SEC's finding of broker reciprocity, a practice which banks vehemently deny.

Greater disclosure of trust department investments and procedures would not only confirm or refute suspicion about malfeasance; disclosure might also have a prophylactic effect, discouraging practices that banks might engage in secretly, but which they would halt if forced to face public scrutiny. Bankers themselves, at least in their public statements, do not openly oppose more disclosure of the trust department investments and procedures. The American Bankers Association declares: "We have no objection to supplying significant and meaningful information that will serve the public good." [221] However, as of October, 1972, out of over 3,000 bank trust departments, only five (FNCB, Morgan Guaranty, Bankers Trust, Provident National Bank, and Citizens and Southern National Bank) had disclosed *any* information about their holdings.

The Deputy Comptroller for trusts believes that the examination process for trust departments should remain secret. He contends that if breaches of the law were made public, it would result in a loss of public confidence.[222] The Study Group disagrees, especially when violations have been uncovered. Insofar as public confidence is concerned, if a trust department is found in a breach, then cause for a loss of confidence exists. We see no reason why a trust department should be able to advertise its trust services, telling its side of the story, while the regulatory authorities charged with protection of the public refrain from revealing the truth. Certainly, a potential trust client would be interested in knowing a trust department's record, and a current trust client has a right to be put on guard if anything suspicious has been found. The public, too, for whose protection the laws have been enacted, has a right to know when those laws have been violated.

There are those who contend that secrecy is needed because of the confidential nature of the relationship between a bank and a trust client. Insofar as personal trust accounts are concerned, we agree. The Study Group has nowhere recommended that information identifying individuals or the investments in any individual account be disclosed. We have even made an exception to the disclosure requirements in cases where a bank's major holding is the stock of a family-owned business held by that family's trust and not subject to the bank's voting control. We do not, however, believe that the relationship between a bank and a corporate client is subject to the same degree of confidentiality. The distinction lies in that the relationship between the bank and a corporation invariably affects more than just those two parties. Thus, while a loan from bank C to corporation X might not be considered, conventionally, anybody else's concern, it does become the public's business if the corporation has interlocking directors with the bank, if the loan is made with funds from the corporation's pension fund, or if the loan is made for any reason other than as a purely economic investment.

In calling for greater disclosure of trust department investments, the President's Commission on Financial Structure and Regulation recommended that trust departments increase the extent of their reporting to the appropriate regulatory agencies.[223] While additional reporting to the regulators is needed, we also recommend more disclosure to trust clients and the public as a whole.

Trust clients have an immediate interest in the activities of the bank managing their account. To permit clients themselves to judge whether conflicts of interest exist, we recommend they be given specific notification of investments in companies that have commercial ties to the bank, and notification of any action, such as the transfer of trust portfolios to the bank's common trust funds, which primarily benefits the bank instead of the beneficiaries.

The public too has a right to know how trust funds are invested and managed The public treasury subsidizes pension trusts, to the tune of between $3 billion to $8 billion annually in tax exemptions. Personal trusts too are subsidized by virtue of the lower taxes. Since the public pays, the public has a right to know how trust money is used.

The public's right to know also stems from the fact that the way trust funds are invested affects large segments of the public. The 30 million persons enrolled in private pension plans have a direct interest in how those funds are invested. If banks sacrifice pension fund performance to cater to investment needs of their corporate commercial clients, that fact is of concern to all employees enrolled in bank-managed plans.

As institutional investors, bank trust departments along with mutual funds and insurance companies account for almost 60% of all stock market activity. Thus, the trading patterns and investment whims of trust departments can have an impact on the market, directly affecting the interests of the 30 million individuals who are also investors.

As managers of vast wealth, estimated to be $330 billion in June of 1972,[224] bank trust departments can influence a large sector of the American economy. The decision to invest the money almost exclusively in the country's largest, most mature corporations, can mean that smaller companies will not be able to find financing, affecting market entry and competition. By virtue of the stock held in trust and the voting power retained by the trust departments, banks can influence management decisions. Also, trust departments, with their large blocks of stock, can thwart efforts towards corporate reform.

In the last analysis, the public's right to know stems from a principle inherent to the democratic system, that an informed public is the best guarantee that the laws will be enforced. If the regulators become lax, or if they are coopted by the very institutions they are charged with regulating, then it falls to the public to act, as vigilant attorneys general, to ensure that the law is obeyed.

More on Use of Trust Funds (Recommendation No. 17). Our study has noted two salient features about trust department holdings. First, these holdings, especially in the New York banks, are quite large; in at least five banks they exceed $10 billion. Second, trust departments possess enormous control over their trust funds, the largest having complete investment and voting discretion over four-fifths of the monies in the pension accounts. In light of these two features, we must consider whether banks have made the best investment decisions both for their trust beneficiaries and for the community.

As trustees, banks have obligations to beneficiaries, but not to them alone. As Paul Harbrecht, author of *Pension Funds and Economic Power,* observes:

Yet the pension trusts administered by pension officers of banks are becoming so large that their management cannot fail to have a significant effect on the general welfare.[225]

Bank trustees also share in various public subsidies, such as the favorable tax treatment of trusts and New York's monopolistic law [226] which only permits banks to serve as corporate trustees. Because of their impact on the community and because of their support by the community, trust departments owe an obligation to the community.

In terms of fulfilling their obligation to beneficiaries, Dreher's, Hansen's, and Cantor's studies, and the Senate Labor Subcommittee's findings have shown that most banks have not done well as pension trustees. In terms of their obligation to the community, banks have done worse. Trust departments have reduced their holdings of government and state obligations and maintain only about 2% of their portfolios in real-estate mortgages. Trust departments have made no visible effort to exercise their stock voting responsibilities to encourage companies to engage our pressing national problems, like housing, pollution, and discrimination. When bank trust departments have been called upon to take stands on social issues, such as in Campaign GM, almost without exception, the banks not only refuse to challenge corporate management, they also refuse to inform their beneficiaries, those in whose best interest they allegedly are acting, of the issues involved.

What can be done to make trust departments responsive to the community and to enable trust monies to produce a maximum social return? Ideally, if our pension proposal is adopted, independent financial institutions will be established to manage pension monies. Some of these institutions could have as their stated aim the utilization of all or a portion of the fund in projects such as low-cost housing. A worker would choose what institution he wants to manage his pension money. He always has the option of moving his money to a different institution. If a worker objected, either on financial or social grounds, to a manager's investment policies, he could simply withdraw his funds and move it to a manager whose investment policies he found more palatable. Currently, only the employer has a right to determine who manages the pension fund and because of preexisting and coexisting relationships between employer and bank, the employer's choice might not be based on the employees' or the community's interests.

In fact, three factors inhibit a corporate trustee from using trust funds to maximize returns to both the beneficiaries and the community. First, the same conflicts of interest which lead a bank's commercial department to choose a less profitable investment over a more profitable one can also lead a bank's trust department to eschew investments in residential mortgages for investments in an employer's own real estate. Second, it is still too easy for a corporate trustee to excuse its investment policy contending that its fiduciary status forces it to invest in companies that pursue discriminatory or socially irresponsible policies since those are the companies that allegedly produce the highest financial return. Third, a large part of the community to which a trust department should be responsive, namely those workers whose pension plans are managed by the bank, have no say in how their funds are being invested.

Severing trust departments from commercial banks will eliminate many of the conflicts of interest inherent in the present system. Requiring the kinds of disclosures that we have recommended will also go a long way toward pressuring trustees to invest for total return.

When bankers are pressed about their lack of social involvement and their unwillingness to use social benefit as a criterion in their investment policies, they respond, "We'd like to but, as fiduciaries, we are restricted to investing for the maximum financial return for our clients." This view is open to question. As Donald Schwartz, Professor of Law at Georgetown University, notes:

> The trustee's obligation remains that of advancing the best interests of his beneficiaries, but that is not to say that the law requires that profits be maximized. The law makes no such requirement . . . because it is impossible to calculate "maximum profits." [227]

Schwartz observes, "just as corporations cannot realistically ignore social implications in determining what are its best economic interests, neither can a shareholder, nor a trustee acting on his behalf." Schwartz concludes that, "the law seems to point toward this view that enables institutions to favor public interest proposals; certainly there is scant evidence that they do not enjoy this freedom." [228]

Like Schwartz, William Greenough, a member of FNCB's Trust Board, criticizes investment policies that follow an overly narrow view of profit maximization. According to Greenough, "a major—perhaps *the* major—unanswered question is the time span over which maximization should be judged. To be sure, the name of the game is profits, but the game is a long one." [229] If institutional investors adopt a long-term perspective towards their investments, Greenough predicts:

> then the institutional investor can support and nudge corporate managements in their efforts to solve ecological and social problems, efforts which may cause additional expenditures in the short run, but gain effective new sources of social wealth and income from many firms in the long run, and make government mandates and requirements with rigid specifications unnecessary. [230]

Phillip Blumberg, Law Professor at Boston University, similarly cautions against only short-term profit maximization:

> Business expenditures directed toward the social environment in which the business must operate may fulfill business objectives, notwithstanding the absence of short-term return. [231]

Schwartz, in describing the impossibility of defining profit maximization, and Greenough and Blumberg, in advocating a deemphasis of short-term financial gain, all touch on the key aspect of social investment policy, namely that returns cannot be measured only in terms of dollars. Other considerations, such as community health, resulting from pollution-free air; safety, resulting from adequate product testing programs; and legality, resulting from compliance with various laws, are now valid investment criteria. Moreover, it is being recognized that employing these nonfinancial criteria can even have long-run beneficial financial consequences. For instance, installation of a pollution control device will entail an expense for a company that could lower the company's current profit statement. Yet, this expenditure might be more than compensated for by savings to workers and the surrounding community, savings which take the form of fewer cleaning bills, less necessity for paint jobs, and no more doctor bills for eye and lung irritation. Even shareholders stand a chance of benefiting because voluntary pollution control tends to immunize a company from civil litigation by environmentalists and prosecution by law enforcement authorities. The company itself would also enjoy a competitive advantage when inevitable federal regulations force other companies to install such devices, paying higher prices at a later date in a regulated context of installation rather than a comprehensive engineering plan at the outset.

Unless the trust instrument or state law specifies otherwise, a trustee is governed by the "prudent man rule" which places the trustee "under a duty to make such investments as a prudent man would make." [232] Prudence certainly includes investing for the long-term benefit of the community and, in this regard, it is significant to note that courts have applauded other fiduciaries, namely corporate directors, when they have made contributions to the general welfare. In deciding that a corporation has the power to make a charitable contribution even without express statutory authority, a New Jersey court stated:

> It seems to us that just as the conditions prevailing when corporations were originally created required that they serve the public as well as private interests, modern conditions require that corporations acknowledge and discharge social as well as private responsibilities as members of the communities within which they operate.[233]

More recently, this attitude was reaffirmed by a Delaware court which upheld a corporate contribution of more than a half-million dollars to a charitable trust. The court stated:

> Contemporary courts recognize that unless corporations carry an increasing share of the burdens of supporting charitable and educational causes that the business advantages now reposed in corporations by law may well prove to be unacceptable to the representatives of an aroused public.[234]

Financial and legal bases therefore exist for the proposition that fiduciaries can, and even should, consider the welfare of the community in their investment decisions.

Once corporate trustees recognize that their fiduciary status does not restrict them to investments that maximize short-term financial returns at the expense of the long-term welfare of the community, the problem of choosing which investments will best serve the beneficiaries and society remains. To make this determination, we recommend that corporate trustees actually go out and ask the beneficiaries, especially the pension plan participants, what they see as being the major social problems of the day. The corporate trustees would establish a list of those problems felt to be most pressing. Today, such a list might include low-cost housing, pollution abatement, crime control, elimination of racial discrimination, and drug addict rehabilitation. The bank's research department would be asked to investigate what investment opportunities were available to help solve some of these problems. If the return on these investments were equal (all other considerations being the same) to other returns in the market, the trustee should not hesitate making the socially useful investment. If the return were lower, then the trustee should at least ask the beneficiaries directly whether they would be willing to forego some degree of financial gain now in order to help eradicate what they themselves have deemed pressing social problems.

Pension trustees presently have little or no contact with pension plan participants, those whose interests the trustees allegedly are protecting. Employees have no opportunity to voice their needs, or their wants. Even when a corporate trustee knows what beneficiaries want, apparently it just pays lip service:

> Sometimes an employer will request that the pension trustee give consideration to mortgages in areas where the company has plants. In most of these cases, we just write back and say: Yes, we've read your letter. Thank you very much.[235]

Many pension plan participants undoubtedly would have favored some of Campaign GM's proposals, especially those asking General Motors to disclose its auto safety, air pollution, and minority hiring policies. After all, those pension plan participants also have to decide whether to buy GM cars and are forced to breathe air saturated by auto fumes. Yet, with rare exceptions, the bank trustees voted against this modest proposal without even asking the participants. We would favor a system in which pension plan participants would be given some say in how the stock held in their pension plan was voted. We agree with William Greenough that the ideal is to: "Let the people who put up the money to buy the shares—the depositors, the policyholders, the participants—vote their proper proportion." [236] If administrative difficulties prevent voting rights from always being passed through to the employees, pension trustees should be required at least to consult with employee representatives on voting proxies. At least once a year, employees should be polled to determine their attitudes towards the kinds of issues that might arise in proxy fights during the year.

Elimination of conflicts of interest, recognition of responsibilities to the community, and giving a part of the community a say in the way trust funds are used are the first three steps to increasing the social utility of the over $300 billion now in trust departments. Once corporate trustees begin to invest in projects designed to cure social problems, or at least inform the public of problems and capabilities, and once socially injurious ventures are denied financing from institutional investors, major progress will have begun in making our financial institutions responsive to the communities that created them At this point, it remains to be seen whether corporate trustees will accept their public responsibilities. Recent statements by two FNCB Directors and the Chairman of the Board of Chase Manhattan Bank give some cause for hope:

> Many of our actions in the public behalf will—let's face it—take untold hours from our business endeavors and dollars from our profit ledgers. Yet, the call to all of us is plain. Our positive approach is mandatory.[237]
>
> > Charles H. Sommer, Chairman
> > of the Board, Monsanto Company
>
> Business is not only recognizing a moral obligation by such involvement [in the massive problems of urban poverty]. It is helping create a climate in which it stands the best chance of prospering.[238]
>
> > Michael Haider, Chairman of Exxon
>
> At a dinner of a group of friends who know the financial community well, the question was raised: Can a commercial bank afford to respond to the escalating demands for more socially responsible behavior within the present profit oriented market system? My answer was that, given the current business environment, neither banks nor any other business enterprise can afford not to respond.[239]
>
> > David Rockefeller, Chase Manhattan Bank

In short, we agree with Geoffrey Cowan, one of Campaign GM's leaders, when he concluded: "At least we have succeeded in changing their rhetoric. Now if we can only get them to live up to their rhetoric." [240]

VI

Bank Regulation

Introduction

Webster's *Dictionary* defines the word "autonomous" as "having the right or power of self-government." That word describes Citibank's relation to the regulatory process better than any other. Through membership on the National Advisory Committee to the Comptroller of the Currency, frequent business contacts with regulatory agency personnel, and occasional extracurricular social contacts with the people responsible for regulating national banks, Citibank has substantial influence over the regulatory policies that vitally affect its own operations.

In addition to its impact on policy, Citibank also plays a major role in the process by which the regulatory agencies are supposed to investigate bank operations. Though the law requires the Comptroller to examine national banks three times every two years, the 50 largest national banks, and many smaller ones as well, are examined only once a year. Furthermore, relatively few resources are assigned to the examination of Citibank because the Comptroller feels that Citibank's internal audit system is so good. The Comptroller's overriding preoccupation with preventing bank failures induces the examiners to focus almost exclusively on solvency at the expense of evaluating compliance with the law. When questions of law do arise in the course of an examination, the Comptroller sometimes turns to the bank's own lawyers for their opinions and defers to their expertise.

Citibank also has a high degree of autonomy from Federal Reserve monetary policy. Its overseas operation and its creation of a one-bank holding company in 1968 helped the bank to circumvent the Fed's anti-inflation credit restraint program during 1969 and early 1970.

The bank also wields considerable influence in the legislative arena. Senator Jacob Javits of New York has consistently sponsored legislation of substantial importance to Citibank; at the same time, the law firm where until recently Javits was a partner does a substantial amount of work for the bank. FNCB's interests are also championed by its own lobbyist, John Yingling, and various trade and lobbying groups like the American Bankers Association, the Foundation for Full Service Banks, and the Association of Corporate Owners of One Bank.

Citibank's ability to influence the regulatory and legislative process has been an indispensable element in the bank's staggering growth. As long-standing regulatory policies and legislative restrictions have eroded, Citibank has found new freedom to expand into new territories and product markets, thereby increasing its ability to attract more deposits.

1. The Regulatory Structure

Bank panics and failures due to loss of confidence and runs on banks occurred in 1873, 1884, 1893, 1907, and 1933. As a result, a byzantine labyrinth of laws and regulations and a multitude of agencies developed to protect against further panics and crises.

Because both states and the federal government can charter banks many observers refer to our "dual banking system." It would be more accurate to say that there are 50 different banking systems, each having four different types of banks. Banks located in the same state are subject to different agencies and rules according to whether they are (1) national banks, (2) Federal Reserve member state banks, (3) FDIC insured state banks, or (4) uninsured state banks.

A comprehensive discussion of bank regulation is beyond the scope of this report. Instead, our focus will be on a few major aspects of bank regulation—policy formulation and bank examination by the Comptroller of the Currency, the Fed's credit policy, and the legislative response to the one-bank holding company—in order to determine how government regulation affects Citibank, and vice versa. Before analyzing bank regulation in operation, however, it is necessary to briefly describe the overall federal bank regulatory structure comprised of the Comptroller of the Currency, the Fed, and the FDIC.

The Comptroller of the Currency. In 1863, Congress enacted the National Currency Act, designed to help the government raise funds to finance the Civil War. The Office of the Comptroller of the Currency, the first federal regulatory agency, was created to supervise the chartering and operations of national banks, which were authorized to issue bank notes secured by government bonds. The only major restrictions on national bank operations were requirements that they set aside currency equal to 25% of their outstanding notes and submit to periodic examinations of their operations by the Comptroller's office.

Over the years, the responsibilities of the Comptroller's office have expanded dramatically. The Comptroller regulates the structure of the national banking system, by authorizing new charters, branches, and mergers. The Comptroller is supposed to issue a new charter only if the incorporators can show that they have the financial resources and ability to operate a bank and that there is a need for the new bank in the community. The Comptroller also passes upon requests for new branches, subject to state law. The requirement that the Comptroller approve all mergers and acquisitions by national banks enables him to affect the number and size of the national banks in each area.

The Comptroller also promulgates rules and regulations which describe how national banks shall conduct their day-to-day business. This includes defining bank powers, deposit gathering, loan limits to each customer, permissible investments, activities by affiliates and trust departments, payment of dividends, reporting of information, and many other matters.

Direct, on-the-spot supervision of national banks is achieved by periodic examinations. The Comptroller appraises each bank's assets and management, verifies its liabilities, and determines its adherence to the law and sound banking principles. At the close of the examination, the examiners discuss their findings with the officers and sometimes the directors of each bank.

The Comptroller is appointed to a five-year term by the president, with the advice and consent of the Senate, and serves at the pleasure of the president.

The Federal Reserve System. After the bank panic of 1907, Congress created a National Monetary Commission to study and recommend legislation that would prevent overexpansion of credit, ensure liquidity by requiring banks to maintain adequate reserves, and create a more elastic currency. The recommendations of the Commission were enacted into law in the Federal Reserve Act of 1913. The act created 12 regional Federal Reserve Banks supervised by a seven-member central board. To ensure that they would be free from domination by the executive branch, board members were given ten-year terms. The act required every national bank to subscribe to stock of its regional Federal Reserve Bank and become members of the system. State chartered banks were permitted to join. The present General Counsel of the Fed recently noted:

> The essential significance of the Federal Reserve Act for present purposes is that it superimposed on the state and national banking systems a third, hybrid system embracing both state and national banks, under the supervision of a new federal banking agency.[1]

The act provided a rediscount mechanism, called the discount window, to provide liquidity and protection from panics, by giving banks quick and cheap access to borrowed money to help them face unexpected losses of deposits or unusual loan demand. The 1913 legislation also provided for the issuance of new currency, "Federal Reserve notes." These notes were to be secured by the commercial paper discounted by banks at the discount window in the expectation that currency would thus expand and contract depending on credit demands, thereby providing a more "elastic" currency. The act gave the Fed power to specify the reserves that all national and state member banks must set aside against time and demand deposits in order to provide for bank liquidity. The Fed was also given power to examine the operations of state member banks.

The basic structure of the Fed has remained intact; but as the bank panic of 1933 demonstrated, the legislation of 1913 was inadequate and needed strengthening. New Deal legislation increased the terms of board members to 14 years. Legislation expanded the Fed's central bank functions, giving it more detailed power to regulate member bank reserves and broader powers to buy and sell federal government securities in the open market, thereby strengthening the Fed's control over bank credit. The Fed was also empowered to regulate the extension of credit for the purchase of securities. The Fed's supervisory responsibility over bank operations was eventually expanded to give the Fed control over branching by state member banks, the payment of interest on deposits by national and state member banks, interlocking directorates, foreign banking, bank mergers (where the surviving bank is a state member bank), and bank holding companies.

A major purpose of the legislation generated by the Depression was to prohibit commercial banks from speculating in corporate securities. All banks subject to federal regulation (98% of all commercial banks) were prohibited from purchasing stock in corporations or underwriting securities, except for a limited number of government securities.[2] They were also prohibited from paying out dividends in certain situations.[3] National and state member banks (which hold 80% of all commercial bank deposits though they constitute only 43% of the banks)[4] were prohibited from having directors, officers, or employees serve as directors, officers, or employees of securities companies[5] and from purchasing their own stock or making loans with their own stock as collateral.[6] The New Deal legislation also tightened up the restrictions on the amount of money that national banks (34% of all banks with 59% of deposits)[7] can lend to a single customer.[8]

National and state member banks must subscribe to the capital stock of the district Federal Reserve Bank in an amount equal to 3% of their capital and surplus. An additional 3% is subject to call.[9] The national and state member banks receive dividends on their investments.

Each district Federal Reserve Bank has nine directors, divided into three classes, A, B, and C:

> The Class A and Class B directors are elected by member banks, one director of each class being elected by small banks, one of each class by banks of medium size, and one of each class by large banks.
>
> The three Class A directors are required to be representatives of member banks and may themselves be bankers. The three Class B directors must be actively engaged in the district in commerce, agriculture, or some other industrial pursuit and must not be officers, directors, employees, or stockholders of any bank. The three Class C directors are designated by the Board of Governors of the Federal Reserve System. They must not be officers, directors, employees, or stockholders of any bank. One of them is designated by the Board of Governors as chairman of the Reserve Bank's board of directors and one as deputy chairman.[10]

The Federal Reserve System performs a variety of interrelated functions in the American economy:

1. The system provides a payments mechanism through which economic units clear claims on each other. It operates a check collection service for member banks to clear checks drawn on each other and a wire transfer system to transfer large volumes of money quickly over long distances. The Federal Reserve System operates this payment mechanism through a network of 12 district Federal Reserve Banks and 24 branches. These facilities handle shipments of coin and currency to and from commercial banks to enable them to accommodate shifts in the public's preference between the different money forms of deposits and legal tender.[11]

2. The Federal Reserve System also controls monetary policy. This function is accomplished through a variety of devices. The Board of Governors determines reserve requirements for member banks—the percentage of time (e.g., savings) and demand (e.g., checking) deposits that must be deposited by member banks with district Federal Reserve Banks. Changes in reserve rates affect the ability of member banks to extend credit by requiring banks to segregate a greater or lesser amount of their funds into nonearning deposits with the district banks. The board also determines the "discount rate"—the rate member banks must pay to borrow from their district Federal Reserve Banks.

The most important tool of monetary policy is the Fed's "open-market" operation in the government securities market, directed by the open market committee.

This is the way the Fed's open market operations work. To expand bank credit, the Fed *buys* U.S. government securities in the open market and pays for them with a check drawn on a district Federal Reserve Bank. When the seller deposits this check in his own bank account, the funds are credited to the bank's reserve account with its district Federal Reserve Bank. This expands that member bank's ability to extend credit. Conversely, *sales* of securities by the Fed reduce the reserve balances of member banks and thus their ability to extend credit.[12]

The Open Market Committee's meetings, which generally take place every four weeks, are surrounded by an aura of mystery. OMC directives, which determine the system's open-market policy until the next meeting, are not released until 90 days after each meeting because of the extraordinary amount of money that could be earned in the government securities and money markets based on knowledge of how the Fed is conducting its open market operation.[13]

In this connection, it is interesting to note that John J. Larkin, FNCB Senior Vice President in charge of the Bond Division was, before coming to Citibank, in charge of the trading room at the new Federal Reserve Bank of New York, with responsibility for implementing the OMC's open-market policy.[14]

3. The Federal Reserve Banks also provide fiscal agency services for the U.S. Treasury, handling purchases and redemptions of government bonds and transferring tax payments to the Treasury.

4. The Federal Reserve is also responsible for regulating and examining state member banks. Twelve hundred banks (9% of all banks) with $119 billion in assets (22% of all bank assets) are subject to the Fed's supervision.[15] In most states, examinations are performed in conjunction with the state banking departments. In the remaining states, the Fed and the state banking departments conduct alternate examinations.[16]

The Federal Deposit Insurance Corporation. The third federal bank regulatory agency is the FDIC. Quite simply, the FDIC insures bank deposits. FDIC insurance is obligatory for all national and state member banks and optional for state nonmember banks. All but 208 of the nation's 13,681 banks have their deposits insured by the FDIC.

FDIC obtains its capital funds from the regional Federal Reserve Banks and its insurance fund is financed by assessments on insured banks. In addition to its insurance function, the FDIC conducts examinations into the operations of all state nonmember banks to ensure that they are following sound banking principles and obeying the law.[17]

More than 98% of all banks (with over 99% of all deposits) are subject to regulation by one or more of the three federal bank regulatory agencies. There are more insured state nonmember banks than any other type, but these banks are relatively small, holding only 19.3% of deposits. Conversely, only 42.9% of all banks are part of the Federal Reserve System, but they are larger in size and thus account for 80% of all commercial bank deposits. And within the Federal Reserve System,

NUMBER AND DEPOSITS OF COMMERCIAL BANKS BY CATEGORY, DECEMBER 31, 1969

	Number	%	Number and Deposits of Commercial Banks Deposits	%
INSURED BANKS				
Members of Federal Reserve System				
National	4,669	34.1%	$257,843,791,000	58.6%
State	1,201	8.8	94,444,591,000	21.4
Total Fed Members	5,870	42.9	352,288,382,000	80.0
Insured State Non-Members	7,603	55.6	84,701,283,000	19.3
Total Insured banks	13,473	98.5	436,989,665,000	99.3
UNINSURED BANKS	208	1.5	2,999,693,000	0.7
Total all banks	13,681	100.0%	$439,989,358,000	100.0%

SOURCE: Federal Deposit Insurance Corporation, 1969 Annual Report.

national banks are more numerous than state banks and hold most of the deposits.[18]

2. The Office of the Comptroller of the Currency—Pay As You Go Regulation

Policy Formulation

National banks, especially large banks, have a high degree of autonomy for many reasons. One is that the Comptroller's office is supported financially by the banks themselves. Though formally part of the Treasury, the Comptroller's office is not dependent on congressional appropriations. Rather, it is supported by assessments on national banks that are proportional to their assets. Of the Comptroller's 1969 revenues of $32,624,880, more than $30 million or 94%, came from the banks. (Most of the remaining income came from the Comptroller's investments in U.S. government securities.) The ten largest national banks paid more than $10 million; and Citibank's share was over $1,900,000. In addition to the regular assessments, national banks pay $500 for each application to open a branch; [19] $2,000 for each application for a merger, consolidation, or purchase of assets; [20] $140 a day for the examiner in charge and $80 a day for each additional examiner for examinations of affiliates, special examinations, and investigations,[21] and trust examinations; [22] and $1,500 for investigating and processing each application to organize a new bank.[23]

The fact that it does not depend on congressional funding insulates the Comptroller's office from some political pressures. But congressional influence is replaced by the banks' influence, as noted in this typical statement of a former official of the Comptroller's office:

> At most agencies, you find political hacks in key positions up and down the line—guys who aren't very good but get the job because they're well-connected politically. That doesn't happen as much at the Comptroller's office. Congressmen don't carry much weight over there. But bankers do. And so occasionally you'll find the son of some banker who hasn't even graduated from law school working in the front office. But more important than the occasional guy who gets his job because his daddy is a

banker is the fact that when bankers want something, such as a change in policy, the Comptroller's people will try to accommodate them. After all, if Citibank pays 6% of the budget, the Comptroller listens to what George Moore [the former FNCB chairman] has to say. And that holds true for other bankers as well.

When, in the early 1960s, banks started shedding their traditional conservatism in order to accelerate their lackluster growth rates, legislative restrictions on their activities prevented them from expanding as quickly as they wanted. State branching laws hampered their efforts to follow customers into the suburbs and limitations on permissible activities hindered them from expanding services to attract more deposits. James Saxon, President Kennedy's Comptroller, was familiar with the bankers' frustrations. After four years working for the American Bankers Association and five years at First National Bank of Chicago, located in a state that allowed no branching at all, he came to the Comptroller's office eager to use his administrative powers to remove the fetters from the banks. Saxon was articulate, aggressive, fiercely competitive, and very controversial. He foresaw the importance of computers and new, interchangeable financing techniques and he wanted to equip commercial banks to cope with the rapidly changing face of the American economy. He wanted banks to provide more and better services and he felt it was necessary to create more large units capable of competing statewide and nationwide. As one lawyer who served under Saxon put it:

> When Jim Saxon took over the Comptroller's office, he went to George Moore [President of FNCB] and other bankers and said, "I've taken over the stodgiest, most conservative agency in the whole federal government. It needs a face-lifting. What can we do for you to make yours a more efficient operation?" Prior to Saxon, the Comptrollers were all guys like Ray Gidney, who didn't want to rock the ship, who didn't want to be innovative. But Saxon was different. He was smart, articulate, and a fierce competitor himself. And he wanted to shake things up.
>
> It was pretty clear to Saxon that men like George Moore were sophisticated and knew where banking was going. So he asked Citibank to make suggestions and Saxon looked them over and adopted some.
>
> There's a new term in administrative law casebooks— "saxonization" or to be "saxonized." It means to undergo a face-lift.

The basic thrust of Saxon's regulatory philosophy was that banking ought to be left to bankers. This was clearly expressed in the 101st (1963) *Annual Report of the Comptroller,* a document subtitled *Years of Reform—A Prelude to Progress,* which candidly describes Saxon's philosophy of nonregulation in language that sounds as if it had been written by a bank trade association:

> . . . any unique form of bank regulation which is not essential to the preservation of the solvency and liquidity of the banking system must be regarded as a harmful impediment upon the capacity of banks to meet the public requirements which they are designed to serve. . . .
>
> Whenever a restrictive control did not meet this test, we have endeavored to broaden the discretionary powers of the national banks, insofar as this appeared desirable and was permissible under existing law. Whenever existing law appeared unduly restrictive in terms of this basic philosophy, we have advocated legislative changes to the Congress.[24]

Saxon, however, did not always wait for Congress. By bold use of interpretive and administrative powers, he reduced or eliminated many traditional restrictions on the powers of national banks.

As the restrictions on national bank activities started tumbling, state banks began to appreciate the competitive advantages accruing to national banks. In 1965, Chase Manhattan, the largest state bank in the country, converted to a national charter. In 1968, Wells Fargo Bank of California, the largest state bank outside of New York City, and the Wachovia Bank and Trust Company of Winston-Salem, North Carolina, the largest state bank in the southeastern United States, also converted to national charters. According to trade publication reports, the Comptroller's more permissive regulatory posture was a factor in these and many other changeovers to national charters.[25] Between 1960 and 1968, 165 state banks converted to national status.[26]

As the liberalization gained momentum, the state bank regulatory agencies and the Fed started getting pressure from their constituents to follow the Comptroller's *laissez-faire* lead. The bankers' success prompted J. L. Robertson, Federal Reserve Board member, to characterize the bank regulatory process as "competition in laxity." [27]

Many of Saxon's changes were contrary to long-standing congressional policy and conflicted with the interpretations of the same statutory language by other federal bank regulatory agencies. Some of the conflicts were resolved when the Fed, under pressure from its banks, relaxed its interpretations to conform with the Comptroller's policy. In other cases the Comptroller was reversed by the courts. In some others, Saxon's successor, William Camp, reinstated the prior rule, thereby reducing somewhat the tendency for regulatory policy to descend to the lowest common denominator.

For example federal law requires every national bank to follow the branching law of the state in which it is located:

> A national banking association may, with the approval of the Comptroller of the Currency, establish and operate new branches: (1) Within the limits of the city, town, or village in which said association is situated, if such establishment and operation are at the time *expressly authorized* to State banks by the law of the State in question; and (2) at any point within the State in which said association is situated, *if such establishment and operation are at the time authorized to State banks by the statute law of the State in question by language specifically granting such authority affirmatively and not merely by implication or recognition, and subject to the restrictions as to location imposed by the law of the State on State banks. . . .*[28] (emphasis added)

Despite this explicit language, Saxon, in 1963, allowed two national banks in Utah to open new branches contrary to a state prohibition against branching except to convert an acquired bank into a branch. The U.S. Supreme Court, noting the congressional policy to foster competitive equality between state and national banks, overturned Saxon's decision.[29] In another case, Saxon ruled that a separate "drive-in" facility was not a branch, thereby permitting a national bank to circumvent a state prohibition against branching. Once again, the Comptroller was reversed by the courts.[30] In a South Dakota case, however, he ruled that a national bank could convert three acquired banks into branches although they were beyond the 50-mile branching limit of the state law and was upheld when the court found the state rule unlawful.[31]

Federal law allows national banks "located and doing business in any place the population of which does not exceed five thousand inhabitants" [32] to sell insurance. Saxon, however, allowed all national banks to sell insurance "which is incident to banking transactions." [33] The U.S. Court of Appeals for the Fifth Circuit overturned the Comptroller's ruling.[34]

Federal law separates commercial banking from investment banking. Banks may not own corporate stock, and may under-write only the "general obligations" of state, municipal, and county governments. The latter had always been interpreted to mean government securities backed by the "full faith and credit" of an issuer with general powers of taxation. The Comptroller, however, lowered the requirements and allowed banks to un-derwrite certain revenue bonds that were not in the permissible category.* Saxon also ruled that national banks could own stock in subsidiary companies to "engage in activities, which are a part of the business of banking or incidental thereto. . . ." [35] The Fed reexamined the question but adhered to its prior posi-tion that state member banks could not own operating subsidi-aries.[36] As national banks spawned various subsidiaries under the authority of Saxon's rulings, state banks complained that they were suffering a competitive disadvantage. In 1968, the giant Wachovia Bank and Trust Company of Winston-Salem, and Wells Fargo Bank both switched to national charters, stating that the Fed's restrictive position on operating subsidiaries had played a major part in their decisions.[37]

Frank Wille, then New York's Banking Superintendent, whose office regulates Morgan Guaranty, Manufacturers Han-over, Chemical, and Bankers Trust, requested a meeting with the Federal Reserve Board.[38] The day after the meeting, the board announced that it had decided that a state member bank could "purchase for its own account shares of corporations to perform, at locations at which the bank is authorized to engage in business, functions that the bank is empowered to perform di-rectly." [39]

In 1964, Saxon and the Fed again split over whether banks could lawfully acquire stock—this time stock in foreign banks. In 1966, Congress amended the law to ratify the Comptroller's more expansive position.[40] Saxon also ruled that national banks

---

* A revenue bond is paid off from a specific source of funds. For example, Triborough Bridge and Tunnel Authority Bonds are paid from bridge and tunnel toll receipts and are not backed by the general credit of New York City.

could acquire the stock in domestic banks. The Fed refused to go along [41] and in 1967, Saxon's successor, William Camp, reversed the position of the Comptroller's office.[42]

In 1964, Congress required banks to make disclosures of information comparable to those required of other issuers of securities,[43] according to regulations to be established by the various bank regulatory agencies. But the differences between Saxon's limited regulations and the detailed regulations of the Fed and the FDIC made it virtually impossible to compare the financial condition of national banks and other banks. Furthermore, Saxon did away with the long-standing practice of requiring national banks to issue detailed reports of condition four times a year. Rather, he allowed national banks to make very limited disclosure in their three quarterly reports, requiring full information only at year-end. William Camp ironed out both of these conflicts with the Fed after he took over the Comptroller's office in 1966.[44]

Saxon's laxity toward mergers was notorious. Under the Bank Merger Act of 1960 and the 1966 amendments, responsibility for evaluating the competitive impact of bank mergers is divided between the Comptroller, the Fed, and FDIC (depending on whether the surviving bank is a national, state member, or insured state nonmember bank), with the Antitrust Division of the Department of Justice also retaining the right to sue. Although Congress anticipated that the three bank agencies would apply uniform standards in assessing the legality of bank mergers,[45] it soon became apparent that the Comptroller was being much more permissive. One study, compiled by the staff of the Senate Banking and Currency Committee, compared the merger approval rates of the three federal banking agencies with the Antitrust Division and found the Comptroller's office by far the most permissive. The data disclosed that the Comptroller's merger approval rate, based on the number of mergers, is 23% *higher* than the Antitrust Division's, while the rates for the Federal Reserve Board and the FDIC are 11% and 6% *lower,* respectively. Comparing merger approval rates in terms of the assets of the combining banks shows an even greater permissiveness by the Comptroller. The Comptroller's approval rate is 40% above the Antitrust Division, while the FDIC's rate is 22% higher than the Antitrust Division's and the Fed's is 6% lower, despite

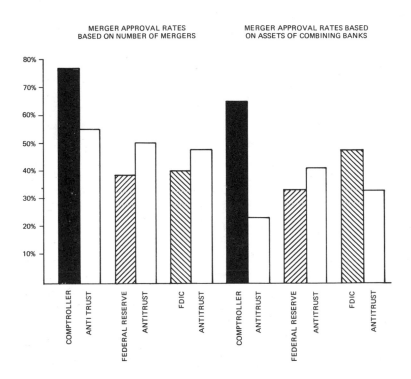

MERGER APPROVAL RATES OF THE 3 FEDERAL BANK REGULATORY
AGENCIES COMPARED WITH THE ANTITRUST DIVISION, 1960 - 1969

the fact that they are all interpreting the same statutory provision.[46]

Perhaps the most flagrant decisions Saxon made were those expanding the scope of permissible bank activity. National banks are permitted to engage only in those activities specifically authorized by Congress, but one provision authorizes banks to exercise "all such incidental powers as shall be *necessary* to carry on the business of banking." [47] The rationale for this restriction is to prevent financial concentration and to avoid conflicts of interest where bank ownership might restrict bank objectivity.

As Comptroller, Saxon ruled that banks could operate "commingled investment funds," the bank equivalent of a mutual fund. Citibank was the first bank to take advantage of this ruling by setting up such a fund whose monies could be—and in part were—invested in the stock of the very same companies that had outstanding loans with the bank. FNCB's attempts to expand into the mutual fund business were quickly curtailed by the Supreme Court's April, 1971 decision ruling that the operation of such a fund violated the prohibition against banks engaging in the securities business.[48]

Another activity that Saxon held to be necessary to carry on the business of banking was the leasing of personal property:

> A national bank may become the owner or lessor of personal property acquired upon the specific request and for the use of a customer and may incur such additional obligations as may be incident to becoming an owner and lessor of such property. Lease transactions do not result in obligations for the purpose of 12 U.S.C. 84.[49]

This ruling opened the way for national banks to compete with commercial and retail leasing and rental companies and provided a means of avoiding the prohibition against lending more than 10% of the bank's capital to a single customer.

The changes in regulatory policy implemented by the Comptroller's office during the 1960s effectively repealed, by administrative fiat, much of the restrictive legislation of the 1930s. Saxon's behavior, and to a lesser extent, Camp's as well, shows how difficult it is to ensure that regulatory agencies—insulated from outside pressure and armed with exclusive access to the information on which policy decisions are based and the support of the business interests their agencies are supposed to regulate— will channel their broad discretionary powers within the guidelines laid down by Congress. Despite the fact that fostering competitive equality between national and state banks is a fundamental policy of the federal banking laws, the Comptroller's unilateral relaxation of long-standing doctrines subverted that policy and pressured the other banking agencies into changing their own regulatory policies in order to restore a semblance of competitive equality.

To characterize Saxon's Administration as "pro-bank" or "bank oriented" is an understatement; in many respects, the bankers themselves—especially the heads of the large national banks—took the initiative in formulating regulatory policy, with the Comptroller's function reduced to ratifying and codifying the practices in which the banks wanted to engage. Saxon's Foreword to the Comptroller's *Manual for National Banks*—the looseleaf compendium of laws, regulations, and rulings affecting national banks—candidly described the symbiotic process by which the rules are made:

> Life has been breathed into the body of bank regulation through the joint efforts of this Office and of the National Banks. The results which have been achieved are as much the product of renewed banking initiative, seeking, in response to public need and demand, to assure the performance of all financial functions, as of our own efforts. . . .
>
> There are now assisting us in our continuing task Advisory Committees to the Administrator of National Banks [the Comptroller of the Currency] and to the Regional Administrators. But we hope that each National Bank will continue to initiate new methods and to explore all opportunities for serving the public. This is the ultimate source from which we must refresh our ideas and reshape our policies—so that, in the emerging future, no proper banking function will go unnoticed or unfulfilled through default or neglect, either by this Office or by the National Banks.
>
> We continue to welcome the thoughts and suggestions of all National Banks—so that we may keep our policies and procedures and this Manual of Laws, Regulations and Rulings abreast of the time, and so that the National Banking System may perform at the highest level of efficiency its vital financial role in the Nation's growth and development.[50]

The bankers' role in the regulatory process was institutionalized in the National Advisory Committee to the Comptroller of the Currency, a group representing the largest national banks, which met periodically with the Comptroller and his staff to discuss and formulate regulatory policy and to develop legislative positions for the Comptroller. The first advisory committee, composed exclusively of bankers, was formed in 1961. In 1962, President Kennedy promulgated an executive order which required Cabinet-level approval of all such industry advisory groups. In addition, the executive order required such committees to maintain a verbatim transcript of proceedings unless the appropriate cabinet officer waived the requirement in favor of minutes.[51] Saxon waited until 1964, however, to request formal authorization to form regional and national advisory committees. Saxon recommended, and Secretary of the Treasury Dillon determined, that "a verbatim transcript would interfere with the proper functioning of the Advisory Committees and that waiver of the requirement of a verbatim transcript is in the public interest." Although the minutes of the National Advisory Committee's (NAC) meetings are scanty—averaging eight double-spaced typewritten pages per three-hour meeting—they do provide a glimpse of the bank regulatory process in action. They show that, as a practical matter, the Comptroller surrendered to the banks responsibility for initiating changes in regulatory policy, formulating rules and regulations, and developing and recommending legislation.

The bankers' proposals involved a wide variety of topics, ranging from detailed, technical changes in bank operating practices to broad legislative policies with significant impact on millions of people. As one would expect, some of the bankers' proposals— especially those involving the technicalities of bank operations —were sound and did not conflict with the broader interests of the public at large. Many others, however, were clearly designed to give the welfare of the banks priority over the interests of those not represented on the National Advisory Committee. In any event, whether the Comptroller's decision to change a particular rule or support a given bill was sound or not, the minutes demonstrate that the Comptroller invariably polled the bankers and sought their concurrence and approval before taking action.

George S. Moore, Citibank's President, was Chairman of the National Advisory Committee and presided over the meetings, which were frequently attended by Ward B. Stevenson, FNCB's Vice President in charge of public relations, E. Sherman Adams, FNCB Senior Vice President in charge of governmental relations, and Lief Olsen, FNCB's chief economist, among other bank employees.[52] The bankers frequently got the Comptroller to do what they recommended, and the Comptroller solicited opinions from the bankers concerning legislation and demonstrated consistent willingness to do their bidding.

In 1967, for example, Congress was formulating Truth-in-Lending legislation, which required creditors to disclose credit costs and how customers could avoid incurring finance charges. Although bankers felt that no Truth-in-Lending law was necessary, they recognized that Congress was going to pass one, so they wanted to make sure that the law was enforced by a government agency sympathetic to their interests. Accordingly, the National Advisory Committee recommended that enforcement of bank compliance with Truth-in-Lending be delegated to the bank regulatory agencies, as shown by the minutes of a National Advisory Committee meeting:

> Discussion of pending banking legislation—

> Truth-in-Lending Bill. There was open discussion about this and the consensus of the Committee was that any bill forthcoming should be policed by the bank regulatory agencies.[53]

Congress went along, and the banks reaped the benefit. For the Comptroller, as the earlier chapters on retail credit demonstrate, has waited for complaints before moving against banks that fail to disclose the required information in the required format, rather than take the initiative to ensure that national banks obeyed the letter and spirit of the law.

The bankers' power to obtain self-serving legislation is exemplified by an addition to the U.S. Criminal Code which makes it a crime knowingly to give a bank false information in a credit application. Citibank's George S. Moore was a prime mover behind this law, as National Advisory Committee minutes show:

> . . . during the discussion it was brought out that there was no federal law against giving a false statement to a National Bank. Chairman Moore felt that some corrective legislation was needed in this area.[54]

Comptroller Camp supported Moore's suggestion and Congress amended the U.S. Criminal Code to make it a crime, punishable by a $5,000 fine and two years in jail,

> . . . to knowingly make any false statement or report, or willingly overvalue any land, property or security for the purpose of influencing in any way the action of . . . any bank the deposits of which are insured by the Federal Deposit Insurance Corporation.[55]

To our knowledge, this is the only federal law which provides criminal sanctions for giving false information to an institution run for private profit.

The bankers on the National Advisory Committee also assumed the burden of drafting the very rules and regulations that are supposed to be part of the Comptroller's regulatory responsibilities, such as the Comptroller's rules on bank accounting.

In 1966, Chairman Moore announced that a committee of bank cashiers and accountants (within the National Advisory Committee) had been appointed to propose changes in bank accounting rules. The Comptroller of the Currency, whose job supposedly is regulation rather than accommodation, even insisted on polling the banks to make sure that the proposed regulations were acceptable.

Despite the objection that the proposed rules gave banks too much discretion to overstate their earnings, the Comptroller duly adopted the rules drawn up by the bankers.

The bankers were so pleased that the Comptroller had become their advocate in the legislative and regulatory spheres that they wanted their man in court as well. So, when bank merger legislation was pending in Congress, George Moore recommended that the law be amended to provide the Comptroller with the statutory right to intervene in suits brought by the Department of Justice to prevent bank mergers deemed anticompetitive. The Comptroller followed Moore's suggestion and supported the provision, which was incorporated into the legislation:

> In any action brought under the antitrust laws arising out of a merger transaction approved by a Federal supervisory agency pursuant to this subsection, such agency . . . may appear as a party of its own motion and as of right, and be represented by its counsel.[56]

Though Comptroller William Camp has been more circumspect than his predecessor in openly expressing his support for expanding the powers of national banks, he too, has demonstrated a sensitivity to bankers' opinions in formulating his legislative endorsements. In 1967, when Congress was considering various measures pertaining to the trust powers of national banks, Camp changed his position to reflect the wishes of the NAC bankers:

> Dean Miller, Deputy Comptroller for Trusts, discussed H.R. 10 [Commingled investment accounts]. He also gave a brief history of the Keogh Bill and the position the Office took at the beginning and . . . [the Comptroller's] current position. Mr. Miller went on to discuss the legislation that is now being promoted (but not introduced as yet) which would specifically exempt Keogh and other pooled pension and profit sharing

trusts and traditional common trust funds but would not affect commingled agency funds. [i.e., bank mutual funds, such as the one operated by FNCB]. Because of certain considerations which were outlined by Mr. Miller, the Comptroller's Office has been asked to reverse its position and actively support this legislation. The Comptroller is presently considering this course of action.[57]

The Comptroller subsequently changed his position and supported legislation that would clearly exempt Keogh trusts (retirement benefit funds for self-employed people) and other types of pooled trusts from certain provisions of the securities laws. He also endorsed a provision in the Mutual Fund Reform Bill (which was never passed) that would have clarified the powers of national banks to go into the mutual fund business.

The Comptroller's willingness to defer to the banks in formulating policy is reinforced by his habit of allowing regulatory agency personnel to be wined and dined by the bankers. Many former officials of the Comptroller's office said that bankers frequently entertain the Comptroller and his staff, as the following remarks by one former official of the Comptroller's office demonstrate:

> When bankers come into town, the people at the Comptroller's office always look forward to being taken out to dinner. It's a big thing for the Comptroller's people and it happens all the time. It's pretty tough to have George Moore take you out to dinner and then turn around and criticize him. Such behavior is not consistent with the role of regulator. It makes the Comptroller look like a prostitute, and in a sense he is, though he does a conscientious job on the examination.
>
> The Comptroller's office has none of the SEC's prophylactic prohibitions against being wined and dined. And this definitely contributes to the fact that the Comptroller is not as enforcement-minded as he should be.

In addition, Saxon's years with the American Bankers Association and the First National Bank of Chicago, according to one former aide who worked closely with the Comptroller, made him aware of the contempt that bankers held for the underpaid administrators who manned the Comptroller's office. So when Saxon took over he sought to increase the status of the officials who worked for the Comptroller's office. As the former aide put it, "Jim said that the bankers fly first class, so we'll fly first class. They eat at the best restaurants and stay at the best hotels, so will we." A small point, perhaps, but significant, because it shows a desire to emulate the men the Comptroller was charged with regulating.

Another reason for the Comptroller's close identification with the banks is the fact that the agency's employees routinely retire to banks or law firms serving bank clients when they are through with government service. Three of the four top policy-making officials recently to leave the Comptroller's Office work for, or represent, national banks. Eighty-five of the 300-plus examiners who left in 1969 work for commercial banks. A survey conducted by the Comptroller's office in 1967 showed that 170 of the 430 examiners who left in 1965 and 1966 went to work for commercial banks. Over 60% of the former officials and attorneys of the Comptroller's office who were interviewed by project members work for, or represent, banks. This revolving door between the Comptroller's office and the banks cannot help but increase the tendency of the Comptroller's personnel to formulate and implement policy in a way that will not jeopardize future employment prospects.

Bank Examinations

The important role played by the large national banks in formulating regulatory policy also prevails in the area of bank examinations. Just as the Comptroller delegates to the bankers on the National Advisory Committee responsibility for gathering data, conducting research, drafting rules and regulations, and formulating the Comptroller's position on legislation, the Comptroller effectively delegates much of his responsibility to examine solvency and ensure compliance with the law to the banks themselves— especially the large banks. The Comptroller ignores the statutory requirement to examine all national banks three times every two years [58] by dispensing with one-third of the required examinations for the 50 largest banks.[59]

The purpose of an examination, as outlined in the Comptroller's *Handbook of Examination Procedure,* is extremely broad:

National Bank examinations are designed to determine the condition and performance of banks, the quality of their operations, the capacity of management, and to enforce compliance with federal laws. All facets of a bank examination, ranging from appraising assets and internal controls to evaluating the soundness of management policies, *have as their end result the determination of liquidity and solvency—present and prospective—and the legality of the bank's acts.* The scope of an examination may embrace every phase of banking activity found in the particular bank under examination or it may concentrate in specific areas of bank activity which deserve and must receive greater emphasis in direct relation to their importance and bearing on the condition of the bank.[60] (emphasis added)

Despite this huge responsibility, however, most people familiar with bank examinations feel that of all the bank regulatory agencies, the Comptroller's office does the best job at examining banks. The following statement was typical:

When I was an attorney at the Comptroller's office, I frequently reviewed examination reports to determine whether certain practices were legal. I also saw plenty of examination reports from the Fed and the FDIC. I always felt that Comptroller's examination reports were much better—more thorough—than those of the other agencies. The Fed, unlike the Comptroller, is not basically an examination agency. It's a central bank and its primary concern is with monetary policy. It's pretty hard to imagine a bank examiner rising to the top at the Fed. And the FDIC is basically an insuring agency that examines small country banks. The Comptroller's office, however, is essentially an examining agency. Comptroller William Camp was an examiner. His deputy is an examiner. They both came up through the ranks and they understand the examining process.

Nevertheless, the Comptroller's resources are limited and the size and complexity of the national banking system make it impossible for him to fulfill all statutory responsibilities with his present resources.

The Comptroller of the Currency employs 1,560 commercial bank examiners based in 14 regional offices. Two-thirds of the examiners are assistant national bank examiners, who do the dull, routine "scut work," as one examiner called it—counting cash, checking securities, collateral, and documentation, and gathering other data. The other third are commissioned national bank examiners who concentrate on evaluating loans.[61] The Second National Bank Region, covering New York and New Jersey, has the largest staff, with 226 commercial bank examiners, 14% of the total; the 310 national banks in the second region control over 19% of all assets in the national banking system.[62]

The amount of resources allocated to each bank examination depends on the size of the bank in terms of its assets, the asset structure, the number of branches, and—most important of all —the Comptroller's opinion of the bank's management and solvency based on prior examinations. If two banks are roughly equal in size, the bank with more loans takes longer to examine because evaluating the creditworthiness of borrowers is slower than counting and checking securities. It is also more time-consuming to examine a large number of small consumer credits than a smaller number of large commercial credits. Examinations also take longer in California, where bank branches are spread out all over the state, than in Illinois, where everything is under one roof.[63] Thus Citibank, which has more branches, more loans, and more consumer credit than Chase, also takes up more of the Comptroller's time. Each man-day spent examining Chase covers $9 million in assets; the same amount of time will cover only $8 million in FNCB's assets.

SELECTED STATISTICS OF FNCB AND CHASE MANHATTAN BANK
(December 31, 1969)

	FNCB	Chase
(1) Total assets	$22,843,320,000	$22,145,000,000
(2) Asset structure		
a. Total loans	$13,240,000,000	$12,999,000,000
b. Consumer credit	$ 1,059,000,000	$ 572,773,000
(3) Number of branches	181	152
(domestic only)		
Man-days expended in 1970 examination	2,866	2,436

SOURCE: FNCC-FNCB, *1969 Annual Report;* Chase Manhattan Bank-Chase Manhattan Corporation, *1969 Annual Report.* FNCC Form 10-K, filed with the SEC, December 31, 1969. Chase Manhattan Corporation, Form 10-K, filed with the SEC, December 31, 1969.

In New York City, the largest banks serve many of the same national and multinational corporations. In smaller cities, however, the largest bank usually gets the cream of the business, the borrowers with better credit. Consequently, in most cities it generally takes more of the Comptroller's resources to examine the second and third largest banks than the largest bank. A bank that has had weak credits in the past generally gets a greater allocation of examination resources. One national bank, for example, with less than 15% of Citibank's assets, takes just as long to examine because its loan officers allegedly are not as expert and its credits have historically been weaker.[64] However, since FNCB is New York's largest plaintiff, and many of FNCB's lawsuits are brought to collect debts in default (arising from loans that violate FNCB's own credit policies) more time and more care, rather than less, should be spent by the Comptroller's examiners when they visit Citibank.

Because solvency is the Comptroller's primary, if not exclusive concern, a relatively small amount of examination resources are allocated to banks, such as FNCB and Chase, in which the Comptroller has a great deal of confidence. Applying the 316,612 man-days spent on national bank examinations in 1970 [65] to the $314,048,000,000 in national bank assets at December 31, 1969,[66] shows that each man must, on the average, examine $1 million of assets per day. At Citibank and Chase, he must cover eight and nine times as much. Especially in dealing with the big banks, the Comptroller uses many shortcuts that effectively shift much of the responsibility from the regulatory agency to the banks themselves.

The Comptroller's *Handbook of Examination Procedure* specifies that the examination force should take control of the bank's assets:

> At the beginning of an examination it is important to obtain immediate control of cash, cash items, clearings, securities on hand, the loan portfolio, collateral to loans and other collateral, customers' safekeeping, deposit ledgers, and all other records and items as may be designated by the Examiner-in-Charge.[67]

This is not possible with the large banks. Even all 226 examiners in the Second Region—and they all go in at the start of a Chase or Citibank examination—cannot possibly obtain control of Citibank's $4,872,000,000 in cash, $3,004,000,000 in securities, and $13,240,000,000 in loans, at any one time. So they sample. The size of the sample depends on the Comptroller's evaluation of the bank's own internal audit procedures and the type of the asset involved. As Justin Watson, the First Deputy Comptroller, put it: "The Examiner-in-Charge reviews the bank's internal audit system. If it's weak, we do more test checks. Citibank has a good audit procedure." [68] A relatively small percentage of the cash is actually counted because, as Mr. Watson noted, "no bank ever failed because of a cash shortage." [69]

The computer has increased the Comptroller's reliance on the banks in the conduct of examination. At first, the Comptroller had trouble dealing with new technology, as a former examiner noted:

> The Comptroller had extreme difficulty in coping with the changeover to computers by a lot of banks. With limited resources, it's been tough for the Comptroller to keep up with the banks in this area. So the examiners had to rely a great deal on the banks to provide the information.

The Comptroller therefore started a computer training program: As Justin Watson observed:

> We have two computer men in each region and computer schools all around to train all the Comptroller's people. Peat, Marwick & Mitchell is assisting in setting up the schools. We're developing audit tapes to test the computers and our e.d.p. [electronic data processing] people work with the banks to work out the test procedures.[70]

The problem is that Peat, Marwick is the accounting firm retained by Citibank and Chase to audit their books.[71] It is a clear conflict of interest for Peat, Marwick to be formulating the procedures by which the Comptroller examines Peat, Marwick's clients and evaluates Peat, Marwick's auditing job. If Citibank or Chase were trying to hide something, their own auditor, responsible for developing the Comptroller's examination procedures and training the Comptroller's personnel, would know how to do it better than anyone else.

The most important part of the examination is the evaluation of the loan portfolio. Citibank's $13,240,000,000 in loans at the end of 1969 accounted for 57% of its assets. Loans subject to criticism are classified as "substandard," "doubtful," or "loss": substandard when the examiner believes that the borrower's current financial condition jeopardizes repayment, doubtful when the examiner thinks that repayment is improbable, and loss when they are deemed uncollectible and no longer to be considered assets of the bank.[72]

A loan is automatically classified as substandard, doubtful, or loss if the borrower (1) is losing money, (2) has a heavy debt to worth ratio (i.e., net worth in terms of shareholders' equity), *and* (3) has a heavy working capital deficit. If only one or two of these factors are present, it is a question of judgment for the examiner.[73]

Even a bank that has a large dollar volume of substandard, doubtful, and loss loans is in excellent condition if it has a large cushion of stockholders' equity to absorb the impact of write-offs. Thus, the lower the percentage of classified assets to capital, the better is the bank's condition. Mr. Watson says that the Comptroller rates each bank's condition according to the following guidelines: [74]

Ratio of Classified Assets to Capital	Rating of Condition
under 10%	excellent
10%–20%	very good
20%–30%	good
30%–40%	fair
over 40%	unsatisfactory

Mr. Watson says that over 80% of all national banks are under 20% (very good or excellent) and that about half of these are under 10% (excellent).[75] Banks with ratios over 40% receive very close supervision from the comptroller.

Surprising as it may seem, two of the three largest national banks—Bank of America and Chase Manhattan—are not in the top 80%. Bank of America's ratio of classified assets to capital is 23% and Chase Manhattan's is 21%. Citibank's ratio, however, is a "very good" 11%:

1970 EXAMINATION RESULTS, BANK OF AMERICA, CHASE, CITIBANK			
	Classified Assets	Total Capital *	Ratio
Bank of America	$336,973,000	$1,437,449,000	23%
Chase Manhattan	342,961,000	1,646,000,000	21%
Citibank	180,621,000	1,701,000,000	11%

*Total capital includes bad debt valuation reserves.

SOURCES:
Bank of America, Application to open branch at Olympic Boulevard and Bundy Drive, Los Angeles, California, filed with the Comptroller, 1970. Chase Manhattan Bank, Application to open branch at Zerega Avenue and Gleason Avenue, Bronx, New York, filed with the Comptroller, 1970. FNCB, Application to open branch at 2100 Grand Concourse, Bronx, New York, filed with the Comptroller, 1970.

In light of the fact that 80% of all national banks have better classified asset to capital ratios than two of the three largest national banks, we suggest that there is no excuse for allocating only 3% of the Comptroller's examination resources to cover the three largest national banks, which have one-fifth of the assets in the national banking system. Bank of America, Chase Manhattan, and FNCB ought to be examined three times every two years, in accordance with the law and the examiners should spend enough time to scrutinize the same areas that are emphasized in the examinations of smaller banks.

Justin Watson, the First Deputy Comptroller, asserts that "examiners spend the amount of time necessary to do the job" [76] of evaluating bank loan portfolios. He says that the Comptroller's office checks all of Citibank's loans between $500,000 and $1 million and 80% of the bank's loans in terms of dollar volume. He explains that the loan portfolio of a bank like Citibank is heavy with good credits of strong companies, credits that are easy to evaluate. Furthermore, he points out that most of the loans are "boilerplate"—standard form agreements—with the blanks filled in and few variations from loan to loan. Finally, he says that credits that were evaluated at the last examination need not be reviewed thoroughly again because checking the repayment progress since the last examination is sufficient.[77]

This rosy view of the examination, however, is not shared by former examiners and attorneys who worked in the Comptroller's office. Most of the examiners described the examination of a multibillion dollar bank as "a monstrous job" that severely taxed the Comptroller's resources. The work is hard and often dull. The hours are long, frequently requiring evenings and weekends in order to finish in time to go on to the next scheduled examination. As one commissioned national bank examiner noted in a statement endorsed time and again by others:

> We never had as much time as we needed. Evaluating credits is a tremendously difficult job, especially if you want to do a good job. And the big banks have enormous amounts of credits. Our coverage was pretty good. We looked at most of the loans, but our look wasn't as thorough as it should have been. If we had more time, we could do a better job.

An attorney noted that violations of law are overlooked because the Comptroller barely has the resources to evaluate solvency:

The basic problem with the examination process is that the Comptroller doesn't have the resources to fulfill his statutory responsibilities. He's supposed to go into every national bank at least three times every two years. But he doesn't have the manpower to look at everything he should. So the primary goal becomes to make sure that each bank is solvent, that the depositors will get their money back. And this means that if a bank is solvent, violations of law get overlooked.

A bank like Citibank, where the Comptroller has confidence in the expertise and sophistication of the lending officers, does not present as much of a regulatory problem as Franklin National, whose lending officers don't do such a good job. When difficult legal questions arise, the Comptroller defers to Shearman & Sterling and Debevoise, Plimpton [Citibank's law firms] because they are hired full-time to thoroughly research difficult legal questions of banking law. He defers to their opinions and doesn't second-guess them.

The Comptroller's *Handbook of Examination Procedure* contains additional evidence of the Comptroller's obliviousness to violations of law. In addition to the three loan classifications, the examiners designate some loans as "other loans especially mentioned." Illegal loans, however, are not placed in this category under the procedures outlined in the Comptroller's *Handbook:*

> The sole test of eligibility for incorporating loans in this schedule must rest on the element of credit risk. Loans should not be listed in this schedule solely because they are in violation of the banking statutes or rulings of the Office of the Comptroller of the Currency.[78]

Furthermore, examiners are instructed not to list in the excessive loan schedule previously excessive loans that have been reduced to the legal limit:

> It is not desired that previously excessive loans, once they have been reduced to a point within a bank's legal loan limit, be continued as "excessive" in the report pending their final liquidation. The bank's management should be informed of their true status, but they should not be repeatedly so classified in the report.[79]

If the Comptroller were seriously interested in enforcing the law, the examination report would contain a comprehensive listing of all excessive loans in order to determine how frequently each bank violates the law, not just how many excessive loans are on the books at the examination date.

Similarly, the Comptroller instructs examiners to ignore preferential loans that depart from sound credit principles, as long as they are not so numerous as to jeopardize solvency:

Poor Selection of Risks

A majority of bankers have several loans or a rather large number of small loans, unimportant to the bank in their aggregate sum, which they regard as warranted loans but as exceptions to their general credit policies because of inherent weaknesses. Because they are recognized by the management as a departure from sound credit principles, and the aggregate of the loans is held to a moderate and unimportant amount, the Examiner need not be unduly concerned. It is when exceptions become the rule, recognized or unrecognized, that important loan problems develop.[80]

The fact that examiners are not instructed to probe deeply into preferential loans to ascertain why banks give favorable terms to certain customers underscores the fact that the Comptroller prefers not to ensure compliance with the law. The Comptroller's overriding concern is solvency; once a bank satisfies the Comptroller's office on that score, the bank is free to violate many of the other banking regulations without a peep from the chief regulator.

Although the Comptroller's *Handbook* directs the examiners to inspect closely the "personal and special accounts of directors, officers and employees *and their interests* . . . for unusual entries or activity, or credit in excess of normal income," [81] Justin Watson indicates that this is not done for large banks such as FNCB:

In your average bank out of New York City, if a director's other companies are borrowing from the bank, the director is more likely to use his influence to get the credit. Generally, there's no conflict of interest involved when Anaconda [whose Executive Committee Chairman was on FNCB's board] borrows from Citibank. . . . Anaconda and Citibank have an old relationship.[82] *

* In this connection it is interesting to note that on June 1, 1971, John B. M. Place, Vice Chairman of Chase Manhattan Bank and a director of Anaconda (James D. Farley, FNCB Executive Vice President, is also a director), became President and Chief Executive Officer of Anaconda to steer the company through the financial difficulties stemming from the Chilean government's expropriation of Anaconda's copper mines. (*Amer-*

We fail to comprehend the logic of Mr. Watson's distinction. Although Anaconda lacks the type of control over Citibank typically enjoyed by directors of smaller banks, an interlocking directorship, it will be recalled, is an important element of the total relationship between bank and customer: loan officers repeatedly asserted that the interlock strengthens the bond between the bank and the corporation. It therefore would be appropriate for the Comptroller to keep close watch over the accounts of directors and their interests to ensure that banks are not making unwarranted extensions of credit. When giant companies get into trouble—as Penn Central and Lockheed did—hundreds of millions of dollars are involved; and these giant companies are the very ones most likely to have "old relationships" and interlocking directorates with banks.

The Comptroller's emphasis on solvency to the exclusion of other considerations is further illustrated by the fact that the examiners do not give special attention to the accounts of large depositors of the giant banks. The Comptroller's *Handbook* calls for close scrutiny of large accounts:

> Also to be identified and separately listed by the Examiner during the proof are accounts with large balances and groups of related accounts, having large balances in the aggregate. This list will assist the Examiner-in-Charge in assessing the potential volatility of the bank's deposit structure and the adequacy of its liquidity position. . . . While the Examiner-in-Charge will determine this amount in the absence of specific instructions, it is good practice during the proof of all deposit accounts, to label all accounts and related deposit balances that together total over 2% of the bank's total deposits.[83]

"This provision," notes Justin Watson, "was written for smaller towns." [84] Mr. Watson indicates that it is not followed in the examination of banks like Citibank, because the Comptroller is confident of the large banks' ability to weather sudden, large withdrawals. Although the liquidity of a giant like Citibank, with over $20 billion in deposits, is not likely to be jeopardized by a large depositor's precipitous withdrawal of funds, large depositors do wield a lot of influence at their banks and can often obtain credit on terms not available to lesser customers. Thus, in the corporate banking chapter it was pointed out that loan officers sometimes grant credit to their profitable accounts—i.e., those with hefty balances—in violation of the bank's credit policies.

An executive of one company claimed that a large New York bank refused to renew the company's credit because one of the bank's largest depositors (one of the 75 largest industrial corporations in America) was trying to buy out the company and the bank wanted to apply pressure in order to help make the company more amenable to the overtures of the prospective purchaser. Whether or not this claim is true—we were unable to verify it independently—the fact remains that banks are under a strong incentive to help their large depositors as much as possible. Accordingly, the Comptroller should not dispense with close scrutiny of the accounts of large depositors merely because bank liquidity and solvency are not at stake.

Finally, the Comptroller makes only superficial inquiry into banks' political contributions. Although until 1972* the U.S. Criminal Code prohibited national banks from making contributions to political candidates,[85] all the Comptroller did to ensure compliance with the law in this area was to examine each bank's expense accounts.[86] Banks, however, use sophisticated, hidden methods of contributing to candidates that such superficial examination will not disclose.

In 1970, the chairman and other senior executives of the National Bank of Commerce of Seattle sent a letter inviting bank officers to contribute to the "League For Good Government." The letter included a schedule of suggested contributions, ranging from $48 per year for those with salaries of $12,000, to $210 per year for those with salaries over $30,000.[87] Although the letter stated that contributions were voluntary, the person who sent a photocopy of the letter to the House Banking and Currency Committee asked a trenchant question: "If you were an officer of the National Bank of Commerce of Seattle, how would

* Public Law 92-225, the Federal Election Campaign Act of 1971, enacted February 7, 1972, amended Sections 591 and 610 of Title 18 of the U.S. Code that deal with political contributions and expenditures. As amended, these sections of the federal criminal law no longer prohibit " . . . a loan of money by a national or state bank made in accordance with the applicable banking laws and regulations and in the ordinary course of business."

you like to receive this letter from a group of your senior officers?" The bank's vice president in charge of governmental relations was "coordinator" of the "clearing committee" [88] that determined who would receive the money.

A similar method of solicitation is alleged to have been employed by Manufacturers Hanover Trust Company (a state-chartered bank). On April 13, 1970, Representative Wright Patman, Chairman of the House Banking and Currency Committee, received the following hand-printed letter: [89]

April 8, 1970

Dear Congressman Patman,

I believe it is illegal for banks to make political contributions to political candidates. The Manufacturers Hanover Trust Company has gotten around this by forcing its 1,000 plus officers to "kick back" 1/2 of 1% of their salary each year.

Checks are drawn to the order of "Robert Isban Special Account." Mr. Isban is a deputy controller. Disposition of the "slush fund" is not disclosed to those who contribute.

Very Truly Yours,
Anonymous

Citibank plays politics by retaining the law firm with which Senator Jacob Javits was associated until 1971 to represent the bank in mortgage transactions. Because the borrower pays the bank's lawyer in New York City real-estate transactions, the payments to the senator's former firm do not show up in the bank's expense account. Senator Javits' old firm does not handle the small, unprofitable transactions, which go to FNCB's salaried collections lawyer, nor the complicated or large transactions, which are handled by Shearman & Sterling, but only the routine, $50,000-$1 million mortgages that do not present unusual problems.* "Deals like these," noted one experienced real-estate

---

* LAWYERS REPRESENTING CITIBANK IN MANHATTAN REAL-ESTATE TRANSACTIONS, 1968–70

	1968	1969	1970
Robert B. Frank			
number of transactions	24	47	23
size of average loan	$15,000	$20,000	$23,000
Javits, Trubin			
number of transactions	30	17	19
size of average loan	160,000	230,000	158,000
Shearman & Sterling			
number of transactions	11	34	39
size of average loan	4,500,000	1,600,000	15,000,000

SOURCE: New York City County Clerk, *Mortgage Records.*

lawyer, "are plums and banks often choose lawyers they want to reward."

Senator Javits has demonstrated a consistent willingness to sponsor measures benefiting his law firm's client. He sponsored, it will be recalled, the National Advisory Committee's study of the problems American banks encounter in expanding overseas, as well as legislation preserving the dual federal-state jurisdiction over foreign banks operating in the United States to ensure that foreign governments are granted reciprocal expansion rights to American banks.[90] When Penn Central, a major Citibank debtor, went bankrupt, Javits quickly introduced a loan guarantee measure [91] that, had it passed, would have saved Citibank $28 million in loan losses in 1970.[92] Senator Javits also successfully introduced and voted for another corporate welfare measure, a $250 million loan guarantee to Lockheed Aircraft Corporation. Lockheed at the time was indebted to FNCB for $30 million [93] and, by his own admission, the senator's law firm had done work for two companies doing business with Lockheed. According to the senator, he saw "nothing in the peripheral connections or in my conscience to prevent me from voting on the (Lockheed) bill." [94]

In 1969, when high interest rates and tight mortgage money were hurting the public image of banks, Senator Javits sponsored a joint resolution authorizing the president to proclaim "National Banking Week." [95] He also testified in 1969 before the House Banking and Currency Committee, defending the banks from criticism for the sharp increases in bank lending rates and endorsing the bankers' favorite solution to tight money, that the Fed remove the Regulation Q ceilings limiting banks' ability to compete for funds in the money market.[96]

Another political contribution in disguise was Citibank's $40,000 1968 prime rate loan to Congressman Seymour Halpern, who happened to be a member of the House Banking and Currency Committee and more than $50,000 in debt when he received the loan. In light of the 12% interest paid on most personal loans, Halpern's 6.75% interest rate saved the congressman $2,000 a year.[97]

One thing is clear, retaining the law firm of a U.S. senator and giving a preferential loan to a U.S. congressman are political contributions in disguise. If the firm of Javits, Trubin were chosen for its legal expertise, why wasn't it entrusted with FNCB's large and difficult transactions? And as far as the loan to Representative Halpern is concerned, how many other people with $50,000 in debts and a $35,000 a year salary could get a $40,000 prime-rate loan? These questions should be answered by a thorough investigation by the Department of Justice.

Senator Javits does not agree that FNCB's directing business to his law firm constituted a political contribution in disguise. Without discussing the merits of the issue, the Senator called such a proposition, "deplorable, reckless, careless and entirely untrue." [98] Nevertheless, three months after the preliminary draft of this study was released, Javits severed his connections with the firm of Javits, Trubin, Sillcocks, Edelman and Purcell. At that time, the senator stated, "the practice of law and being a Senator has become increasingly difficult." [99]

During the summer of 1972, Senator Javits discussed his separation from the firm with the Nader Congress Project:

> I felt that I would make a contribution to the public climate surrounding the work of the Senate, but I have no consciousness of a single thing that I have ever done that was effected or determined by my law partnership. My firm was fantastically scrupulous in not handling federal business, in keeping out of any involvement which would in the remotest way embarrass me—but, nevertheless, I felt the time had come to terminate that.[100]

The Comptroller's laxity in not scrutinizing banks for political contributions also extends to the Comptroller's regulation of trust departments. The trust departments of all national banks are placed under the direct supervision of the Comptroller's office. As we have seen from the trust chapter, practices such as broker reciprocity and use of inside information go completely unregulated by the Comptroller. A major problem in some of the larger banks is that the banks' commercial departments often have interests that conflict with the banks' trust departments. For these conflicts to be perceived, it seems axiomatic that the Comptroller should examine a bank's commercial department and trust department concurrently. The Comptroller, however, examines these two departments separately, at different times, and with different examiners. The scope of the Comptroller's trust examinations must not only be broadened; it must be co-ordinated with the examination of the banks' commercial activities.

Consonant with the outmoded and superficial bank examination procedures, the Comptroller's enforcement machinery is also inadequate to make banks obey the laws, rules, and regulations. Despite all of his talk about modernizing the century-old Comptroller's office, one thing Saxon did not do is give the agency modern enforcement tools, such as the power to issue injunctions against unsound or illegal banking practices. So the Comptroller's personnel must employ roundabout enforcement methods. One such device is the regulation requiring each bank to pay the cost of conducting special examinations or investigations (currently at the rate of $140 per day for the examiner-in-charge and $80 per day for each assistant). If a regular examination discloses unsound practices that the bank refuses to discontinue, the Comptroller sometimes calls a special examination, which continues until the practice is corrected, while charges to the bank mount up. Since banks are concerned with their reputation, this device is somewhat effective. However, by merely increasing its advertising budget, a bank can cosmeticize any blemish caused by a slap on the wrist by the Comptroller. Assuming that a Comptroller really did want to regulate, having the power to enjoin illegal banking practices would be indispensable.

Another limitation is that while the Comptroller can criticize loans and make the bank write them off, it cannot force the bank to get rid of them. In one case, Roy Cohn, Ed Krock, Victor Muscat, and some other entrepreneurs who gained a certain measure of local fame during the takeover of New York's Fifth Avenue Coach Lines,* acquired control of one state and two national banks in the Chicago area. As most of Cohn's operations were based in New York and Florida, the Comptroller's office suspected that the banks would be used to make out-of-territory loans. Accordingly, Thomas DeShazo, Deputy Comptroller, according to a former official of the Comptroller's office, spoke to Cohn, pointed out that the needs of the community was one of

---

* This and other transactions of Roy Cohn have been investigated by the SEC and the Department of Justice.

the factors considered in granting a bank charter, and expressed the hope that the Illinois banks would not be used to finance Cohn's New York and Miami business dealings. Cohn, a smart attorney who was well aware of what he could and could not do, told DeShazo that he'd do as he pleased, confident that the Comptroller's office couldn't stop him.

It was an unusual move for the Comptroller's office to have criticized Cohn for failing to meet the needs of the community by extending out-of-territory loans. For the most striking thing about the Comptroller's policy—or, more accurately, nonpolicy —on this subject, is the high degree of autonomy that bankers have as to how they shall use depositors' money. But then, Roy Cohn's apparent reputation makes him a safe target for criticism.

Some effort to remedy the enforcement problem has been made by the promulgation of a "cease and desist procedure" to require banks to cease activity deemed by the Comptroller to violate the laws, rules, and regulations. According to Justin Watson, however, the Comptroller's office has initiated cease and desist proceedings fewer than 15 times and only in cases involving willful activity that constitutes a conflict of interest,[101] leading one former staff attorney to characterize the Comptroller as "a very reluctant regulator." In those few cases, Watson says, the banks agreed to abandon the activity complained about; therefore the Comptroller was not obliged to issue a formal order. That was fortunate, because the procedure has been so junked up with hearings, secrecy requirements, and appeal rights that the banks can delay and drag out the proceedings for years.

Commercial banks and their regulators have lost sight of the fundamental fact that banks are not like other corporations. Their basic function—the operation of the nation's payment mechanism—is a public trust, conferred by government charter and controlled, at least in theory, by the government's power to define the boundaries of permissible activity and examine bank operations for solvency and compliance with the law. The Comptroller, however, has delegated his regulatory responsibilities to the banks themselves. The large banks conduct the research on which changes in regulatory policy are based, draft rules and regulations, formulate legislative proposals for the Comptroller, and virtually conduct their own examinations. As a result, the money-market banks are essentially autonomous and the overriding regulatory touchstone has become the banks' self-interest.

If banks are to serve broader interests, there must be some basic changes in the regulatory process. The assessments on banks must be increased to enable the Comptroller to examine all national banks three times every two years, as the law requires. The scope of the examination must be broadened, especially for the large banks, to include areas presently ignored.

Accordingly, the examiners should investigate where banks are lending their money, to assess whether community needs are being met. The examiners should scrutinize the accounts of bank directors and their interests to ascertain whether interlocked companies are getting preferential credit terms in violation of sound banking principles. The accounts of major depositors must be checked to increase the likelihood of discovering unsound or discriminatory practices intended to avoid a loss of deposits. All loans that are exceptions to the bank's general credit policies should be examined to identify political contributions and other violations of the law. Examination of the trust and commercial departments should be coordinated to deter the trust department from making loans to and investments in commercial customers in derogation of the trust beneficiaries' interests. Coordinated examinations would also help the Comptroller ensure that the trust department does not utilize inside information possessed by the commercial side.

The problem with the Comptroller's office is that everything is subordinated to ensuring solvency. And vigorous enforcement of some laws can conflict with that priority. Thus, if the Comptroller were to move aggressively against bank credit card statements that violate truth-in-lending laws, it might encourage widespread consumer class action lawsuits to recover bank finance charges imposed in violation of the law. Though Citibank can afford to lose such a lawsuit, there are undoubtedly banks that cannot. Preferential loans to politicians may yield legislation or government deposits that help strengthen the bank. Similarly, a trust department that performs well because it has inside information is also likely to help the bank's balance sheet and income statement. Therefore, the Comptroller's overriding concern with bank solvency undermines enforcement of the law.

Because of this conflict between solvency and legality, it is doubtful whether a mere increase in examination resources would make the Comptroller's office more enforcement minded. A thorough change in the responsibilities of the nation's oldest regulatory agency is called for. Responsibility for formulating regulatory policy, conducting bank examinations, and enforcing the law should be divided between the Federal Reserve, the Comptroller, and government enforcement agencies to ensure the assertion of priorities other than bank solvency and profits.

Responsibility for formulating policy and promulgating regulations on permissible bank powers should be transferred to the Fed. This is especially appropriate because the Fed has the responsibility of defining the permissible activities of bank holding companies under the 1970 amendments to the Bank Holding Company Act. This would prevent the Comptroller's office from attempting to subvert—through expansive interpretation of the laws regulating banks—restrictions that the Fed places on bank holding company activities. It would also tend to homogenize the ground rules for all banks, thus fostering the competitive equality between state and national banks that Congress has declared to be national policy.

The Comptroller, on the other hand, should have exclusive responsibility for examining all insured banks, national or state, since he evidently does the best examining job of the three federal bank regulatory agencies, at least as far as solvency is concerned. But because the Comptroller does not examine compliance with the law carefully, the FTC and the Department of Justice should also participate in bank examinations to investigate legal questions. This would increase the likelihood of discovering political contributions, violations of truth-in-lending, and other behavior which the Comptroller has been so reluctant to investigate. It would also eliminate the present tendency of the Comptroller's personnel to defer to the banks' lawyers when practices involving borderline questions of legality are discovered.

3. Cat and Mouse—The Fed's Attempt to Control Inflation

The causes of inflation are simple and should be easily understood. Whenever the supply of money exceeds the supply of goods available, prices go up. In the 16th Century the Incan gold caused a sharp inflation in Spanish prices because the money supply in Spain exceeded the goods available for purchase.[102]

—*George S. Moore, Former Chairman, First National City Bank*

The law gives commercial banks a monopoly over checking account deposits and guarantees banks the interest-free use of these deposits. Government insurance creates the confidence in banks. Government deposits are an important source of funds for commercial banks; on June 30, 1970, Citibank's $729,463,000 of interest-free federal, state, and local government funds amounted to 10% of its domestic demand deposits.[103] The Fed's "discount window" enables banks to meet unexpected withdrawals without having to liquidate their loans and investments. In short, the protective umbrella of the government allows banks to attract more deposits and to use them with much greater flexibility than they otherwise could. An aggressive bank like Citibank can, thanks to the government, strain its liquidity to the limit in order to put as much money as possible into loans. In 1961, Citibank loaned out 58¢ on each dollar deposited. By 1969, Citibank was lending out 75¢ on each dollar deposited.[104]

The protection given each bank in the interest of financial stability and security gives rise to an obligation on the part of banks to comply with the policy objectives of the Fed, obeying the spirit as well as the letter of the laws, rules, and regulations. This is just what Citibank has not done.

In 1969, the Fed tightened reserve requirements, discount rates, and its open-market policies in an effort to control inflation, as the Federal Reserve Bank of New York noted in its *1969 Annual Report:*

Even before 1969 began, it was clear that the primary task confronting monetary policy would be to restrain the strong and growing inflationary pressures in the economy. During the year the Federal Reserve System, applying all the major instruments of policy, sharply curtailed the rate of growth of bank credit and the money supply, and financial conditions tightened to a degree not experienced in many decades.[105]

In Washington, the Fed noted that it had almost stopped the growth of two important parts of the monetary system, the money stock and bank credit:

> During the second half of 1968 these two variables had increased at seasonably adjusted rates of 7 and 15 percent, respectively. But over the corresponding period of 1969 the growth rate for each dropped to less than 1 percent.[106]

Citibank and other large banks, however, did everything possible to avoid the impact of the Fed's policies. The New York Fed called it "a costly 'cat and mouse' game":

> . . . the large banks, in an effort to maintain their earning assets, sought out and exploited gaps in System regulations to secure nondeposit funds—such as Euro-dollars, the proceeds of repurchase agreements against loans, and funds derived from commercial paper sales by bank subsidiaries and affiliates. The System in turn amended, or proposed amending, its regulations to close such gaps.[107]

Citibank, for example, "borrowed" over $1 billion from its foreign branches to expand its loans to its domestic customers. Citicorp, FNCB's holding company, issued almost $1 billion in commercial paper and used the proceeds to "purchase" loans from Citibank, thereby enabling the bank to make more loans.[108] These activities enabled Citibank to continue expanding its loan portfolio. On the whole, the banking industry responded to the anti-inflation policy adopted by the Fed; bank credit growth dropped from 11% in 1968 to 3.3% in 1969. Citibank, however, increased its bank credit by more than 12% in 1969.[109] The Fed's efforts to restrain bank credit were designed to combat inflation. Restricting bank credit reduces the ability of people, corporations, and governments to buy goods and services—that is, it reduces demand. And a reduction in demand, so goes the theory, tends to reduce inflation. But credit restraint also strikes at the heart of bank profits; interest on loans accounted for 75% of Citibank's operating revenue in 1969. Rather than follow Federal Reserve policy, therefore, Citibank has been the leading innovative force in developing new sources of funds to meet the credit demands of its customers.

Indeed, Citibank admits that accommodating the needs of its long-standing customers takes precedence over compliance with the Fed's anti-inflation policies. "It is highly unrealistic to expect individual banks willingly to refuse loans to borrowers who have maintained idle balances at banks in the expectation that they could get credit when needed," proclaimed Citibank's *Monthly Economic Letter*.[110] And to drive home its point, from early 1969 to mid-1970, when the Fed's policy of restraint was in force, Citibank increased its loan portfolio by $2,800,000,000, more than 24%.[111] In order to support this expansion, Citibank became the leader in developing and exploiting new ways of generating loanable funds. The history of Citibank's creation of the Certificate of Deposit (CD) provides a good example.

CERTIFICATES OF DEPOSIT

The 1950s saw little deposit growth in New York City. Three recessions plagued the economy and loan demand was weak. The exodus to the suburbs had begun and it was not until 1960 that the New York State laws were amended to allow branching into suburban Westchester and Nassau counties by the big New York City banks. In the early 1960s, however, reduced tax rates (which free more income for private spending) and accelerated depreciation and the investment tax credit (tax incentives to encourage business investment in new plant and equipment), brought responses from the economy and loan demand picked up. Faced with the need for additional funds, Walter Wriston and Senior Vice President John Exter invented the negotiable certificate of deposit (CD). Available in denominations starting at $100,000 and paying interest rates of 1.25% to 1.75% above the passbook savings accounts available to the average saver, negotiable CDs were designed to attract the funds of corporations, which were becoming increasingly sophisticated in maximizing income from their excess cash. Technically CDs were time deposits (and consequently required to remain deposited for 30 days); but they achieved rapid and widespread acceptance in money markets because maturity dates could be tailored to the specific needs of the corporate depositors. Furthermore, they were negotiable; if the original depositor wanted its money before maturity, it could sell the CD to another "depositor" for the duration.

Federal Reserve Regulation Q limited the amount of interest that banks could pay on CDs. At first, the Regulation Q interest rate ceiling didn't matter, for the 6.25% ceiling was above what the banks had to pay to attract CD deposits. By 1966, CDs amounted to $18 billion of bank "time" deposits. But interest rates escalated in the late 1960s, and short-term Treasury bills and short-term commercial paper, which were not subject to any interest rate limits, became much more attractive than CDs. Depositors withdrew from CDs; by the end of 1969, a total of $13.5 billion had left CDs for greener pastures. The bankers sought to have the Regulation Q interest rate ceilings raised. The Fed refused to budge. By using Regulation Q to limit the amount of interest that banks could pay on CDs, the Fed prevented the banks from attracting new CD deposits. And this, in turn, would limit the banks' ability to make new loans—at least that's what the Fed wanted. But Citibank soon found another way to squirm out from under the Fed's control; Citibank turned to the Eurodollar market.

EURODOLLARS

A Eurodollar is an American dollar on deposit outside of the United States. Massive overseas spending by the United States for the Vietnam War, overseas activities by American multinational corporations, and the excess of American imports over exports have resulted in approximately $50 billion of Eurodollar deposits in Europe, Canada, Japan, Switzerland, Vietnam, and Nassau. This market is international and, consequently, is not regulated. Regulation Q interest rate ceilings do not apply. A foreign holder of a dollar could, in 1969, convert it to the local currency and receive, say 7% interest, or deposit the dollars with the local branch of an American bank and receive up to 11% interest. Furthermore, these funds are not subject to Federal Deposit Insurance Corporation assessments and, until May 1969, the banks did not have to set aside any part of their Eurodollar borrowings as reserves. Since CDs were no longer paying attractive interest rates an American multinational corporation could deposit Eurodollars with one of Citibank's European offices and receive an interest rate that would be illegal between the same parties in the United States. Citibank could then funnel these funds to its domestic branches and use the

money to make loans in the United States, often at the "prime
rate," which was well below Citibank's cost of borrowing in
the Eurodollar market.

Citibank and the other large banks moved aggressively into
the Eurodollar market. In the first six months of 1969, as billions
of dollars were fleeing from CDs, money-market banks increased their Eurodollar borrowings by approximately $5 bil-
lion. Citibank's holdings amounted to $1.4 billion. The Fed did
not anticipate that the big banks would use the Eurodollar
market to avoid the impact of credit restraint on such a large
scale, apparently underestimating Citibank's willingness to absorb short-term losses to preserve its long-term relationship with
large corporations.

Citibank admits, perhaps with a touch of pride concerning its
resourcefulness, that its activities were designed to avoid the impact of the Federal Reserve credit restraint program and that
its behavior took the Fed by surprise:

> JOHN EXTER (FNCB senior vice president and international
> monetary advisor): As interest rates rose above the Regula-
> tion Q ceilings we found it impossible to increase our de-
> posits in the U.S. In fact, we couldn't hold our deposits.
> J. HOWARD LAERI (FNCB vice chairman): Which was the way
> the Fed was planning it.
> EXTER: *But I don't think they really wanted the Eurodollar
> market to grow that way.* (emphasis added)
> LAERI: Well, all right.
> EXTER: So what happened was, since there was no Q ceiling
> abroad and the more restricted the Q ceilings became, the
> greater incentive we had to take deposits overseas.
> STEVE ROSEN (Task Force law student): A company with
> an office in London could place deposits with First Na-
> tional City Bank in London and obtain a CD?
> EXTER: A lot of that was done.[112]

Eurodollars were an extremely expensive way to attract loanable funds. As the money market banks relied more and more
on this international dollar pool, their cost of funds rose and
their overall profit margins shrank. To offset the higher cost of
obtaining funds, major commercial banks, on June 9, 1969,

raised the prime lending rate one full percentage point to 8.5%, thus adding one more rung to the spiral of inflation that the Fed was trying to combat. Another reason for increasing the prime rate, according to Citibank's *Monthly Economic Letter,* was to reduce the demand for bank credit.

> The obligation to honor credit commitment . . . weighed much more heavily in the decision [to raise the prime rate] than did the need to offset the high cost of money.[113]

Also, in June, 1969, the Fed acted to limit Eurodollar borrowing by American banks by imposing a 10% reserve requirement on all Eurodollar borrowings that exceeded the daily average amount of Eurodollars held by each bank in the four weeks ending May 28, 1969. While this amendment to Regulation D allowed the continuation of a large reserve-free Eurodollar base ($1.4 billion for Citibank), it effectively added 10% to the cost of additional Eurodollar borrowings by each bank, and thus motivated the money-market banks to develop new sources of funds.

BANK HOLDING COMPANY COMMERCIAL PAPER

Despite the elimination of CDs and the high cost of Eurodollars as sources of loanable funds, money-market banks were not ready to conform to the Fed's credit restraint program. In late 1968, Citibank formed a holding company, Citicorp. The bank stock was exchanged for holding company stock, and Citicorp, 99% of whose assets were Citibank, was interposed between the regulatory authorities and the bank. The formation of the holding company created a loophole in Regulations Q and D that the Fed had not anticipated. Although the short-term notes of First National City *Bank* were subject to interest-rate ceilings and reserve requirements under Regulations Q and D, the notes of First National City *Corporation* were not. Citicorp sold its own commercial paper in the money markets and used the proceeds to purchase loans from Citibank. This provided the bank with additional funds for new loans and a new way to avoid the impact of credit restraint.

The sale of commercial paper by bank holding companies expanded rapidly following the imposition of reserve requirements on additional Eurodollar holdings. As of May, 1969, just prior to the Eurodollar changes, there was only $800 million worth of bank holding company commercial paper outstanding. A year later, the outstanding paper had jumped almost ten-fold to $7.5 billion, $888 million of which was FNCC's paper.[114]

THE PENN CENTRAL BANKRUPTCY

Despite their every effort, the big banks were gradually being brought to heel by the Fed. But on Sunday, June 21, 1970, an event occurred that forced the Fed—just as its anti-inflation policies were beginning to work—to open up the gates of credit once again. On June 21, 1970, the Penn Central Transportation Company, a subsidiary of the Penn Central Company, the nation's eleventh largest nonfinancial company, with $6.9 billion in assets, filed a petition for "reorganization" (read bankruptcy) in the U.S. District Court in Philadelphia, becoming the largest bankrupt in the history of the United States.

After the Penn Central filed for reorganization, there was widespread speculation that corporations that had been borrowing in the $38 billion commercial paper market would have trouble "rolling over" (refinancing) their commercial paper in the wake of the Penn Central's failure to roll over its own "prime" rated paper the month before.* As commercial paper (short-term unsecured notes) comes due, companies must sell more paper in the market to pay off the maturing paper. If investors

---

* The "prime" rating Penn Central paper received from Dun & Bradstreet raises serious questions about Dun & Bradstreet's ability to stay on top of the financial developments in the 650 companies whose commercial paper it rates, not to mention the 2,800,000 U.S. companies whose overall creditworthiness it evaluates. D&B had also given its "prime" rating to the commercial paper of Four Seasons Nursing Homes of America, Inc., and King Resources. Four Seasons filed a bankruptcy petition a week after Penn Central, and King Resources announced a month later that it was having trouble paying its bills. According to executives contacted by the *Wall Street Journal*, D&B "cuts corners" in its investigations, "relies too much on what a company's management says and doesn't do enough independent checking." There is also a tendency to assume that larger companies are better risks. As the *Wall Street Journal* notes:

> Though a big company may be no sounder than a small one, large firms historically have been considered more reliable issuers of commercial paper than small concerns. "Until Penn Central, most people assumed that a company is solid if it's big and its name is instantly recognizable," one commercial paper analyst says. (*Wall Street Journal*, June 13, 1970.

refuse to reinvest, the borrower must come up with the cash from somewhere. So several coordinated steps were taken by various government agencies to give the banks additional funds to lend to hard-pressed companies.

On June 23, two days after the bankruptcy petition was filed, the Fed suspended the Regulation Q ceilings on some CDs.[115] The Fed also informed banks that borrowing at the discount window would be an "appropriate" method of easing financial strains caused by the Penn Central failure. District Federal Reserve Bank officials were instructed to remain in "exceptionally close touch" with banks that might be affected by unusually heavy demands for credit. The Fed thus stood ready to act as a lender of last resort and help banks meet the additional credit demands expected due to uncertainty in the commercial paper market. After the Penn Central failure, there was a 90% jump in borrowings at the discount window. The Fed also used its open-market operations to add $1,200,000,000 to member bank reserves in the four weeks following the Penn Central filing.[116] Finally, the Treasury helped out by increasing its bank deposits by $2 billion. Of that amount $873 million went to the large New York City banks and $182 million to Citibank.[117]

Immediately following the suspension of Regulation Q, money center banks boosted CD interest rates by 1.5% to levels that were competitive with Treasury bills, corporate commercial paper, and other money-market instruments. In the three months following the change in Regulation Q, money-market banks increased their CDs by over $4 billion.

Having abandoned—as a result of the Penn Central crisis— all semblance of influence, much less control, over CDs the Fed moved in August, 1970, to assert some sort of regulation over bank holding company commercial paper, a move it had been considering for ten months. In October, 1969, the Fed had issued a press release proposing to apply Regulation Q interest-rate ceilings to bank holding company commercial paper.

This trial balloon generated such strong opposition from the money-market banks, that the Fed backed off from applying Regulation Q to the banks' latest credit restraining avoidance device. Rather than apply Regulation Q to bank holding company commercial paper, which is what it had done to bank notes in the preholding company days, the Fed merely amended Regulation D to impose reserve requirements (a 5% time deposit rate on long-term paper and a 17.5% demand deposit rate on short-term paper). The Fed offset this increase in reserve requirements by reducing the reserve requirements on large CDs from 6% to 5%. The net effect of these two moves was to decrease required reserves by $350 million, thereby freeing additional funds for loans.

Conclusion

First National City Bank tries to circumvent Federal Reserve policy because it is profitable to do so. It subverted the spirit and purpose of the regulations because, despite the Fed's indications that it wanted to reduce total demand by slowing down business investment through credit restraint, the business community continued its investment plans and Citibank strained its liquidity to meet the loan demand those investments entail. As Citibank sees its own continued growth and profitability in terms of developing and preserving long-term relationships with its corporate customers, the bank placed its relationship with its corporate customers above its responsibility to observe government policy. John Exter, the Citibank senior vice president who developed the negotiable CD with Walter Wriston, put it this way:

> It's not what the Federal Reserve wants that's important, it's what the Federal Reserve does and the Federal Reserve continually expands its own credit and under our system when the Fed creates credit, we create credit because the Fed gives us the reserves. We live in a fractional reserve system and we have a competitive urge to create as much credit as we can. We want to create more than Chase.[118]

James Meigs, a Citibank vice president in charge of domestic economics, said that when the Fed, in December, 1966, started feeding money to the banking system to prevent a recession from setting in, Citibank concluded that the tight money period was over and, accordingly, made extensive credit commitments.[119] Some of these commitments, however, were long term and would last well beyond the time when the bank might have anticipated a further period of restraint by the Fed. Therefore, when the Fed tightened up again at the end of 1968, Citibank found itself unable to live up to its long-term commitments and follow Fed policy at the same time. The bank pursued its own self-interest at the expense of Fed policy.

Citibank's senior lending officers claim that the bank's credit Policy Committee spent many long meetings rationing loans and denying new requests for credit in an effort to comply with Fed policy. But the damage had already been done; the bank had already promised more than it could deliver in tight money. While the bank may have turned down requests for loans from new customers, it did everything possible to meet new requests from old customers. Balances are the name of the game in commercial banking, and an old customer that has maintained them gets the loan, even if the bank has to borrow in London at 11% to lend domestically at the 8.5% prime rate.

Citibank admits that past promises and long-range relationships dominate in a collision with Fed policy. "Every effort has been made to cooperate with the Federal Reserve authorities in their program to control the level of bank credit in this country," said Citibank in its *1969 Annual Report*. "However, the necessity to honor prior commitments and to respond to the needs of customers who have had long-established relationships with us has resulted in some further increase in the loan portfolio." That "some further increase" was more than 12% in 1969 alone.

As Arthur Burns pointed out in a speech to the Association of Reserve City Bankers in April, 1970, his first major speech after becoming chairman of the Fed, the practice of making binding commitments "for large amounts of credit tied to a conventional prime rate" insulates a lot of credit from the impact of monetary policy.

> If bankers were to limit their commitments to totals they felt sure they could finance in periods of tight money, and if they charged at least as much for commitment take-downs as they themselves were paying for additional funds, I suspect that some of our nation's battles against inflation would be easier to win.[120]

William McChesney Martin, Arthur Burns's predecessor, noted that the banks' circumvention of Fed policy had several harmful consequences:

> In addition to delaying the impact of monetary restraint, these new devices used by banks to raise funds have been undesirable

on other grounds. For one thing, these sources of funds have
been available mainly to the larger banks in the System, and
especially to those who have branches abroad or affiliated holding companies. Consequently, the incidence of monetary restraint in the banking system has been unevenly distributed. Additionally, the amount of funds brought in by our banks through
Eurodollar borrowing has been so massive that it has threatened
to disrupt the money and capital markets of our European trading partners and to put excessive strains on the international
reserve positions of some countries.[121]

Despite Arthur Burns's call for the banks "to limit their credit
commitments to totals they felt sure they could finance in periods of tight money," the Fed has taken no action to make bank
lending policies more responsive to government monetary policy.
To reduce the time lag between changes in monetary policy and
the banks' compliance, and to ensure that the impact of monetary
policy is evenly distributed throughout the economy, the Fed
should limit bank credit commitments by formulating and publishing specific guidelines defining, for different types of banks,
appropriate rates of credit commitment and expansion. The Fed
should publicize the names of banks that violate the guidelines,
a practice that would be quite a deterrent in light of bankers'
preference for maintaining "low visibility."

This would place direct pressure exactly where it is needed—
on banks' commitment of funds. It would require the banks to
make more realistic, less speculative assessments of their sources
of funds. Finally, it would induce the banks to make their customers aware of the impact that Fed policy would have on their
investment plans—to make them realize that as soon as the Fed
tightened up on monetary policy, not 12 months later, the availability of bank credit would be restricted.

The formulation, implementation, and evaluation of monetary
policy is an art of enormous complexity and difficulty. It becomes an impossible task if Citibank, which single-handedly
makes nearly 5% of the nation's bank loans, and the other
large banks pursue their own narrow self-interest without regard for the consequences. Inevitably an aggressive bank like
Citibank will try to find and exploit loopholes in the complex
regulatory structure; the rewards for success are great. And
once one bank discovers a new loophole the others must follow

suit or lose ground in the never-ending race to grow larger and more profitable.

The federal government does a lot for banks—especially for the big ones. The government gives commercial banks a monopoly over checking deposits and guarantees them the interest-free use of these funds. Government insurance gives the people a sense of security and encourages them to use the banks. Government deposits on which the banks pay no interest is another direct government gift to banks; in Citibank's case, it amounts to the annual interest-free use of over $700 million. In return for such subsidies, the least the government has a right to ask for is cooperation with its fiscal and monetary policies. If the banks cannot be induced to comply voluntarily with the letter and spirit of Fed actions, then the regulatory structure and the regulators must be strengthened to guarantee compliance.

4. Congress Makes a Law—The One-Bank Holding Company Legislation of 1970

While the Fed was trying to get the banks to comply with its actions, Congress, too, was trying to bring banks under effective control. One of the ways that the big banks escaped the Fed's anti-inflation policies was to create one-bank holding companies, which could issue commercial paper. These companies were subject to no government regulation at all. The 1969–70 legislative fight over regulating them involved the most important piece of banking legislation since the 1930s. At stake was the future shape of the American banking industry and with it, the structure of the economy itself.

Following the financial collapse of the 1930s, Congress tightened up restrictions on bank involvement in commercial enterprises, prohibited banks from selling corporate securities, and restricted them to activities deemed "incidental" to banking. In the 1960s, encouraged by Comptroller of the Currency James Saxon, banks began to expand into insurance, travel services, leasing data processing, mutual funds, and other areas, a development that generated strong opposition from established companies in those fields. As courts gradually expanded the rights of aggrieved competitors to sue, and frequently determined that banks were exceeding their powers, banks looked for new ways to broaden their activities.

The one-bank holding company became the vehicle for side-stepping the restrictions on bank activities. As banks were rebuffed in their attempts to provide a broader range of services for their customers, they created new parent corporations that could own and operate the banks and still be free to engage in activities prohibited to banks.

The Bank Holding Company Act of 1956 gave the Fed responsibility for regulating companies owning or controlling *two* or more banks. The statute required multibank holding companies to seek the Fed's approval before acquiring new subsidiaries and allowed the acquisition of nonbanking companies "all the activities of which are or are to be of a financial, fiduciary, or insurance nature . . . so closely related to the business of banking or of managing or controlling banks as to be a proper incident thereto . . ." [122]

The 1956 statute was designed primarily to preserve the traditional separation between banking and commerce and to prevent concentration of financial resources. However, holding companies that owned only one bank were not subject to Fed regulation. Consequently, one-bank holding companies were free to acquire subsidiaries without Fed approval. This exemption was justified on the ground that one-bank holding companies were generally small family enterprises, located in rural areas, that did not pose a threat of undue economic concentration—at least not outside the communities where they were located. In 1965, the 550 unregulated one-bank holding companies owned or controlled banks that had less than 5% of the nation's commercial bank deposits. [123]

FNCB played a more important role in the one-bank holding company movement than any other bank. It was the first major money-market bank to form a one-bank holding company. Its use of the holding company as a diversification tool has enabled it to expand into more new fields than any of its competitors. And its bold attempt to take over a large insurance company played an important part in convincing virtually everyone, from

Wright Patman to Richard Nixon, that some form of regulation was necessary.

In August, 1968, FNCB announced that it was forming a one-bank holding company to take over ownership of the bank. Approval by the Comptroller of the Currency, a ruling by the IRS that the transaction would be nontaxable, and formal approval by the shareholders followed. On October 31, 1968, stock in FNCC was exchanged on a share-for-share basis with stock in the bank.[124] By the end of the year, Bank of America (ranked #1), Chase Manhattan (#2), Manufacturers Hanover (#4), Morgan Guaranty (#5), Chemical (#6), Continental Illinois (#8), and First National Bank of Chicago (#9) announced that they too were forming one-bank holding companies. Within a few months, more than $100 billion, or 23% of all commercial bank deposits, had come under the control of new one-bank holding companies.

For bank executives, the holding company had great advantages: increased management autonomy, independence from shareholders, freedom to expand the range of corporate activities, and freedom from geographical restrictions.

Federal law provides that shareholders of national banks shall have cumulative voting rights:

> In all elections of directors, each shareholder shall have the right to vote the number of shares owned by him for as many persons as there are directors to be elected, or to cumulate such shares and give one candidate as many votes as the number of directors multiplied by the number of his shares shall equal, or to distribute them on the same principle among as many candidates as he shall think fit.[125]

This gives minority shareholders the power to obtain representation on the board of directors of a national bank. Prior to the reorganization, holders of 4% of Citibank's stock could elect one person to the bank's 25-man board of directors. While the board was still controlled by shareholders holding a majority of the voting stock, minority shareholders were able, in theory, at least, to obtain representation. The reorganization did away with cumulative voting rights.

"We just think it's an easier way to operate," explained Citibank's Secretary, Carl Desch.[126] Well, Mr. Desch is probably right, it probably is easier for Citicorp's management to run things the way they want if they are not held accountable to groups of their shareholders. But, in our opinion, the elimination of cumulative voting is a blatant circumvention of the law.

The creation of a bank holding company also gave management new freedom to expand geographically. The leasing operation was split up between the bank and two new subsidiaries of the holding company, First National City Leasing, Inc., and Citicorp Leasing International, Inc., in order to take advantage of the new-found geographic freedom:

> This subsidiary permits us to do some leasing work in some of the states we weren't able to before, Florida, for example, where the bank couldn't perform those kinds of leasings, and it also permits us to [form] an international organization to do the same kind of leasing abroad.[127]

The separation, however, is a pure formality—at least as far as domestic leasing is concerned. The same people direct and staff the Bank's Equipment Leasing Department and the holding company's domestic leasing subsidiary. Brian Livsey, Vice President in charge of the Bank's Equipment Leasing Department and President of the subsidiary, frankly admitted that the two operations were one:

> We in fact have two budgets. Obviously, for our internal purposes, we combine the two. And we think it's great to work two hands. But we do prepare two different budgets and then they merge for our day-to-day working purposes.[128]

Tax considerations determine whether a given transaction goes on the books of the bank or the subsidiary. Once again, Brian Livsey:

> . . . the tax implications of some leases are better suited to the Bank as a vehicle and if there are no tax implications it makes it better suited to the other. . . . If there is no depreciation, there is no point particularly in putting it in the Bank. So we tend to put the few finance leases we do in FNCL [First National City Leasing, Inc.] . . . with no depreciation benefits.[129]

The holding company also gave Citibank new flexibility in its operation of its travellers check business. When a customer buys travellers checks, the funds go into the general investment or lending pool until the travellers checks are redeemed—a period of time known as "float"—and are thereby made available for loans and investments.[130] Because travellers checks may be redeemed at any time, the Federal Reserve Board classified them as demand deposits and requires banks to set aside 17.5% as reserves. When Citibank created the holding company, the travellers check operation was transferred to a holding company subsidiary, FNCB Services Corporation, in order to avoid the reserve requirements, as Carl Desch explains:

QUESTION: Now, I understand that travellers checks were recently changed from the bank to the holding company. What was the advantage gained to the bank by doing that?

ANSWER: Well, for one thing, there was the advantage of giving us an opportunity of putting travellers checks, for example, in travellers offices if we chose to do it some day down the line outside the New York City area. Maybe Don [Colen, Vice President in charge of Public Relations] has a better reason for knowledge of that one. It does eliminate, it does give us an opportunity to have funds in the holding company that we can use for further expansion. It has some advantage in that reserve requirements are somewhat different.

QUESTION: Exactly what are the reserve requirements for a travellers check organization that's run by the holding company?

ANSWER: Well, there are no reserve requirements. . . .[131]

FNCB wasted no time in trying to expand into new fields. Before 1968 was over, it announced a joint agreement and plan of merger between FNCC and the Chubb Corporation, an insurance organization engaged in property, casualty, and life underwriting with assets of $605 million.[132] The merger was never consummated. The Antitrust Division of the Department of Justice announced its intention to oppose the merger and FNCC abandoned it. One thing, however, was clear: left unregulated, the one-bank holding company would completely change the American banking industry—and the entire economy as well.

On February 17, 1969, Representative Wright Patman (Democrat, Texas), Chairman of the House Banking and Currency Committee, introduced a bill to plug the one-bank holding company loophole, setting the stage for the most important battle over bank legislation since the 1930s. Patman's bill adopted the standard of the 1956 multibank holding company law, which permitted the firms to acquire

> "shares of any company, all the activities of which are of a financial, fiduciary, or insurance nature and which the [Federal Reserve] Board has determined to be so closely related to the business of banking as to be a proper incident thereto. . . ." [133]

In a statement issued on March 24, 1969, President Nixon recognized the need for legislation to preserve the distinction between banking and commerce:

> Left unchecked, the trend toward the combining of banking and business could lead to the formation of a relatively small number of power centers dominating the American economy. This must not be permitted to happen; it would be bad for banking, bad for business, and bad for borrowers and consumers.
>   The strength of our economic system is rooted in diversity and free competition; the strength of our banking system depends largely on its independence. Banking must not dominate commerce or be dominated by it. [134]

But the administration bill, proposed by Charls E. Walker, Under Secretary of the Treasury and former Executive Vice President of the American Bankers Association, was more permissive than Patman's bill. It allowed one-bank holding companies to acquire shares in any company engaged exclusively in activities that have been determined "(1) to be *financial or related to finance* or of a fiduciary or insurance nature, and (2) to be *in the public interest* when offered by a bank holding company or its subsidiaries." [135] (emphasis added)

Citibank originally opposed any limits on one-bank holding companies, saying that either bill would give the Fed "veto power" over expansion into new activities. To FNCB, the key issue was whether banks were to be confined to traditional areas of bank activity or be allowed to provide any financial service that a bank customer desired:

> The one bank holding company is the culmination of the banker's frustration over the last 10 years in which he attempted to be market- or customer-oriented within a product-oriented environment. This is the critical issue. . . . [136]

FNCB has always strived to convey the impression that in meeting its customers' needs, it does not intend to go beyond financially related (bankers like to use the term "congeneric") services, as Walter Wriston, FNCB-FNCC Chairman told the Senate Banking and Currency Committee:

> We do not seek to expand beyond the confines of financially related businesses. We are not equipped to run a department store or a manufacturing company, and we do not want to. We believe, however, that we are singularly well-equipped to provide a wide variety of financial services that the average American now needs or will require in the days to come.[137]

Despite the public disclaimers of any intention to enter non-financial fields, the formation of the holding company gave FNCB the power to do what it wanted, as the 1968 Proxy Statement announced:

> At the present time, it is not anticipated that First National City Corporation will engage in operations unrelated to commercial banking or financial fields, although it has broad power and could do so in the event that, at any time in the future, its Board of Directors should determine that such course of action would be desirable.[138]

During April and May of 1969, the House Banking and Currency Committee held exhaustive hearings on the proposed legislation. A staggering array of bankers, holding company executives, representatives of national, state, and independent bankers' associations, data processors, travel agencies, insurance agents, state and federal agency officials, university professors, and private citizens submitted information and opinions pertaining to every conceivable legislative formula. The hearings comprise over 1,600 pages of testimony, statements, and exhibits.

The bill reported out by the committee in July, 1969, embodied a compromise between the formulas proposed by Patman and the administration. The test adopted allowed a bank holding company to retain or acquire shares in a company performing any activity that the Fed determined to be

> functionally related to banking in such a way that its performance by an affiliate of the bank holding company can reasonably be expected to produce benefits to the public that outweigh possible adverse effects.[139]

On November 4 and 5, 1969, Representative Patman took the floor of the House and offered a series of amendments that virtually rewrote the bill. With superbly organized forces and strong antibank public opinion stemming from high interest rates, a tight mortgage market, and massive letter writing campaigns by the data processors, travel agents, and insurance agents, Patman obtained passage of a much more restrictive bill:

> A bank holding company or any subsidiary thereof may carry on any activity of a financial or fiduciary nature if the Board finds, on the record after opportunity for hearing, that the carrying on of the activity in question . . . will be functionally related to banking and can reasonably be expected to produce benefits to the public, such as greater convenience, increased competition, or gains in efficiency, that outweigh possible adverse effects such as undue concentration of resources, decreased or unfair competition, conflicts of interest, or unsound banking practices.

In addition, the bill contained an explicit "laundry list" of activities from which banks and their holding companies were to be excluded, except in specific, narrowly defined situations involving traditional banking functions. The forbidden activities were underwriting, insurance (except in situations such as writing credit-life insurance), travel agency services, auditing and other accounting services, data processing (except in situations such as payroll preparation for customers or the utilization of excess computer capacity) and leasing property (unless the lessee paid the entire cost of the property and received ownership for little or no cost at the end of the lease).

The House of Representatives vote was 351 to 24 in favor of the bill.

The banks, especially the large banks, were stunned. Citibank called the House-passed measure "punitive." Bank of America said the bill "would stem the flow of creativity by banks that has become so necessary for meeting the needs and vast changes of our increasingly complex society." Nat Rogers, President of the American Bankers Association, was "disappointed that the House did not support the work of its committee, which had given weeks and months to the study of this issue." A representative of a large Chicago bank holding company called the bill a "monster" and said there should be a "regrouping" of forces to "go to work on the Senate." [140] The margin of the industry's defeat at the hands of Representative Patman galvanized the bank into action, as one bank lobbyist noted:

> Occasionally, I still have a nightmare, and, once again, I am up there in the House gallery watching Wright Patman lead the massacre on the floor. But then I wake up and get to thinking it might be the best thing that has happened to us in a long time.[141]

When the bill went to the Senate the large banks stepped up their lobbying efforts on several fronts. The American Bankers Association (ABA) was called in. This organization, with more than 13,000 members accounting for 97% of the nation's commercial banks, has ten registered lobbyists who have frequent contact with the congressional banking committees, the regulatory agencies, and the Treasury. The banks also brought in their own lobbyists. FNCB's registered lobbyist is John Yingling, a former staff member of the Senate Banking and Currency Committee who now receives $60,000 a year from FNCB.[142] Like Yingling, the lobbyists employed by the other banks and banking organizations had similar experience with those groups they now were trying to influence.

In order to bolster their claim that the public wanted banks to become financial supermarkets, the banks, through their Foundation for Full Service Banks, commissioned pollster Louis Harris to conduct a national survey of 3,000 households, and 809 "leaders" in business, the professions, government, education, and the mass media to find out what people wanted their banks to do. Predictably, the "leaders" roundly endorsed further expansion of bank activity:

> Forty-seven per cent of the public would like to see all banks go to a single monthly statement for all business transacted with their banks;
>
> Thirty-seven per cent would like help from their bank in preparing their income taxes;
>
> Fifty-eight per cent of public leaders favor banks going into the data processing service business;
>
> Forty-four per cent [leaders] want banks to offer travel services;
>
> Fifty-three per cent of the leaders and 33 per cent of the general public favor banks going into mutual funds;
>
> Thirty-six per cent of the leaders would like banks to go into life insurance selling.

RECENT COMMERCIAL BANK LOBBYISTS

Name	Retained By	Previous Experience with Treasury, the Fed, or Congressional Banking Committees
Matthew Hale	American Bankers Association	General Counsel, Senate Banking and Currency Committee
John W. Holton	American Bankers Association	Board of Governors, FRB, 1957
John F. Rolph, III	American Bankers Association	Assistant General Counsel Treasury, 1952
Charles R. McNeill	American Bankers Association	
Charles T. O'Neill	American Bankers Association	Treasury, 45 years
William T. Heffelginger	American Bankers Association	
Charles O. Zuver	American Bankers Association	
Willis W. Alexander	American Bankers Association	
Robert L. Bevan	American Bankers Association	Staff member, Senate Banking and Currency Committee, 1955–61
James B. Cash	American Bankers Association	
Roy W. Terwilliger	American Bankers Association	Chief Clerk, Senate Banking and Currency Committee, 1955–60
John H. Yingling	First National City Bank	
	Association of Corporate Owners of One Bank	
Robert James	Boston Safe Deposit & Trust Company	
Owen V. Frisby	Bank of America	
Alexander Christie	Chase Manhattan Bank	
	Bankers Trust	
	CIT Financial Corporation	

James W. Riddell	CIT Financial Corporation	
Donald L. Rogers	Association of Registered Bank Holding Companies	Assistant Counsel, Senate Banking and Currency Committee, 1953–58
Forrest J. Prettyman	Association of Registered Bank Holding Companies Bank of New York	
Miller & Chevalier Leva, Hawes, Symington, Martin and Oppenheimer	CIT Financial Corporation	
H. Stewart Dunn (Ivins, Phillips & Barker)	Wilmington Trust Company	
Lewis G. Odom	CIT Financial Corporation	Staff Director, Senate Banking and Currency Committee, 1967–68
Esther Peterson	Amalgamated Clothing Workers Union	

SOURCE: Frank V. Fowlkes, "Washington Pressures/The Big-Bank Lobby," *CPR National Journal*, December 6, 1969, p. 297. Fowlkes, "Financial Report/Bank Lobby Scores in Senate," *CPR National Journal*, July 18, 1970, pp. 1541–2.

> By 65 per cent [Americans] believe that one bank holding
> companies will allow banks to have a full and positive impact on
> the community.[143]

The results of this poll were, of course, distributed in Washington
while the bank holding company legislation was pending.

The Senate committee hearings which began in May, 1970,
were shorter than those held in the House.[144] From the start, it
was apparent that Patman's "laundry list" would be deleted. So
the major emphasis of the lobbying efforts focused on the "functionally related" language. Yingling, who said that this language
was the heart of the bill, urged, along with the other bank lobbyists, adoption of the "functionally related" formula, but without the list of prohibited activities. The data processors, travel
agents, and insurance agents wanted the "closely related" language in lieu of the deleted laundry list. The differences between
the two formulations, however, were hard to detect, as Congressman Patman noted:

> Some claim . . . [functionally related] means the same thing as
> closely related, but I'm afraid of it. I think the big banks think
> they are on to something. It excites my curiosity why they are so
> eager for it if it means the same thing.[145]

The banks won a decisive 11 to 4 victory in the Senate committee on this issue.[146]

During the Senate committee's consideration of the one-bank
holding company legislation, the banks got their own laundry list
of special amendments to protect themselves from the impact of
the legislation. One such amendment, sponsored by Senator Harrison Williams, exempted conglomerate companies that owned
banks with assets under $3 million, or assets under $50 million
that constituted less than 25% of the parent's assets. This
amendment, referred to contemptuously by Senator William
Proxmire as "the green stamp" amendment because of its similarity to a proposal circulated earlier by Robert Oliver, lobbyist
for Sperry and Hutchinson, the S & H Green Stamp company,
was opposed by the Fed and the Department of Justice. Under
Secretary of the Treasury Walker, however, said that "enact-
ment of the Williams Amendment would not defeat the basic
purpose of the legislation." Senator John Tower of Texas tried
but failed to get the exclusion raised to exempt owners of $100

million banks—a change that would have exempted the Texas Bank of Houston. The "green stamp" amendment, however, was included in the committee's version of the bill.[147]

CIT Financial Corporation, the conglomerate owner of the $1.4 billion deposit National Bank of North America, lobbied for time to divest banking or nonbanking assets should the Fed rule that they were not "functionally related." The House bill required divestiture within two years, unless the Fed allowed an additional three years. CIT wanted ten plus three, and received five plus five, from the Senate committee.[148]

Union Bank of Los Angeles, with $1.7 billion in deposits, had contracted in January, 1969 to acquire an insurance brokerage firm. The "grandfather clause"—the cutoff date for nonconforming acquisitions—had been moved by the Senate committee to March 24, 1969 (from the House bill's 1956 date). This was still too early to save Union Bank's acquisition. So Senator Alan Cranston (Democrat, California) introduced an amendment, adopted by the committee, that made binding commitments equivalent to acquisitions for grandfather clause purposes.[149]

A variety of other amendments were also lobbied into the bill. Bank of America's lobbyist, Robert James, sought an exemption for nonconforming foreign businesses that did most of their activities overseas. Senator Proxmire, however, limited the effect of this exemption with an amendment requiring the foreign business's activities in the United States to be only incidental to its foreign business. John Yingling, on behalf of the Boston Safe Deposit and Trust Company, sought an exemption for banks that did no commercial lending; Senator Brooke introduced the amendment that was adopted by the Senate Committee. Finally, an amendment to exempt banks owned by labor unions, protecting such investments by the Amalgamated Clothing Workers Union and the United Mine Workers, was put forth by Esther Peterson, a former special assistant to President Johnson for consumer affairs, and adopted by the committee.[150] One lawyer on the Senate Banking and Currency Committee noted that "any bank willing to send a lobbyist to Washington got something." [151]

On August 10, 1970, the Senate Banking and Currency Committee reported out the bill, which came to the floor of the Senate on September 16, 1970. The Senate retained the committee's version of the "functionally related" test, but pushed the grandfather clause, which the committee had pegged at March 24, 1969, back to June 30, 1968. This change meant that FNCB and the other giant banks that formed holding companies in late 1968 and early 1969 would have to divest themselves of all nonconforming acquisitions.

With the House and Senate bills so far apart on the major provisions, the task of writing a compromise bill fell to a conference committee composed of members of the House and Senate banking committees. The membership on the conference committee was vitally important. In the Senate, Chairman Sparkman had the option of having a five- or seven-man delegation. As the rules dictate that conference committee members must be chosen according to seniority, Sparkman could have prevented Muskie and Brooke, who generally favored stricter regulation of holding companies, from sitting on the committee by limiting the Senate's delegation to five members.[152] Sparkman chose a five-man Senate delegation consisting of himself, Harrison Williams, William Proxmire, Wallace Bennett, and John Tower. The House delegation, headed by Patman, included William Barrett, Leonor Sullivan, Henry Reuss, William Widnall, Albert Johnson, and J. William Stanton.

On November 18, 1970, the conferees started three weeks of negotiations intended to resolve the differences between the two bills while 10-20 reporters and lobbyists congregated in the halls outside the meeting room.[153] The meetings were so stormy that at one point, Senator Wallace Bennett walked out. By December 9, however, agreement had been reached. The "laundry list" was deleted. In its place appeared the "so closely related" formula of the 1956 legislation, but modified by a list of additional factors that the Fed was to consider:

> In determining whether a particular activity is a proper incident to banking or managing or controlling banks the Board shall consider whether its performance by an affiliate of a holding company can reasonably be expected to produce benefits to the public such as greater convenience, increased competition, or gains in efficiency, that outweigh possible adverse effects, such as undue concentration of resources, decreased or unfair competition, conflicts of interest, or unsound banking practices. . . .

Furthermore, the statute explicitly differentiated between acquisitions of established businesses and starting up new businesses;

this gave the holding companies a basis for arguing that they should have greater latitude to begin a new business, thus bringing new competition to a particular market, than to acquire an existing business.

When courts interpret the meaning of legislation, they often look to the "legislative history," which includes statements made by legislators at the time a particular statute was passed. So when the compromise bill came to the floor of the House, Representative Patman sought to strengthen the legislative history by arguing that the rejection of the "functionally related" test and adoption of the 1956 "so closely related" formula showed a congressional intent strictly to limit bank holding companies from entering new areas of activity. Representative Widnall (Republican, New Jersey), however, a consistent champion of bank expansion, pointed out that the additional factors the Fed was to consider indicated a congressional intent to provide new "flexibility" in evaluating the proper areas for bank and bank holding company activity. Only time will tell how the Fed and the court interpret the statute.

Other provisions of the restrictive House bill were also modified by the conference committee. The House had set the grandfather clause at May 9, 1956, thus requiring all subsequent acquisitions by bank holding companies to conform to the "closely related" test; the Senate's date, June 30, 1968, was adopted by the conferees. The conferees, however, rejected the formula of the original "green stamp" amendment, giving the Fed broad discretion to determine which long-standing, nonconforming acquisitions might stand. The conferees gave CIT and other companies ten years to divest themselves of their nonconforming acquisitions, preserved Bank of America's foreign business exemption, Boston Safe Deposit's exemption for banks not engaged in commercial banking (i.e., trust companies), and the Amalgamated Clothing Worker's exemption for labor unions.[154]

After two years of intense battling, both houses of Congress quickly and overwhelmingly approved the conference bill and President Nixon signed the law before the end of 1970.

The large number of factors that the Fed must consider in deciding the appropriate areas for bank holding company activity gives broad interpretative discretion. In effect, the statute directs the Fed to balance the various factors in arriving at its decisions and decide whether increases in convenience, competition, and efficiency stemming from the holding company activities outweigh undue concentration of resources, decreased or unfair competition, conflicts of interest, and unsound banking practices.

The Fed's first set of proposed regulations, issued in January, 1971, allows banks to act as insurance agent and insurer "principally in connection with extensions of credit by the holding company or any of its subsidiaries." [155] While the word "principally" creates ambiguity, it indicates an intention to go beyond the narrow credit-life insurance allowed by the House version of the bill. Similarly, the proposed regulations allow holding companies to provide bookkeeping and data processing services "provided that the value of services performed by the company . . . is not a principal portion of the total value of all such services performed." [156] Holding companies would also be allowed to act as investment or financial advisors and to lease personal property "where the initial lease provides for payment of rentals that will reimburse the lessor for the full price of the property."

After hearings on the proposed regulations, the Fed, in May, 1971, promulgated its first implementing regulations under the Bank Holding Company Act Amendments of 1970. The regulations allow bank holding companies to make loans, operate as industrial banks, service loans for others, perform the functions of a trust company, act as investment or financial advisor, make equity and debt investments in economic development companies, and lease personal property. Still under consideration are two of the most controversial activities, those relating to insurance and data processing.[157]

The Future of Bank Holding Companies

Within a month after the new bank holding company took effect, the large New York City banks started expanding their banking operations into territories from which they had long been excluded. On February 4, 1971, FNCC announced its plan to form a new bank subsidiary to operate in rapidly expanding suburban Suffolk County. By November, 1971, Citibank (Suffolk), N.A. was in operation. That same month, FNCC announced its plan to acquire the Silver Creek National Bank, thirty miles from Buffalo, New York. The following month, FNCC decided to acquire the State Bank of Honeoye Falls, fifteen miles south of Rochester, New York. In February, 1972, FNCC announced its plan to acquire the National Exchange Bank of Castleton-on-Hudson, ten miles south of Albany. In June, 1972, FNCC concluded agreements to acquire the First Trust and Deposit Company of Oriskany Falls, and then, in August, 1972, FNCC agreed to acquire the Central Valley National Bank in Central Valley, New York. Actually, in June, 1971, the New York State Legislature had passed a law providing for statewide branching starting January 1, 1976. By creating six new subsidiaries under the aegis of a holding company, FNCC had accomplished the same result four years earlier.

The holding company device also enables geographic expansion into new states. Thus FNCC's Citicorp Systems, Inc., a data processing subsidiary, is based in Boston; Advance Mortgage Corporation, a mortgage servicing company acquired in 1970, has offices in Atlanta, Chicago, Cincinnati, Cleveland, Dayton, Denver, Harrisburg, Indianapolis, Los Angeles, Oakland, Pittsburgh, Riverside (California), San Diego, San Jose, Seattle, and Washington, D.C., in addition to its head office in Detroit.

When bank holding companies expand by acquisition, or by starting up new subsidiary firms, the fact that the activity is carried on by a bank or bank affiliate affords significant competitive advantages over independent competitors. Banks and their affiliates can accumulate vast pools of capital at extremely low cost; even a prime-rate loan is more expensive than the terms available to a bank holding company's subsidiaries. This is because the operations of the holding company subsidiaries—in leasing, for example—are so intertwined with those of the bank and the holding company, sharing personnel, quarters, equipment, and funds with the bank and/or the holding company, that affiliates have cost advantages that are unavailable to nonbank competitors. And these advantages are *structural*. They exist by virtue of the affiliate's ties to the bank even if the bank treats its nonbank competitors with model fairness and impartiality.

Although the law requires 100% to 120% collateral when a bank holding company or its subsidiaries borrow from their bank affiliate,[158] there is no restriction when affiliates borrow from the holding company. Thus, FNCC, with more than $2 billion of its own assets at December 31, 1970,[159] can channel funds derived from FNCB dividends and its own borrowings (in the commercial paper market, for example) to its subsidiaries. By December 31, 1970, FNCC had advanced over $114 million to its subsidiaries, up from a mere $2 million the year before and had made $439 million in loans, up from zero at December 31, 1969.[160] The holding company, therefore, has already become a substantial financial intermediary in its own right, based, of course, largely on its relationship with FNCB.

In addition to the structural cost advantages enjoyed by banks and their affiliates by virtue of their access to low-cost funds, the manner in which banks and affiliates price their services affords an additional advantage that the independent competitors cannot match. Services, it will be recalled from Chapter III, are designed primarily to attract deposits and increase the bank's total relationship with its corporate customers. For many services, no fees are charged provided the customer maintains adequate deposit balances in the bank. And even where fees are charged, they are set with the primary goal of increasing the bank's overall relationship with the customer. So Citibank can afford to lose money or make less profit on its services if the overall account or the long-term future relationship looks profitable.

The so-called anti-tying provision of the bank holding company legislation does not effectively prohibit banks or their holding company affiliates from charging lower rates to depositors. Although there is a general prohibition against *banks* granting credit or reducing the fee for services on the condition that the customer utilize additional credit or services of the bank or affiliate, there is an exemption for loans, discounts, deposits, and trust services.[161] Therefore, banks can continue to provide free or low-cost services to depositors. Furthermore there is no limitation whatever in the statute on the freedom of bank *affiliates* to provide free or low-cost services to bank depositors. The legislation, therefore, does not touch a major competitive advantage of banks and their affiliates—the ability to attract business from independent competitors by providing free or lower-cost services if the customer brings in his deposits with his other business.

Although the Fed's implementing regulations plug the gap for affiliates by requiring them to observe the same restrictions on tying and price variations applicable to banks, the exemption for deposits allows bankers and their affiliates to continue to price their services according to the customer's deposit balances. Independent competitors—data processors, for example—will find it difficult to compete on equal terms with such loss-leading packaged deals, no matter how good their own services may be. As every company has to bank somewhere, there will be a strong incentive for customers of independent data processors to save money by taking their data processing business to a bank that provides depositors with data processing free of charge or for a lower fee.

Citibank has already started developing advanced data processing systems for its customers, apparently without any pressure to show a profit, as noted by Carl Desch, Senior Vice President and Cashier of FNCB and Secretary and Treasurer of FNCC:

> Citicorp Systems is a little group which is based in Cambridge up in Boston and they're working on developing better computer programs and systems and procedures and so forth. They're a peculiar kind, just like a horse which is a peculiar kind or a doctor who is a peculiar kind of specialist. This is what they're developing. Developing work for ourselves and opening a service center. . . .
>
> Well, they're the MIT kind of guy, you know, who is scientifically oriented and they lay out computer systems, better techniques for arriving at management information work, etc. Nothing mysterious about it, that's what they do. We house them up there because they're close to the schools, and they're available up there. I don't know, 30, 40 people we have. *It hasn't made any money, be assured. In fact, so far it's cost us money.*[162] (emphasis added)

As long as these activities attract deposits and strengthen existing relationships, FNCB and other banks are likely to continue such operations without too much concern for the individual profit and loss figures of each subsidiary. As these same competitive advantages apply to every field that banks and their affiliates enter, the future does not look bright for independent competitors.

The Fed's first set of guidelines indicates that retailers may soon join the ranks of the insurance agents, travel agents, data processors, and mutual funds that have long opposed bank expansion into their fields. This is because the banks' rapidly expanding leasing activities may eventually make many retailers superfluous, at least those who sell high-priced consumer durable goods such as automobiles and appliances. Although most of FNCB's leasing activities have thus far involved multimillion dollar capital goods, such as aircraft, railroad rolling stock, and computers, demand for leasing services in the "middle market" —which FNCB defines as goods costing from $10,000 to $1 million—is increasing rapidly. After the "middle market," the next step will be the development of leasing services for consumer goods. While Citibank has not yet opened leasing windows in the branches to serve the individual customers of the Personal Banking Group, Brian Livsey, vice president in charge of FNCB's leasing operation, indicates that the conceptual work in developing a retail leasing operation has already been done:

> But now, we're getting an increasing flow of inquiries in what we call the middle market, the smaller ticket market. Although we know the whole product conceptually, but operationally we have to provide a vehicle that can profitably—because we have to look after the stockholders too—profitably handle small leases. And, down the road, as I think I mentioned, there is a small unit in the personal bank but there isn't a leasing window. In fact, *if you did walk in for, to lease one of these [pointing to the tape recorder] or a typewriter or something else a personal bank customer might want, the vehicle is there.* If you will, we're in a passive response market, but the demand is growing there and our mission is to provide a product to meet the demands of all the bank's customers.[163] (emphasis added)

Leasing, like credit cards, provides 100% financing. It differs from credit cards, however, in that title to the goods remains with the lessor, who can thus take advantage of depreciation and investment tax credit benefits not available to retailers or the individual owner of a color television set or an automobile. In addition, the banks' ability to buy at wholesale prices with volume discounts may provide additional savings which, if passed on to lease customers, will substantially undermine the ability of retailers to compete with bank leasing departments.

In the short run, individual lessees may benefit from the lower cost of leasing compared to borrowing and buying. But the long-run consequences raise fundamental questions concerning the future shape of the American economy. Although leasing is a form of finance and thus arguably appropriate for banks and their affiliates under the new legislation, will this new activity result in a *de facto* destruction of Congress's long-standing policy of separating banking from commerce? Will leasing services and terms for various products hinge on the bank's total relationship with the manufacturer of the products in the same way that other bank services depend on the "total account relationships"? Will retailers, data processors, and other competitors of banks be at a substantial competitive disadvantage in their efforts to compete with banks and their affiliates, thus increasing the trend toward concentration of America's business resources?

We think that these questions will eventually be answered affirmatively as banks start to expand their activities in new fields. Leasing is clearly just one area into which banks want to expand. In addition to the areas permitted under the Fed's first set of proposed guidelines, the banks have already asked permission to acquire savings and loan associations, credit bureaus, financial advertising or financial public relations companies, armored car and messenger companies, property management companies, custom house brokers, freight forwarders, industrial and urban development companies, business and farm management consulting companies, agencies for the training or employment of financial personnel, and economic or financial consulting companies.[164]

Congress enacted legislation to prohibit bank holding companies from controlling companies whose activities are unrelated to banking. Despite the restrictions on bank ownership of commercial enterprises, the ever-expanding definition of bank related activities will enable banks to influence effectively, if not actually control, corporate behavior in other more oblique ways.

Bank affiliated data processing operations will provide corporate executives with the latest in sophisticated management information systems on which to base their decisions. Bank affiliated management consulting companies will help corporate executives formulate their options and choose between various alternatives. Bank affiliated leasing operations and commercial loan officers will provide the financing necessary to implement corporate decisions.

Expanded bank involvement with corporate decision making will further erode the separation between banking and commerce. In addition to the excessive concern with balances and the scope of the entire relationship that bankers already exhibit in evaluating "creditworthiness," the new dimension of the banks' increasing involvement in formulating the very spending plans that bank lending officers are called upon to evaluate will be added. These developments indicate that the Fed should proceed cautiously in allowing banks and their affiliates to extend the scope of their activities.

To preserve what is left of the diversity and countervailing economic powers that exist in our economy, further expansion by banks and their holding companies should be prevented. The incentive for banks to maximize growth to compensate for their narrowing profit margins, their ability to marshal vast sums of capital at wholesale cost, and their practice of attracting deposits with low-priced, packaged deals means that banks will quickly dominate any market they enter. And because a move by one large bank into a new field usually means that the others are close behind, structural changes in banking and newly entered markets will occur with extreme rapidity, and on a broad scale.

Accordingly, in applying the statutory formula of the Bank Holding Company Act amendments, the Fed should give the highest priority to preventing an "undue concentration of resources, decreased or unfair competition, conflicts of interest or unsound banking practices." [165] And this means giving bank holding companies a very heavy burden of proving that the "benefits to the public such as greater convenience, increased competition or gains in efficiency" [166] clearly outweigh the negative effects. If the Fed does otherwise, it may safely be forecast that in coming years, banks and their holding companies will obtain more influence than they already possess over an ever-increasing segment of the American economy.

Although this book has focused primarily on one bank, the problems described here are by no means unique. Discriminatory personnel policies, bankers who are unable to explain services adequately, deceptive retailing practices, corporate favoritism, social apathy, misuse of others' wealth, and political influence are problems that permeate the banking world. We hope our exposing of these problems will galvanize the reader to action. We have made numerous recommendations; yet, in the final analysis, the hope for a better banking system lies with conscientious individuals who will stand up at tellers' windows and sit down at executives' desks to demand the service and honesty which their bank owes them and which, we believe, it has the potential to render.

Appendix

Summary of Major Recommendations

First National City Bank

Expand JOBS program to increase upgrading of entry level clerical employees.

Increase promotion opportunities for women, blacks, and other groups that have experienced discrimination.

Describe cost and operation of services in brochures and advertisements.

Abandon cross-selling and volume oriented employee incentive program until branch organization and service can handle the increased volume.

Improve implementation of credit granting standards.

Screen merchants accredited for Master Charge to eliminate those who engage in fraudulent advertising, sales, and service practices.

Utilize warranty provision in Master Charge Sellers Agreement to force merchants, instead of cardholders, to bear the cost of fraud and other illegal practices.

Compile list of merchants engaging in poor advertising, sales, and service practices by sending complaint forms to cardholders every month and turning information over to government consumer protection agencies.

Supervise collection personnel closely to minimize abusive collection practices.

Prohibit calls—and threats of calls—to employers of defaulting debtors.

Hire salaried process servers.

Diversify board of directors to include independently chosen representatives of employees, individual customers, small and/or mid-sized corporate customers, pension fund beneficiaries, and New York City.

Help arrest trend toward greater concentration of economic resources by abandoning merger brokerage services, enforcing loan agreement covenants that prohibit mergers, and declining to finance mergers and acquisitions.

Increase investments in small, neighborhood businesses in order to foster grass-roots economic development.

Advertise and solicit local economic and minority business development loans.

340 APPENDIX

Require loan officers to provide managerial assistance to minority enterprises on a routine basis.

Radically expand commitment of managerial, financial, and technological resources to foster improvement in areas such as housing, local economic development, and mass transit in the communities from which the bank draws its funds.

Describe and publicize consumer credit granting criteria.

Warn settlors of the trust department's proclivity to dispose of unique assets and small closely held businesses in FNCB-managed trusts.

When advertising its fiduciary service, disclose the average number of years the same manager can be expected to supervise an account.

Inform beneficiaries of the existence and extent of the bank's commercial dealings with companies in which the bank invests the beneficiary's account.

Without necessarily sacrificing performance, invest trust funds and exercise stock voting responsibilities to engage the nation's pressing social problems.

New York City, New York State, and other states and municipalities

Inaugurate "zero balance" bank accounts in order to minimize cost of obtaining banking services.

Adhere to competitive bidding for all short-term borrowings.

Require FNCB and other city pension fund advisors to provide an accounting of demand deposits purchased through allocation of commissions on pension fund transactions.

Remove the bankers from the MTA and replace them with citizens who are free from conflicts of interest.

Hire nonbank data processors to handle New York City personal income tax processing and have the city retain back-up computer tapes.

Investigate FNCB and Chase Manhattan Bank credit files to check for misuse of income tax return data.

Comptroller of the Currency

Have all national banks, not just those against whom complaints have been lodged, revise billing statements in order to maximize the clarity and completeness with which the required information is disclosed.

Require banks applying for permission to open new branches to demonstrate that they are providing a satisfactory level of customer service in the existing branches.

Prohibit a trust department from advertising that it is providing individualized investment services unless it actually is.

Require that trust departments obtain the informed, written consent of beneficiaries before liquidating trust portfolios for the purpose of investing them in the banks' own common trust funds.

Require that banks disclose the profitability of their trust activities, broken down by services rendered, but not including "credits allowed for deposits."

Require disclosure of a bank trust department's 20 largest stock holdings, holdings over $10 million, holdings constituting more than 5% of a public corporation's stock, and holdings of the bank's own stock.

End equity kickers.

Investigate reciprocity to determine if banks have breached their fiduciary obligations to their trust beneficiaries.

Replace Peat, Marwick and Mitchell with independent consultant to formulate examination test procedures pertaining to computers.

Increase assessments and examination resources.

Examine all banks three times every two years as the law requires.

Examine to whom and where banks are lending money in order to assess whether community needs are being met.

Scrutinize thoroughly all accounts of directors and their interests at all banks.

Scrutinize thoroughly accounts of major depositors at all banks.

Scrutinize thoroughly all loans that are exceptions to a bank's general credit principles.

Coordinate the examination of trust departments with the examination of commercial departments.

Federal Reserve Board

Require commercial banks to maintain residential mortgage loan portfolios equal to two-thirds of their passbook savings deposits.

Investigate reciprocity to determine whether the practice has violated the prohibition against payment of interest on demand deposits.

Formulate and enforce credit commitment guidelines to ensure that the banking system retains flexibility to respond to changes in monetary policy.

Require bank holding companies to provide cumulative voting.

Place a heavy burden of proof upon bank holding companies to show that benefits of expansion clearly outweigh possible negative consequences.

U.S. Department of Justice

File a class action type lawsuit against FNCB on behalf of default judgment debtors who were served improperly.

Investigate conglomerate merger movement in terms of impact on competition in the banking industry.

Investigate prime rate changes, exchange of customer information, and price fixing through syndicate loan agreements.

Investigate FNCB's retention of Javits, Trubin, Sillcocks, Edelman and Purcell and FNCB's prime rate loan to Representative Seymour Halpern to determine whether prohibitions against political contributions have been violated.

Securities Exchange Commission

Examine FNCB's personal and employee-benefit trust investment services to see if, as it appears, accounts are being managed in an assembly-line fashion.

Internal Revenue Service

Investigate financing for World Trade Center to determine if banks took illegal income tax deduction for interest paid on Port Authority time deposits.

Legislative Recommendations

Expand the right of consumers to file class-action lawsuits.

Create fully taxable, subsidized state and municipal securities to reduce government borrowing costs.

Amend New York State and City corporate income tax laws to tax banks at the same rate as other businesses.

Require New York State to process New York City personal income tax returns.

Hold congressional hearings on frequency, scope, and depth of bank examinations.

Reorganize responsibilities of bank regulatory agencies:

Fed—to define permissible bank activities, formulate operating rules and regulations, and pass on all bank mergers;

Comptroller of the Currency—to rule on branch and charter applications and to examine all insured banks;

FDIC—to administer deposit insurance program;

FTC—to enforce consumer related policies, such as truth-in-lending and fair advertising.

Remove tax subsidy for generation-skipping trusts.

Permit beneficiaries, on a showing of due cause, to move testamentary trusts from one to another corporate fiduciary.

Hold pension trustees to strict fiduciary standards, including ensuring that no self-dealing occurs and that participants are fully informed of all aspects of their plans, especially of underfunding.

Sever trust departments from commercial banking institutions and encourage the establishment of private, competitive, cooperative, insured financial institutions, regulated by the SEC, to manage pension monies.

Prohibit a bank's exercising voting control over its own stock held in its trust department.

Require that profits resulting from trust funds left uninvested in the commercial side of a bank be distributed to beneficiaries of the trusts that generated the deposits.

Rebuttal and Surrebuttal

Rebuttal

New York, N.Y., June 20 [1971]—First National City Bank today characterized the Nader report on the bank as a "painstakingly detailed and wide-ranging study which is unfortunately based on serious misconceptions about the proper role of the banking system and a frightening cynicism about other people's ethics.

"Nevertheless, the report will be given careful consideration in our continuing reappraisal of Citibank's policies and practices," Chairman Walter B. Wriston said.

"Indeed, a great deal of information was taken directly from selected parts of two surveys commissioned by Citibank to audit the level of service to customers and employees' working conditions and compensation. The results of both surveys were used to make improvements that were already underway at the time the Nader men were interviewing bank personnel. A preliminary reading of the Nader report suggests some additional points which appear to have merit and which we will carefully consider.

"We are surprised, however, that important sections of the report cover areas the student investigators never discussed with bank officials during two months of interviews, especially in view of the charge of our failure to cooperate.

"We find it hard to understand why the law students failed to question us on these subjects, but relied instead on incomplete and incorrect information obtained from sources that are in many cases questionable.

"It is difficult to know how to respond to a 500-page report which is on both sides of many issues. For example, we are alleged to have abandoned the tax-exempt bond market on one page, while our preference for tax-exempt securities is given as our reason for supporting the World Trade Center on another page.

"We are told that our record of credit extension is very good in one breath, but that our craving for growth has led us to condone sloppy credit procedures in another.

"We are accused of shoveling funds to our corporate customers at the expense of the small consumer, while at the same time we are supposed to be foisting unwanted credit upon the poor.

"We are blamed in one breath for failing to help the City of New York deal with its massive problems, and in the next castigated for permitting our officers to serve on municipal and regional groups attempting to work on those problems.

"One page cites the inability of a senior officer who sat on a company's board to get that company's business for FNCB, while on another page there is an allegation that directors control business.

"We will be glad to respond to either position, but it is impossible to respond to both.

"It is difficult to react to a report which affects concern for the privacy of individuals because Citibank administers New York City tax collections under a contract forbidding use of the information for any other purpose, and at the same time demands information about the private affairs of Citibank's depositors and borrowers; which flogs the bank as laggard in the areas of black and female employment in which it has, in fact, been a leader by quoting at length from a study that the bank itself commissioned precisely to inform itself about personnel policy problems in order to solve them.

"The law students make some definitive legal judgments with which more experienced lawyers disagree.

"Although in the short run, we may have some difficulty in catching up with the report's distortions, over the long run we hope to improve our performance as a result of learning how we look to outsiders who certainly gave us no quarter."

In response to the Nader report, Citibank highlighted a number of major Nader distortions and inconsistencies.

Cooperation with the investigators—Mr. Nader charges that Citibank gave his task force "very limited" cooperation. This "very limited" cooperation included the participation of Citibank officers in the areas selected by the investigators themselves in 53 interviews lasting hundreds of hours, providing the task force with mountains of documents bearing on every facet of bank operations and policy, and giving them tape recordings of every interview so that the facts about the bank would be readily available to the student investigators.

At the outset, Citibank offered to provide the law students with the same information it regularly furnishes to interested stockholders and responsible members of the press, subject to the bank's obligation to protect the confidentiality of customer relationships and the necessity for withholding information of value to Citibank's competitors.

Bank customers' right to privacy and their expectation that it will be respected is protected by fundamental legal and constitutional safeguards. The U.S. government itself may not violate this right and private investigators, however highly motivated, have no privileges greater than the law prescribes.

Project Director David Leinsdorf agreed to abide by these rules, yet the report flays the bank because it withheld information Citibank is prohibited by law from revealing and which would obviously jeopardize the bank's position opposite its competitors.

Citibank's collection methods—The report criticizes FNCB for bringing more suits to collect on delinquent personal loans than any other New York City bank—"adjusted for the volume of consumer credit outstanding," says Mr. Leinsdorf, "more than double the rate of suit of any other bank."

Despite its seeming precision, this statement is a gross distortion of the facts. Citibank makes almost as many personal loans as all four of its major competitors put together, and nearly three times as many personal loans as its nearest competitor. It follows logically, therefore, that we do sue more than any other bank because, in addition to having such an enormous volume, Citibank's personal loan portfolio differs significantly from those of its major competitors in that it contains a much larger number of unsecured loans. On these loans, unlike those secured by collateral which can be liquidated without resort to the courts, if a borrower (on an unsecured note) defaults and declines to make alternative arrangements, the bank's only resource is to institute suit.

The facts supporting the above statement are derived from information supplied by the New York State Bankers Association as of December 31, 1969, and are attached as Appendix A to this memorandum.

On the question of so-called "sewer service," Citibank rejects the allegation that it is careless about notifying delinquent borrowers that legal action has been started and resents the name-calling comparison to a firm which the report identifies as "one of the most notorious default judgment creditors in New York City." Citibank deals with one process serving company, the Aetna Judicial Service. Citibank's policy is to require Aetna to make four attempts at varying hours to serve the borrower personally before resort to indirect or substitute service.

In each and every case where a borrower or co-signer disputes the server's affidavit that the summons was delivered, Citibank requires a detailed report from the company. If the report is not entirely satisfactory, service is vacated and the legal proceedings abandoned. In addition, if a number of complaints are received involving a particular process server, Aetna is instructed never to use that person for Citibank business.

In 1970, charges or complaints of improper service were made a total of 35 times. While Citibank is not content with any complaints at all, the facts simply do not sustain the lurid picture painted in the Nader report. If the Nader men will supply us with names and addresses of those improperly served, we will immediately move to correct the situation. The handful of allegations are already being investigated.

Response to monetary restraint—The attached table indicates loan-to-deposit ratios for New York City and country banks for 1969, the restraint year when FNCB and other large banks allegedly failed to cooperate with the objectives of the Federal Reserve. As the year 1969 progressed and the Fed persistently accelerated its efforts to restrain growth of bank loans, Citibank steadily reduced the rate of growth of its loans—indeed, just about keeping in step with the "aver-

LOAN-TO-DEPOSIT RATIOS,
COMMERCIAL BANKS, 1969

	New York City	Country Banks
December, 1968	67.2%	57.6%
January, 1969	73.1	59.2
February	75.7	59.9
March	76.1	60.3
April	72.3	60.2
May	76.8	61.4
June	73.9	61.6
July	84.9	63.3
August	82.4	63.6
September	84.4	63.7
October	80.7	63.2
November	79.8	63.5
December	77.3	62.2

NOTE: Data for last Wednesday of each month, except for June and December for which the dates are end-of-month call report dates. Loans include interbank (federal funds) loans and liquid money-market loans. Deposits are gross, without adjustment for bank float. Country banks include only those that are members of the FRS. New York City banks are those classified as reserve city banks (11 out of about 40 banks doing a fairly full commercial banking business in the city).

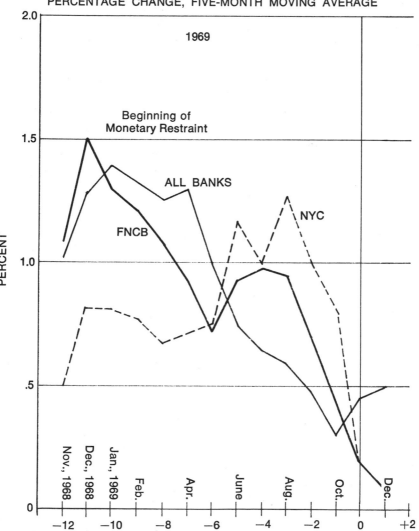

BUSINESS LOANS SEASONALLY ADJUSTED
PERCENTAGE CHANGE, FIVE-MONTH MOVING AVERAGE

age" countrywide bank, and slightly faster than the average of all New York banks. (see chart)

The New York City Employee Pension Fund—The report, by some perverse logic, indicts Citibank for serving as advisor on $2.7 billion of bonds and $105 million of stocks in the municipal employee pension funds without charging a fee. The report quotes the New York City comptroller's office as stating that Citibank has done "an excellent job" and that income has been increased by about $15 million per year as a result of changes made with the advice of FNCB and the other advisors.

It is alleged that "Citibank used the commissions generated by the NYC pension fund transactions to buy deposits for the bank. Halsey Stuart & Company was selected by Citibank to handle corporate bond transactions for the city pension funds in return for Halsey Stuart's checking account deposits."

The fact is that during the approximately two years that Citibank has been advising the comptroller without charging a fee, total bond transactions initiated by Citibank with brokers of our choice involved $8 million face value of bonds. (All other transactions were initiated directly by the comptroller's office without consultation with Citibank as to the choice of broker/dealer.) Not a single one of the Citibank initiated orders was placed with Halsey Stuart. (As a sidelight, Citibank's total commission business with Halsey Stuart during 1970 arising from all accounts under our management was under $30,000.)

The Nader document therefore is patently absurd in claiming that "millions of additional dollars would thus be available for pensions" if the income alleged to have been generated by deposits attracted by brokers business from the city pension funds were to be turned over to the funds. Assuming a normal ¼ % imputed commission (bonds are traded net of commission) on the $8 million of transactions we directed, the total commissions were $20,000. As a public service for these funds Citibank made a unique exception to its normal management fee which would have approximated $125,000/$150,000 per annum. For this saving to the taxpayers, we are attacked.

Personnel Policy—The report's contention that the vast majority of our clerical staff earn less than $6,500 is grossly in error. The average salary for our nonofficial staff, which includes many young and unmarried employees, significantly exceeds that figure. Also the report's estimates as to the wage levels of various officer groups are greatly exaggerated.

Moreover, the allegations that wage levels in banks are not competitive with other industries conflict with the Department of Labor's study completed in August, 1970:

The rapid increase in bank employee salaries in the New York area over the past five years has narrowed and in some cases eliminated the gap in earnings levels compared with other industrial rates. For example, in the latter part of 1964, salaries of secretaries, typists, and keypunch operators in the banking industry were somewhat below comparable cross-industry scales in the area but by November, 1969 they had closed the gap and actually *had slightly higher earnings than their counterparts studied in a representative cross-section of private industry.*

In another area, the Opinion Research Study that the report quotes so voluminously concludes:

A large majority of clerical staff members view the Bank favorably as a place to work. This view has not changed much since the 1966 survey, indicating that Citibank has done a reasonably good job of maintaining basic staff morale. This is especially encouraging in light of the fact that in recent years the levels of favorable response on questions like this have generally declined.

In contradiction of the report's contention that opportunities for advancement are limited, last year, the 15,900 nonofficial employees in New York received 16,512 merit salary increases in addition to 7,400 promotional increases.

As to the report's comments regarding Citibank's participation in the JOBS program, we will merely point out that Citibank is the nation's single largest participant in the training of office clerical employees under this program and that, beyond the reimbursement Citibank receives from the Department of Labor, this program costs the bank nearly three times the normal hiring and training costs for each employee.

ADDITIONAL MEMORANDUM ON COLLECTION AND LENDING POLICIES

This memorandum expands on the discussion of Citibank's personal lending policies and collection methods contained in the accompanying press release.

On the next page is a table derived from information supplied by the New York State Bankers Association indicating the number of loans outstanding as of December 31, 1969 and comparing the personal loan portfolio of Citibank with combined totals of its four major competitors.

These figures show:

* Citibank makes more unsecured loans than its four major competitors combined—344,835 against 326,122. These loans, unlike loans made against collateral, which can be liquidated without resort to the courts, are made on a personal signature, with or without co-signers. If the borrower defaults and declines to

make alternative arrangements, the bank's only recourse is to institute suit.

 * Citibank also makes more FHA property improvement loans
than its four competitors combined—38,903 to 33,722—and in
fact has the largest FHA portfolio of any U.S. bank. Under FHA
policies, a bank is required to pursue all of its collection remedies
before making a claim to FHA. As a practical matter, this means
that delinquent loans must be pursued in the courts.

NUMBER OF PERSONAL FINANCE ACCOUNTS OUTSTANDING
AT FIVE NEW YORK CITY BANKS,
LEADERS IN THE CONSUMER LOAN FIELD
(Information on combined totals of four major bank competitors as
of Dec. 31, 1969 supplied by New York State Bankers Association)

	FIRST NATIONAL CITY BANK		FOUR MAJOR COMPETITORS COMBINED	
Loan Classification	Number	Percent of Total	Number	Percent of Total
Unsecured Signature Loans	344,835	70.02	326,122	58.0
FHA	38,903	7.91	33,722	6.0
Auto—Direct	49,418	10.03	69,739	12.4
Indirect	11,592	2.35	34.114	6.1
Home Appliances	2,472	.5	1,395	.2
Property Moderni-zation Own Plan	6,531	1.33	10,205	1.8
Installment Loans to Small Business	13,205	2.68	51,663	9.2
Miscellaneous	25,519	5.18	35,089	6.3
TOTAL	492,475	100.00	562,049	100.0

Another important factor to be considered in making comparisons
is the differing loan charge-off requirements that apply to national and
state banks. Because of its status as a national bank, Citibank is required to charge off delinquent loans as bad debts when they fall 90
days in arrears, a requirement that compels relatively prompt legal
action when a debtor makes no effort to pay. In contrast, three of Citibank's four principal competitors are state banks with a charge-off
cycle of 180 days instead of 90 days, and the fourth bank has only
recently gone on a 90-day cycle.

   The figures cited in the Nader report are also distorted by inclusion
of suits involving credit card delinquencies. In 1969, Citibank had a
very large lead over any of its major competitors in the credit card
business, and naturally it had many more credit card delinquencies to
cope with. Credit card accounts are not reflected in the figure shown
in Appendix A; if they were, Citibank's position as leader in the field
of personal finance in 1969 would have been even more apparent.

   Contrary to what Mr. Leinsdorf and his associates appear to believe, Citibank institutes suit on delinquent loans only after efforts to collect or obtain agreement on an alternative payment schedule have failed to elicit any meaningful response. Customers in financial difficulty are given every opportunity to work out problems with the bank's cooperation. The three collection form letters attached provide concrete examples of the bank's attitude in dealing with delinquent borrowers. (The first is used when loan payments are in arrears, the second on loans which have been called or "matured," and the third on loans which have been charged off as bad debts.)

The Nader report is also in serious error with regard to the alleged impact of Citibank's lending and collection policies on persons of lower income. Relying on interviews with "332 New York City debtors"—presumably of various financial institutions—conducted by Professor David Caplovitz, the Nader report concludes that persons with incomes of $6,000 or less account for 70% of the debtors sued by First National City Bank. Citibank could find no indication in the report of sampling technique employed by Professor Caplovitz, but to check the facts, Citibank itself made an analysis of a random sample of 550 loans that had been called or "matured" in a typical month. The analysis revealed that only 153 accounts or 27.8 percent of the total had incomes of less than $6,000 while 150 or 27.3% had incomes in the $6,000 to $7,500 bracket, 21.6% had incomes from $7,500 to $10,000, 13.5% earned between $10,000 and $15,000, 4.4% had incomes exceeding $15,000 and 5.5% did not specify income.

In contrast to the Nader report's complaint that FNCB over-extends credit to poor people, here are the views of George Wiley, executive director of the National Welfare Rights Organization (on WNBC-TV's "For Women Only," January 5, 1970): "I realize that there are dangers of credit. The problem is, however, we feel that the credit industry has been too discriminatory in not extending credit to some of the people who actually need it most . . . For example, credit is good for smoothing out peaks and valleys of the economy, and the people who have the most problem about that are the people who have the least money because they have the greatest need to be able to budget large expenditures and to such people credit is normally not extended. . . . Many of them are excellent credit risks."

First National City Bank's credit policy is to lend to individual borrowers if we can expect to be repaid. Citibank turns down many loans and suggests smaller loans in many cases based on an estimate of the prospective borrower's financial circumstances. That Citibank's judgment on these matters is reasonably sound is shown by the fact that the bank's delinquency record is as good or better than that of other New York State and New York City banks:

NEW YORK STATE BANKERS DELINQUENCY REPORT
(Based on number of loans)

	New York State	Greater New York	FNCB
January 31, 1970	2.2	2.0	2.0
January 31, 1971	2.9	2.7	2.5
April 30, 1971	2.3	2.1	2.0

Overextension of credit makes no sense from a profit standpoint (which Citibank is elsewhere accused of emphasizing unduly). A recent sample of 4,000 loans indicates that the average loss on a bad loan amounts to $534, nearly 10 times the average profit of $56 on a good loan.

FIRST NATIONAL CITY BANK

PERSONAL FINANCE DEPARTMENT
810 7TH AVENUE
NEW YORK, N.Y. 10019

TELEPHONE (212) 559-3211
ADDRESS MAIL TO
  BOX 1136, GRAND CENTRAL STATION
  NEW YORK, NEW YORK 10017
IN REPLYING PLEASE REFER TO FILE NO.

Dear

Undoubtedly you have been concerned about your existing loan and we are writing to suggest it might be beneficial to change the terms of payment.

If possible we will extend a new loan to you, one that will require a smaller monthly payment and give you a little time before the next payment becomes due. You will not receive any additional money but will have a fresh start with an obligation that might be more comfortable to handle.

To save time, we have filled out all the figures on the enclosed form. All you have to do is complete the application, sign the papers, and send them back. We will make every effort to put the loan through.

To make sure your papers get to the right person, please use the enclosed envelope which needs no postage.

Yours truly,

John E. Muller
Assistant Vice President

Enclosure

P.S.: If, in the interim, you have made a satisfactory arrangement please disregard this letter.

FIRST NATIONAL CITY BANK

PERSONAL FINANCE DEPARTMENT
810 7TH AVENUE
NEW YORK, N.Y. 10019

TELEPHONE (212) 559-3211
ADDRESS MAIL TO
BOX 1136, GRAND CENTRAL STATION
NEW YORK, NEW YORK 10017
IN REPLYING PLEASE REFER TO FILE NO.

Dear

Sometimes through unexpected expenses or temporary loss of income, or a combination of both, borrowers find it impossible to keep up to date on their obligations. Frequently they presume that we are not interested or are inflexible and do not let us know that they have a financial problem. They don't realize that we might be able to help. Or, they may have made the effort only to be frustrated in their attempt to reach the person handling their account.

Perhaps you have experienced some such difficulty in connection with your loan. Although it became necessary to mature the loan and demand payment of the entire balance, we would nevertheless welcome an opportunity to discuss a new schedule of repayment with you. If you are employed, we would consider your application to refinance the balance. This would reduce the amount of your monthly payments, provide additional time and, we hope, assist you in adjusting your financial affairs.

Our representative handling your account is Mr.   who can be reached by telephone at 559-   . If you will call him within the next day or two, while he has your file on his desk, he will be glad to discuss the details. Should it be inconvenient for you to telephone him, you may complete and return the attached request for an application.

Needless to say, it is important that we hear from you promptly.

You may be assured that it is our sincere desire to be helpful to you in this regard.

Very truly yours,

FIRST NATIONAL CITY BANK

PERSONAL FINANCE DEPARTMENT   TELEPHONE (212) 559-3211
        810 7TH AVENUE   ADDRESS MAIL TO
    NEW YORK, N.Y. 10019   BOX 1136, GRAND CENTRAL STATION
                                      NEW YORK, NEW YORK 10017
                                      IN REPLYING PLEASE REFER TO FILE NO.

Dear

Temporary loss of income or unexpected expenses, or a combination of both, sometimes make it impossible for borrowers to keep up to date on their obligations. They very often presume that we are not interested in hearing about their financial difficulties, or are so inflexible that we are unwilling to discuss a possible solution.

Our representative handling your account is Mr.   who can be reached by telephone at 559-   . He will have your file on his desk during the next few days and if you call him, he will be pleased to discuss your particular problem with you. Needless to say, it is important that we hear from you promptly.

You may rest assured that it is our sincere desire to be helpful and every effort will be made to suggest a solution which will be mutually satisfactory.

Very truly yours,

Surrebuttal

For Release: Thursday AMs
        November 4, 1971

Contact: Donald Etra

Attached please find the Nader Study Group's response to Walter Wriston's statements concerning the Citibank Report.

As you know, two weeks ago, Mr. Wriston, Chairman of First National City Bank, refused further cooperation with the Nader group, using as an excuse that the report contained errors. The attached response highlights the unfounded nature of Mr. Wriston's reaction.

During the summer of 1970, a Study Group, sponsored by the Center for the Study of Responsive Law, began to study the First National City Bank. The group's goal was to examine the bank and to analyze its impact on the community.

Part One of the Citibank Report was released in the Spring of 1971.

Walter Wriston, Chairman of First National City Bank, responded to this report by alleging that it contained "contradictions."

It is noteworthy that, except for one instance,* Mr. Wriston has not denied any of the factual observations made by the Report. Rather, he has listed claimed inconsistencies which upon closer examination are found to be more apparent than real.

More importantly, Mr. Wriston has not responded to the fundamental assertion that a bank holds a position of public trust in the community. This trust arises out of the special privileges conferred upon banks, specifically money-creating power and a monopoly over demand deposits.

The Study Group would now like to reply to Mr. Wriston, examining the so-called contradictions, and clarifying some points that Mr. Wriston overlooked.

1. FIRST ALLEGED CONTRADICTION

Mr. Wriston: "We are alleged to have abandoned the tax-exempt bond market on one page, while our [FNCB's] preference for tax-exempt securities is given as a reason for supporting the World Trade Center on another page."

The Facts: In 1970-71 Citibank substantially withdrew from the municipal bond market. In 1968, however, Citibank used tax-exempt investments to its own great advantage by investing in the World Trade Center.

In 1970, Citibank's holdings of state and municipal securities dropped to 4.3% of assets, an all-time low. In the first quarter of 1971, Citibank's ownership of state and municipal securities plummeted another $270,000,000, to 3.1% of assets, a smaller percentage than in any of the 100 largest American banks.

Banks' substantial withdrawal from the municipal market decreases the price of existing outstanding securities, and increases the interest rate that the municipality will have to pay on new issues. In short, actions like that taken by Citibank increase New York City's cost of borrowing funds. This increased cost must be borne by New York City's citizens.

When the opportunity presents itself to make a profit from New York City, FNCB does not hesitate. Let us examine the case of the World Trade Center, a project of the Port of New York Authority.

In 1968 Citibank loaned the Port Authority $39 million, but the Port Authority had to redeposit $6 million in Citibank as an interest-free compensating balance. Citibank earned 4.25% tax-exempt interest on the full $39,000,000 loan.

---

* Commission-generated deposits from the New York City Pension Fund.

4.25% of $39,900,000 is $1,695,750. Since there was a $6 million compensating balance, all that Citibank actually advanced the Port Authority was $33,900,000. Thus, when Citibank received $1,695,750 return on its $33,900,000 loan, it was actually making 5% on its investment. This was a tax-free return. A tax-free loan at 5% return is equivalent to a taxable loan of more than 10%. A return of more than 10% is sufficient to tempt any bank back into the tax-exempt market, and was especially so in December, 1968, when banks could only charge their prime-rate corporate customers 7.5%.

2. SECOND ALLEGED CONTRADICTION

Mr. Wriston: "We are told that our record of credit extension is very good in one breath, but that our craving for growth has led us to condone sloppy credit procedures in another."

The Facts: We never disputed the fact that Citibank was putting its funds to work to earn money. What was questioned was the lack of tight controls and the deception employed in the *details* of credit extension. For example:

1. Citibank does not provide clear disclosure of credit cost information. For instance, Citibank failed to disclose the 12% Checking Plus interest rate in its ads and omitted this information from the descriptive brochures that it had available at its branches.

2. The format that Citibank uses to bill its credit customers emphasizes the item "total minimum payment due" instead of the item "total balance." Such a format may deceive Citibank's credit customers, causing them inadvertently to obligate themselves to needless and excessive finance charges. Such a practice is a violation of the Truth-in-Lending Act and Regulation Z of the FRB.

3. Based on Citibank's own 1970 study:
   Only 35% of Citibank's platform personnel could adequately explain the requirements for Ready Credit.
   Only 46% of Citibank's bankers could spell out the costs of Master Charge.
   44% of the platform officers did not clearly explain the rules for making payments on unpaid Checking Plus balances.

4. Citibank had limited, if any, screening procedure for those to whom they sent unsolicited credit cards.

5. Citibank does not adequately scrutinize the merchants whom it signs up to participate in Master Charge. When customers are swindled by fraudulent merchandising schemes (as were 160 Master Charge users in the Astro Sewing Machine fraud described in the re-

port), Citibank disclaimed all responsibility for the deceptive practices of the seller, the very seller that Citibank aggressively signed up to participate in the Master Charge Program.

6. Citibank claims that credit is granted only after a thorough evaluation of current economic strength has been made. According to a recent study by Professor Caplovitz of Columbia University, about 30% of Citibank's defaulting debtors obtain credit in violation of Citibank's own debt-to-income guidelines.

3. THIRD ALLEGED CONTRADICTION

Mr. Wriston: "We are accused of shoveling funds to our corporate customers at the expense of the small consumer, while at the same time we are supposed to be foisting unwanted credit on the poor."

The Facts: Available information supports the contention that, relative to their deposits, corporations are favored over individuals. The contention is supported by a comparison of the loan-to-deposit ratios at Citibank's branches in residential areas, with the loan-to-deposit ratios at Citibank's branches in the business districts, where deposits are mainly those of large corporate depositors.

Residential Area	Loans	Deposits	Loan-to-Deposit Ratio
Bensonhurst	$ 36,000	$ 3,226,000	1.1%
Washington Hts.	4,400,000	25,700,000	17.0%
Castle Hill	587,000	28,993,000	2.0%
Luna Park	32,000	747,000	4.3%

Business District	Loans	Deposits	Loan-to-Deposit Ratio
Rockefeller Plaza	126,300,000	222,000,000	57.0%
J. C. Penney Bldg.	58,000,000	78,000,000	75.0%
181 Montague St.	49,700,000	58,600,000	85.0%

The unwanted credit that Citibank "foists," through aggressive and misleading advertising, on the poor is in the form of high interest rate consumer loans. What is needed greatly are the lower interest rate (although still higher than the prime rate given to corporations) residential mortgage loans. Residential mortgage loans comprise less than 2% of Citibank's assets, compared to 13% for all commercial banks.

It is fair to state that Citibank is not alone among big banks in shoveling loans to corporate customers. The ABA's study of consumer credit in banks showed that in 1969, banks with deposits of $5 million and over carried installment credit equal to only 10.2% of their total loans and discounts. The smaller banks had larger percentages of consumer credit, running over 20% of loans and discounts for the small banks, and, in one category as high as 27.1%.

4. FOURTH ALLEGED CONTRADICTION

Mr. Wriston: "We are blamed in one breath for failing to help New York City with its massive problems, and in the next castigated for permitting our officers to serve on municipal and regional groups attempting to work on those problems."

The Facts: By ignoring a large part of New Yorkers' residential needs, and by allocating an insufficient amount of capital for minority business loans, Citibank fails to help New York with two of its major problems. Instead of using its representation on public bodies to help the public, Citibank uses its representation on municipal groups to benefit Citibank, at the expense of New York City and New Yorkers.

Citibank's $450 million residential mortgage loan portfolio is only one-third the size of its $1.4 billion in passbook savings. Residential mortgage loans comprise less than 2% of Citibank's assets, compared with 13% for all commercial banks.

According to Sidney Davidson, FNCB Vice-President in Charge of Urban Affairs, Citibank's total equity investment in black enterprises is a mere $250,000, most of which is in one particular venture.

Citibank uses its representation on public bodies to bail out bank customers. Such was the case when Eben Pyne, a senior vice president at Citibank, sat on a special committee which recommended that New York State purchase the Long Island Railroad for $65 million from the Pennsylvania Railroad. In 1965, the LIRR owed Citibank's debtor, the Pennsylvania Railroad, $76.1 million. Of the $65 million paid by New York to the Pennsylvania Railroad, $60 million was given in consideration for cancellation of LIRR's debt to the Pennsylvania Railroad.

Similarly, when the MTA, of which Mr. Pyne is also a member, considered the question of a fare increase at the beginning of 1970, Mr. Pyne voted for the increase, instead of asking the city to pay for the deficit from its own revenues. It is not without significance that at the time of the vote, Citibank and other banks had not yet begun to withdraw substantially from the municipal bond market. Thus the banks had an interest in keeping the New York City treasury free from extra demands in order to protect the price of their holdings of city bonds. While the MTA is not to be thought of as wholly representing banking interests, one should note that seven out of the eleven members of the MTA were either officers or directors of banks.

5. FIFTH ALLEGED CONTRADICTION

Mr. Wriston: "One page cites the inability of a senior officer who sat on a company's board to get that company's business for FNCB, while on another page there is an allegation that directors control business."

The Facts: The inability of that one senior officer to get the company's business for the bank was cited as the exception to the prevailing rule that directors bring business to the bank in return for the bank's more-than-generous services furnished to the directors' own corporations.

At the end of 1969, Citibank had interlocking directorates with 40 of America's top 300 largest corporations.

As of 1968 Citibank had one director interlock with Pan American World Airways. Two of Pan Am's employee benefit funds were managed by Citibank. In at least one syndicated loan agreement, Citibank loaned Pan Am $18 million at the prime rate for eight years.

As of 1968 Citibank had two director interlocks with Consolidated Edison Company of New York. Citibank manages one of Con Ed's employee benefit funds and holds 6.1% of an issue of Con Ed's stock.

The list continues. The Study group directs those interested to the tabulation found in Representative Wright Patman's 1968 study of *Commercial Banks and Their Trust Departments.* Patman's tabulation is entitled *Interlocking Relations between First National City Bank, New York, N.Y., and Major Corporations.*

6. CITIBANK'S WITHHOLDING OF INFORMATION

To justify Citibank's withholding of information from the Study Group, Mr. Wriston states that Citibank withheld information that it was prohibited by law from revealing. The report indicates over 25 separate items that Citibank refused to reveal, including:

Loans to directors in lump sum totals

Loans to affiliates in lump sum totals

The geographic distribution of the mortgage portfolio and a breakdown by the type of building

The names of companies whose pension funds it manages

The profitability of the bank's major divisions

Mr. Wriston, what law prohibits Citibank from revealing the above?

7. COLLECTION METHODS

Mr. Wriston has yet to deny that Citibank is New York City's number one plaintiff, that in 1969 Citibank sued 10,000 people, and that in 1970 it sued 15,000. In the majority of cases those sued were earning under $5,000, and had neither the financial ability nor the legal expertise to challenge the suits. Even if one accepts Mr. Wriston's "explanation" that Citibank has three times the number of personal loans as its nearest competitor, its record is still far from exemplary because it institutes five times as many suits as any other bank.

Mr. Wriston states that Citibank provides customers every opportunity to work out problems with the bank's cooperation and sues only after efforts to collect have failed to elicit meaningful response. The Study Group hopes that the bank will adhere to this new policy and discontinue the practices of harassing debtors' families, causing debtors to lose their jobs through the garnishment of wages, and reneging on offers to refinance.

The new form letters, which Mr. Wriston attached to his response, include offers to refinance debts. We hope that Citibank will inform judgment debtors who chose to refinance that refinancing will entail a 24% boost in the size of the debt, to cover attorney's fees and court costs.

"SEWER SERVICES"

Mr. Wriston asks the Nader Study Group to provide him with the names of those defendants who were victims of "sewer service," i.e., those who never received summonses because the server merely threw the papers away. The report itself gives examples, complete with names and addresses of prospective defendants improperly served. Addresses were furnished to show that some of the defendants lived several miles from each other, but that each was allegedly served by the same server at the same time. The report questions how one man could be in two or three places at once, and then swear to the fact in an affidavit. The report cites two process servers who served Citibank's summonses and who were subsequently convicted of violating summons service laws.

Most importantly, the Nader Report questions why Citibank takes a passive role, waiting for complaints, rather than assuming affirmative supervision for service of its own summonses, particularly in light of what it and other financial institutions know about the disgracefully widespread and unconstitutional practice of "sewer service."

8. RESPONSE TO MONETARY RESTRAINT

The Study Group Report charges Citibank with failure to cooperate with the objectives of the Fed's monetary policies. Mr. Wriston has responded:

As the year 1969 progressed, and the Fed persistently accelerated its efforts to restrain growth of its loans, Citibank steadily reduced the rate of growth of its loans–indeed, just about keeping in step with the 'average' countrywide bank, and slightly faster than the average of all New York banks.

The record, however, shows that from early 1969 to mid-1970, when the Fed's policy of restraint was in force, Citibank increased its loan portfolio by $2,800,000,000, more than 24%. Citibank's *Monthly Economic Letter* for June, 1969 states

> It is highly unrealistic to expect individual banks willingly to refuse loans to borrowers who have maintained idle balances at banks in the expectation that they could get credit when needed.

As to the extent of Citibank's cooperation in relation to other banks, the Study Group Report notes: The drop in total credit *growth* (loans and investment) from 11% in 1968 to 3.3% in 1969, shows that, on the whole, the banking industry responded to the anti-inflationary policy adopted by the Fed. Citibank, however, increased its bank credit by more than 12%, four times the national average. To circumvent the Fed's monetary policies, Citibank and the other large banks moved aggressively into the Eurodollar market. Since this market is international, Regulation Q interest rate ceilings do not apply and banks are free to pay the market rates of interest on their Eurodollar borrowings. In the first six months of 1969, banks increased their Eurodollar borrowings by $5 billion. Citibank's holdings amounted to $1.4 billion. The Fed had not anticipated that the big banks would use the Eurodollar market to avoid the impact of credit restraint.

Walter Wriston, in a 1970 speech, boasted: "In spite of a discriminatory Regulation Q, we were successful in hanging on to most of our customers by finding other pools of liquidity to tap."

9. NEW YORK CITY EMPLOYEE PENSION FUND

Mr. Wriston: "It is alleged that 'Citibank used the commissions generated by the NYC pension fund transactions to buy deposits for the bank. Halsey Stuart & Company was selected by Citibank to handle corporate bond transactions for the city pension funds in return for Halsey Stuart's checking account deposits.' "

In the one flat denial Mr. Wriston makes to the report, he states, "Not a single one of the Citibank initiated orders was placed with Halsey Stuart." *

The Study Group: Before making our allegations of broker reciprocity, the Study Group interviewed members of the brokerage

---

* At a press conference in June, 1971, the Task Force conceded that the naming of Halsey Stuart could be wrong, but noted that Citibank has not provided evidence that the bank does not engage in reciprocity.

firm in question and personnel in the New York City Comptroller's office.

In an interview with a member of the Study Group, a responsible supervisor in the Bond Division of Halsey Stuart said:

> First National City Bank, as pension adviser to the City, selects Halsey for its purchasers of corporate bonds. Halsey Stuart banks at First National City, and at many other banks. We have to put our money somewhere, and the reciprocal dealing just preserves our ongoing relationship with Citibank.

Citibank's use of reciprocity on the city pension fund was also confirmed by personnel in the New York City Comptroller's Bureau of Investments.

Mr. Wriston has pointed out that Citibank's total commission business with Halsey Stuart during 1970 was under $30,000. This figure should be interpreted in light of some of the observations made by the SEC *Institutional Investor Study* of 1970. This study noted:

> An increase of $1 in commissions paid by a trust department and received by a broker was estimated to be accompanied, on the average, by an increase of $4.26 in the broker's deposits in the bank. The relationship found between commissions paid and brokers' deposits does not disclose who initiates the arrangement.

10. PERSONNEL POLICY

WORKING CONDITIONS

Mr. Wriston cites the platitudinous conclusion of the 1970 Opinion Research Study which states that "a large majority of clerical staff members view the bank favorably as a place to work." The body of the Opinion Study revealed otherwise. Oppressive working conditions was a major grievance of Citibank's 4,937 Operating Group clericals, who constitute 88% of the Operating Group work force. The Operating Group clericals complained of inadequate space and equipment, too much noise, uncomfortable temperatures, too many rush jobs, and insufficient staff to handle the work load.

TURNOVER

Citibank employees quit in droves. In 1969, more than one out of every three employees—or 6,000 people—left the bank. In the recession year of 1970, when employment was hard to to find, the turnover dropped slightly to 29%, but 5,000 people still left the bank.

ADVANCEMENT

Jobs entailing high levels of responsibility, discretion, and compensation are closed to thousands of qualified Citibankers. Although more than half of Citibank's employees are women and more than 35% are black, there is not one woman or black vice president in the Corporate Banking Group, the department that handles most of the bank's money and deals.

Of the 288 officers in the Corporate Banking Group at July 1, 1969, there was one black and three women, all assistant cashiers in nonlending jobs.

Trust Department Study
Letters and Questionnaires

Letter and Questionnaire Sent to FNCB Directors and Trust Board Members

December 23, 1971

Mr. George S. Moore
——— 79th Street
New York, New York 10021

Dear Mr. Moore:

By way of introduction, I am working for the Center for Study of Responsive Law, Ralph Nader's research organization. I am presently directing a project on bank trust departments.

The purpose of the study is to examine how a trust department works. What are its functions and how well does it fulfill its goals? We will attempt to analyze the impact of trust activities on the community; because, when a bank has investment discretion over several billions of dollars, its choice of investments will affect more people than just the trust beneficiaries.

More importantly, we are seeking to determine what *should* be the role of a bank trust department.

Your experience, both as an executive of First National City Bank and as a member of that bank's Board of Directors, has undoubtedly given you many opportunities to consider the questions that we are seeking to understand. I have enclosed a list of those questions for your response.

I am certain that you realize, for a complete understanding of the issues involved, we must have the insights of men of experience like yourself.

Thank you for your thoughts and time.

Sincerely yours,

Donald Etra

Questions about Bank Trust Departments

1. Can an institution be responsive to the personal needs of beneficiaries?
2. Does a bank's commercial relationships influence investments made by the bank's trust department?
3. Do members of the bank's board influence investment decisions of the bank?
4. When a bank is appointed trustee of a pension fund, what should be its role with respect to the employees covered by the fund and the employer corporation?
5. Does broker reciprocity still take place?
6. Why are trust departments a part of commercial banks?
7. Should trust departments be a part of commercial banks?
8. What should the role of a bank be towards the community in which it does business?
9. If you were a legislator, what changes in the present system of banking would you suggest?

Please reply to: Donald Etra
Center for Study of Responsive Law
P. O. Box 19367
Washington, D.C. 20036

Letter and Questionnaire Sent to Beneficiaries of Trusts Managed by FNCB

CENTER FOR STUDY OF RESPONSIVE LAW
P.O. BOX 19367
WASHINGTON, D.C. 20036

December, 1971

Dear

By way of introduction, I am working for the Center for Study of Responsive Law, Ralph Nader's research organization. During the past several years, we have received complaints from beneficiaries of trusts managed by banks. These beneficiaries have stated that the bank was either mismanaging the trust, or was not responsive to the personal need of the beneficiaries. Often, many who wrote us expressed the fear that because they were just individuals while the bank was so large and powerful, they could do nothing.

The Center for the Study of Responsive Law has decided to investigate the situation. Essentially, we want to know whether banks are doing a good job as trustees.

We have chosen to write you because you are a beneficiary, or at least a potential beneficiary, of a trust created by the estate named below.* As a beneficiary of a trust managed by a bank, you can tell us whether the bank has handled your interests satisfactorily. Here is an opportunity for you as an individual to be heard.

We rely on your response to the attached questionnaire so that your interests, and the interests of others in a similar position can be represented.

Naturally, because of the personal nature of this inquiry, we are not asking you to identify your questionnaire in any way unless you choose to do so voluntarily. Also, please be assured that we do not want to make any personal gain from this study; we just want to find out what the situation is and to report the facts.

Thank you for your cooperation.

Sincerely yours,

Donald Etra

*Estate of _____

Trust Beneficiary Questionnaire

1. Please state which bank was appointed trustee for this trust?_____
2. How often, if ever, has the bank reported to you about the performance of this trust?_____
3. Has the bank ever discussed its investment policies with you?
   _____
4. Does the bank ever tell you which brokers it chooses to make stock transactions for this trust? _____
5. Has the bank ever suggested that they put the trust assets in a common trust fund? _____
6. Has the bank ever told you when it has interests in some of the companies whose stock it buys for your trust? _____
7. Has the bank been responsive to your personal needs as a beneficiary? _____
8. Have you been satisfied with the bank's overall performance? If so, why, if not, why not? _____

_____

_____

On the back of this sheet please add any additional comments that you feel might help our study. We have enclosed an envelope for your convenience. Thank you; we deeply appreciate your cooperation.

*Letter Sent to Approximately 400 Companies Whose Employee
Benefit Plans Are Managed by FNCB*

November 8, 1971

Dear Sir:

By way of introduction, I am directing a project for the Center for
the Study of Responsive Law on the role of banks as trustee or co-
trustee for employee pension funds. As you know, thousands of employees are participants in pension funds. That their interests be protected is of vital importance to every employer and citizen.

From publicly available information, we note that your corporation
has a pension fund account with First National City Bank. In that
connection, we would like to ask you the following questions:

1. As background information, we would appreciate a description
   of your plan, including:
   a) How many employees are covered and how large is the fund?
   b) Is the fund managed separately or is it managed as part of a
   larger pool?
   c) How soon do pension benefits vest in the beneficiaries, and are
   the benefits portable?
   d) What has been the rate of return from your fund over the past
   five years?
   e) Are D-1 and D-2 forms filed with the Department of Labor? If
   so, please send us the latest of these forms.
2. When your corporation was establishing the fund, did you first approach the bank or did the bank first approach you?
   a) In negotiating the terms of your fund, did First National send
   you any "boiler-plate" clauses relating to responsibilities and liabilities that they wished to have in the trust agreement?
   b) Does your corporation use the bank for other services, including financing, corporate deposits, as a corporate trustee for bondholders, or as a stock transfer agent?
   c) Who managed the fund before First National took over?
3. How often and how specifically does the bank report to you on the
   progress of the fund?
   a) Do you make periodic reports to the employees?
   b) Please send us the brochure or description of the fund which
   is made available to the employees.
4. Who controls investment policy for the fund?
   a) What information does the bank give you when it suggests certain investments?

b) Does your corporation have any policy concerning investment of the fund's money in your own corporation's stocks?

c) How is the fund presently invested? Please list the major stock-holdings, bondholdings and other investments.

5. Who decides the voting policies for the proxies held by the fund?

6. In your opinion, has the bank provided personalized or exemplary services? If so, please give examples.

7. Have you ever had any problems with the bank's management of the fund? If so, please explain.

8. Has it ever been discussed to invest a portion of the fund to finance public housing, education, mass transit or other socially beneficial projects? What would be the minimum return you would expect from such investments?

If you are unable to answer any of the above questions, please explain to us why. We are confident you will understand the importance of our project and thank you for your cooperation. Upon completion of our study, we will be glad to furnish you with our conclusions.

Sincerely yours,

Donald Etra
Project Director

Notes

Introduction

1. Letter of Carl Desch, FNCB Vice President and Cashier to David Leinsdorf, July 3, 1970.
2. Conference with J. Howard Laeri, FNCB Vice Chairman, Carl Desch, FNCB Senior Vice President and Cashier, and Reade Ryan, Shearman and Sterling, June 30, 1970 (hereafter, "June 30 Conference").
3. *Ibid.*
4. Interview with William Spencer, FNCB President, November 24, 1970.
5. FNCC, "Minutes of Annual Stockholders Meeting," March 30, 1971 (hereafter, 1971 "Annual Meeting"). Letter of David Leinsdorf to Walter Wriston, FNCB Chairman, September 18, 1970. Letter of J. Howard Laeri, FNCB Vice Chairman, to David Leinsdorf, October 30, 1971.
6. David Leinsdorf, letter of September 28, 1970. J. Howard Laeri, letter October 30, 1970.
7. June 30 Conference.
8. Interview with Walter Wriston, *op. cit.*
9. 1971 Annual Meeting, p. 7.
10. June 30 Conference.
11. 1971 Annual Meeting, p. 51.
12. *Ibid.*
13. Interview with Walter Wriston, *op. cit.*
14. June 30 Conference.
15. David Leinsdorf, Letter of September 28, 1970. J. Howard Laeri, Letter of October 30, 1970.
16. *Ibid.*
17. June 30 Conference.
18. Interview with Walter Wriston, *op. cit.*
19. As of 1970.
20. David Leinsdorf, Letter of September 28, 1970. J. Howard Laeri, Letter of October 30, 1970.
21. *Ibid.*
22. *Ibid.*
23. *Ibid.*
24. June 30 Conference.
25. Conversation with Carl Desch, Senior Vice President and Cashier, March, 1971.
26. Interview with Walter Wriston, *op. cit.*
27. David Leinsdorf, Letter of September 28, 1970. J. Howard Laeri, Letter of October 30, 1970.
28. June 30 Conference.
29. Letter of Carl Desch, FNCB Senior Vice President and Cashier, to David Leinsdorf, February 10, 1971.
30. Interview with William Spencer, FNCB President, November 24, 1970.

31. Interview with John Heilshorn, FNCB Senior Vice President, Corporate Planning and Management Information, August 13, 1970.
32. *Ibid.*
33. *Ibid.*
34. Interview with John Porta, FNCB Vice President, Capital Goods, July 10, 1970.
35. Interview with Roy Dickerson, FNCB Senior Vice President, Capital Goods, Information Systems and Transportation Division, July, 1970.
36. Interview with George M. Lingua, Senior Vice President, Institutional Investment Division, August 3, 1970.
37. Interview with John Mosier, FNCB Vice President, Branch Installment Loan Coordination and Training, July 17, 1970.
38. 1971 Annual Meeting, p. 51.
39. *Ibid.*
40. *Ibid.,* p. 52.
41. *American Banker,* May 18, 1971, p. 18.
42. *Comptroller's Manual for National Banks,* 2 C.F.R. §9.18(b) (5) (iv).

I. Citibankers

1. Cresap, McCormick, and Paget (hereinafter Cresap), *Third Service Shopping Program,* 1970.
2. Conversation with Robert Feagles, FNCB Senior Vice President, Personnel Administration, May 18, 1971.
3. First National City Bank (hereafter "FNCB"), *Salary Policy and Administration Guide—Non-Official Staff,* June, 1969; interview with Robert Feagles, FNCB Senior Vice President, Personnel Administration, August 10, 1970.
4. R. David Corwin, *New Yorkers in the Banking Industry: A Minority Report* (1970), p. 97. Corwin's note indicates that this information comes from the bank that has the lowest turnover rate of all New York City banks employing more than 8,000 people, which is Citibank. In any event, Corwin indicates that there are very minor differences between the employment practices of the different banks.
5. *Ibid.*
6. U.S. Department of Labor, Bureau of Labor Statistics, *Three Standards of Living for an Urban Family of Four,* Spring, 1970.
7. *American Banker,* March 15, 1971, p. 3. Conversation with Robert Feagles, *op. cit.*
8. FNCB, Operating Group Personnel, Employee Relations, 1970 *Attitude Survey Analysis, Operating Group Clericals,* based on results of employee attitude survey conducted in 1970 by Opinion Research Corporation, Princeton, N.J., October 30, 1970.
9. Corwin, *op. cit.,* p. 60.
10. Interview with Robert Feagles, *op. cit.*
11. *Ibid.*
12. *Ibid.*
13. Corwin, *op. cit.,* p. 90.
14. Cresap, *op. cit.*
15. The Task Force surveyed 21 FNCB branches located in different parts of Manhattan.

16. FNCB, *Meet the Innovators,* telephone directory with photographs of all officers in the Corporate Banking Group, July 1, 1969.
17. *Ibid.* We tried to get a more up-to-date tabulation, but FNCB claims that it doesn't maintain personnel records on the basis of race and thus could not provide us with recent information on this subject. In fact, FNCB does maintain information on the ethnic composition of its employees (see FNCB, *1970 Attitude Survey Analysis, Operating Group Clericals,* Response Report). Based on FNCB's willingness to provide as much favorable information as possible, it seems reasonable to assume that if the distribution of blacks and women in this group had changed substantially since July, 1969, the bank would have provided a more recent profile of its corporate lending officers.
18. FNCB, *Meet the Innovators,* p. 39.
19. Conversation with Robert Feagles, *op. cit.*
20. *Ibid.*
21. FNCB, Salary Administration Unit, *Officer Salary Structure and Increase Increments (Guidelines),* July, 1969.
22. FNCC, *Notice of Annual Meeting of Stockholders,* February 23, 1971.
23. Cresap, *op. cit.*
24. *Ibid.*
25. *Ibid.*
26. *Ibid.*
27. *Ibid.*
28. *Ibid.*
29. *Ibid.*
30. FNCC–FNCB, *Minutes of Annual Stockholders Meeting,* March 31, 1970.
31. *American Banker,* May 5, 1971, p. 3.
32. Cresap, *op. cit.*
33. *Beverly Wadsworth* v. *First National City Bank, et al.,* No. CSF 224 33–70, State of New York, State Division of Human Rights.
34. *The New York Times,* March 24, 1972.
35. "Address by William Spencer to the Association of Governing Boards of Universities and Colleges," *American Banker,* May 31, 1972, p. 5.
36. *American Banker,* March 23, 1972, p. 2.
37. *American Banker,* May 19, 1972, p. 1.
38. Corwin, *op. cit.,* p. 15.
39. *The New York Times,* Business Section, November 29, 1970, p. 8.
40. *Ibid.*
41. FNCB, "Watch Out, Harry. Here Comes Another Truckload," reprinted from *Citibank Magazine,* 4 (1969).
42. Conversation with Peter J. Wolfe, Vice President, Services Division, during tour of Operating Group, February, 1971.
43. *Ibid.*
44. FNCB, *Attitude Survey Analysis,* Operating Group Clericals; Operating Group Officers; Operating Group Supervisors, 1970.
45. FNCB, *Attitude Survey Analysis, Operating Group Clericals,* 1970.
46. *Ibid.*
47. *Ibid.*
48. *Ibid.*
49. *Ibid.*

50. *Ibid.*
51. *Ibid.*
52. *Ibid.*
53. *Ibid.*
54. *Ibid.*
55. *Ibid.*
56. *Ibid.*
57. Corwin, *op. cit.*, p. 107.
58. *Ibid.*, p. 95.
59. *Ibid.*, p. 106.

II. Retail Banking for Individuals

1. New York Civil Court, *Docket Book "F,"* 1969, 1970.
2. Letter of Carl Desch, Cashier and Senior Vice President, to David Leinsdorf, April 12, 1971.
3. *See* Cresap, McCormick, and Paget, *Second Service Shopping Program,* 1963 [hereinafter cited as "Cresap, *Second Program*"], pp. I–1.
4. Letter of Carl Desch, FNCB Cashier and Senior Vice President, to David Leinsdorf, April 12, 1971.
5. Cresap, *Second Program,* Exhibit II–3.
6. *Ibid.*, Exhibit II–4.
7. *Ibid.*, Exhibit II–6.
8. *Ibid.*, Exhibit IV–1.
9. *Ibid.*, pp. VI–4, VI–18.
10. FNCC-FNCB, 1970 *Annual Report.*
11. Cresap, McCormick, and Paget, *Third Service Shopping Program,* 1970 (hereinafter cited as "Cresap, *Third Program*").
12. *Ibid.*
13. *Ibid.*
14. *Ibid.*
15. *Ibid.*
16. FNCB, "Ready Credit," Brochure # ADV 664, July, 1970.
17. Cresap, *Third Program.*
18. *Ibid.*
19. *Ibid.*
20. *Ibid.*
21. *Ibid.*
22. *Ibid.*
23. *Ibid.*
24. FNCB, "Golden Growth Bonds," Brochure # ADV 664, August, 1969.
25. Cresap, *Third Program.*
26. *Ibid.*
27. *Ibid.*
28. *Ibid.*
29. *Ibid.*
30. See Comptroller of the Currency, Branch Applications.
31. Cresap, *Third Program.*
32. FNCC, Form 10k, Schedule III, filed with the Securities and Exchange Commission, December 31, 1969.
33. Chase Manhattan Corporation, Form 10k, Schedule III, filed with the SEC, December 31, 1969.

34. Manufacturers Hanover Corporation, Form 10k, Schedule III, filed with the SEC, December 31, 1969.

35. Chemical New York Corporation, Form 10k, Schedule III, filed with the SEC, December 31, 1969.

36. Federal Deposit Insurance Corporation (FDIC) *1969 Annual Report,* pp. 264–65.

37. Interview with John Mosier, FNCB Assistant Vice President, Branch Installment Loan Coordination and Training, July 17, 1970.

38. Interview with John Reynolds, FNCB Senior Vice President, Branch Administration, and Peter G. Wodtke, FNCB Vice President, Personal Finance Department, August 20, 1970.

39. Interview with John Mosier, *op. cit.*

40. Interview with John Reynolds and Peter G. Wodtke, *op. cit.*

41. Interview with John Mosier, *op. cit.*

42. Interview with John Reynolds and Peter G. Wodtke, *op. cit.*

43. Interview with John Mosier, *op. cit.*

44. Interview with John Reynolds and Peter G. Wodtke, *op. cit.*

45. FNCB, "Checking Plus," Brochure # ADV 636 REV, June, 1969.

46. *Ibid.*

47. FNCB, "Personal Checking Accounts," Brochure # ADV 526 REV 6/70.

48. Cresap, *Third Program.*

49. *Ibid.*

50. Interview with John Reynolds, FNCB Senior Vice President, Branch Administration, and Thomas J. Clough, FNCB Vice President, Credit Supervision, July 24, 1970.

51. *Ibid.*

52. Interview with John Reynolds and Peter G. Wodtke, *op. cit.*

53. *Ibid.*

54. Interview with John Mosier, *op. cit.*

55. *Caplovitz files.* Interview with John Reynolds and Peter G. Wodtke, *op. cit.*

56. *Caplovitz files.*

57. Interview with John Reynolds and Thomas Clough, *op. cit.*

58. Interview with John Reynolds and Peter G. Wodtke, *op. cit.*

59. *Caplovitz files.*

60. *Ibid.*

61. *Ibid.*

62. *Ibid.*

63. *Ibid.*

64. Interview with FNCB customer who asked to remain anonymous.

65. *Caplovitz files.* Eleven of the 35 FNCB debtors were over the limit.

66. Interview with John Reynolds and Peter G. Wodtke, *op. cit.*

67. During the summer of 1970, the Task Force did extensive research on the cases filed by FNCB during 1969 in the New York City Civil Court. We counted a total of 10,671 cases filed by FNCB in 1969. Our research included two random surveys. In one survey, we examined 1,000 cases, selecting every tenth case (hereinafter "1,000 Case Survey"). In the other, we examined 100 cases, selecting every one-hundredth case (hereinafter "100 Case Survey"). The 95% default judgment ratio was computed from the 1,000 case survey.

68. Conversation with J. Howard Laeri, FNCB Vice Chairman, February 3, 1971.

69. FNCB, *1965 Annual Report*, p. 7.
70. FNCB, *1967 Annual Report*.
71. Interview with Edward H. Gottlieb, Vice President, First National City Charge Service, and Ludwig Dosch, Assistant Vice President, First National City Charge Service, August 10, 1970.
72. Letter from John D. Gwin, Deputy Comptroller of the Currency, to James H. Harris, Senior Vice President, Chase Manhattan Bank, February 18, 1971.
73. Fed Regulation Z, *Truth-in-Lending*, section 226.7(b)(9).
74. Gwin, *op. cit.*
75. National Advisory Committee to the Comptroller of the Currency, *Minutes of Meeting,* November 1, 1967, p. 4.
76. FNCB, *1967 Annual Report*, p. 6.
77. FNCB-FNCC, *1970 Annual Report,* p. 11.
78. Interview with Ludwig Dosch and Edward Gottlieb, *op. cit.*
79. Interview with John Reynolds and Thomas Clough, *op. cit.*
80. Interview with Ludwig Dosch and Edward Gottlieb, *op. cit.*
81. *Ibid.*
82. FTC Consent Order C-1737.
83. Letter of Philip G. Schrag, Consumer Advocate, New York City Department of Consumer Affairs, to Ralph Nader, July 8, 1970.
84. *Ibid.*
85. *Ibid.*
86. Interview with Philip G. Schrag, Consumer Advocate, New York City Department of Consumer Affairs, July 30, 1970.
87. *Ibid.*
88. Interview with John Reynolds and Thomas Clough, *op. cit.*
89. Address by George Mitchell, member of the FRB, to the American Bankers Association Card Conference, 1972.
90. Interview with Ludwig Dosch and Edward Gottlieb, *op. cit.*
91. *Ibid.*
92. 100 Case Survey, *op. cit.*
93. *Ibid.*
94. U. S., Congress, Senate, Subcommittee on Financial Institutions, Banking and Currency Committee, *Bank Credit and Check Credit Plans: Hearings,* October, 1968.
95. *Ibid.*
96. Interview with Ludwig Dosch and Edward Gottlieb, *op. cit.*
97. *Ibid.*
98. *Ibid.*
99. *Ibid.*
100. Compare Chemical Bank, "Don't Get A Credit Card Until You Read This," Brochure number ADV 265, June, 1969 with FNCB, "Apply Now," Brochure number F.C.C., June, 1970.
101. FNCB, "Apply Now," *op. cit.*
102. Interview with John Reynolds and Thomas Clough, *op. cit.*
103. *Ibid.*
104. FNCB, "Apply Now," *op. cit.*
105. FNCB, *1969 Annual Report*.
106. Cresap, *Third Program*.
107. E. Heinemann, "National City Alters Credit Card Links," *The New York Times,* September 9, 1971.

108. Telephone conversation with Edward Gottlieb, November 21, 1972.
109. *American Banker,* November 10, 1971, p. 2.
110. U. S., Congress, House, Subcommittee on Consumer Affairs, Banking and Currency Committee, *Consumer Credit Regulations: Hearings,* February, 1969.
111. *Ibid.*
112. Interview with Philip Conway, FNCB Vice President, Finance Companies and Factors, August 11, 1970.
113. *Ibid.*
114. 100 case survey.
115. FNCB, form number DPC 583 REV. 12-69.
116. FNCB, form number CHS 511 * REV. 12-69.
117. FNCB, form number CMS 512 REV. 12-69.
118. *Caplovitz files.*
119. *Ibid.*
120. Interview with FNCB debtor who insisted on remaining anonymous.
121. This incident was recounted by a close personal friend of DL.
122. *Caplovitz files.*
123. Caplovitz, *op. cit.,* pp. 12–30.
124. *Ibid.,* pp. 12–31.
125. New York City Civil Court, *op. cit.*
126. *Ibid.*
127. *Ibid.*
128. Interview with Robert B. Frank, FNCB attorney, July 28, 1970. Letter of Edward Gottlieb, FNCB Vice President, to Mark Foster, August 18, 1970.
129. New York State Retail Installment Sales Act, Section 413(5).
130. Interview with Philip Schrag, *op. cit.*
131. *100 Case Survey.*
132. Interview with Robert B. Frank, *op. cit.*
133. Interview with Robert B. Frank; *100 Case Survey.*
134. Interview with Robert B. Frank, *op. cit.*
135. *1,000 Case Survey.*
136. Interview with Robert B. Frank, *op. cit.*
137. *Ibid.*
138. *Ibid.*
139. *Ibid.*
140. *Ibid.*
141. *Ibid.*
142. New York Civil Court Docket # 112933.
143. New York Civil Court Docket # 112929.
144. New York Civil Court Docket # 1129xx.
145. New York Civil Court Docket # 99194.
146. New York Civil Court Docket # 99190.
147. New York Civil Court Docket # 99203.
148. New York Civil Court Docket # 99209.
149. New York Civil Court Docket # 118433.
150. New York Civil Court Docket # 118441.
151. United States Attorney's Office, Southern District of New York.
152. *Ibid.*
153. *Ibid.*
154. 70 Civ. 179.

155. *1,000 Case Survey.*
156. "Address by James Farley to the Bank and Consumerism Conference," reprinted in *American Banker,* February 10, 1972, p. 7.
157. Telephone conversation between James Farley and Donald Etra, November 30, 1972.
158. Interview with Lloyd Milliken, attorney, New York State Attorney General's Office, August 13, 1970.
159. *1,000 Case Survey.*
160. *Caplovitz files.*
161. *Ibid.*
162. *Ibid.*
163. Interview with Robert Frank, *op. cit.*
164. *Ibid.*
165. *The City Record,* June 26, 1970, p. 158.
166. Interview with John Reynolds and Thomas Clough, *op. cit.*
167. Walter B. Wriston, FNCB-FNCC Chairman, "The Riskless Society Reexamined," May 28, 1969.
168. Interview with Walter Wriston, October 2, 1970.

III. Wholesale Banking for Corporations

1. FNCB, *1965 Annual Report.*
2. FNCB, *Annual Reports,* 1966–70.
3. FNCB Overseas Division, *The Criteria and Philosophy of Bank Term Lending,* 1968.
4. *Ibid.,* p. 2.
5. FNCB, *Summary of Major Services,* filed with branch applications at Comptroller of the Currency, 1970, p. 16.
6. *Ibid.,* p. 4.
7. FNCB, *Rules Governing the Extension of Credit,* September 16, 1969.
8. Interview with Robert Rice, FNCB Vice President in charge of Money Allocation Committee, July 28, 1970.
9. *Ibid.*
10. *Ibid.*
11. FNCB Overseas Division, *op. cit.,* pp. 4–5.
12. Interview with Roy Dickerson, FNCB Senior Vice President in charge of Transportation, Aerospace and Information Systems Division, July, 1970.
13. Interview with William Herbster, FNCB Senior Vice President in charge of Corporate Services Division, August 8, 1970.
14. Interview with William Herbster, *op. cit.*
15. *Ibid.*
16. FNCC-FNCB *1969 Annual Report,* p. 27.
17. *American Banker,* December 11, 1970, p. 1. See also *American Banker,* December 18, 1970, p. 3.
18. FNCB *Annual Reports,* 1965–70.
19. Standard and Poors, *Corporation Records, The New York Times,* September 12, 1970, p. 35.
20. *Ibid.*
21. Standard and Poors, *Corporation Records.*
22. Chase Manhattan Bank, Application to open a branch at 65th Street

and Fort Hamilton Parkway, Brooklyn, New York, filed with the Comptroller of the Currency, October, 1970. Branch applications contain loan and deposit figures on nearby branches of the applicant and its competitors.

23. FNCB, Application to open a branch at Broadway and 170th Street, New York, New York, filed with the Comptroller of the Currency, October, 1970.

24. Chase Manhattan Bank, Application to open a branch at Zerega Avenue and Gleason Avenue, Bronx, New York, filed with the Comptroller of the Currency, October, 1970.

25. Chase Manhattan Bank, Application to open a branch at 65th Street and Fort Hamilton Parkway, Brooklyn, New York, filed with the Comptroller of the Currency, September, 1970.

26. FNCB, Application to open a branch at Avenue of the Americas and 47th Street, New York, New York filed with the Comptroller of the Currency, 1967.

27. *Ibid.*

28. FNCB, Application to open a branch at Cadman Plaza Development, Henry Street, Brooklyn, New York, filed with the Comptroller of the Currency, 1968.

29. FNCB, Application to open a branch at 152 Middle Neck Road, Great Neck Estates, Town of North Hempstead, New York, filed with the Comptroller of the Currency, April, 1970.

30. FNCB, Application to open a branch at 238–44 Main Street, White Plains, New York, filed with the Comptroller of the Currency, August, 1970.

31. FNCB Overseas Division, *op. cit.*, p. 2.

32. *American Banker,* March 2, 1971, p. 1.

33. FNCC-FNCB *1968 Annual Report,* pp. 14–15.

34. Interview with Thomas Wilcox, FNCB Vice Chairman in charge of urban affairs, August 12, 1970.

35. Interview with Sidney Davidson, FNCB Vice President in charge of "Urban Affairs," July 31, 1970.

36. *Ibid.*

37. Interview with John Davies, Manager of "Urban Affairs," Chase Manhattan Bank, August, 1970.

38. Interview with Douglas Ades, "Urban Affairs" Officer, Chemical Bank, August, 1970.

39. Interview with John Davies, *op. cit.*

40. Interview with Sidney Davidson, *op. cit.*

41. *Ibid.*

42. Interview with Thomas Wilcox, *op. cit.*

43. Interview with Sidney Davidson, *op. cit.*

44. S. Reid, *Mergers, Managers and the Economy,* 1968.

45. U.S., Congress, Senate, Subcommittee on Antitrust and Monopoly, Senate Judiciary Committee, Hearings, November 4, 1969.

46. See Standard and Poors *Corporation Records.*

47. Conversation with Richard Davis, Executive Vice President, Harder Bank and Trust, Canton, Ohio, March, 1971.

48. Newspaper Enterprise Association, Inc., *The 1971 World Almanac and Book of Facts.*

49. Comptroller of the Currency, Regulations, 12 C.F.R. Section 1.3. 12 U.S.C. § 24.

50. Joseph Poindexter, "A Whole New Groove in Banking," *Dun's Review,* April, 1969, pp. 39–41.
51. Comptroller of the Currency, 12 U.S.C. § 24.
52. Joseph Poindexter, *op. cit.,* p. 40.
53. *Ibid.*
54. See Standard and Poors, *Corporation Records.*
55. *Ibid.*
56. Standard and Poors, *Corporation Records.*
57. Civil Aeronautics Board, *Long and Short Term Non-Trade Debt,* Schedule B-46, December 31, 1970.
58. *The New York Times,* Business Section, December 27, 1970, p. 3.
59. *Aviation Week & Space Technology,* March 1, 1971, p. 9.
60. Civil Aeronautics Board, *Impact of New Large Jets on the Air Transportation System, 1970–73,* p. 20.
61. *Ibid.,* p. 21.
62. *American Banker,* December 16, 1970, p. 3.
63. Interview with Brian Livsey, FNCB Vice President in charge of Leasing Department, July 21, 1970. Pan American World Airways, Inc., Prospectus for issue of 11¼% Guaranteed Loan Certificates, Due October 29, 1986, October 22, 1970.
64. Interview with Brian Livsey, Trans World Airlines, Inc., Prospectus for issue of 10% Guaranteed Loan Certificates due May 15, 1985, December 4, 1969.
65. Interview with Brian Livsey, American Airlines, Prospectus for issue of 10% Guaranteed Loan Certificates, Series B, Due December 1, 1988, September 22, 1970.
66. *Forbes Magazine,* April 1, 1971, p. 49.
67. Interview with Brian Livsey, *op. cit.*
68. *American Banker,* May 18, 1971, p. 18.
69. U.S., Congress, House, Banking and Currency Committee, Staff Report for the Subcommittee on Domestic Finance, *Commercial Banks and Their Trust Activities: Emerging Influence on the American Economy,* July 8, 1969.
70. Standard and Poors, *Register of Corporations, Directors and Executives,* 1971.
71. *Ibid.*
72. Civil Aeronautics Board, Form B-41, December 31, 1970. Standard and Poors, *Corporation Records.*
73. Standard and Poors, *Corporation Records.*
74. *The New York Times,* December 31, 1970, p. 1.
75. *American Banker,* May 5, 1971, p. 3.
76. *The New York Times,* February 8, 1971. *Wall Street Journal,* March 19, 1971, p. 27.
77. See Civil Aeronautics Board Financial Advisory Committee, *op. cit.*
78. Berkeley Rice, *op. cit.,* p. 86.
79. Walter B. Wriston, "The Riskless Society Re-examined," an address at Goldsmiths' Hall, London, May 28, 1969, p. 5.
80. *Ibid.,* p. 8.
81. FNCC, Notice of Annual Meeting of Stockholders, February 23, 1971.
82. Standard and Poors, *Register of Corporations, Directors and Executives,* 1970, 1971.
83. 12 U.S.C. Section 84.

84. 12 U.S.C. Section 83.
85. 12 U.S.C. Section 371(c).
86. 12 U.S.C. Section 161.
87. 12 U.S.C. Section 56, 60.
88. Federal Reserve Board, Regulation Q. See generally, 12 U.S.C. Section 93.
89. Comptroller of the Currency, *Handbook of Examination Procedure,* I, p. 13.
90. See generally, Comptroller of the Currency, *Duties and Liabilities of Directors of National Banks,* October, 1969.
91. FNCC, List of Stockholders, February 16, 1970. American Society of Corporate Secretaries, *Nominee List.*
92. *Ibid.*
93. Newspaper Enterprise Association, Inc., *op. cit.,* p. 49.
94. FNCB, *1966 Annual Report,* p. 10.

IV. Banking for Government

1. New York City Budget, 1970–71 Fiscal Year, *City Record,* June 26, 1970.
2. New York City Comptroller.
3. *Wall Street Journal,* April 14, 1971, p. 23.
4. New York City Budget, 1970–71 Fiscal Year, *City Record,* June 26, 1970.
5. New York City Finance Administration.
6. Federal Reserve Bank of New York, *1969 Annual Report,* p. 6.
7. Federal Deposit Insurance Corporation (FDIC), *1970 Annual Report.*
8. FNCC, Form 10K, Schedule III, filed with the Securities and Exchange Commission, December 31, 1970.
9. FNCC, *Minutes of Annual Stockholders Meeting,* March 30, 1971, p. 52.
10. "FNCC-FNCB, *1970 Annual Report,*" *American Banker,* May 18, 1971, p. 18.
11. *Perotta Report,* p. 12.
12. Interview with James Allen, FNCB Vice President, Municipal Bond Portfolio, July 22, 1970.
13. FDIC, *1969 Annual Report; 1970 Annual Report.*
14. Interview with W. F. Fyfe, Assistant Treasurer, Pan American World Airways, July 15, 1970. Interview with Brian Livsey, FNCB Vice President, Leasing, July 21, 1970.
15. *American Banker,* January 21, 1971, p. 4.
16. Federal Reserve Board, *Bulletin,* March, 1971, pp. A 45, A 34.
17. *American Banker,* January 21, 1971, p. 4.
18. *Ibid.*
19. Federal Reserve Board, *Bulletin,* March, 1971, p. A 34.
20. *The New York Times,* November 6, 1970, p. 69.
21. *Perotta Report,* p. 10.
22. *The New York Times,* November 6, 1970, p. 69.
23. *Perotta Report,* p. 9.
24. *The New York Times,* November 6, 1970, pp. 1, 69.
25. New York City Charter, § 1523, 1524.

26. Letter from Abraham D. Beame, Comptroller of the City of New York, September 30, 1971.
27. Telephone conversation with Malcolm Strickler, Finance Administration, November 16, 1972.
28. FDIC.
29. New York Clearinghouse Association, *Quarterly Report,* June 30, 1970.
30. Interview with Harry Tishelman, New York City Deputy Finance Administrator, August 27, 1970.
31. *Ibid.*
32. Interview with Lawrence Small, FNCB Vice President, New York City Personal Income-Tax Processing, August 25, 1970. Conversation with Robert H. Aten, New York City Finance Administration, April 1, 1971. Conversation with Walter Kraus, former FNCB Vice President in charge of New York City Personal Income-Tax Processing, April, 1971.
33. *Ibid.*
34. *Ibid.*
35. Interview with Harry Tishelman, *op. cit.* Conversation with Walter Kraus, *op. cit.*
36. *Ibid.*
37. Conversation with Walter Kraus, *op. cit.*
38. Robert H. Aten, New York City Finance Administration, memo to Jay Kriegel, Aide to Mayor Lindsay, *re* "Nader Staff Interest in City Finance Administration Activities," April 1, 1971.
39. Robert H. Aten, *op. cit.* Conversation with Walter Kraus, *op. cit.*
40. *American Banker,* October 29, 1971, p. 1.
41. *American Banker,* March 6, 1972, p. 3.
42. New York City Comptroller, *New York City Retirement Systems,* December, 1970, p. 18.
43. *Ibid.*
44. Conversation with Henry Walter, Assistant to New York City Comptroller, April 9, 1971.
45. Interview with Julian Buckley, Third Deputy Comptroller, Pension Fund Investments, July, 1970.
46. *Ibid.*
47. Conversation with Henry Walter, *op. cit.*
48. *The New York Times,* November 10, 1972.
49. *American Banker,* November 14, 1971, p. 1.
50. *The New York Times,* August 3, 1971, p. 40.
51. Interview with Eben W. Pyne, FNCB Senior Vice President, Regional Centers Division I, July 31, 1970.
52. Penn Central Transportation Company, *1969 Annual Report,* filed with Interstate Commerce Commission.
53. Special Committee on the Long Island Railroad, *A New Long Island Rail Road,* February, 1965.
54. *Ibid.*
55. Levitt letter published in "The Rape of the LIRR," by Sam Schein; accuracy confirmed by Comptroller Levitt.
56. William J. Ronan, William A. Shea, "Report to the Governor and the Legislative Leaders on a Reasonable Price of the Long Island Rail Road by the State of New York from the Pennsylvania Railroad," June, 1965.

57. *Ibid.*
58. Interview with Eben W. Pyne, *op. cit.*
59. *Wall Street Journal,* October 28, 1970.
60. *Memorandum of Intent* among the Metropolitan Transportation Authority, Connecticut Transportation Authority, and Penn Central Transportation Company, *In Re* Penn Central's New Haven Division West End Suburban Passenger Train Service, November 25, 1969.
61. Port of New York Authority (hereafter "PONYA"), *1968 Annual Report,* p. 1.
62. *Ibid.*
63. PONYA, *1969 Annual Report.*
64. DLMA, *Planning for Lower Manhattan,* 1969, p. 6.
65. *Ibid.,* p. 3.
66. Letter of James M. Kennelly, Executive Assistant to PONYA Director of Public Affairs, to David Leinsdorf, December 9, 1970.
67. *Ibid.*
68. Letter of James M. Kennelly, PONYA, to David Leinsdorf, February 3, 1971.
69. Interview with R. G. Jacobs, *op. cit.*
70. James M. Kennelly, Letter of February 3, 1971, *op. cit.*
71. PONYA, *1968 Annual Report,* p. 5.
72. Interview with James H. Allen, *op. cit.*
73. 26 U.S.C. §265(2). IRS Regulations, §1.265-2 (1968).
74. CCH–*Standard Federal Tax Reports,* Regulations, §1.265-2, paragraph 2232.033.
75. 26 U.S.C. §265 (2).
76. PONYA, *1969 Annual Report,* p. 51.
77. See Richard C. Blodgett, *op. cit.* Theodore Kheel, "How the World Trade Center is Strangling New York," *New York Magazine* (May, 1969). *The New York Times,* Real-Estate Section, October 18, 1970, p. 1.
78. Theodore Kheel, *op. cit.*
79. PONYA, *The World Trade Center,* p. 1.
80. DLMA, *op. cit.,* p. 18.
81. *Ibid.* New York City Planning Commission, *Standards for Rapid Transit Expansion: A Report to the Mayor and the New York City Planning Commission,* 1968.
82. DLMA, *op. cit.,* p. 18.
83. Cloverdale and Colpits, *Report to DLMA,* January, 1967, p. 8.
84. Public Authority Laws of New York State, §1219(a)(2)(a).
85. J. Toby, New York City Budget Bureau, Memo to D. A. Grossman, Deputy Director of the Budget, "Claimed and Reasonable Surpluses, Triborough Bridge and Tunnel Authority," December 10, 1968, and attachments.
86. Interview with Eben W. Pyne, *op. cit. The New York Times,* February 10, 1968.
87. Memo of New York City Transit Fare Committee, February 7, 1969.
88. J. Toby, *op. cit.* Wiebe and Prince, Metropolitan Transit Authority, Memo to William J. Ronan, March 29, 1968.
89. FNCB Economics Department, *Public Transportation in the New York Region,* 1970, p. 8.
90. New York City Transit Fare Committee, Notes of Meeting, March 11, 1970.

91. Interview with Eben W. Pyne, *op. cit.*
92. FNCB Economics Department, *op. cit.*, p. 30.
93. FNCB Economics Department, *op. cit.*, p. 13.
94. New York Clearinghouse Association, *op. cit.*
95. 12 U.S.C. section 548.
96. James Papke, Temporary Commission on City Finance, Research Note 14, Task Force II, *Inequalities In New York City Business Taxation: The Treatment of Banks,* August 12, 1965, p. 2.
97. *Ibid.,* p. 3.
98. Conversation with Harry Tishelman, New York City Deputy Finance Administrator, May 5, 1971.
99. R. David Corwin, *New Workers In the Banking Industry, A Minority Report,* June, 1970, p. 11.
100. New York Clearinghouse Association, *Quarterly Report,* December 31, 1970.
101. See *Forbes* Magazine, January 1, 1971.
102. Interview with Thomas Wilcox, FNCB Vice Chairman, August 12, 1970.
103. Interview with Dr. Frank Kristoff, Director of Housing Programs, New York State Urban Development Corporation, July 14, 1970.
104. Interview with Dr. Michael Tietz, Director, RAND Corporation Urban Affairs Institute, June 23, 1970.
105. See New York Clearinghouse Association, *Weekly Reports of Member Banks.*
106. U.S., Congress, Senate, Subcommittee on Financial Institutions, Banking and Currency Committee, *Deposit Rates and Mortgage Credit; Hearings,* September 9, 10, and 22, 1969.
107. FDIC, *1970 Annual Report.*
108. FDIC, *Summary of Accounts.*
109. FDIC, *1970 Annual Report.*
110. *Ibid.*
111. FNCC-FNCB, Minutes of Annual Stockholders Meeting, March 30, 1971, p. 66.
112. Conversation with Patrick J. Mulhern, Vice President, FNCB Cashier's Administration, May, 1971.
113. FNCC-FNCB, Minutes of Annual Stockholders Meeting, March 30, 1971, p. 66. FNCC-FNCB, *1970 Annual Report.*
114. FDIC, *1970 Annual Report.*
115. Interview with William Gavin, FNCB Assistant Vice President, Residential Mortgages, July 20, 1970.
116. See *The New York Times,* January 22, 1971.
117. Conversation with Jean Richards, Public Relations Officer, Chase Manhattan Bank, May, 1971.
118. FNCC-FNCB, *1968 Annual Report,* p. 12; *1969 Annual Report,* p. 6.
119. FNCC-FNCB, *1970 Annual Report,* p. 16.
120. Interview with Robert Graham, FNCB Senior Vice President, Real Estate and Construction Industries Division, July 10, 1970.
121. FNCC-FNCB, *1970 Annual Report,* p. 16.
122. Interview with Tony Sanders, Assistant to New York City Commissioner of Development, July 17, 1970.
123. Interview with Robert Graham, *op. cit.*
124. Interview with William Gavin, *op. cit.*

125. *Ibid.* Interview with Robert Graham, *op. cit.*
126. *Ibid.*
127. Federal Reserve Board, *Bulletin,* March, 1971, A 53. FNCC-FNCB, *Annual Reports,* 1966–70.
128. FNCB, *Monthly Economic Letter,* November, 1969, p. 129.
129. *Ibid.*
130. 12 U.S.C. §371(b).
131. 12 U.S.C. §462.
132. FDIC, *1970 Annual Report.*
133. *Ibid.* FDIC, *Summary of Accounts,* June 30, 1970.
134. FNCB, *Officers of the First National City Organization Residential Addresses—Domestic.*

V. In Citibank We Trust

1. "The Investment Management Group of First National City Bank, Review of 1971, p. 29 [hereinafter cited as "Review of 1971"].
2. *Trust Assets of Insured Commercial Banks—1970,* Board of Governors of the *Federal Reserve System, Federal Deposit Insurance Corporation,* Office of the Comptroller of the Currency, p. 68.
3. U.S., Congress, House, Subcommittee on Domestic Finance, Committee on Banking and Currency: *Staff Report, Commercial Banks and their Trust Activities: Emerging Influence on the American Economy,* 90th Cong. 2d Sess., 1968, Vol. I, p. 33.
4. *Trust Assets of Insured Commercial Banks—1970, op. cit.,* p. 68.
5. U.S., Congress, House, *H.R. Doc. no. 64, Institutional Investor Study Report of the Securities and Exchange Commission,* 92d Cong., lst Sess., 1971, [hereinafter cited as *Institutional Investor Study*].
6. FNCB, *Corporate Policy Manual,* § 10.3A, dated October 1, 1970.
7. J. Ruskay and R. Osserman, *Halfway to Tax Reform* (1970), pp. 136–7.
8. U.S., Congress, Joint Publication Committee on Ways and Means of the House and Committee on Finance of the Senate: *Tax Reform Studies and Proposals U.S. Treasury Department,* 91st Cong., 1st Sess., 1969, Part 1, p. 43.
9. New York Banking Law, §131(3)(McKinney, 1966)
10. "Attorney's Reference File of Will and Trust Forms, Fourth Edition," distributed by FNCB's Investment Management Group, pp. 18–21.
11. "The Corporate Fiduciary's Power to Vote its own Stock," *68 Columbia Law Review,* 116, at 126 (1968).
12. *Ibid.,* p. 124.
13. FNCB's "General Policy Concerning Executorships and Trusteeships," June 1969, as found in "Attorney's Reference File," *op. cit.*
14. Surrogate's Court Procedure Act, §2309.
15. *Ibid.*
16. "Attorney's Reference File," *op cit.,* p. 16.
17. *In Re City Bank Farmers Trust Company,* 68 N.Y.S. 2d 43, at 46 (1947).
18. *Institutional Investor Study, op. cit.*
19. *Commercial Banks and Their Trust Activities: Emerging Influence on the American Economy, op. cit.*
20. Interview with Howard Scribner, Vice President of Chase Manhattan Bank, December 13, 1971, New York, New York.

21. Interview with Thomas Theobald, Executive Vice President, FNCB, Summer 1970.
22. Interview with Thomas Theobald, *op. cit.*
23. FNCB, "Reasons for Naming a Bank an Executor of Your Estate."
24. See "Performance, Power, and the Public Interest—the Forces of Change Bearing upon Bank Trust Departments," by James Byrne, American Banker Reprint Service, 525 West 42nd St., New York, 1968.
25. Interview with Dean Miller, Deputy Comptroller for Trusts, December 7, 1971, Washington, D.C.
26. Advertisement of FNCB, attached as Exhibit "B" to SEC's Complaint for Injunction, *Securities and Exchange Commission* v. *First National City Bank, et. al.,* 70 Civ. 517, U.S.D.C., S.D.N.Y., February, 1970.
27. Advertisement of FNCB, attached as Exhibit "C" to SEC Complaint, *Ibid.*
28. SEC Complaint, *Ibid.,* paragraph 13(a).
29. Such a provision might be considered by New York courts to be invalid as contrary to public policy and EPTL §11–1.7 (McKinney's 1967); See *Application of Burden,* 5 Misc. 2d 558, 160 N.Y.S. 2d 372 (1957); *Application of Uran,* 24 Misc. 2d 1069, 204 N.Y.S. 2d 840 (1960); *In Re Brush's Estates,* 46 Misc. 2d 277, 259 N.Y.S. 2d 390 (1965).
30. "Attorney's Reference File," *op. cit.* p. 38.
31. "Turnover in Common Stock Investment for Trust Accounts," by Yates Eckert, Vice President, Fidelity Union Trust Company, Newark, New Jersey, *Trusts & Estates* Vol. III, p. 36, Jan. 1972.
32. *Institutional Investor Study, op. cit.,* Vol. 2, p. 460.
33. "Turnover in Common Stock Investments for Trust Accounts," *op. cit.,* p. 37.
34. Interview with Frank Barnett, December 15, 1971, New York.
35. Interview with Howard Scribner, *op. cit.*
36. *Institutional Investor Study, op. cit.,* Vol. 2, p. 460.
37. Report of the Trust and Investment Division, Morgan Guaranty Trust Company, 1972, p. 8.
38. Letter from Alexander Jackson, Vice President FNCB, to Mrs. R., dated April 22, 1970.
39. Letter from Mrs. R. to Alexander Jackson, dated April 27, 1970.
40. Letter from Arthur Mittwoch, Vice President FNCB, to Mrs. R., dated May 5, 1970.
41. Interview with Richard Johnson, November 24, 1971, New York.
42. "How Trust Officers See Themselves," by Don Howard, President, Don Howard Personnel Inc., *Trusts & Estates,* Vol. 109, p. 171, (March, 1971).
43. See *Securities and Exchange Commission* v. *Texas Gulf Sulphur,* 258 F. Supp. 262 S.D.N.Y. (1966); 401 F. 2d 833, (2nd Cir. 1968); cert. denied, 394 U.S. 976 (1969).
44. "Insider Trading in Stocks," 21 *Business Lawyer* 1009, at 1011 (1966).
45. *SEC Staff Study of the Financial Collapse of the Penn Central Company* (1972), p. 405.
46. FNCB, "The Anatomy of an Investment," p. 11.
47. "Insider Trading in Stocks," *op. cit.,* p. 1018.
48. *Ibid.*

49. *Trustees of Bakery Drivers Local 802 Pension Fund* v. *The Chase Manhattan Bank,* Complaint filed in the Supreme Court of the State of New York, Index No. 08309/1971; *Trustees and Administrator of the Welfare and Pension Fund of Local 701, Mid-Jersey Trucking Industry* v. *Bankers Trust Company,* Complaint filed in U.S.D.C. E.D.N.Y.; *Local 734 Bakery Drivers' Pension Fund Trust and Chicago District Council of Carpenters' Pension Fund* v. *Continental Illinois National Bank and Trust Co.,* 72 Civ. 2551, U.S.D.C.,N.D.Ill., filed October, 1972.
50. *In the Matter of Cady, Roberts,* 40 SEC 907 (1961).
51. Securities and Exchange Act of 1934, 15 USC §78, 17 C.F.R. §240.12b–2.
52. *J. P. Morgan & Co.,* 10 SEC 119,136 (1941).
53. *Commercial Banks and their Trust Activities, op. cit.*
54. *Ibid.,* Vol. I, Table 76. pp. 711–716.
55. *Ibid.,* p. 713.
56. Interview with Frank Barnett, *op. cit.*
57. *Trust Assets of Insured Commercial Banks—1970, op. cit.,* p. 68.
58. *Institutional Investor Study, op. cit.,* Vol. 2, p. 426.
59. Interview with Edward Ryan, Vice President, Chase Manhattan Bank, December 13, 1971, New York.
60. FNCB, "General Policy Concerning Executorships and Trusteeships," *op. cit.,* June, 1969.
61. Surrogate's Court Procedure Act, §2307.
62. Surrogate's Court Procedure Act, §2309.
63. Interview with Reese Harris, former Chairman of the Trust Committee, Manufacturers Hanover Trust Company, July 17, 1970, New York.
64. Interview with Thomas Theobald, Summer, 1970.
65. Citizens and Southern National Bank, *Report of the Trust Department,* July 31, 1972, p. 16.
66. Interview with Robert Hoguet, December 15, 1971, New York.
67. Address by Reese Harris to trust divisions of the California and Texas bankers associations, in *American Banker,* July 3, 1972, p. 11.
68. *Recommended Cost Accounting Procedure,* American Bankers Association Trust Division, 1949, p. 32.
69. *Ibid.,* p. 34.
70. "A Statement of Principles of Trust Institutions," adopted by the Executive Committee of the Trust Division of the American Bankers Association, April 10, 1933.
71. Telephone conversation between Donald Etra and C. Arthur Weis, August 28, 1972.
72. Interview with Frank Barnett, *op. cit.;* Interview with Richard Furlaud, President Squibb-Beech Nut, January 12, 1971, New York.
73. Interview with Howard Scribner, *op. cit.*
74. "Cooperation between Trust and Commercial Officers," by Helmut Andresen, Executive Vice President, U.S. Trust Co., *Trusts and Estates,* Vol. 107, p. 436, (May, 1968).
75. *Commercial Banks and their Trust Activities, op. cit.,* Vol. I., p. 1.
76. *Trust Assets of Insured Commercial Banks—1970, op. cit.,* p. 68.
77. Paul Harbrecht, *Pension Funds and Economic Power* (1959), p. 4.
78. Letter from Robert C. Wilson, Jr., Secretary, Allied Chemical Corporation, dated November 23, 1971.

79. Letter from H. P. Tanner, Vice President, Wild Heerbrugg Instruments, Inc., dated November 11, 1971.

80. Letter from H. Yakubowish, Regional Manager, Kaar Electronics Corporation, dated November 12, 1971.

81. Letter from W. F. Fyfe, Assistant Treasurer, Pan American World Airways, dated November 15, 1971.

82. President's Committee on Corporate Pension Funds and Other Private Retirement and Welfare Programs, *Public Policy and Private Pension Programs: A report to the President on Private Employee Retirement Plans* (Washington, D.C., 1965), p. 17.

83. U.S., Congress, Senate, Subcommittee on Labor, Committee on Labor and Public Welfare, *Hearings: Examination of Private Welfare Plans* 92nd Cong., 1st Sess. (Pursuant to S.Res. 35, §4), October 12 and 13, 1971, Part 2, p. 394 [hereinafter cited as Hearings before the Senate Subcommittee on Labor].

84. M. S. House, *Private Employee Benefit Plans: A Public Trust,* State of New York Insurance Department, 1956, p. 105 (cited in Harbrecht, *op. cit.,* p. 59).

85. U.S., Congress, Senate, Subcommittee on Labor, Committee on Labor and Public Welfare, *Preliminary Report of the Private Welfare and Pension Plan Study, 1971,* 92nd Cong., 1st Sess. November 1971, p. 5.

86. Harbrecht, *op. cit.,* p. 38.

87. Interview with Kevin Keenan, Vice President, First Pennsylvania Banking and Trust Company, February 14, 1972, Philadelphia, Pa.

88. Interview with Frank Barnett, *op. cit.*

89. Interview with Robert Hoguet, *op. cit.*

90. See *Rosenfeld v. Black,* 319 F. Supp. 891 (1970), 445 F. 2d 1337 (2d Cir. 1971); Investment Company Act of 1940, 15 U.S.C. §36.

91. Labor Management Relations Act, 61 Stat. 156 (1947), 20 U.S.C. 185(a)(1952).

92. Harbrecht, *op. cit.,* p. 45.

93. Specimen Form of Trust Agreement of Chase Manhattan Bank, as found in Harbrecht, *op. cit.,* p. 318.

94. Harbrecht, *op. cit.*

95. Hearings before the Senate Subcommittee on Labor, *op. cit.,* p. 402.

96. Harbrecht, *op. cit.,* p. 79.

97. Hearings before the Senate Subcommittee on Labor, *op. cit.,* p. 209.

98. *Commercial Banks and Their Trust Activities, op. cit.,* Vol. I., p. 524.

99. *Institutional Investor Study, op. cit.,* Vol. 3, pp. 1044–5.

100. "The Anatomy of an Investment," p. 13.

101. Official Transcript of Proceedings before the SEC, File No. 4–147, *In the Matter of the Structure, Operation, and Regulation of the Securities Markets,* October 20, 1971, p. 922.

102. U.S., Congress, Subcommittee on Fiscal Policy, Joint Economic Committee, *Hearings: Investment Policies of Pension Funds,* 91st Cong., 2d Sess., April, 1970, p. 176 [hereinafter cited as JEC Hearings].

103. JEC Hearings, *op. cit.,* p. 119.

104. Harbrecht, *op. cit.,* p. 112.

105. JEC Hearings, *op. cit.,* pp. 119–20.

106. *Institutional Holdings of Common Stock 1900–2000* by Robert M. Soldofsky, Bureau of Business Research, Graduate School of Business Administration, the U. of Michigan, 1970, p. 111.

107. *Institutional Investor Study, op. cit.,* Vol. 2, p. 424.
108. *Trust Assets of Insured Commercial Banks—1970, op. cit.,* p. 68.
109. *Commercial Banks and Their Trust Activities, op. cit.,* Vol. I, p. 550.
110. *Ibid.,* p. 128.
111. *Ibid.,* p. 192.
112. *Ibid.,* p. 194.
113. See plaintiffs' complaint in *Aviation Consumers Action Project* v. *First National City Bank, et. al.* Docket 24593 before CAB, filed July 6, 1972.
114. Interview with Thomas Theobald, Summer, 1970.
115. Report of the Investment Division Morgan Guaranty Trust Company, May, 1972, p. 13.
116. "Campaign GM—Round II, Scoresheet," Project on Corporate Responsibility, 1609 Connecticut Avenue, N.W., Washington, D.C., May 20, 1971, p. 2.
117. "IMG Review of 1971," p. 5.
118. *Ibid.,* p. 20.
119. Survey was conducted for FNCB by the Opinion Research Corporation, which interviewed 1,378 persons. Detailed results of the survey were not made public but were referred to in a speech by William Spencer, FNCB President, on May 25, 1971.
120. *American Banker,* June 1, 1972, p. 15.
121. JEC Hearings, *op. cit.,* p. 207.
122. *Ibid.,* p. 208.
123. A. S. Hansen, Inc., *Employee Benefit Fund Investment Performance 1965–1971* (1972).
124. William Dreher. "Expanding the Actuaries' Role in Pension Fund Management," *Institutional Investor,* Vol. V, No. 8 (August, 1971), p. 30.
125. *Ibid.,* p. 32.
126. Letter from John Kajander, Vice President, Employer Relations, Pennzoil United, Inc., dated December 15, 1971.
127. Letter from Kenneth D. Hutcher, Chairman, Investment Committee, Tennessee Valley Authority Retirement System, dated November 16, 1971.
128. Letter from V. J. Motto, Assistant Treasurer, Standard Oil Company of New Jersey, dated December 13, 1971.
129. Response to questionnaire was returned completed but unsigned by Mutual Marine.
130. Letter from Thomas Waaland, Vice President and Treasurer, Corning Glass Works, dated November 23, 1971.
131. *Business Week,* September 11, 1971, p. 92.
132. Telephone conversation between John Masten and Donald Etra, June 2, 1972.
133. Telephone conversation between Alan Brightman and Donald Etra, June 2, 1972.
134. See Remarks by Ralph Nader before the Association of Private Pension and Welfare Plans, Inc., Washington, D.C., July 14, 1971.
135. *Meinhard* v. *Salmon,* 249 N.Y. 458, 464, 164 N.E. 545, 546 (1928).
136. *Trust Assets of Insured Commercial Banks—1970, op. cit.,* p. 5.
137. Remarks by Donald I. Baker, Deputy Director of Policy Planning, Antitrust Division, Department of Justice, "Banking and Bigness— And the Search for a Better Tomorrow," Prepared for delivery at

Federal Bar Association Convention, Washington, D.C., September 17, 1970.

138. *Institutional Investor Study, op. cit.,* Vol. 2, pp. 470–1.

139. Letter from Donald Baker, Director of Policy Planning, Antitrust Division, Department of Justice, July 20, 1972.

140. Interview with Dean Miller, Deputy Comptroller for Trusts, December 7, 1971, Washington, D.C.

141. Remarks by Dean Miller before the Midwinter Trust Conference of the American Bankers Association, New York., February 7, 1972.

142. *Ibid.*

143. The Report of the President's Commission on Financial Structure and Regulation (1971), p. 101.

144. Interview with Thomas Theobald, Summer 1970.

145. FNCB, *Corporate Policy Manual,* §70.37, entitled "Selection of Brokers," dated November 10, 1970, authorized by FNCB president.

146. Meeting with Raymond Sampson, December 21, 1971, New York.

147. Interview with William C. Greenough, Chairman, College Retirement Equities Fund, Teachers Insurance Annuities Association, January 4, 1972, New York.

148. Interview with Richard Furland, *op. cit.*

149. Interview with Frank Barnett, *op. cit.*

150. Telephone conversation between Samuel Calloway and Donald Etra, December 8, 1971.

151. Telephone conversation between C. W. Farnam and Donald Etra, December 17, 1971.

152. *Perdita M. Schaffner* v. *Chemical Bank,* 70 Civ. 5323, (S.D.N.Y., filed December 4, 1970).

153. Letter from Edward Ryan, Vice President, Chase Manhattan Bank, dated December 28, 1971.

154. Helmut Andresen, "Cooperation between Trust and Commercial Officers," *Trusts and Estates,* Vol. 107 (May, 1968), p. 434.

155. Telephone conversation between Helmut Andresen and Donald Etra, June 14, 1972.

156. Letter from Gene L. Finn, SEC Chief Economist, September 14, 1972.

157. See *Schaffner* v. *Chemical Bank, op. cit.,* and *Ruskay* v. *Morgan Guaranty Trust Company,* 70 Civ. 5455, (S.D.N.Y., 1970).

158. *Schaffner* Complaint, paragraph 10.

159. *Annual Survey of Trust Department Income and Expense 1971,* Federal Reserve Bank of New York, Table III.

160. Interview with George Lingua, August 3, 1970, New York.

161. Proceedings C.F.A. Research Seminar, "Pension Fund Investment Management," Charlottesville, Va. (1968), p. 132 [hereinafter cited as C.F.A. Seminar].

162. Citizens and Southern National Bank, *Report of the Trust Department,* July 31, 1972, p. 9.

163. Comptroller's Manual for National Banks, 12 C.F.R. 9.10.

164. Form CC-1440-OX, p. T–4, Revised January 1969, U.S. Treasury, Comptroller of the Currency.

165. Remarks by Dean Miller, February 7, 1972, *op. cit.*

166. *Finance, the Magazine of Money* (February, 1972): Vol. 90, No. 2, p. 64.

167. *Berry* v. *McCourt,* 1 Ohio App. 2d 173, 204 N.E. 2d 235 (1965).

168. *New England Trust Co.* v. *Triggs,* 135 N.E. 2d 541 (1956).
169. *Lynch* v. *Redfield,* 88 Cal. Rptr. 86; 9 Cal. App. 3d 293 (1970).
170. *In Re McKay's Estate,* 5 Misc. 123, 25 N.Y.S. 725 (1893).
171. *Annual Survey of Trust Department Income and Expense 1971, op. cit.*
172. *Institutional Investor Study, op. cit.,* Vol. 5, p. 2720.
173. JEC Hearings, *op. cit.,* pp. 208–9.
174. *Bakery Drivers Local 802* v. *Chase Manhattan Bank, op. cit.*
175. From Plaintiffs' Complaint in *Local 802, etc., op. cit.*
176. *Institutional Investor Study, op. cit.,* Vol. 5, p. 2720.
177. *Local 701, Mid-Jersey Trucking Industry* v. *Bankers Trust Company, op. cit.*
178. "Review of 1971," pp. 23–5.
179. *Institutional Investor Study, op. cit.,* Vol. 5, p. 2716.
180. Letter from Office of the Chairman, Eastman Kodak Company, dated January, 1972.
181. Letter from Robert Oelman dated January 7, 1972.
182. Telephone conversation between John deButts and Donald Etra, December 22, 1971.
183. 12 U.S.C. §73.
184. Comptroller's *Manual for National Banks,* 12 C.F.R. 9.12 (a).
185. Restatement of Trusts 2d, §170(n).
186. *Scott on Trusts,* §170.15.
187. FNCC List of Stockbrokers, February 16, 1970, American Society of Corporate Secretaries, *Nominee List.*
188. *Institutional Investor Study, op. cit.,* Vol. 5, p. 2729.
189. Anaconda Company, Form 8K for period ending July 31, 1971, filed with the SEC.
190. Allied Chemical Corporation, Form 8K for period ending May 31, 1971, filed with the SEC.
191. Monsanto Company.
192. Harbrecht, *op. cit.,* p. 49.
193. CFA Seminar, *op. cit.,* p. 14.
194. Hearings before the Senate Subcommittee on Labor, *op. cit.,* p. 443.
195. See New York Estates Powers and Trusts Law §11–2.2 (McKinney Supp. 1970).
196. U.S., Congress, Senate, Subcommittee on Labor, Committee on Labor and Public Welfare, Preliminary Report of the Private Welfare and Pension Plan Study 1971, Case History No. 33, November, 1971, p. 18.
197. Hearings before the Senate Subcommittee on Labor, *op. cit.,* p. 726.
198. Interview with Richard Furlaud, *op. cit.*
199. Interview with Preston Bassett, February 14, 1972, Philadelphia, Pennsylvania.
200. Remarks of Dean Miller, *op. cit.*
201. *Ibid.*
202. CFA Seminar, *op. cit.,* p. 137.
203. *Comptroller's Manual for National Banks,* 12 C.F.R. §9.12(d).
204. Address by Peter N. Prior, Senior Vice President, Hartford National Bank & Trust Company, third ABA Trust Operation and Automation Workshop, March, 1972.
205. Interview with Frank Barnett, *op. cit.*
206. See Henry Harfield, "Texas Gulf Sulphur and Bank Internal Pro-

cedures Between the Trust and Commercial Departments," *The Banking Law Journal* (October, 1969).

207. *Rippey* v. *Denver United States National Bank,* 273 F. Supp. 718, D. Colo. (1967).

208. *Commercial Banks and Their Trust Activities, op. cit.,* Vol. I, p. 780.

209. *In Re Estate of Frederika Bailey Ferris,* Probate Court, Cuyahoga County, Ohio, Doc. 557 No. 553648 (May 7, 1962).

210. *Commercial Banks and Their Trust Activities, op. cit.,* Vol. I, p. 785.

211. U.S., Congress, House, Committee on Banking and Currency, Staff Report: *The Penn Central Failure and the Role of Financial Institutions,* 92d Cong., 1st Sess., January 3, 1972.

212. *Ibid.,* p. 314.

213. *Ibid.,* p. 335.

214. *Ibid.,* p. 336.

215. SEC, Staff Study of the Financial Collapse of the Penn Central Company (1972), p. 431 [hereinafter cited as SEC Penn Central Study].

216. *Ibid.,* p. 437.

217. Letter from Stanley Sporkin, Deputy Director, SEC, dated October 16, 1972.

218. Letter from Robert B. Fiske, Jr., Davis Polk & Wardwell, September 11, 1972.

219. *SEC Penn Central Study, op. cit.,* p. 446.

220. *Local 734 Bakery Drivers' Pension Fund Trust and Chicago District Council of Carpenters' Pension Fund* v. *Continental Illinois National Bank and Trust Co., supra* note 68.

221. Remarks of John M. Cookenbach, Chairman, Trust Division, ABA, November 11, 1971.

222. See Remarks of Dean Miller, Deputy Comptroller for Trusts, Buies Creek, North Carolina, November 11, 1971.

223. *Report of the President's Commission on Financial Structure and Regulation* (1971), p. 102.

224. See Remarks of the Hon. Wright Patman, Chairman, House Banking and Currency Committee, June 20, 1972.

225. Harbrecht, *op. cit.,* p. 100.

226. New York Banking Law, Section 131(3).

227. Schwartz, "The Public Interest Proxy Contest: Reflections on Campaign GM," 69 *Michigan Law Rev.* 421 at 501 (1970).

228. *Ibid.,* p. 502.

229. W. C. Greenough, *Social Change and the Institutional Investor* (unpublished).

230. *Ibid.*

231. P. E. Blumberg, "Corporate Responsibility and the Social Crisis," 50 *Boston U. Law Rev.* 157, at 205 (1970).

232. 3 Scott, *Law of Trusts 1805–06,* 3d ed., (1967).

233. *A. P. Smith Mfg. Co.* v. *Barlow,* 13 N.J. 145, 98 A2d 581 at 586 (1953).

234. *Theodora Holding Company* v. *Henderson,* 257 A2d 398, at 404, Del. Ch. (1969).

235. C.F.A. Seminar, *op. cit.,* p. 71.

236. W. C. Greenough, *op. cit.*

237. P. E. Blumberg, "Corporate Responsibility and the Social Crisis," 50 *Bost. U. Law Rev.* 157, at 160 (1970).

238. *Ibid.,* p. 162.

239. David Rockefeller, "Banks Must Respond to Social Concerns," *The New York Times,* July 18, 1971, Section 3, p. 12.

240. D. E. Schwartz, "Corporate Responsibility in the Age of Aquarius," 26 *The Business Lawyer,* 515, at 523 (1970).

VI. Bank Regulation

1. Howard H. Hackley, "Our Baffling Banking System," *Virginia Law Review,* December, 1967, p. 576.

2. 12 U.S.C. Sections 24, 335.

3. 12 U.S.C. Sections 55, 56, 324, 1828(c).

4. FDIC, *1969 Annual Report.*

5. 12 U.S.C. Section 378.

6. 11 U.S.C. Sections 83, 324.

7. FDIC, *op. cit.*

8. 12 U.S.C. Section 84.

9. 12 C.F.R. Section 209.1 (1970).

10. Federal Reserve Board (hereafter "Fed"), *The Federal Reserve System: Purposes and Functions,* 1963, p. 19.

11. Fed, *op cit.*

12. Interview with John J. Larkin, FNCB Senior Vice President, Bond Division, July 29, 1970.

13. See Alan R. Holmes, Senior Vice President, Federal Reserve Bank of New York and Manager of the System Open Market Account, "A Day at the Trading Desk," FRB *Monthly Review,* October, 1970. Federal Reserve Bank of New York, *Open Market Operations,* July, 1969.

14. *Ibid.*

15. FDIC, *op. cit.*

16. Fed, *1969 Annual Report,* p. 308.

17. FDIC, *op. cit.*

18. *Ibid.*

19. 12 C.F.R. §8.3 (1969).

20. 12 C.F.R. §8.4 (1968).

21. 12 C.F.R. §8.5 (1965).

22. 12 C.F.R. §8.6 (1969).

23. 12 C.F.R. §8.8 (1965).

24. Comptroller of the Currency (hereinafter, "Comptroller"), "Years of Reform: A Prelude to Progress," in *101st Annual Report,* 1963. pp. 1–2.

25. *Journal of Commerce,* May 17, 1968, p. 4. *American Banker,* June 17, 1968, p. 1.

26. Howard Hackley, "Our Discriminatory Banking Structure," *Virginia Law Review,* December, 1969, p. 1459.

27. J. L. Robertson, "Federal Regulation of Banking: A Plea for Unification," 31, *Law and Contemporary Problems,* 690 (1966).

28. 12 U.S.C. Section 36.

29. *First National Bank* v. *Walker Bank & Trust Company,* 385 U.S. 252 (1966).

30. *Jackson* v. *First National Bank of Valdosta,* 246 F. Supp. 134, D.C. Ga. (1965).

31. *Livestock State Bank* v. *South Dakota State Banking Commission,* 80 S.D. 491 (1964).

32. 12 U.S.C. Section 92.
33. Comptroller, *Rulings,* ¶7110.
34. *Saxon* v. *Georgia Association of Independent Insurance Agents,* 399 F.2d 1010 (5th Cir., 1968).
35. Comptroller, *Rulings,* ¶7376.
36. Hackley, "Our Discriminatory Banking Structure," *op. cit.,* pp. 1446–7.
37. *Journal of Commerce,* May 17, 1968, p. 4. *American Banker,* June 17, 1968, p. 1.
38. U.S., Congress, House, Committee on Banking and Currency, *Hearings on Federal Reserve Rulings Regarding Loan Production Offices and Purchases of Operating Subsidiaries,* 1968, pp. 33, 34.
39. 12 C.F.R. §250.14 (1968).
40. 12 U.S.C. §601.
41. 12 C.F.R. §250.140 (1969).
42. Hackley, "Our Discriminatory Banking Structure," *op . cit.,* p. 1451.
43. 15 U.S.C. Section 78a–78hh (1964).
44. Hackley, "Our Discriminatory Banking Structure," *op. cit.,* pp. 1454–5.
45. *Ibid.,* 1457.
46. Senate Banking and Currency Committee.
47. 12 U.S.C. Section 24.
48. *American Banker,* April 6, 1971, p. 1.
49. Comptroller, *Rulings,* ¶3400.
50. Comptroller, *Manual for National Banks,* 1966, pp. iii–iv.
51. Executive Order 11007.
52. National Advisory Committee (hereinafter, "NAC"), *Minutes,* December 6, 1965.
53. NAC, *Minutes,* November 1, 1967, p. 4.
54. *Ibid.,* p. 3.
55. 18 U.S.C. Section 1014.
56. 12 U.S.C. Section 1828(c)(7)(D).
57. NAC, *Minutes,* May 24, 1967, pp. 3–4.
58. 12 U.S.C. Section 481.
59. Conversation with Justin Watson, 1971.
60. 12 U.S.C. 481.
61. Interview with Justin Watson and Thomas DeShazo, *op. cit.*
62. *Ibid.*
63. *Ibid.*
64. Interview with Justin Watson and Thomas DeShazo, *op. cit.*
65. Conversation with Justin Watson, February, 1971.
66. Comptroller, *1969 Annual Report.*
67. Comptroller, *Handbook of Examination Procedure* (hereinafter "Handbook"), I, p. 2.
68. Interview with Justin Watson and Thomas DeShazo, *op. cit.*
69. *Ibid.*
70. *Ibid.*
71. FNCC-FNCB, *1970 Annual Report,* p. 62. Chase Manhattan Corporation-Chase Manhattan Bank, *1970 Annual Report,* p. 25.
72. Comptroller, *Handbook,* III, pp. 11–12.
73. Interview with Justin Watson and Thomas DeShazo, *op. cit.*
74. Conversations wtih Justin Watson, May 24, 28, 1971.
75. *Ibid.*

76. *Ibid.*
77. *Ibid.*
78. Comptroller, *Handbook,* III, p. 12.
79. *Ibid.,* III, p. 109.
80. *Ibid.,* III, p. 9.
81. *Ibid.,* I, p. 52.
82. Interview with Justin Watson and Thomas DeShazo, *op. cit.*
83*l* Comptroller, *Handbook,* I, p. 53.
84. Interview with Justin Watson and Thomas DeShazo, *op. cit.*
85. 18 U.S.C. §608, 610, 611.
86. Interview with Justin Watson and Thomas DeShazo, *op. cit.*
87. "League for Good Government," letter of April 3, 1970, to Officers of National Bank of Commerce, Seattle, signed by Senior Management.
88. *Ibid.*
89. Anonymous letter to Representative Wright Patman, Chairman, House Banking and Currency Committee, April 8, 1970.
90. NAC, *Minutes,* June 15, 1966, p. 8; October 13, 1966, p. 3; May 24, 1967, p. 4.
91. *American Banker,* June 24, 1970, pp. 2, 28.
92. FNCC, Minutes of Annual Stockholders Meeting, March 30, 1971, p. 9.
93. *Wall Street Journal,* May 4, 1971, *American Banker,* June 8, 1971, p. 3.
94. *The New York Times,* September 19, 1971, p. 37.
95. SJR 43, January 22, 1969.
96. U.S., Congress, House, Committee on Banking and Currency, *Hearings: Investigation of Increase in Prime Interest Rate,* June, 1969.
97. *Wall Street Journal,* July 29, 1969. *The New York Times,* July 30, 1969, pp. 1, 20. *American Banker,* March 8, 1971, pp. 1, 16.
98. *The New York Times,* September 9, 1971, p. 37.
99. *Ibid.*
100. Profile of Senator Jacob Javits, *Nader Congress Project,* 1972, p. 17.
101. Conversation with Justin Watson, May, 1971.
102. U.S., Congress, House, Committee on Banking and Currency, *Hearings: Investigation Of Increase In Prime Interest Rate,* George S. Moore, Chairman, FNCB, June–July, 1969, p. 109.
103. New York Clearinghouse Association, *Quarterly Report,* June 30, 1970.
104. FNCB, *Annual Reports,* 1965–69.
105. Board of Governors of the Federal Reserve System, *1969 Annual Report,* p. 3.
106. Federal Reserve Bank of New York, *1969 Annual Report,* p. 22.
107. *Ibid.,* pp. 6–7.
108. FNCC-FNCB, *Report of Condition,* June 30, 1970.
109. FNCC-FNCB, *1969 Annual Report.*
110. FNCB, *Monthly Economic Letter,* June, 1969, p. 62.
111. FNCC-FNCB, *1969 Annual Report.* FNCC-FNCB, *Report of Condition,* June 30, 1970.
112. Interview with John Exter, FNCB Senior Vice President, International Monetary Advisor, July 29, 1970.
113. FNCB, *Monthly Economic Letter,* July, 1969, p. 78.
114. FNCC-FNCB, *Report of Condition,* June 30, 1970.

115. *American Banker,* June 24, 1970.
116. *Business Week,* October 24, 1970, pp. 24, 54.
117. New York Clearinghouse Association, *Weekly Reports,* June 17, 1970, June 24, 1970.
118. Interview with John Exter, *op. cit.*
119. Interview with James Meigs, FNCB Vice President, Domestic Economics, July 17, 1970.
120. *American Banker,* April 7, 1970, p. 22.
121. U.S., Congress, Senate, Banking and Currency Committee, Subcommittee on Financial Institutions, *Hearings: Deposit Rates and Mortgage Credit,* September 9, 1969.
122. 12 U.S.C. Section 1843(c)(8).
123. U.S. Congress, House, Committee on Currency and Banking, *Hearings: Bank Holding Company Act Amendments on H. R. 6778,* Part 1, p. 1.
124. FNCC-FNCB, *1968 Annual Report,* pp. 3, 7.
125. 12 U.S.C. §61.
126. Interview with Carl Desch, *op. cit.*
127. Interview with Carl Desch, *op. cit.*
128. Interview with Brian Livsey, FNCB Vice President, Leasing, July 21, 1970.
129. *Ibid.*
130. Interview with Fred A. Stecher, FNCB Vice President, Travelers Check and Travel Service Divisions, July 27, 1970.
131. Interview with Carl Desch, *op. cit.*
132. Chubb Corporation, *1968 Annual Report,* p. 14.
133. Bank Holding Company Act of 1956, §4(c)(8).
134. *Bank Holding Company Act Amendments op. cit.,* p. 85.
135. *Ibid.,* p. 88.
136. U.S., Congress, House, Committee on Banking and Currency, *Hearings on H. R. 6778, FNCC Statement,* May 20, 1969.
137. U.S., Congress, Senate, Banking and Currency Committee, *Walter Wriston, FNCC-FNCB Chairman, Statement,* May 26, 1970.
138. FNCB, *Proxy Statement, op. cit.*
139. U.S., Congress, House, Committee on Banking and Currency, *Report on H. R. 6778,* July 23, 1969, p. 15.
140. *American Banker,* November 7, 1969, p. 1.
141. *American Banker,* July 24, 1970.
142. Interview with Thomas Wilcox, FNCB Vice Chairman, August 12, 1970.
143. FNCB, *Citibank Magazine,* Number 3, 1970.
144. Frank V. Fowlkes, *"Washington Pressures/The Big-bank Lobby,"* (hereinafter "Big Bank Lobby") *CPR National Journal, December* 6, 1969.
145. Fowlkes, *Financial Report,* p. 1539.
146. *Ibid.,* pp. 1539–40.
147. *Ibid.,* pp. 1538–43.
148. *Ibid.*
149. *Ibid.*
150. *Ibid.*
151. Timothy D. Naegele, Assistant Counsel, Senate Banking and Currency Committee, Speech to 40th New England Bank Management Conference, October 9, 1970.

152. Fowlkes, *Financial Report,* p. 1543.
153. *American Banker,* December 24, 1970, p. 6.
154. Bank Holding Company Act Amendments of 1970.
155. *American Banker,* January 17, 1971, p. 15.
156. *Ibid.*
157. Fed Press Release, May 27, 1971.
158. 12 U.S.C. §371(c).
159. FNCC, Form 10K, filed with the SEC, December 31, 1970.
160. *Ibid.*
161. Bank Holding Company Act Amendments of 1970, §106(b).
162. Interview with Carl Desch, *op. cit.*
163. Interview with Brian Livsey, *op. cit.*
164. *American Banker,* April 5, 1971, pp. 1, 22.
165. Bank Holding Company Act Amendments of 1970, §4(c)(8).
166. *Ibid.*

Index

ABA. *See* American Bankers Association
acquisition loans, 92–93, 96
acquisitions, 94, 95–97
Advance Mortgage Corporation, 331
adversary proceeding, 55–57, 65
Aetna Judicial Service, 57, 58, 345–346
aircraft and airline industries. *See* banks; Boeing; Lockheed
airline credit syndicate, 102–103
Allegheny Airlines, merger between Mohawk Airlines and, 75
Allen, James H., 121, 146, 147
Allied Chemical Corporation, 244; pension plan of, 239, 240
Allison Distributing Corp., 42
American Bankers Association (ABA), 194–195, 256, 323, 324, 349
amortization, 72
Anaconda Company, 249–295; pension plan of, 201, 239
Andresen, Helmut, 195–196; on broker reciprocity, 224–225
Antitrust Division (Department of Justice), 97, 220, 278, 319
anti-tying provision, 332–333
asset protection, 72
Association of the Bar of the City of New York, 140
Astro Sales Corporation, 40–42, 50, 356–357
Aten, Robert H., 133–134
Atlantic Richfield, acquisition of Sinclair Oil by, 96
automobile loans, 26

Baker, Donald, 220
bank-client relationship, 72–73
bankers, role of, in the regulatory process, 280–286
Bankers Trust Company, 105, 112, 125, 127, 132, 142, 144, 145, 146, 151*n,* 163, 164, 196; and broker reciprocity, 224; conflict of interest case against, 230; and economic development loans, 88–89, 90
bank examinations, 286–300
bank holding companies, control over corporate activities by, 335–336. *See also* one-bank holding companies
Bank Holding Company Act

Amendments of 1970, 303, 330, 336
Bank Holding Company Act of 1956, 316
bank loan portfolios, xxvi, xxxi; examination of, 290–296
Bank of America, xxiv, 291, 317, 329
bank panics and failures, 266, 268
bank regulation, xxix–xxxiii, 265–267. *See also* bankers; bank examinations; Comptroller of the Currency; regulatory agencies; regulatory structure
banks, and the aircraft and airline industries, 101–108, 209; four different types of, 266; growth of, xxi–xxiii, 69–70; investment of pension trusts in employer's assets by, 241, 242–245; as pension trustees, 199–201; political contributions by, 296–299; and the Port Authority, 144–148; preferential tax treatment of, in New York, 153–154; as a public trust, xxiii, xxix, xxxii, 301, 355; and the regulatory process, 286; and the securities business, 269, 277–278, 279–280; services to large corporations by, 76–79; and transportation policy, 150–153; as trustees or executors of estates, 167–170; and the World Trade Center, 141–143, 149. *See also* Bank of America; Chase Manhattan; Citibank; Manufacturers Hanover; Morgan Guaranty Trust
BANs. *See* Bond Anticipation Notes
Barnett, Frank, 189, 195, 223–224, 248
Bassett, Preston, 244
Batten, William M., 109, 232, 235–236
Beame, Comptroller Abraham D. (Abe), 126
beneficiaries, trust, opinions of Citibank, by, 171–174, 176, 177, 183–184, 185–186; rights of, 253
black capitalism, 86–87, 88–89
blacks, as employees of Citibank, xxv, 1, 2, 9, 17, 363. *See also* minority employees
block purchases, 174–175